Business Systems and Organizational Capabilities

Business Systems and Organizational Capabilities

The Institutional Structuring of Competitive Competences

Richard Whitley

OXFORD
UNIVERSITY PRESS

OXFORD
UNIVERSITY PRESS

Great Clarendon Street, Oxford OX2 6DP

Oxford University Press is a department of the University of Oxford.
It furthers the University's objective of excellence in research, scholarship,
and education by publishing worldwide in

Oxford New York

Auckland Cape Town Dar es Salaam Hong Kong Karachi
Kuala Lumpur Madrid Melbourne Mexico City Nairobi
New Delhi Shanghai Taipei Toronto

With offices in

Argentina Austria Brazil Chile Czech Republic France Greece
Guatemala Hungary Italy Japan Poland Portugal Singapore
South Korea Switzerland Thailand Turkey Ukraine Vietnam

Oxford is a registered trademark of Oxford University Press
in the UK and in certain other countries

Published in the United States
by Oxford University Press Inc., New York

British Library Cataloguing in Publication Data

Data available

Library of Congress Cataloging in Publication Data

Whitley, Richard.
  Business systems and organizational capabilities : the institutional
structuring of competitive competences / Richard whitley.
     p. cm.
  ISBN 978–0–19–920518–9
  ISBN 978–0–19–920517–2
  1. Comparative organization.   2. Comparative economics.
3. Competition.   4. Business enterprises.   I. Title.
  HD30.55.W47 2007
  338—dc22   2007025806

Typeset by SPI Publisher Services, Pondicherry, India
Printed in Great Britain
on acid-free paper by
Biddles Ltd, King's Lynn, Norfolk

ISBN 978–0–19–920517–2 (hbk.)
ISBN 978–0–19–920518–9 (pbk.)

1 3 5 7 9 10 8 6 4 2

Preface

Twenty-first-century capitalism continues to exhibit considerable differences between dominant systems of economic coordination and control at the same time as international economic interdependence is increasing. The governance of leading firms, and the kinds of competitive competences they develop, remain quite diverse between institutional contexts, while cross-national competition and coordination have grown in many industries. In this book, I suggest how we can understand this combination of diversity and integration by extending and developing the comparative business systems framework in three major ways.

First, by considering more systematically than before the particular circumstances in which distinctive business systems and innovation systems are likely to become established and reproduced at national levels of collective organization, together with an examination of how changing endogenous and exogenous pressures have affected the major kinds of business systems that developed in many OECD states during the postwar period. Particularly important in this respect have been the intensification of cross-national competition and expansion of international institutions governing economic activities.

Second, by identifying the key mechanisms through which different institutional regimes can affect the nature of organizational capabilities that dominant firms develop, and how these competences enabled companies to deal with different kinds of risks and opportunities in particular technologies markets. Variations in authority sharing with employees and business partners are seen here as the central phenomena connecting macro-institutional analyses with recent work on the theory of the firm to account for continuing divergences in patterns of sectoral specialization and performance in differently organized market economies. Particular attention is paid to the development of different kinds of innovative capabilities and project-based firms in societies dominated by contrasting institutional regimes.

Third, by extending this approach to understanding the institutional structuring of competitive competences to the analysis of multinational companies, particularly of the circumstances in which such firms are likely to develop distinctive transnational organizational capabilities and so become different kinds of companies from their more domestically focused competitors. In many, if not most, cases of cross-national managerial coordination, these conditions rarely exist, and so the extent to which multinational firms do indeed constitute distinct organizational forms and strategic actors is much less than is sometimes claimed.

The book therefore broadens the scope of the comparative business systems framework to incorporate issues of change, innovation, and multi-levelled governance, on the one hand, and deepens its analysis by attempting to show how different institutional arrangements governing economic activities can be expected to generate different outcomes for firms and economies. This has led to some further distinctions being drawn between forms of economic coordination and control in addition to those discussed in my *Divergent Capitalisms* (Oxford University Press, 1999), such as those dominated by project networks and financial conglomerates, and some descriptions of firm types altered and/or elaborated, particularly project-based, managerially coordinated and cooperative hierarchy. In the introductory chapter, I outline the reasoning behind these changes and summarize the underlying dimensions for comparing competing forms of economic organization with their dominant strategic actors.

Earlier versions of many of these chapters were presented to meetings of Standing Working Group One of the European Group for Organization Studies on 'The Comparative Study of Economic Organization', which has been a major source of intellectual debate and development on these topics over the past 10 years. Others have been presented to conferences and seminars at the Universities of Manchester, Rotterdam, Uppsala, and Warwick, the Massachusetts Institute of Technology and INSEAD, as well as to the Institute of International Business, Stockholm School of Economics. I am grateful for the comments and suggestions received on these occasions, and am especially indebted to Laszlo Czaban for his helpful comments on all the chapters in this book.

Parts of Chapter 2 and Chapter 11 were previously published in Glenn Morgan *et al.* (eds.) *Changing Capitalisms?* (Oxford University Press, 2005), parts of Chapter 3 in E Lorenz and B-A Lundvall (eds.) *How Europe's Economies Learn* (Oxford University Press, 2006), parts of Chapter 6 in *Organization Studies* (24 (5), 2003, 667–95), parts of Chapters 7 and 9 in

Industrial and Corporate Change (11 (3), 2002, 497–528 and 15 (1), 2006, 77–99 respectively), parts of Chapter 8 in *Research Policy* (33 (1), 2004, 89–106), parts of Chapter 10 in Glenn Morgan *et al.* (eds.) *The Multinational Firm* (Oxford University Press), and parts of Chapter 12 in the *Journal of Management Studies* (40, 2003, 639–68). I am grateful to Oxford University Press, Blackwell Publishing, Elsevier Limited and Sage Publications for permission to reproduce this material. In all cases I have revised the original papers, in many cases substantially, to integrate the arguments and evidence more effectively and remove redundancies.

Contents

Contents

Figure

List of Tables

Abbreviations

ABB	Asea Brown Boveri Engineering Group
APV	Aluminium Plant and Vessel Engineering Group
BASF	Badische Analin und Soda Fabrik Chemical Group
BWS	Bretton Woods System
CAD	Computer Aided Design
CAM	Computer Aided Manufacturing
CIM	Computer Integrated Manufacturing
CRM	Customer Relationship Management
DNA	Deoxyribo Nucleic Acid
EC	European Commission
ECJ	European Court of Justice
ECSC	European Coal and Steel Community
ERP	Enterprise Resource Planning
ETUC	European Trade Unions Confederation
EU	European Union
EUROFER	European Confederation of Iron and Steel Industries
FDI	Foreign Direct Investment
FTP	File Transfer Protocol
GATT	General Agreement on Tariffs and Trade
GDP	Gross Domestic Product
GHR	Global Human Resources
GSM	Global System for Mobile Communications
JIT	JIT Electronics
LDP	Liberal Democratic Party
MFN	Most Favoured Nation
MITI	Ministry of International Trade and Industry

MNC	Multi-National Corporation
NGO	Non-Government Organization
NYSE	New York Stock Exchange
OECD	Organization for Economic Cooperation and Development
PBF	Project-Based Firm
PTT	Post, Telephone and Telegraph Administration
R&D	Research and Development
SME	Small and Medium Enterprise
TRIPS	Trade-Related Aspects of Intellectual Property Rights
UNICE	Union of Industrial and Employers' Confederations of Europe
WTO	World Trade Organization

Part I

Introduction

1

The Comparative Analysis of Competing Capitalisms

Introduction

A major feature of post-Second-World-War capitalism has been the development and relative success of different systems of economic organization in the industrialized market economies. The prevalent ways in which economic activities are coordinated and governed in, for example, France, Germany and Japan, continue to differ greatly from those dominant in the USA and UK, as well as varying considerably between themselves (see, e.g., Amable, 2003; Hollingsworth, 1991; Lincoln and Gerlach, 2004; Schmidt, 2002). It also seems likely that whatever forms of market economy eventually become established in China, they will both differ significantly from those institutionalized elsewhere and also vary in significant respects between different localities within the country (King and Szelenyi, 2005; Krug and Hendrischke, 2007; Wank, 1999).

Despite the claims of some globalization enthusiasts, these differences are no more likely to become reduced and converge to a single type of market economy in the twenty-first century than similarly varied forms of capitalism did in the internationalized world economy of the late nineteenth century (Hirst and Thompson, 1996; Kenworthy, 1997; 2005; Koechlin, 1995; Wade, 1996). In particular, the idea that the prevalent American variety of capitalism will come to dominate the world economy by virtue of its superior efficiency, which was widely held in the heyday of Fordism, is as flawed as the notion that Japanese capitalism would sweep all before it, as was popularly thought in the 1980s (Boyer and Durand, 1997; Djelic, 1998; Vogel, 1988).

Indeed, insofar as globalization is creating common financial pressures for leading companies and state élites in the major OECD economies,

3

these forces are just as likely to increase the heterogeneity of policy responses and firm strategies as to decrease it, as indeed happened in the early part of the twentieth century. States in institutional regimes that provide competitive advantages for some firms in particular technologies and markets seem unlikely to abolish these in favour of different kinds of currently fashionable policies in the hope of becoming more successful overall. Equally, leading firms that have developed specific organizational capabilities as a result of being effective in different institutional frameworks will probably respond to increasing international competition by improving these capabilities rather than trying to compete in the same way across international markets. Slavishly imitating what is considered to be current 'best practice' by, for instance, imitating lean production techniques is impossible to do without some translation (Liker *et al.*, 1999), and also implies an inability to innovate successfully. By always trying to follow the industry leader, companies will never reap first mover advantages and would be permanently condemned to competing on other firms' terms.

The continuing differences in the ways that economic activities are organized and governed across market economies emphasize the variety of economic rationalities and performance standards in the world economy today. They also suggest that competition between firms from different kinds of market economies is as much between alternative frameworks as within a single one (Hall and Soskice, 2001a; Quack and Morgan, 2000). Contrary to some economic reasoning that assumes the dominance of a single standard for determining efficient performance throughout all market economies, this pluralism of competitive competences and logics of economic action highlights the diversity of criteria for evaluating the performance of firms that have become established in different societies (Hodgson, 1996).

Once it is accepted that there are a wide variety of different ways of organizing market economies, and that there are no good theoretical or empirical reasons to believe that these will converge to a single model on the basis of its superior efficiency, it becomes important to analyse why such differences have developed, and how they have led to varied economic outcomes. This in turn requires: (a) the identification of the key differences between the major forms of economic organization that have come to dominate industrial capitalist societies, especially those established since the end of the Second World War, (b) an explanation of why these divergences have developed in different kinds of societal contexts, and (c) an account of how they have resulted in contrasting

patterns of sectoral and technological specialization in differently organized market economies. Central to this last concern is an investigation
into how different kinds of societal institutions governing business activities encourage firms and other strategic actors to develop varied organizational capabilities that enable them to compete effectively in different
kinds of industries and markets.

A further major issue to be considered is how significant internal and
external pressures, such as changes in domestic dominant coalitions,
in state structures and policies, and in the wider geo-political environment, affect particular forms of economic organization. In the cases
of the particular kinds of business systems established in the postwar
capitalist economies under the Bretton Woods system (BWS) governing
international financial flows, these pressures include: changing patterns
of sectoral specialization, urbanization and social stratification, the oil
price rises of the 1970s and attendant inflation, the collapse of the BWS
and the increasing internationalization of competition, capital flows and
managerial hierarchies, together with the collapse of the Soviet Union.

In the past few decades, a number of scholars have focused on the
first two of these concerns, mostly at the macro-institutional level, and
compared various types of capitalism (Hall and Soskice, 2001b; Orru *et al.*,
1997), social systems of production (Hollingsworth and Boyer, 1997), and
political economies (Crouch and Streeck, 1997). Others have considered
how different nation states and regions developed variously characterized
national innovation systems that encouraged contrasting patterns of technological specialization and change (Braczyk *et al.*, 1998; Edquist, 1997;
2005; Nelson, 1993), while researchers in the French regulationist school
have examined the varieties of 'post Fordist' systems of innovation and
production (Amable, 2003; Boyer, 2004).

Work in the comparative business systems framework has concentrated
rather more on integrating the macro-institutional level of analysis with
more microanalyses of firm governance and behaviour to account for
the major variations in postwar patterns of economic organization. This
approach was developed first of all to explain differences between East
Asian postwar capitalisms (Whitley, 1992a), and then considered variations in the organization of Western European economies (Whitley,
1992b; Whitley and Kristensen, 1996; 1997) and the emerging market
economies of Eastern Europe (Czaban and Whitley, 1998; Whitley *et al.*,
1996; Whitley and Czaban, 1998).

Over much the same period there has been a renewal of interest in how
firms develop distinctive competitive competences, building on the work

of Edith Penrose (1959) and George Richardson (1972; 1998). Amongst other results, this has led to the development of the dynamic capabilities theory of the firm (Dosi *et al.*, 2000; Teece *et al.*, 1994) and a more dynamic analysis of the relationships between firms and markets (Langlois, 2003; Langlois and Robertson, 1995), often, though, without considering the institutional context in which different kind of firms develop varied capabilities.

By integrating these accounts of how different kinds of firms develop different kinds of organizational capabilities with the comparative analysis of institutional regimes and business systems, we can begin to understand the processes through which differently organized market economies generate varied economic outcomes. Amongst other issues, this involves analysing the circumstances in which distinctive business and innovation systems become established at the national level of collective organization, and encourage leading national firms to develop particular kinds of capabilities. Additionally, given the significant endogenous and exogenous changes that have taken place since the end of the postwar *trentes glorieuses,* it is important to consider how dominant institutions and business systems may have altered such that predominantly national forms of economic organization have become less cohesive and reorganized. In particular, the significance of increasing economic internationalization for established institutional regimes, business systems and firms needs to be analysed.

Before exploring these concerns in more detail, it is important to discuss some of the central concepts and issues involved in comparing competing forms of capitalism, particularly the key ways in which market economies can be contrasted, the nature of different kinds of strategic actors in them, and the role of ideal types of socio-economic organization in explaining diversity and change. Accordingly, in this chapter I summarize the major ways in which the organization and control of economic activities in capitalist societies can be compared, and how different business systems vary in their dominance of market economies through their association with particular kinds of societal institutions. Initially, I describe the key dimensions that distinguish different ways of organizing and controlling market economies and then discuss their combination as eight ideal types of business system. The varied kinds of strategic actors that exercise authority in these are then distinguished, together with the different kinds of connections between dominant institutions and prevalent patterns of economic organization at different levels of analysis.

The Comparative Analysis of Market Economies

As numerous comparative studies have shown, a key way in which market economies continue to vary concerns how economic activities and resources are coordinated and governed, and by which kind of corporate agent or firm (see, e.g., Amable, 2003; Hollingsworth and Boyer, 1997; Piore and Sabel, 1984). In particular, the legal status of incorporated companies and the extent of their monopolization of economic coordination and strategic decision making differ considerably between political economies, as the discussion in Paul DiMaggio's *The Twenty-First Century Firm* (2001a) highlights. The formal boundaries of Chinese family businesses, Japanese large firms and small enterprises in tightly clustered Italian industrial districts, for instance, often do not identify the key strategic actors in these national and regional economies (Crouch *et al.*, 2001, 2004; Redding, 1990; Westney, 2001a).

Furthermore, as Roy (1997), and others (e.g. Dobbin, 1994) have shown, the nature of the privately owned US corporate form has changed considerably over the past two hundred years. It was fiercely contested throughout the nineteenth century, and continued to be shaped by political struggles in the twentieth. There is no particular legal and financial construction of the limited liability company that is demonstrably superior to all other ones in all market economies and institutional contexts (Milhaupt, 2003). Different states have institutionalized the privilege of limited liability for corporate actors in diverse ways, with varied obligations to different stakeholders and society as a whole (Roe, 2003).

The nature of the firm as the key collective economic actor is therefore variable across differently organized market economies, and cannot be assumed to be basically the same regardless of its political and social context. Rather, leading firms' governance, direction and capabilities differ significantly between capitalist societies, and the comparative analysis of market economies has to consider these differences as phenomena to be explained rather than presuming that they are essentially negligible. In particular, the idea that the publicly quoted company is the same kind of dominant strategic actor in all advanced industrial societies, and that business groups, networks and other forms of inter-firm alliance have no strategic capabilities as distinct economic actors is not tenable (Biggart and Guillen, 1999; Granovetter, 2005; Powell, 2001).

This means that any comparative framework for analysing market economies has to take the nature and strategic significance of legally defined firms as empirically variable and theoretically problematic. In particular, the roles of other kinds of authoritatively coordinated groups, such as inter-firm networks, in structuring decisions and becoming significant economic actors under particular conditions needs to be considered. Such inter-firm networks and business associations differ in their formalization and centralization of authority between integrated business groups, German cartel offices in the prewar period (Herrigel, 1996: 60–8) and those institutionalized in some Italian industrial districts and local production systems whose communal governments, technical colleges and local banks provide 'collective competition goods' (Crouch *et al.*, 2001, 2004).

The importance of these kinds of networks and associations in some societies led Langlois and Robertson (1995: 9–11) to suggest that market economies could be usefully compared in terms of two basic, and independently varying, dimensions: the degree of ownership integration and the extent of coordination integration. The postwar South Korean (henceforth Korean) economy represented high levels of both dimensions as it has been dominated by the large managerially integrated and highly diversified conglomerates called *Chaebol* (Amsden, 1989; Steers *et al.*, 1989), while economies dominated by financially oriented holding companies can be seen as being high in ownership coordination but low in organizational integration. The sorts of venture capital networks dominating Silicon Valley at the end of the twentieth century represent intermediate degrees of both dimensions in this approach (Langlois and Robertson, 1995: 124–7; cf. Crouch, 2005: 130–43).

A similar concern with contrasting organizational forms at the end of the twentieth century led Paul DiMaggio to compare firms, networks and markets in terms of the degree of explicit coordination of economic activities and the extent of domination by some actors over others (2001b: 213–15). Spot markets are low on both of these dimensions, oligopolistic markets—in the late twentieth century USA at least—are dominated by large multidivisional companies but do not manifest much explicit collaboration, while Japanese vertical *keiretsu* exhibit both considerable domination and explicit integration of supply chains. Various kinds of inter-firm networks, such as those in different industrial districts, Silicon Valley and the Japanese inter-market groups represent intermediate combinations of these two characteristics.

Two underlying themes dominate these sorts of comparisons. First, that markets are often much more organized around medium- to long-term relationships between formally independent firms than is assumed in many accounts of market economies. Second, that activities in legally constituted firms are often less hierarchically integrated through central direction and rules than is supposed in many textbook accounts of managerial control. Thus, markets could, and often do, manifest relatively stable patterns of coordination and control of economic activities without being formally integrated through common ownership, and hierarchical firms sometimes organize themselves internally in quasi-market-like fashion, as well as varying greatly in the autonomy granted to sub-units, project teams and individual employees (Imai and Itami, 1984). Furthermore, many of these variations appear to constitute distinct patterns of economic organization that dominate particular industries and/or entire national economies.

If we assume that the minimum requirement of a market economy is that it institutionalizes private property rights and a governance regime that facilitates spot market based transactions between autonomous actors controlling resources and activities by virtue of their legally defined status, then a major contrast between them becomes how much, and in what ways, economic activities are coordinated and directed through non-spot market exchanges, such as sustained collaboration in inter-firm networks and associations and formal authority relations of subordination and control. Crucial to such coordination, and to the constitution of distinct collective actors that are able to act as cohesive organizations under unified direction, is some degree of collective subordination to a common source of authority.

Such authoritative coordination of activities involves individuals, groups and organizations accepting the right of some agency, whether informal network, cartel office or managerial hierarchy, to control the allocation and use of economic resources, including labour power. This authority need not be absolute, of course, and may be organized horizontally through cooperative networks as well as vertically in a formal hierarchy, but necessarily implies the partial subordination of individual actors to the choices of some agency through jointly agreed processes, however informal and asymmetric such agreements may be. It is through such collective subordination to some common decision making authority that agents are able to function as organized strategic actors.

In this sense, networks of firms, partnerships and project teams exercise authority over economic actors in a comparable, but distinct, manner to managerial hierarchies, and economies where such 'horizontal' coordination is prevalent can be quite highly integrated even in the absence of

9

large ownership based companies. Equally, as many holding companies and 'hollow' firms (Teece *et al.*, 1994) illustrate, high levels of ownership coordination in an economy need not necessarily imply strong central integration of economic activities through formal rules and procedures administered by a unified bureaucracy within such formally constituted entities.

Market economies vary significantly, then, in both: (a) the extent of authoritative coordination and direction of economic activities, and (b) the ways that this is achieved. Given the importance of private ownership in capitalist societies, and the key role of companies in providing a vehicle for investment in the production of goods and services and appropriating surpluses, a central means of authoritative integration is clearly through unified ownership. Such ownership integration can be further divided into two sub dimensions: its degree or intensity and scope. Considering first the degree of ownership integration in an economy, this refers here to the extent that leading companies integrate subunits and activities systematically through organizational routines and central direction, and act as unitary entities. The more market-like are relationships between the organizational subunits of leading firms, and the more they function as a nexus of contracts, as in some financial holding companies, the lower is the extent of ownership integration in an economy in this sense.

Secondly, the scope of ownership integration here refers to the range of assets and activities typically controlled by leading companies. It is considerable in economies dominated by large conglomerates, such as the postwar Korean *Chaebol*, that are highly vertically integrated and control activities in many different, often unrelated, sectors. A narrower scope of ownership integration exists in an economy when dominant firms are more specialized, control a limited range of different kinds of businesses within industries, and rarely diversify widely into technologically or market unrelated areas.

The second broad means by which authoritative coordination is achieved in market economies is, or course, through alliances and networks of economic actors, whether individuals, families or variously structured and demarcated firms. Key to this mode of economic coordination is the sharing of authority such that actors are constrained in the short to medium term by common interests and concerns that restrict their individual pursuit of private profit where it could harm the collective interests of the network. Such alliance integration also varies on the two dimensions of degree and scope.

A high degree of alliance integration in an economy implies that many actors delegate substantial powers to third parties, including collective organizations of which they are members, and enter into long-term partnerships that involve mutual commitments and risk sharing. An obvious example of an economy dominated by such close inter-firm connections is found in the alliance capitalism of postwar Japan (Gerlach, 1992; Lincoln and Gerlach, 2004), which highlights the asymmetric nature of some of these groupings. Low levels of alliance integration are found where owners and managers of firms rarely share authority with business partners, business associations or other third parties, or collaborate with competitors, and most inter-firm relationships are conducted on an arm's length, ad hoc and low commitment basis.

The scope of alliance integration refers here to the range of different kinds of activities and assets involved in forming and maintaining such alliances. These vary from highly specific sharing of particular resources for limited purposes, as in many networks in the high technology industries of the USA, to much broader and more diffuse sharing of information, technologies and opportunities across a large number of industries, as in the postwar Japanese inter-market groups.

In principle, these four sub-dimensions of authoritative coordination and control of economic activities in market economies can vary independently of each other. Considering the interconnections between the degree and scope of ownership integration, for instance, economies dominated by large conglomerates can manifest different degrees of administrative integration within these firms according to their centralization of strategic decision making and establishment of common organizational routines and personnel management practices across divisions and subsidiaries.

However, some combinations of these two sub-dimensions of ownership integration seem likely to be less stable than others. For example, economies dominated by relatively small and specialized companies in related markets and technologies, are unlikely to display low levels of organizational integration and central direction given the narrow range of their activities and ease of direct control. Thus, the combination of limited ownership scope with low intra-firm integration is unlikely to be sustained.

Similarly, the degree and scope of alliance coordination and control may differ considerably in how they are connected in different market economies, with networks between companies based on a limited range of interests and activities varying greatly in the intensity of commitments between them. Again, though, firms that develop wide-ranging relationships with suppliers, customers and other actors—which typically involve information sharing on a considerable number of different kinds of activities—seem unlikely to do so on a short-term basis in which commitments are limited. To coordinate a wide range of activities with other companies typically requires considerable knowledge of, and trust in, their competences and commitments, and so substantial levels of cooperation over time. This suggests that economies where alliances between firms are wide-ranging are likely also to exhibit quite strong commitments between business partners.

The same considerations apply to the combination of different levels of ownership and alliance integrations. While economies dominated by large firms can display varying levels of alliance integration, as the examples of postwar Japan and the USA exemplify, certain combinations of the scale and scope of ownership and alliance integration are less likely to be established. For example, developing long-term and wide-ranging alliances between companies involves considerable trust and cooperation in which organizations share some authority. This will be difficult to accomplish when firms are weakly integrated and relatively fragmented because the commitment and reliability of the whole organization becomes questionable. Large holding companies run more as financial investment vehicles than as integrated organizations are also unlikely to engage in long-term alliances in which they share authority with networks or associations because of the variety and distinctiveness of their interests and capabilities. Joint coordination of activities may be feasible in financial terms, but organizational integration on a continuing basis between such fragmented enterprises will be difficult to maintain.

Another combination of these characteristics that is improbable as a stable feature of market economies is high levels of ownership integration of very diverse activities with extensive and long-term alliances. This is because large firms controlling a wide range of assets and activities in different industries will be able to access complementary assets and capabilities internally, as well as managing risks by investing in sectors with contrasting product life cycles and different kinds of technologies and demand patterns. Thus, economies dominated by large vertically integrated and diversified conglomerates are unlikely to be characterized by long-term alliances between leading firms. Equally, where such alliances are firmly established, large companies are unlikely to diversify widely into quite unrelated technologies and markets.

Table 1.1. Eight ideal types of business systems

Type of Business System	Level of Ownership Integration		Level of Alliance Integration	
	Degree	Scope	Degree	Scope
Fragmented	High	Low	Low	Low
Project network	High	Low	Some	Low
Coordinated industrial district	High	Low	Considerable	Some
Financial conglomerate	Low	High	Low	Low
Integrated conglomerate	High	High	Low	Low
Compartmentalized	Considerable	Considerable	Limited	Low
Collaborative	Considerable	Considerable	Considerable	Some
Highly coordinated	High	Some	High	High

Varieties of Business Systems

These points suggest that there are a limited number of distinct and stable ways of organizing market economies in terms of their patterns of authoritative coordination and control of economic activities. If we consider the stereotyped Marshallian district of small, highly specialized firms to represent the traditional ideal type of an economy coordinated by short-term, singular and largely anonymous transactions as one, rather fragmented, type, a further seven can be distinguished in terms of the degree and scope of ownership and alliance integration, as listed in Table 1.1. Here, the extent of authoritative coordination prevalent in a market economy is described on a five point scale of: low, limited, some, considerable and high.

These ways of organizing economic activities in market economies represent distinct idealizations of authoritative coordination of business activities. They can be described as separate kinds of business systems that vary in the degree to which authority is used to organize economic activities, and how authority patterns are related to ownership. As ideal types they become established to varying extents in different institutional environments at different levels of collective organization and jurisdiction, such as subnational regions, nation states and transnational groupings. Each kind of business system is dominated by different kinds of collective strategic actors that are governed to varying degrees by diverse interest groups, and develop different kinds of organizational capabilities in pursuit of different priorities. These actors are authoritatively coordinated organizations that are able to exercise varying levels of control over their members' activities. The key features of these eight ideal types of business system will now be briefly discussed.

Beginning with economies characterized by relatively low levels of authoritative coordination and control through ownership, and varying degrees of inter-firm collaboration and cooperation, we can distinguish between project network kinds of business system from the more highly fragmented type. While the latter are dominated by relatively small- and medium-sized units of ownership coordination whose owner-managers are reluctant to share authority with each other, the former are characterized by networks of relatively specialized firms that share some resources and engage in joint activities. However, authority sharing between firms is here restricted to specific projects and opportunities—and so is limited in its scope. Inter-firm commitments tend to be short term and narrowly focused rather than long-lasting and wide-ranging.

Project network business systems are therefore quite fluid in terms of market entry and exit, and often in employment relations as well, but nonetheless are more coordinated in terms of sharing information, investment opportunities and expertise for a variety of purposes than fragmented ones. This coordination is often accomplished through venture capital and business lawyer networks, as suggested in the case of Silicon Valley in the late twentieth century (Kenney and Florida, 2000; Langlois and Robertson, 1995: 126–7; Suchman, 2000), labour unions, as in the case of some film production networks (Christopherson, 2002b), or geographical proximity and technical communities as perhaps in the cases of the London advertising industry and the New York new media sector (Grabher, 2002a, 2002b, 2004a; Heydebrand and Miron, 2002).

Coordinated industrial district types of business system, on the other hand, display a greater degree of alliance integration, both in terms of the extent of commitment between business partners and in the scope of activities coordinated through alliances. Whether territorially circumscribed or more bounded by particular technologies and markets, these networks of competing and collaborating small- and medium-sized companies share resources and opportunities with a more stable set of partners, albeit one in which firm founding and dissolution are quite common as skilled staff switch between employee, entrepreneurial and employer roles. Often allied through cooperative marketing and distribution organizations, and/or technology development consortia, firms in such districts also share substantial 'collective competition goods' (Le Gales and Voelzkow, 2001) provided by local governments, training organizations, local financial institutions and similar district based agencies.

In some countries the key coordinating role in developing such districts has been played by the local Chamber of Commerce, as in the machine tool industry of Sakaki township in Nagano prefecture in Japan (Friedman, 1988: 187–99). Such high levels of inter-firm cooperation are often maintained and reproduced by political and other barriers to entry, so that large companies cannot easily turn a district dominated by a network of small innovating firms into one dominated by networked firms (Burroni and Trigilia, 2001; Crouch and Trigilia, 2001).

Turning next to consider economies dominated by larger ownership units, these vary considerably in their degree of internal organizational integration and in the scope of, and commitment to, inter-firm alliances, as well as in the prevalent connections between investors and controllers of firms. Two types of conglomerate business systems can be distinguished. Financial conglomerate business systems are dominated by large, diversified holding companies that rarely integrate the disparate activities conducted by subsidiary companies through company wide procedures, routines and careers. Organizational knowledge, capabilities and skills are primarily generated and improved through the integrated direction of business activities by the managers of subsidiary firms rather than by those at the holding company level, who focus mostly on financial asset allocation and performance monitoring. From the point of view of the dynamic capabilities theory of the firm, such holding companies, often controlled by small groups of large shareholders, constitute 'hollow' firms (Teece *et al.*, 1994).

In contrast, integrated conglomerate business systems are dominated by large and widely diversified companies that do integrate their varied activities systematically to ensure that effective transfer of knowledge and skills between subsidiaries and sectors. They combine high levels of authoritative integration of economic activities within and between industrial and service sectors through centralized control of people and money with limited cooperation and collaboration between conglomerates. The postwar Korean *chaebol* appear to be quite similar to such integrated business groups, as do perhaps some French *groupes industriels* (Amsden, 1989; Bauer and Cohen, 1981; Fields, 1995; Janelli, 1993), in their high levels of owner-manager control, diversification and integration of organizational abilities across subsidiary companies. Such centralized and highly diversified groups tend not to develop alliances with each other, and often use their market power to squeeze smaller suppliers.

Compartmentalized business systems are similar to conglomerate ones in their high levels of ownership coordination and limited extent of alliance integration, but differ in their more restricted scope of diversification across disparate sectors and dominant pattern of ownership. Here, large, organizationally integrated firms dominate largely oligopolistic markets and diversify into cognate fields where their skills and knowledge appear to offer economies of scale and scope, but do not usually combine major activities in totally unrelated areas. Additionally, while formal internal controls may be quite centralized in such companies, operational delegation to divisional managers is often greater than that in integrated conglomerates. Overall, the degree and scope of ownership integration in these kinds of business systems are somewhat less than in the previous type, but the general pattern of inter-firm relationships is equally adversarial, with collaborations restricted to specific business deals on a typically short-term basis. Ownership, though, tends to be more widespread, not to say fragmented, with most investors operating at a considerable cognitive and social distance from the top managers of large companies (O'Sullivan, 2000; Tylecote and Conesa, 1999).

In the two remaining distinct kinds of business system that can be distinguished by their degree and scope of authoritative integration of business activities, considerable ownership integration is combined with some, though varying, alliance integration. As in compartmentalized ones, both collaborative and highly coordinated business systems are dominated by large companies that have diversified into mostly technological and market related industries—but not into highly unrelated ones. However, these firms additionally collaborate and cooperate with each other and with business partners on a considerable range of issues, such as training, wage bargaining, technology development and technical standards, much more than is usually the case in compartmentalized business systems. They also tend to have closer and more committed relationships between investors, banks and top managers than is common in the latter systems.

These two types of business system do, however, differ from each other in terms of the extent of vertical ownership integration and reliance on alliance integration to coordinate supply chains and activities across sectors. In collaborative business systems, large companies integrate a considerable range of complementary activities within their sectors through unified ownership and authority hierarchies, but also collaborate with suppliers, customers and competitors over a number of activities, and share authority with powerful employers' and trade associations. They also cooperate with smaller, more specialized firms in a variety of fora, including conducting joint technology development activities, and tend to be less opportunistic than large firms in compartmentalized business systems in taking advantage of them.

Large firms in highly coordinated business systems tend, on the other hand, to rely more on alliances and obligational contracting than unified ownership to integrate supply chains within sectors. These often involve long-term commitments in which knowledge, employees, authority, and sometimes capital, are shared between customers and suppliers on a continuing basis. Additionally, some large companies form large business groups of legally separate firms coordinating activities across many industrial and service sectors, as in the postwar Japanese inter-market groups that integrate banks, manufacturing and other firms from most of the major sectors in the economy (Gerlach, 1992).

Within-company authority sharing is also quite high in these kinds of business system, with high levels of employer–employee commitment, and highly integrated organizational systems that ensure the development of strongly firm-specific knowledge and skills. Organizational careers in these kinds of firms also tend to be more integrated across functions and departments than in the large companies dominating compartmentalized and collaborative business systems, which further facilitates the generation of highly firm-specific knowledge and commitment. As a result of this high level of authority sharing within and between large companies and their major business partners, economic activities in these kinds of business systems are more strongly coordinated through authority relationships than they are in any of the other ones considered here.

Business Systems and Strategic Actors

As this discussion emphasizes, these different kinds of business systems are dominated by quite different kinds of firms, with contrasting ownership structures, authority patterns and organizational capabilities. They also vary considerably in the variety and types of dominant strategic actors that control resources and exercise authority, such that the corporate form combining legal personality, investor ownership, unified authority, limited liability and transferability of shares (Kraakman, 2001) represents only one amongst many feasible centres of authority in market economies. Strategic actors are here understood as authoritatively coordinated organizations that are able to exert sufficient control and decision

Table 1.2. Varieties of strategic actors in different business systems

Type of Business System	Variety of Strategic Actors	Types of Strategic Actors
Fragmented	Low	Owner controlled specialist firms
Compartmentalized	Low	Isolated hierarchies
Integrated conglomerates	Low	Owner controlled conglomerates, plus state elite-firm owner networks
Financial conglomerates	Some	Holding companies, major subsidiaries
Project networks	Some	Specialist firms, business services providers, local and dispersed reputational networks
Industrial districts	Considerable	Owner controlled specialized firms, local states, cooperatives, reputational networks, training and technical colleges, labour unions
Collaborative	Considerable	Most of these, plus employers' and trade associations, labour unions
Highly coordinated	Many	Most of these, plus inter-market groups, vertical networks and trading companies

making power over the activities of their members to constitute separate units of collective economic direction.

In many business systems, networks of firms, business groups, trade associations and similar alliances are able to exert enough authority over legally independent companies to constitute strategic actors in this sense. In such cases, authority over strategic decisions is dispersed among a number of collective actors rather than necessarily being monopolized by a single type of legally and financially defined organization. While, then, legally constituted private companies exist in all market economies as key units of capital accumulation and unified ownership, the extent to which this particular organizational form monopolizes the direction of economic activities varies considerably, as is summarized in Table 1.2. I now briefly discuss how these ideal types of business systems differ in the nature and variety of dominant strategic actors.

Beginning first to consider business systems in which there are few different kinds of strategic actors exercising authority over economic resources and activities, this is especially the case in fragmented and compartmentalized ones. In the former ones, they are small- and medium-sized firms that typically concentrate authority in the hands of owner-managers with little or no sharing of authority with broader inter-firm networks. Similarly, in compartmentalized business systems, authoritative integration of economic activities is concentrated in large companies operating at arm's length from each other and other collective actors such as investing groups and state agencies. As reflected in many economic accounts of market economies, these strategic actors can be seen as 'islands of planned coordination in a sea of market relations' (Richardson, 1972: 883), or isolated hierarchies of authoritative order amidst the disorder of shifting and uncertain markets.

While dominant strategic actors in integrated conglomerate business systems also tend to monopolize the authoritative coordination of economic activities, owners and top managers of these kinds of firms often form close networks with state elites since they typically become dominant in societies where the state plays a leading role in economic development (Schmidt, 2002; Woo, 1991). These state-business networks can become distinct strategic actors when they control scarce resources, such as subsidized credit during high growth periods, and play a major part in the formulation and implementation of economic policies in dominant developmental institutional regimes, as discussed in Chapter 2.

Where more weakly integrated holding companies dominate a market economy, the variety of strategic actors is greater since both the parent firm and its major subsidiaries are able to act as separate centres of economic authority, albeit to varying degrees. Especially where the former focuses on financial control and in effect decentralizes substantial operational and strategic authority to its main operating units, these latter can develop considerable autonomy in pursuing their own interests, often in distinct industries. As they become more successful, they on the one hand generate surpluses that enable them to act more independently of the parent company and, on the other hand, develop specific knowledge of specialized technologies and markets that in practice make it difficult for top managers to intervene effectively in their strategic decisions.

Although, then, the holding company managers in this situation may be able to make broad decisions about capital allocation between sectors, they share considerable authority with subsidiary managers, and rely greatly on the information provided by them. Similar issues arise, of course, in many multidivisional companies in compartmentalized business systems, as described in Freeland's (2001) account of strategic management in General Motors, but authority is more formally divided in many holding companies, and parent company management rarely has the extensive staff and information gathering resources that are typical of the Chandlerian enterprise in the more compartmentalized business system of the twentieth-century USA.

In the case of business systems with greater degrees of alliance coordination, inter-firm networks, trade associations and business groups can become strategic actors in addition to individual companies. Although varying considerably in their stability, and the extent to which they have a central administrative staff that can exercise authority over member firms, all such alliances involve some sharing of authority with other groups that are able to act on behalf of all the companies involved. The most informal and fluid networks have to be able to exert some control over entry and exit, to govern appropriate conduct in matters of dispute, and to mobilize resources and members in pursuit of new opportunities if they are to function as distinct strategic actors. Thus, not all high-technology networks in the USA, or putative industrial districts, constitute strategic actors in this sense, although many do when they institutionalize procedural routines and norms for developing new start-ups, organizing capital raising and monitoring performance, as in the case of venture capitalists and business lawyers in Silicon Valley and elsewhere (Kenney and Florida, 2000; Suchman, 2000).

By establishing distinct 'rules of the game' for highly risky new ventures, such networks of specialist providers of business services become authoritative coordinators of innovative activities in particular localities, albeit with limited centralization of authority and limited capacity to act strategically as a single organizational unit. Informal networks of entrepreneurs can also develop some collective authority over their shifting membership in less formally institutionalized environments, as seems to be the case in some parts of China (Hendrischke, 2007). Here, the network exercises some control over business entry and exit, and is able to mobilize resources to support members seeking to take advantage of new opportunities, often by controlling access to scarce resources such as land use, subsidies and information about trading possibilities.

More stable and visible agents of supra-company economic coordination and control are established in many industrial districts or local production systems (Crouch et al., 2001, 2004), where local governments, banks and other providers of credit and/or loan guarantees, training colleges and distribution/marketing cooperatives provide collective competition goods for local companies. While sometimes conflicting with each other, and often failing to act in concert or control firm behaviour effectively, these agents nonetheless are able to exert some authority over companies, allocate scarce resources and encourage cooperation in pursuit of collective goals, thus limiting short-term opportunism and enabling the district as a whole to generate distinctive collective competences and retain some control over their benefits. The more cohesive they become in working together and exercising authority, the more the district becomes a distinct strategic actor.

Similarly, strong employers' groups and trade federations can exert considerable authority over member companies, especially in highly corporatist societies. Often staffed by permanent officials who are responsible for developing agreements with labour unions and state agencies, establishing particular rules of the game for governing competition and cooperation between member firms, and monitoring performance, these long-term associations can function as separate strategic actors pursuing distinctive collective goals on behalf of their membership, and sometimes disciplining the more wayward companies. In collaborative business systems, then, there are quite a wide range of different kinds of strategic actors, so that conventional, legally constituted firms are only one source of authoritative coordination of economic activities.

This variety of strategic actors, and concomitant limited significance of the legally defined corporate form, is even more marked in highly coordinated business systems where sectoral and inter-market business groups are quite stable and exert considerable authority over member companies. As Westney (2001a) has emphasized, in Japan such groups exchange information, capital and employees between legally independent companies, to the extent that their organizational boundaries become highly permeable and authority is shared between a number of different entities. Accountability for decisions and performance in such complex groups can be difficult to assign, especially for outsiders, as assets are moved between firms in the interests of the group as a whole. In the case of the postwar Japanese economy, strategic actors have included suppliers' associations, general trading companies, bank-dominated business groups, business associations and other alliances in addition to legally constituted companies (Fruin, 1992; Smitka, 1991; Yoshino and Lifson, 1986). As a result, decision making often involves multiple negotiations between a number of collective actors, and responsibility for outcomes can be highly opaque.

Institutions and the National Specificity of Business Systems

As numerous comparative studies have shown these different ways of organizing market economies become dominant in different institutional contexts (see, e.g., Amable, 2003; Hollingsworth and Boyer, 1997; Whitley, 1992a). In explaining, then, the varied importance of these different ideal types of business system in particular market economies, it is crucial to identify the key institutions that encourage differences in the levels of ownership and alliance coordination and in the nature of key strategic actors. These institutions govern the nature of private property rights, authority and trust relations, access to finance, the development of skills and knowledge, and labour relations (Whitley, 1999). Additionally, the informal and formal rules governing the organization of interest groups and their competition for resources in particular jurisdictions are important factors in accounting for differences in patterns of authoritative coordination and control of economic activities (Amable, 2003).

Different kinds of business systems can be expected to develop and dominate particular market economies as a result of variations in these key institutional arrangements, and in the nature of dominant socio-political coalitions. The more complementary are the dominant institutions, in the sense of encouraging similar patterns of firm governance and behaviour, in any one jurisdiction, the more likely that a distinctive pattern of economic organization will become established there. Many of the more distinctive forms of capitalism in the postwar period have been identified at the national level, for instance, because of the dominance of the nation state as the central unit of political-economic organization, competition and control (Amable, 2003; Hollingsworth *et al.*, 1994, 2002). For much of the twentieth century it has been the nation state that determined the nature of private property rights, the rules governing commercial contracts, the rights and obligations of private companies, and it was national institutions that dominated the governance of capital, labour and product markets.

Furthermore, the prevalence of the modern democratic nation state as the dominant focus of political mobilization and competition since 1945—albeit in quite varied and changing ways—has meant that economic interests and socio-economic groups seeking to influence policies and practices have tended to organize nationally, and political-economic choices are more influenced by their expected implications for national constituencies and stakeholders than for regional or transnational ones. Dominant political-economic coalitions are accordingly most likely to be constituted, and to act strategically, at the national level, particularly where the powers of local and regional authorities are weaker than those of national ones.

It is also important to note that under the post-Second-World-War arrangements for managing the international economy agreed at the Bretton Woods conference in 1944, national economies were largely insulated from each other and governed by predominantly national institutions reflecting the choices of powerful nationally organized groups (Menz, 2005; O' Riain, 2000; Schmidt, 2002). As Gilpin (2000: 66) puts it: 'At the time of the BWS (Bretton Woods System) founding, economists assumed that the domestic and international realms were in large part independent of one another... national economies were closed economies... connected by trade flows and exchange rates.' Throughout most of the three postwar decades of continuing, relatively high, economic growth in the major industrialized economies, each state was able to manage 'its' own market economy as it wished within the overall rules of the international economic order established at Bretton Woods and policed by the US dominated institutions.

Consequently, many of the key institutions governing the constitution and behaviour of economic actors, including property rights regimes and the organization of capital and labour markets, were nationally specific and quite variable between countries. This has meant that the governance of leading companies, their dominant strategic goals and how they pursued these have differed considerably between nationally distinct institutional regimes, thus generating different kinds of capitalism at the national level. Most of the diverse systems of economic coordination and control that became established in the postwar period did so within nation states, although this did not mean that each of them dominated all parts of national economies to the same extent, or that every country was dominated by its own, separate and distinct form of economic organization. Together with the strong role of the state in coordinating, and in some cases directing, economic development in many East Asian societies in the postwar period, these features of many market economies made it quite appropriate to compare the dominant forms of economic organization in East Asia and elsewhere as nationally specific business systems whose characteristics could be explained in terms of national institutional features and histories (Whitley, 1992a, 1992b).

However, the extent to which national institutional arrangements dominate regional and local ones varies between countries, sectors and over time. Not all the advanced industrialized states, for instance, have established predictable and reliable legal systems for organizing and governing companies, or for prescribing and sanctioning particular forms of competitive behaviour. In the case of Italy, Farrell and Holten (2004) have suggested that the limited ability of the state to provide reliable collective competition goods encouraged many firms and socio-economic groups to focus on local communities and agencies for support, as well as relying on traditional means of dealing with uncertainty and risks. As a result, in many parts of Italy local governance has become more significant for the development of distinctive patterns of economic organization, such as coordinated industrial districts.

Equally, strong national institutions governing capital and labour markets that standardize the behaviour of actors across industries and regions do not exist in all market economies. Indeed, recent moves to decentralizing wage bargaining and deregulate other aspects of the industrial relations system in some, but by no means all, European countries (Bowman, 2002; Pontusson and Swenson, 1996; Thelen and Wijnbergen, 2003; Vogel, 2001) could suggest a weakening of such national governance norms where they had previously been strongly institutionalized.

Additionally, while some states can have quite strong national institutions governing private property rights and securities markets, they may permit considerable variation in other rules affecting corporate governance and employment relations, as occurs between some state regulations in the USA for instance. This can result in some local differences in the latter areas. Finally, many state agencies pursue sector specific policies for particular public policy reasons that can encourage 'deviant' patterns of collaboration and risk sharing, as arguably has happened in countries where the state has developed strong 'mission-oriented' technology policies (Ergas, 1987) and supported new industries based on them, as will be discussed further in Chapter 3.

Within some general set of national institutions governing economic activities, then, there may be a number of local and sectoral differences that enable contrasting characteristics of business systems to become established in particular localities and industries. Despite the dominant role of national institutions in structuring the organization of economic activities constituting the 'default' option for most of the richer countries since 1945, in practice the extent of such pre-eminence, and the degree to which they have helped to standardize patterns of economic organization throughout national economies, have varied considerably between states and over historical periods. As a result, the prevalence of particular patterns of authoritative coordination and control in national economies has often differed between territorial levels, jurisdictions and sectors, with some characteristics being quite nationally homogenous, but other ones being more heterogenous between subnational regions and industries (Kenworthy, 2005).

These variations and changes in the degree of national homogeneity of dominant institutions, and in their related patterns of economic organization, highlight four important points about the comparative analysis of competing capitalisms. These concern: (a) the contingent nature of nationally specific business systems, (b) the need to distinguish between ideal types of economic organization and empirical analyses of concrete economies, (c) the identification of the causes and consequences of significant institutional and economic change, and (d) the nature of the connections between dominant institutions, business system characteristics and economic performance.

Considering first the contingent nature of nationally dominant business systems, once it is recognized that the relationships between national boundaries and institutions and prevalent forms of capitalism are empirically variable rather than being necessarily isomorphic, then it becomes important to investigate how and why particular kinds of business system come to dominate certain national economies, as well as how they change. The national homogeneity and standardization of key institutions, together with the nature of dominant political-economic coalitions of interest groups, are clearly critical in such analyses, as will be further discussed in Chapter 2.

Second, comparative analyses of economic systems rely on ideal types of socio-economic organization that are rarely, if ever, manifested as a totality in any one empirical situation. Whether considering 'liberal market economies', 'social democratic' systems of innovation and production, or 'highly coordinated' business systems, these are all abstract constructs that focus on particular combinations of properties of socio-economic phenomena, which are much more coherent and systemic than the everyday behaviour and rules of the game that we observe in practice (Crouch, 2005: 68–73). As such, they hypostatize certain logics of action that underlie empirical practices and help to explain them.

It is important, then, to distinguish clearly between these idealized constructions and any empirical realization of combinations of elements from different ones in particular societies. To understand how and why various forms of economic organization become established, reproduced and changed in different territories and jurisdictions, and have varied outcomes, we construct these ideal types that highlight specific aspects resulting from underlying mechanisms and processes. Any concrete economy can be understood as the site of competing kinds of business system and economic rationalities, supported by different institutions and interest groups that struggle to establish their economic logics and rules of the game as the dominant ones.

Third, dominant business systems can, and do, change, as can institutions. Thus, currently dominant ways of organizing economic activities in any given jurisdiction may well become transformed as a result of both internal conflicts and external pressures. How and why economic systems and the key institutions governing them change have become the focus of considerable debate in recent years as many firms, markets and institutions have developed cross-nationally and previously stable business systems within national boundaries seen as liable to alter some of their key characteristics (see, e.g. Campbell, 2005; Morgan *et al.*, 2005; Streeck and Yamamura, 2003). Additionally, the establishment and growth of some transnational institutions, notably within the European Union but also more generally as in the case of the World Trade Organization, highlights the growing complexity of multi-levelled governance of economic activities in many parts of the world (Bache and Flinders, 2004), as will be analysed further in Chapter 5.

Fourth, the national variability of dominant institutions, forms of authoritative coordination of economic activities and relative success in particular industries have highlighted the role of institutional frameworks in accounting for differences in economic performance. Sometimes summarized in terms of the comparative institutional advantages of differently organized societies (Hall and Soskice, 2001), the connections between institutional arrangements, firm governance and behaviour and competitive success have been emphasized in studies of differences in national innovative performance across sectors (Casper *et al.*, 1999; Soskice, 1999). These processes are analysed in more detail in Part III of this book.

We can begin to address these concerns in the comparative analysis of competing capitalisms and how they change by extending the comparative business systems framework in three ways. First, to identify more explicitly the processes through which distinctive business systems and innovation systems become dominant at the national level, as well as the conditions in which increasing transnational governance can be expected to affect their cohesion and scope. In particular, to show both how different institutional regimes and political-economic alliances sustain these varied systems of economic organization, and how specific kinds of endogenous and exogenous pressures can result in changes to them.

Second, to incorporate the dynamic capabilities theory of the firm with institutionalist approaches to the analysis of organizations and economic change so that we can specify the processes through which different macro-institutional environments encourage different kinds of firms to develop varied competitive competences and dominate particular industries. Third, to consider how the internationalization of firms, markets and some institutions is leading to significant changes in the nature of dominant firms and their competitive competences, especially the circumstances in which different kinds of multinational companies are likely to develop novel organizational capabilities as a result of operating in varied institutional contexts.

Outline of the Book

These three sets of issues form the basis of the three main parts of this book. The next part deals with complementarities and changes in institutional regimes at different levels of collective organization, and how these affect the establishment and modification of dominant business systems and innovation systems in different countries, regions and industrial sectors. It consists of four chapters identifying the circumstances in which distinctive business and innovation systems can be expected to dominate national economies, and how these change with shifts in their institutional environments, particularly the growth of international governance.

The first chapter in this part considers the kinds of states and associated institutional regimes that are likely to generate different kinds of dominant business system at the national level, with contrasting types of strategic actors, governance structures and organizational capabilities. The extent to which business system characteristics are nationally standardized and homogenous across sectors and regions can be expected to vary considerably between these contrasting institutional regimes.

The next chapter extends this approach to the analysis of innovation systems and suggests how different institutional factors help to explain the establishment of six distinct varieties of these at the national level in certain circumstances. Particular combinations of state structures and policies, public science systems and dominant institutions governing economic activities are likely to generate nationally varied patterns of innovation and technological change.

In analysing changes in national institutional regimes and allied forms of economic organization since the breakdown of the BWS, it is important to identify the major endogenous factors, and their linkages with exogenous ones, that were critical in different political-economies, especially the changing nature of dominant interest groups. It has been especially when these endogenous pressures were complementary in their implications for the constitution and behaviour of economic actors with exogenous ones that they have had significant effects on prevalent patterns of economic organization at the national level. Particularly important in this respect have been changes in the institutional constraints on short-term economic opportunism and in the kinds of collective competition goods provided by different regional, national and transnational agencies. These interconnections and their consequences for nationally dominant business systems are explored in Chapter 4.

One of the key exogenous factors encouraging changes in these business systems has been the growing internationalization of business regulation, as documented by Braithwaite and Drahos' *Global Business Regulation* (2000). Another, more variable, influence is the increasing coordination of trade and related economic policies by nation states, especially within the EU and various regional trade agreements. While these have tended to be viewed as forces that reduce the power and distinctiveness of national institutions in structuring economic activities, and so the variability of nationally dominant business systems, their nature and consequences are more varied and complex than is commonly assumed (see, e.g. the papers in Weiss, 2003b). In Chapter 5, I suggest how we could begin to analyse the changing transnational governance of economic activities in the late twentieth and early twenty-first century and its likely effects on established patterns of economic organization.

The four chapters in part two explore the connections between institutional regimes, firm type and behaviour in more detail, focusing especially on how variations in dominant institutions encourage different kinds of firms to develop distinctive competitive capabilities that are more effective in certain kinds of industries. These chapters suggest how the analysis of societal institutions could be integrated with recent work in the theory of the firm to understand how different institutional environments encourage companies to become competitive in different kinds of industry by developing varied kinds of organizational capabilities through contrasting forms of authority sharing. This helps to explain how societies with dominant institutions resembling particular ideal types of institutional regimes can be expected to become specialized in different sorts of industries and subsectors.

The first chapter in this part explores the roles of authority sharing and organizational careers in encouraging skilled employees and business partners to contribute to the development of firm and network specific dynamic capabilities. Variations in commitment between investors, managers and employees, in particular, are seen as crucial to the explanation of how different kinds of firms generate diverse competitive competences. These variations in turn are connected to differences in dominant institutional features, especially those constraining short-term economic opportunism and providing collective competition goods such as skilled labour power.

This kind of analysis of the relationships between the institutional environment of firms and the capabilities they develop can be combined with studies of innovation systems to account for differences in prevalent innovative competences between market economies. In Chapter 7, I suggest that four major approaches to the generation of such capabilities can be distinguished in terms of how firms learn about new processes, products and services, which lead to different patterns of innovation. These approaches are more or less likely to be adopted by leading firms in economies governed by different institutional frameworks, especially when combined with different kinds of public science systems and modes of training researchers.

In Chapter 8, Steven Casper and I further develop this framework to account for significant national differences in the relative success of entrepreneurial technology firms in two high-risk industries: biotechnology and computer software. By suggesting how such firms develop different kinds of competences to deal with variations in appropriability and competence destruction risks in different subsectors of these industries, we are able to show how the diverse institutional frameworks governing business activities in Germany, Sweden, and the UK in the 1990s led to different patterns of relative success in these subsectors. The seemingly anomalous case of middleware internet software in Sweden can be, at least partially, accounted for by the coordinating role of Ericsson and changes in its employment and intellectual property policies.

The growing significance of inter-firm networks and project-based firms in many industries, which some claim heralds major changes in dominant economic forms (Powell, 2001), is analysed in Chapter 9. Rather than assuming that all such enterprises are basically the same, I suggest that it would be fruitful to distinguish between four ideal types of project-based firms in terms of the singularity of their goals, on the one hand, and the separation and stability of the division of labour, on the other hand. These ideal types vary in their importance across subsectors with different output characteristics, such as appropriability, modularity and technological cumulativeness, and processes, such as client involvement. They also are more or less likely to become prevalent in contrasting institutional environments, which means that the establishment of the

Silicon Valley type of economic organization as the dominant form is improbable in many societies.

In the final part of this book I suggest how we can extend this integration of the institutionalist analysis of organizations and the capabilities theory of the firm to study the internationalization of companies in the twenty-first century. The three chapters of this part focus on multinational companies (MNCs) as potentially distinctive kinds of organizations, examining in particular the conditions under which firms from different institutional regimes are likely to develop different internationalization strategies and varied transnational firm-specific capabilities.

In Chapter 10, I consider how the three ideal types of firm that become dominant in different kinds of institutional regime described in Chapter 6 could be expected to internationalize their operations, especially the extent to which their foreign subsidiaries are encouraged to develop novel kinds of distinctive knowledge and competences that could lead to changes in the parent company. From this analysis, it seems clear that MNCs from differently organized home economies will vary considerably how much they could 'learn from abroad' and alter as a result of operating across national boundaries. They also are likely to differ significantly in how they manage subsidiaries in host economies with contrasting business environments.

The processes through which different kinds of MNCs might develop firm-specific transnational organizational capabilities are further explored in Chapter 11 where I suggest how firms from four quite differently organized home economies could be expected to share authority with, and provide international organizational careers for, staff in their foreign subsidiaries. Essentially, the argument follows the logic outlined in Chapters 6 and 7 in that the generation of transnational collective competences that are specific to the MNC depends greatly on the encouragement of high levels of commitment to the parent company from foreign employees, over and above that engendered to each national unit. Given the limited extent of such international authority sharing and provision of organizational careers in most of the six major kinds of MNC identified in these terms, this commitment seems likely to be restricted in degree and scope, and so most international companies will only rarely develop distinctive kinds of transnational knowledge and capabilities as a result of operating in different national contexts. This means that the MNC cannot be expected to be a distinctive kind of firm simply because it controls activities in different nation states.

Japanese companies are often portrayed as being particularly reluctant to share authority with foreign nationals and to integrate their careers with domestic staff. However, the ways that firms from this highly coordinated market economy have internationalized their operations in the postwar period vary between sectors and over time (Westney, 2001b). Some of the significant differences between Japanese banks and car manufacturers in this regard are discussed in Chapter 12, which reports some results of a study of Japanese and Korean firms in the UK conducted with Glenn Morgan, Bill Kelly, and Diana Sharpe. Most of the banks have remained highly domestically embedded in the sense that their competitive competences are closely interdependent with the Japanese postwar institutional context and have proven difficult to extend to overseas markets. In contrast, although the core competences of leading Japanese car manufacturers are also strongly embedded in their domestic environment, these can be, and have been, extended to foreign plants and subsidiaries through considerable investment in training and close supervision by expatriate managers and engineers. In both cases, however, the extent to which these companies have learnt from abroad has been limited—as seems also to have been the case in some Japanese pharmaceutical firms (Lam, 2003)—and their development of novel transnational organizational capabilities remains rather restricted.

Part II

The Changing Nature of National Capitalisms: Institutional Regimes, Business Systems, and Innovation Systems

2

The Contingent Nature of National Business Systems: Types of States and Complementary Institutions

Introduction

As emphasized in the previous chapter, the extent to which the key institutions governing economic relationships are nationally specific and complementary in their implications for economic actors can vary considerably. As a result, the institutionalization of coherent forms of economic organization as distinctive kinds of business systems at the national level is a contingent, not necessary, phenomenon. They could, and have been, established at sub-national levels in Germany, Italy and elsewhere (Crouch *et al.*, 2001; 2004; Herrigel, 1996). Not all national market economies, then, are dominated by a single kind of business system throughout all regions and sectors, and not all cohesive and stable business systems are nationally specific and bounded. The nature of firms, their strategies and capabilities frequently vary between sectors, technological regimes and regions within countries, and can also overlap across national boundaries (Braczyk *et al.*, 1998; Breschi and Malerba, 1997; Whitley, 1999).

Such variable connections between national boundaries and forms of economic organization raise questions about the circumstances in which distinctive business systems become established and reproduced at the national level. More generally, how do different kinds of institutional arrangements at different levels of social organization help to constitute economic actors and regulate their behaviour in contrasting ways, and what are the consequences of changes in such arrangements, especially for economic performance?

In dealing with these kinds of questions, there are two aspects of the institutions governing property rights, capital, labour and product markets that are particularly important. First, their relative strength and stability at different levels of collective organization. Second, their degree of coherence and complementarity in encouraging particular economic rationalities and patterns of behaviour throughout national market economies. Institutional arrangements in, say, labour markets are complementary with those in capital markets in this sense if they reinforce actors' preferences for specific strategies and actions in those domains, such as relational financing (Aoki, 2001: 310–26). As Deeg (2005a) suggests, complementarity implies a logic of synergy whereby the influence of institutions in one domain of action is strengthened by institutional arrangements in another one.

The establishment and reproduction of distinctive and cohesive business systems at national, subnational or transnational territorial levels depends, then, on the strength and complementarity of the key institutions governing economic activities at each level, relative to those established at different levels. This suggests that when some national institutions become less dominant relative to cross-national ones, as in the European Union, the national specificity of economic systems may be reduced. Their cohesion and distinctiveness are especially likely to decline when the governing principles of institutional arrangements at the national and international levels are contradictory in their implications for economic actors, as discussed in Chapter 5.

In attempting to understand how and why different patterns of economic organization become established and reproduced at different levels of collective organization, then, a key issue is how strong and complementary are governing institutions at those levels and how much they generate similar kinds of actors to manage their interrelationships in similar ways across sectors, regions and size classes of firms. At the national level, this involves consideration of the nature and role of states, especially their internal cohesion and ability to pursue consistent policies regarding the organization and regulation of capital and labour markets.

As well as providing a stable and predictable environment for economic actors to make strategic decisions, an important feature of states concerns the extent of their involvement in the development and organization of economic actors. As Evans (1994: 9–10) points out, most, if not all, states in industrial capitalist societies, are involved in improving national competitive advantages, often by encouraging the development of particular kinds of firms and capabilities. They differ, though, in how they attempt to do this, and in their capacity to implement their policies effectively. These differences affect the extent to which distinctive kinds of national business systems become standardized across regions and sectors.

In order to clarify the circumstances in which we would expect different kinds of states with complementary institutions to lead to contrasting varieties of firm governance structures, authority sharing and organizational capabilities becoming institutionalized throughout their economies, this chapter identifies four ideal types of states that combine with particular features of allied institutions to constitute particular institutional regimes. These differ especially in how much they organize and develop economic actors in standard ways throughout national political economies. In general, the more states organize and homogenize: (a) the nature of legitimate economic actors, (b) the rules governing their interaction, and (c) the organization of interest representation, the more we would expect them to develop nationally distinctive business systems.

In the next section, I summarize the key features of four kinds of states that vary considerably in the extent to which, and ways in which, they promote specific paths of development. Such broad contrasts between types of states do downplay the significance of internal conflicts and susceptibility to fragmentation between political factions, bureaucratic elites and other groups within states, as well as differences in electoral systems and the organization of political parties, but this seems to me justified for the purposes of considering how different kinds of states are likely to affect the establishment of contrasting kinds of business systems at the national level. Subsequently, I suggest how these different kinds of states and national institutional arrangements are likely to encourage varying degrees of standardization of firm governance structures and strategies across sectors, and how these in turn generate nationally distinctive forms of authority sharing, commitment and organizational capabilities in different kinds of firms.

Types of States and Complementary National Institutions

The development of cohesive business systems at the national level depends, inter alia, on states establishing stable rules of the game governing economic decision making. However, the ways in which they do so, and the kinds of rules that they entrench, vary considerably between different kinds of states as the extensive literature on comparative political economy illustrates (see, for example, Amable, 2003; Hart, 1992; Schmidt,

2002). In considering how different kinds of states are likely to: (a) encourage the establishment and reproduction of distinctive national business systems, and (b) help to standardize these across sectors and sub-national regions, two features are critical.

First, the extent to which the state is actively involved in coordinating and steering economic development, especially in helping to construct particular kinds of organizational capabilities, varies greatly between the arm's length approaches of most liberal market economies and the *dirigiste* policies of highly active states. While the former focus on establishing clear rules of the competitive game within which varied kinds of economic actors are free to pursue their objectives as they wish, the latter are more concerned to develop particular kinds of actors and sectors. In Evans' (1994: 77–81) terminology, what are here termed arm's length states perform custodial roles that concentrate on establishing and applying rules as remote policing agents, while more promotional states take active steps to develop new industries and skills as direct producers, midwives and supporters. These often involve providing financial and other types of assistance and sanctioning failure of specific firms and groups, as well as organizing markets to support entry into new industries.

Second, states differ greatly in the extent to which they actively encourage and structure independent intermediary associations representing the interests of different groups that become involved in policy formulation and implementation. While arm's length states usually leave it up to individual firms, unions and other groups to organize as they wish, more promotional ones tend to standardize interest group representation in particular ways that facilitate the state's coordinating role. These latter do, however, vary greatly in: (a) how they do so, (b) for which interests, and (c) how autonomous such associations are from the state, as the extensive literature on corporatism illustrates (see, e.g., Crouch, 1999: Chapter 12; 2003; Katzenstein, 1985; Streeck and Schmitter, 1985). Where states are quite constrained in their attempts to construct national competitive advantages by powerful and relatively autonomous social groupings, as perhaps is the case in Denmark (Karnoe, 1999; Kristensen, 1992; 1994; Martin, 2006; Pedersen, 2006), the less likely they are to develop nationally specific and homogenous business systems with similar characteristics throughout the country and across all sectors.

Variations in states' developmental policies suggest at least three major varieties of promotional states can be distinguished in terms of how they encourage and support the development of independent interest groups of different kinds and involve them in economic policy development and implementation. In what might be termed dominant developmental states such as South Korea since 1961 or postwar France up to the 1980s, industry associations and similar groupings do sometimes form, but these usually function as agents of the state rather than as autonomous representatives of distinct interests (Fields, 1995; Kim, 1997; Schmidt, 2002; Woo, 1991). On the whole, such states do not support the establishment of independent peak associations that could challenge its decisions or interfere with its direct links with owners and top managers.

More collaborative promotional states, on the other hand, do support intermediary associations with greater autonomy, often by delegating some powers to them and granting them representational monopolies in dealing with state agencies, either on a formal or informal basis. However, they differ in terms of their recognition and involvement of labour union federations in economic policy making. Business corporatist states tend to work most closely with associations of large companies, such as the *keidanren* in Japan (Eccleston, 1989; Pempel, 1998; Samuels, 1987), and rarely encourage peak associations of labour unions to become involved in policy making. Inclusive corporatist states, on the other hand, are more concerned to mobilize unions at the national level to deal with distributional issues and manage incomes policies. In both cases, the active involvement of business associations by the state tends to encourage their standardization as state agencies seek predictable and reliable partners for achieving their development goals.

A further logically possible kind of state would combine a regulative, arm's length approach with highly centralized economic policymaking and implementation. However, this seems empirically and theoretically unlikely to be stable. Since arm's length states are primarily concerned to establish formal rules of the game that are neutral between economic actors and outcomes, they are not inclined to build direct links on a continuing basis to particular firms or to encourage business dependence on state agencies, except perhaps in areas of major state responsibility, such as defence and security, where state procurement policies inevitably affect firm development. On the whole, then, effective arm's length states do not seek to structure firms' strategies or behaviour, but prefer to operate remotely and allow 'market forces' to determine outcomes.

These four ideal types of states, arm's length, dominant developmental, business corporatist and inclusive corporatist, develop different kinds of approaches to the regulation and management of capital and labour markets, as well as institutionalizing varied political cultures and legal systems. These different approaches lead to variations in the standardization of interest group formation, labour relations and skill formation systems, especially between inclusive corporatist states and arm's length ones.

These different kinds of states combine with other institutional variations to constitute distinct institutional regimes governing economic activities within national jurisdictions. These institutional regimes organize leading economic actors and other interest groups, and the rules governing their cooperation and competition, in particular ways that also vary in their national standardization and homogeneity. They include: the nature and reliability of the legal system, especially the specification and regulation of property rights, the norms governing authority relations, market boundaries and behaviour, interest group formation and interaction, and the skill formation system. Different kinds of regimes encourage different patterns of economic organization to become dominant at the national level, especially in the areas of corporate governance, authority sharing and the kinds of organizational capabilities that leading companies develop. The key features of these four types of states and associated institutions are summarized in Table 2.1 and will now be further discussed.

Since states are political entities, they institutionalize particular conceptions of power and authority that impinge upon relations of subordination elsewhere in market economies, particularly within firms. While, then, cultural norms governing authority are not always standardized within national boundaries, and are often shared between liberal democratic societies, the ways in which state elites justify their status and claims to subjects' loyalty tend to be specific to particular countries. In particular, the extent to which relations between politicians, and the state more generally, and the public are understood in largely contractual terms, as distinct from paternalistic or communitarian ones, differs considerably between societies.

The more that political authority is seen to rest on services rendered between equal and remote transacting partners who do not directly share collective interests, the more likely that authority within other organizations will also be viewed as primarily contractual. Conversely, political and bureaucratic elites in more promotional states often justify their roles in paternalistic terms that encourage paternalism within companies. Inclusive corporatist states, however, are more likely to invoke communitarian norms that treat citizens as equals and emphasize the common interests of all members of the polity.

Similarly, where states are trusted by most citizens to follow the 'rule of law' and pursue the collective interests of society as a whole rather than

Table 2.1. State types and complementary institutions

Key Characteristics	State Types			
	Arm's Length	Dominant Developmental	Business Corporatist	Inclusive Corporatist
Active involvement in economic development	Low	High	Considerable	Considerable
Active encouragement of business associations	Limited	Limited	Considerable	Considerable
Active encouragement of labour associations and organization of representation	Limited	Low	Limited	Considerable
Complementary Institutions				
Prevalent norms governing subordination	Contractual	Paternalist	Paternalist	Communitarian
Reliability of legal system and formal institutions	Considerable	Varied	Varied	Considerable
Strength of minority property rights	Considerable	Limited	Limited	Limited
Strength of arm's length competition policies	Considerable	Limited	Limited	Limited
Market segmentation and entry constraints	Limited	Considerable	Considerable	Considerable
Standardization of interest group representation	Low	Some	Some	Considerable
Standardization of labour relations	Limited	Varied	Varied	Considerable
Standardization of skill formation system	Low	Varied	Limited	Considerable

those of the political class or individual politicians, trust in other institutional arrangements is likely to be high, including those dealing with economic transactions and disputes. Since the legal and justice systems of states remain the central institutions regulating economic activities, their efficacy and reliability are critical factors governing the management of transactional uncertainty and the longevity of investment horizons, as well as the nature of employer–employee commitments. National variations in these systems affect the ways in which owners deal with managers and other employees, as well as economic opportunism more generally. While most societies with industrialized market economies, or OECD states, have developed relatively effective legal systems, how these operate in practice and how willing firms are to rely on them for settling disputes vary considerably across countries in ways that affect firm governance and behaviour. In particular, their autonomy, cost, speed and reliability differ.

States with predictable legal systems develop varied relationships with different kinds of institutions governing financial markets and competition that often complement and reinforce their encouragement of economic opportunism or commitment and cooperation between particular groups of economic actors. Three aspects of these institutions are especially important: their protection of minority shareholders, their facilitation of trading ownership and control of companies in a largely anonymous market, and their regulation of competition. While these are often correlated in terms of their impact on firm structures and behaviour, they are not necessarily so. It is quite possible, for example, to have a financial system with formally equal shareholders, as in postwar Japan, that has a very weak market for corporate control because of limited mechanisms reinforcing this formal 'constitutional' governance regime (Aguilera and Jackson, 2003).

On the whole, arm's length states seem more likely to establish relatively transparent capital markets, in which all participants are formally equal and funds are priced and allocated through market processes, than are promotional ones seeking to mobilize capital for specific goals. They should, then, be more concerned to protect the rights of minority shareholders, while the latter develop close links to major block holders who can cooperate effectively in achieving state policy goals. Similarly, while arm's length states typically insist that firms are distinct, legally separate entities competing in a large anonymous market, and legislate against collusion and cooperation, promotional ones often encourage them to collaborate and share risks in developing new markets, skills and technologies. Even where anti-cartel legislation promoting competition has been passed, such countries have differed considerably in the vigour with which they enforce it, as the cases of Germany and Japan show (Berghahn, 1986; Djelic and Quack, 2005; Gao, 2001: 144–9; Sheridan, 1993).

In addition to such norms encouraging flexible trading relationships, states vary in the extent to which they regulate market entry and exit and encourage collective means of settling disputes through trade associations. Segmented markets with strong industry and trade associations are less likely to be developed in arm's length states because they will be seen as preventing market forces acting throughout an economy, while encouraging collusion that may be against the perceived public interest. Conversely, some promotional states often view such groupings as essential to risk sharing and technological progress, as well as being important agencies for state-backed economic growth. By organizing market entry and exit for developmental goals, such states are able to structure incentives for firms to develop effective capabilities in new industries and to exit old ones with limited losses.

The organization and standardization of interest group representation, as well as the nature of the skill formation system, can additionally complement the effects of state types and policies on the organization of economic activities and encouragement of opportunistic behaviour. Considering first business associations, these vary in their domination of different sectors, their national heterogeneity and the scope of services that they provide for their members. On the whole, arm's length states leave the organization and roles of such associations to individual companies, and rarely support attempts to establish monopolistic groupings in each sector that could co-ordinate training initiatives, diffuse new technologies and set standards. As a result, business associations in these kinds of market economies often compete for membership, rarely represent all the leading firms in an industry or other unit of collective organization, and are usually unable to discipline their membership or guarantee their support for agreed policies. Their ability to provide valuable collective competition goods is therefore limited.

Dominant developmental states are often suspicious of independent intermediary associations that could compete with state authority in developing and implementing economic policies, and so rarely support their development by delegating substantial powers to them. Where they exist then, such groupings are typically limited in their authority and unable to co-ordinate activities independently of state direction. Authority sharing between firms is unlikely to be high in countries dominated by such states, and opportunism in seeking state support considerable.

More collaborative promotional states, on the other hand, actively enlist business association support in carrying out economic policies, and often delegate substantial powers and resources to organizations that monopolize representation and other roles. Because such states encourage firms to join particular organizations and to form federations that unite major interest groups, these associations are usually able to exert considerable influence over their members and to constrain opportunistic behaviour. Authority sharing within such groupings is therefore much greater than that between firms in countries with other kinds of states, especially where companies that remain outside them are seen as weak and/or exploitative and so most firms join them for reputation effects (Culpepper, 1999; 2001).

Considering next the institutions governing labour unions, these vary greatly in their homogenization of forms of representation within a country and the extent to which they encourage workers to join them. Again, arm's length states rarely specify the particular forms that labour representation should take or support their attempts to monopolize membership in particular industries or crafts. Beyond specifying the rules governing labour relations, especially strike actions; most such states restrict their regulation of labour representation. As a result, this is often quite heterogeneous, especially between skilled trades and unskilled workers, between sectors, especially between public and private employers, and manufacturing and service industries, and between professional highly qualified labour and manual workers.

Dominant developmental states usually take more active measures to discourage and/or control union organization, particularly when that would threaten state development policies, and sometimes attempt to structure union organization by forbidding certain forms. The South Korean state, for example, at one time encouraged enterprise unions and prohibited industrial ones. Mostly, such states either attempt to prevent them being formed at all or else ensure that they do so under state tutelage and in effect become an arm of the state's development policy (Deyo, 1989; Kim, 1997; Woo, 1991). In either case, they rarely influence firms' strategies very much and, when independent, often oppose owners and managers in a zero sum approach.

Collaborative promotional states sometimes encourage more positive union attitudes and delegate certain welfare functions to them, thus increasing union membership. Business corporatist ones do, however, differ from inclusive corporatist states in the degree to which they support particular forms of labour representation and involve them in policy development and implementation. In the former countries, the state delegates most aspects of labour management and social welfare to private companies, especially the largest ones, and does not usually encourage the formation of national union federations or standardized systems of labour representation throughout the economy. The coordination of wage bargaining across firms and sectors is here left to privately organized groups, albeit, no doubt, with considerable informal state assistance to ensure that developmental objectives are not compromised.

As a result, the national standardization of labour representation and bargaining systems across sectors and firm type remains restricted in business corporatist states, and the involvement of labour unions in economic policy making and implementation is limited. In Japan, for example, after the strikes of the early 1950s, the state encouraged enterprise based unions rather than industrial and craft based ones and did not involve national union federations in policy discussions (Cusumano, 1985; Gao, 2001; Garon, 1987).

In many of the European corporatist states, on the other hand, unions are more standardized in their organizational basis and form strong federations that negotiate with both employers' associations and state agencies. Inclusive corporatist states establish formal mechanisms to coordinate wage bargaining and economic policy development. Typically organized through national employer and union federations such public-private collaboration is often quite centralized and based upon relatively formal, standardized systems of labour representation, both within enterprises and sectors. Consequently, these kinds of states develop quite nationally cohesive and distinctive patterns of labour organization that encourage firms to work together as well as to engage in continuous discussions with unions and state agencies.

Similar differences can be found in the skill formation systems of different states. Arm's length states tend to develop rather heterogeneous and changeable ways of developing, assessing and certifying practical skills and expertise, often relying on 'market forces' to guide the establishment of training programmes and evaluation of their outputs. Whether these are organized around apprenticeships, professional examinations or educational establishments, the state here usually prefers to delegate skill formation processes to a variety of groups and organizations, with little attempt to establish a nationally standardized system. As a result, flexibility and responsiveness to market changes are often high, but signalling of competences in labour markets is difficult and time consuming, often leading to high rates of labour turnover (Crouch et al., 1999; Marsden, 1999).

Dominant developmental states often take a more active part in organizing skill formation processes, but usually within the state system. Standardization of training in state technical schools and similar organizations can therefore be considerable in such countries, but resources are not always substantial and the prestige of the expertise gained may be limited. Since neither employers nor unions are usually involved in these processes, the practical utility of the skills produced may be restricted, and, again, firms have to find out through experience how to assess and use them. Additionally, since the state here typically monopolizes the provision and assessment of practical skills, the speed with which training programmes respond to market changes is often limited.

Collaborative states are more willing to involve companies directly in skill formation, usually with state agencies playing a coordinating role, for example through a national skill testing and certification system as in Japan (Crouch *et al.*, 1999). Again, though, they differ in how much they involve labour representatives and standardize training provision. In the business corporatist countries, states tend to delegate most training provision to employers and do not standardize training programmes. Such 'segmentalist' skill formation systems typically rely on public schools and universities to produce a highly educated workforce that can be trained for company purposes in house (Thelen and Kume, 2001). Since the larger firms can invest more resources in such training and offer more credible commitments to long-term employment, their staff tend to become more highly skilled and to contribute more to firm-specific knowledge and competences.

Inclusive corporatist states, on the other hand, develop more homogenous skill formation systems that integrate state schools with employer provided training, usually with the active participation of labour unions and workplace representatives. While the extent of employer provided training varies between, say, Germany and Sweden, it is usually cooperatively planned and monitored by representatives of employers, unions and state agencies. Skills are therefore quite highly standardized and well understood by firms and unions. Such cooperation may limit the speed of response to market changes but does ensure rapid introduction of new standards and courses once they have been agreed. Furthermore, it encourages the generation of relatively broad skills that enable future learning, rather than those that are limited to the performance of specific tasks.

In general, then, skill formation is quite standardized in these kinds of societies and is built upon considerable employer-union collaboration. Again, opportunism in labour markets is constrained by complementarities between state policies, the nature of the institutions governing financial flows and bargaining systems that encourage commitment between economic actors.

Types of States, Complementary Institutions, and the National Homogeneity of Business Systems

The combination of these institutional features with the four ideal types of states constitute particular kinds of institutional regimes that govern economic activities within their national borders in different ways, and so can be expected to generate nationally distinct dominant business systems and firm types. However, although such institutional regimes generally encourage particular kinds of governance structures and firm strategies to become prevalent in national political economies, they do vary in the extent to which all aspects of these are standardized systematically throughout the economy, especially across industrial sectors and between firms of different sizes.

It is also worth emphasizing that national institutions in particular countries often differ considerably in their complementarity in reinforcing certain forms of economic organization and firm behaviour, and discouraging others. Relatively arm's length relations between large banks and companies, for example, can be combined with a legislative framework that severely restricts the market for corporate control and grants the incumbent top management considerable protection against hostile takeovers, as in the Netherlands (van Iterson and Olie, 1992). Together with largely corporatist public-private relationships and strong unions, this tends to encourage authority sharing and employer–employee commitment in that country, despite some limited institutional pressures towards arm's length contracting. Similar sorts of variations in the extent of institutional complementarity between state strength and promotional policies, bank-firm connections and the organization of labour markets seem to explain differences in the cohesion and homogeneity of Finnish and Danish business systems and firms in much of the postwar period (Kristensen, 1992; 1996; 2006; Lilja *et al.*, 1992; Lilja and Tainio, 1996).

In any empirical case, then, contradictions between dominant institutional arrangements can be expected with respect to firm governance, strategies, authority sharing and employer–employee commitments, and their associated organizational capabilities, but these vary in their strength and scope over time and between countries. Generally, the greater they are, the more opportunity that firms' top managers have for developing idiosyncratic characteristics and distinctive strategies and capabilities (Hancke and Goyer, 2005; Herrigel and Wittke, 2005). When these kinds of contradictions are considerable and linked to powerful competing socio-economic groups, the likelihood of institutionalizing a cohesive national business system is limited because they permit different sectoral and regional interests to follow contrasting paths of development.

Bearing such possible empirical contradictions between institutions within national boundaries in mind, I now consider how these four distinct kinds of ideal states and their complementary institutions can be expected to establish and reproduce nationally distinct standardized forms of economic organization and firm behaviour. The kinds of governance structures, inter-firm and employment relations and organizational capabilities that are likely to become established in these states, as well as their variability across sectors, are summarized in Table 2.2, and will now be further discussed.

Examining first arm's length states with complementary institutions limiting commitments between economic actors, these establish formal rules of competition and cooperation without greatly restricting and standardizing the nature of economic actors, the organization of interest groups or the movement of resources and skills between markets. Such rules are usually generic across markets. They impose few limits on the kinds of owners or managers that can enter particular kinds of markets, or on the kinds of strategies they follow and how they implement them. Equally, the structure and boundaries of interest groups, as well as their relationships with their members, are typically not specified, so that employers' groups, unions and professions are heterogeneous in their governance and operations. This means that the relative influence of such groups on firms' priorities and strategies can vary within and between such countries, as can their pursuit of growth or profit goals and investment in developing different kinds of organizational capabilities.

Within the broadly arm's length relationships between major economic actors in these kinds of societies, for example, the autonomy of managers from shareholders to invest in the development of routines and collective expertise to realize economies of scale and scope can differ considerably over time and across sectors. In the case of the USA, Lazonick and O'Sullivan (1996; 1997) have suggested that, during much of the twentieth century, capital markets provided relatively patient capital to large companies able to pay out steady dividends. This enabled many of them to develop substantial managerial hierarchies and invest in innovative capabilities. Subject, then, to the general constraints of capital market expectations and market for corporate control, senior managers in these kinds of states can have considerable freedom to determine strategies and change direction.

Additionally, the organization of labour relations is often left open in such societies, with multiple possibilities available to firms. Heterogeneity in employer–employee relationships is therefore quite high, especially between sectors and firms of different sizes. As a result, market economies dominated by these kinds of institutions exhibit a preference for arm's length relationships between owners, managers and employees, but permit a wide variety of firm type and commitment within this general framework (Jacoby, 2005).

Table 2.2. Types of states and associated business system and firm characteristics

Associated Business System and Firm Characteristics	Types of States			
	Arm's Length	Dominant Developmental	Business Corporatist	Inclusive Corporatist
Governance Structures				
Fragmentation of large firm ownership	High	Low	Limited	Limited
Commitment of largest shareholders	Low	High	Considerable	Considerable
Strategic autonomy of large firms	Considerable, within capital market constraints	Limited by state	Considerable, limited by business partners and state	Some, limited by business partners and employees
Inter-Firm Relations				
Extent of authority sharing with other firms	Limited to short-term alliances	Limited, except for state-coordinated alliances	Considerable among large firms, limited in SMEs	Considerable
Employment Relations				
Authority sharing with skilled staff	Varies between sectors and firm types	Generally limited	Some in larger firms	Considerable in most firms
Long-term employer/employee commitments	Low	Some for managerial staff, limited otherwise	Considerable in larger firms, limited elsewhere	Considerable in most firms
Organizational Capabilities				
Variability across sectors	Considerable	Considerable	Limited	Limited
Prevalent types	Coordinating, reconfigurational in some firms	Coordinating in state-supported firms	Coordinating and learning in large firms	Coordinating and learning

Consequently, while the overall extent of authority sharing between business partners, employers and most employees tends to be limited in such societies, sectoral differences as well as changes over time in particular industries, can be considerable, as Herrigel and Wittke suggest (2005). This is especially likely when different technological regimes encourage contrasting patterns of managerial behaviour and the state pursues particular policy 'missions', in areas such as defence and healthcare. Even within the same sorts of industries, distinct differences in economic organization can develop between regions with contrasting histories and environments, as Saxenian (1994) has emphasized in her discussion of Route 128 firms and Silicon Valley (see, also, Kenney, 2000). Characteristics of both project network and compartmentalized business systems have, then, become dominant in different parts of the US economy in the late twentieth century.

Given the heterogeneity of skill formation systems and labour representation characteristics of such societies, it is not surprising that considerable variations occur in the organization of, say, financial and professional service companies, capital intensive industry, high technology new firms and light industry. The extent to which countries such as the UK and USA have established nationally standardized and stable forms of owner control, inter firm relations and employment policies across all sectors remains, then, questionable, despite their overall tendency to favour an arm's length version of industrial capitalism (Dobbin, 1994; Hollingsworth, 1991).

Turning now to consider countries where the state has tended to follow more active promotional policies and organize interest groups more directly, these establish a 'thicker' institutional environment for companies that encourages greater similarity in many aspects of economic organization (Hollingsworth and Streeck, 1994). However, the considerable differences between types of promotional states and associated institutional arrangements affect the degree of standardization of economic organization patterns and firm strategies across sectors and regions, especially inter-firm collaboration and employment relations.

In state dominated institutional regimes there are likely to be considerable differences between companies and sectors supported by the state and those that are relatively neglected. While the former are often able to obtain cheap credit for expansion in line with state objectives, and so grow without diluting owners' control, the latter usually have to rely on their own resources and so typically are unable to compete in capital-intensive sectors. Similarly, while the state may assist the former to obtain licenses for new technologies and import scarce components, the latter are likely to experience much greater difficulty in accessing key resources for entering new industries. As a result, state supported firms and sectors will probably grow faster in the more capital intensive and innovation based industries, be able to attract better educated staff and invest in developing distinctive organizational capabilities. They will therefore tend to be larger, more diversified and have stronger coordinating abilities than less favoured companies.

However, their high level of dependence upon state agencies and susceptibility to changes in state policies and personnel mean that such firms have to deal with high levels of political risk and often develop quite particularistic relations with the political executive and bureaucratic elite. These can be more personal than organizational and encourage strong levels of owner control over firm strategies and behaviour. Who owns and controls these companies matters to the state in such societies, as does which industries they enter and on what conditions. An important characteristic of successful companies is therefore their ability to develop and maintain close connections with political, and perhaps bureaucratic, elites, and to fulfil their objectives.

Because of continued access to cheap credit, at least during periods of rapid growth, continuing direct owner control is facilitated in these state supported enterprises. Given the dominant role of the state and its predominantly top down, if not paternalistic, pattern of political control and mobilization, their internal authority relations are also likely to be centralized with little authority sharing, especially over issues of finance, strategy and personnel. Collective learning and continuing incremental innovation based on individual employee problem solving and knowledge enhancement are limited in these circumstances. Equally, competition for state support between these companies is likely to restrict their ability to cooperate with each other, and thus authority sharing between business partners will also be restricted in these sectors. Interfirm connections are therefore more limited and short-term than in more decentralized economies.

In the less favoured sectors, firms are likely to be smaller, slower growing and owner dominated. As the history of the *chaebol* in South Korea shows, much of their growth has been achieved through acquiring small and medium-sized enterprises (SMEs) with the help of state subsidized credit, and many smaller firms have been subject to predatory behaviour by them (see, for example, Fields, 1995; Woo, 1991). This uncertain and unsupportive environment seems likely to encourage opportunism by economic actors as well as strong owner control of most companies and a reluctance to share authority, even with managers who might develop coordinating capabilities. Consequently, the establishment of managerial hierarchies and distinctive organizational capabilities in these enterprises will remain limited.

Business corporatist states develop considerable collaboration between state agencies, the banking system, and large companies in managing economic development, as in the postwar Japanese developmental state (Aoki and Patrick, 1994; Gao, 2001; Johnson, 1982; Okimoto, 1989; Samuels, 1987). Individual shareholder interests are typically weakly represented in large companies' dominant coalitions in these kinds of societies relative to those of top managers and other long-term core employees. Additionally, state supported and strong business associations encourage cooperation between many of the larger firms, who also are not prevented from forming alliances within and across sectoral boundaries to block hostile takeovers and share investments in new developments. Growth goals correspondingly dominate those focused on investor returns in most large companies.

Although such states may support some small businesses, as did the Japanese in the pre-war period, albeit somewhat ineffectually (Friedman, 1988: 162–6), and more systematically with specialized financial institutions in the 1950s and 1960s (Patrick and Rohlen, 1987), promotional states in general find it easier to work with large companies and cohesive associations that can implement agreed policies effectively. As Patrick and Rohlen (1987: 369) suggest: 'government economic policymakers (in Japan) apparently see small and medium-size-enterprise more as a problem than as a source of economic growth and vitality...on the whole.... MITI's policy approach (to SMEs) is defensive.' There are often therefore considerable differences in the degree of collaboration between companies and opportunism more generally between large and small firms in such countries, especially where the more conservative political parties do not rely greatly upon small business owners' support.

This is especially so in employment relations and labour representation practices that are largely left up to individual firms and business groups. While firms do often develop common norms about poaching skilled workers and exchange information on wage rates, sometimes encouraged by state agencies seeking to limit 'excessive' competition (Gao, 2001), they are much more able to pursue idiosyncratic labour management practices than their counterparts in collaborative regimes. Consequently, inter-firm differences tend to be stronger in this regard, especially since unions are less standardized in their organizational forms and more enterprise specific. It should be noted, though, that in Japan at least, what Clark (1979) terms the 'society of industry' exerts quite strong institutional pressures on the larger firms to conform to dominant norms of employment policy.

State coordination of large firms' strategies and restriction of opportunism by employers here encourages them to invest more in training and long-term commitments to skilled employees than do most small firms. Consequently, significant variations in employment policies and bargaining procedures develop between firms of different sizes in these kinds of market economy. While large employers tend to pay higher wages than their smaller competitors in most economies, this is especially likely in business corporatist states where bargaining and many other aspects of labour relations are decentralized to individual companies and firms attempt to retain scarce skilled workers.

Such variation in labour management practices between employers is further reinforced by the lack of a state supported and standardized skill formation system in these kinds of economies. The development and evaluation of practical skills are essentially in the hands of individual firms, who vary in the resources they can devote to training as well as their ability to retain staff. Large firms are more able to attract better educated workers by offering long-term career prospects, higher pay and more training in a variety of roles. Because skills are highly firm specific here, they restrict labour mobility, which in turn further enhances employer–employee commitment. As a result, employees are more willing to contribute to long-term organizational learning on a continuous basis, thus further improving collective capabilities and knowledge in ways that smaller firms find difficult to imitate.

Inclusive corporatist states, on the other hand, encourage the institutionalization of common kinds of employment relations, workplace representation and skill formation systems across sectors and regions so that companies tend to follow similar procedures and deal with similar types of unions, works councils etc. The management of labour relations is, therefore, quite highly structured by collective rules and norms in such institutional regimes. This means that most companies are enmeshed in collaborative relationships with competitors, suppliers and customers, as well as with unions and other labour groupings.

Consequently, they are encouraged to develop relatively long-term commitments to established business partners, including skilled workers, that favour growth goals and incremental rather than radical innovation.

However, because skills are developed, assessed and certified by joint public-private agencies, and standardized around particular technologies and sectors rather than being largely idiosyncratic to firms, commitment to individual employees tends to be less than in countries that delegate more to firms. In the case of countries such as Germany where sectoral bargaining systems and strong employers' associations restrict both employer and employee opportunism, these standardized skills and occupational identities have not led to as much labour mobility as is common in the fluid labour markets of arm's length business environments, and so organizational learning tends to be greater (Marsden, 1999; Soskice, 1999; Streeck, 1992).

As in other financial systems with limited protection of minority shareholder rights and bank credit financed growth, these kinds of institutional arrangements facilitate the continuation of large blockholder control of companies as they grow, as well as close, relatively long-term, relationships between banks and industrial firms. Together with weak enforcement of any competition legislation that might prevent alliances and cooperation between companies, often because of a history of effective cartelization and rationalization through cooperative agreements as in Germany (Berghahn, 1986; Djelic and Quack, 2005; Herrigel, 1996), these interconnections encourage considerable collaboration between companies and the pursuit of long-term growth goals rather than short-term profitability.

However, these states often also develop specialized agencies and programmes to support small firms and protect them against predatory actions of large competitors, especially by limiting price competition and supporting technology transfer and cooperative research and development in 'diffusion-oriented' technology policies (Abramson et al., 1997; Ergas, 1987; Morris-Suzuki, 1994). Such efforts limit the differences between large and small firms and further the homogeneity of firm type and behaviour in these kinds of societies.

Overall, then, the more corporatist is the political system, the more owners, managers and employees are likely to be organized in similar ways and deal with each other according to relatively standardized procedures. Firms in highly corporatist environments will be more constrained to follow institutionalized conventions and should vary less in their governance structures, priorities and capabilities than those in less organized societies. Sectoral, regional and size differences between companies should be less marked in these kinds of regimes than in other ones. Because the institutions governing labour and capital markets typically encompass small and medium-sized firms as well as large ones here, more companies are likely to follow similar policies and practices—and so develop similar kinds of organizational capabilities than where states focus on larger firms and do not establish stable mechanisms for managing labour relationships.

It is particularly in such societies, then, that nationally distinctive patterns of economic organization are most likely to be developed and reproduced, and that most firms are likely to follow similar patterns of authority sharing and employer–employee commitment, including the sorts of employment practices identified by Marsden (1999) as key features of employment systems. The national specificity and cohesion of business systems should be greatest in societies where the state takes a leading role in orchestrating economic development with systematically organized and standardized forms of interest group representation and bargaining on a continuing basis.

Conclusions

This account of the key contingencies affecting the establishment of nationally dominant business systems has emphasized three main points. First, the establishment of cohesive and distinctive business systems at the national level is greatly affected by the degree to which the national institutions governing capital and labour markets dominate those at other levels, and are complementary to state structures and policies in their implications for the constitution of key economic actors and the prevalent ways in which owners, managers and employees deal with each other. Especially important here is the extent to which they reinforce tendencies to opportunism and adversarial competition between discrete actors or constrain such behaviour and encourage long-term commitments.

Second, the homogeneity and national distinctiveness of economic coordination and control patterns across technologies, markets and localities reflects the standardization of key institutions within national borders and differences between countries. The more that the formal institutions governing economic transactions, interest group formation, employment relations, skill development etc apply throughout an economy, the more likely that the nature and behaviour of economic actors will be similar in different industries and regions.

Such institutional standardization is linked, third, to the nature of the state and the economic policies followed by its elites. The more active and cohesive is the state in organizing and mobilizing major interest groups in the formulation and implementation of economic policies, the more likely that forms of representation and political-economic bargaining processes will become relatively standardized, particularly the ways that owners, managers and employees compete and cooperate. Corporatist states encourage and legitimate certain kinds of group formation and collective action to a greater extent than do arm's length ones, and so build more stable and common patterns of interaction between major economic actors.

In sum, the national specificity and distinctiveness of business systems depends on the extent to which characteristics of states and related institutions are complementary in their implications for firms and markets, as well as the active structuring and coordination of interest groups and their interrelationships by state agencies. As long as the nation state remains the primary unit of political competition, legitimacy and definer and upholder of private property rights, in addition to being the predominant influence on labour market institutions, many characteristics of business systems will continue to vary significantly across national boundaries, albeit not always constituting highly integrated and consistent coordination and control systems. Similar factors affect the development and reproduction of particular kinds of innovation systems in different institutional regimes and nation states, as will be discussed in the next chapter.

3

Constructing Innovation Systems:
The Roles of Institutional Regimes
and National Public Science Systems

Introduction

In addition to numerous comparisons of business systems, social systems of production and varieties of capitalism since the 1980s, there have been many discussions about the nature and significance of different innovation systems (see, e.g. Braczyk *et al.*, 1998; Edquist, 1997; 2005; Lundvall, 1992; Nelson, 1993). However, few of these accounts have agreed about the precise nature of these systems and their key components, whether they are predominantly national, regional or sectoral, or the relative importance of societal institutions and technological regimes in generating them (Breschi and Malerba, 1997; Guerrieri and Tylecote, 1997; Malerba and Orsenigo, 1993; Whitley, 2000a). This is partly because many authors have been reluctant to specify precisely the nature of innovation systems, their key components and variable characteristics (Carlsson *et al.*, 2002; Edquist, 2005). Additionally, relatively little attention has been paid to how the distinctly national ones may be changing, especially as a result of growing economic and political integration across national borders.

In seeking to understand how different kinds of innovation system have become established at subnational, national and transnational levels of collective organization, and are changing, it is important to identify the key characteristics of their components and explore how these combine to constitute distinctive types that become established in different institutional environments. Similarly to the business systems discussed in the previous chapter, such systems of innovation develop nationally or regionally depending on both the strength of key institutions at those levels of collective organization and their complementarity in reinforcing particular features and rationalities of actors. In this chapter, I suggest: (a) a way of distinguishing between systems of innovation in terms of three key dimensions, (b) how these characteristics can be expected to vary across distinctive institutional regimes, and (c) how different types of innovation systems can be expected to become established and reproduced at national, sectoral and international levels of socio-economic organization.

First, I shall outline the key characteristics of innovation systems that stem from variations in how economic actors develop and diffuse innovations, and suggest how these combine to form six distinct ideal types. Next, I shall suggest how these six types of innovation systems are likely to become established in particular kinds of institutional regimes governing economic activities. Finally, I shall consider the institutional conditions that can be expected to produce distinctive national innovation systems. Essentially, I argue that coherent and distinctive kinds of innovation systems only become established when strong and complementary institutions develop at transnational, national, or regional levels. In the case of the EU, this implies that the relative weakness, and often contradictory nature, of many European institutions and policies are likely to limit their impact on well-established national patterns of innovative activity and the development of a transnational European system of innovation.

The Nature and Characteristics of Different Innovation Systems

Much of the literature on systems of innovation emphasizes the importance of different processes of knowledge production and dissemination, as well as varied patterns of interactive learning between groups and organizations in developing and commercializing new processes, products and services (e.g. Carlsson *et al.*, 2002; Lundvall *et al.*, 2002). Additionally, a common theme in many comparisons of national innovation systems concerns the nature of state science and technology policies, and of the organization of university and other publicly supported research. Any consideration of the nature of innovation systems needs, then, to identify the main types and characteristics of knowledge developers and users in different contexts and how they are coordinated to generate distinctive kinds of innovations (Kaiser and Prange, 2004).

The key components of innovation systems are usually taken to include firms of different kinds, their organization into research consortia, business associations etc., public and private research organizations, education and training systems and various providers of infrastructural services such as venture capitalists and lawyers, as well as the major institutions governing their behaviour. Variations in their central characteristics, such as governance structures and organizational capabilities, and in how their activities are coordinated lead to the constitution of distinctive systems of innovation.

The critical innovative agent in market economies is the private company. They generate new knowledge from current operations by employees through 'learning by doing', as well as from directed search for new processes and products through dedicated research and development activities (Coriat and Weinstein, 2002). However, as emphasized in Chapter 1, the nature and behaviour of firms vary greatly between countries, regions and cultures. In considering how different innovation systems develop and change, then, it is especially important to identify the central differences in how firms learn and develop new knowledge. Two characteristics dealing with the sources of new knowledge and how it is integrated into the organization are particularly important.

First, there is the extent to which owners and managers learn from various groups of employees, business partners and other organizations within and beyond their industry, and develop organization specific routines for integrating new knowledge from these groups. These differences affect the kinds of collective capabilities they develop and how they use them to produce new goods and services, as will be explored further in Chapter 6. The extent to which companies involve employees in problem solving activities and actively incorporate their knowledge—as well as that of business partners and other external organizations—into the development of new products, processes and services constitutes, then, a major differentiating characteristic of systems of innovations in market economies. It can be termed the degree of authority sharing between economic actors because it implies a willingness to delegate authority over, and actively encourage involvement in, innovation development and problem solving activities.

This characteristic distinguishes firms that rely considerably upon the skills and activities of their skilled workforce to improve production technologies and introduce new products from those that rely primarily on technologists' and managers' learning, both about current processes and new opportunities. Many 'artisanal' enterprises in Italian industrial districts, parts of Denmark and elsewhere appear to resemble the former, while Taylorist and Fordist firms resemble the latter (Andersen and Kristensen, 1999; Chandler, 1990; Crouch *et al.*, 2001; Kristensen, 2006). Additionally, of course, many large companies in continental European countries and Japan integrate shop floor learning with that of engineers and managers (see, e.g. Fujimoto, 2000). They thus effect greater levels of knowledge integration within the firm than either artisanal or Fordist companies.

Such 'internal' authority sharing and involvement of skilled staff in collective problem solving is often, but not always, combined with 'external' cooperation and knowledge sharing with other companies and organizations in particular kinds of socio-political environments. As discussed in the previous chapter, in relatively 'thick' institutional contexts, this can involve collaboration with competitors in dealing with industry specific issues such as training, union negotiations and standards setting. Knowledge development and learning in these kinds of regions and countries occur repeatedly between owners, managers and technical experts of separate companies as well as within them.

In contrast, the kinds of technology alliances and similar inter-firm collaborations that are becoming more widespread in particular industries in more arm's length institutional regimes, tend to be narrower in scope, restricted in time and subject to more rapid shifts in partners (Powell, 2001). Inter-firm learning here is therefore more limited in scope and longevity, and based more upon individual agreements and labour mobility than collective ones, as in much of Silicon Valley and Silicon Alley (Almeida and Kogut, 1999; Angel, 2000; Christopherson, 2002b; Grabher, 2002a).

Second, innovative firms differ in the extent to which, and how, they learn from the formal knowledge production systems of their domestic economy and, more recently, those of other countries. While most rely on the education and training system to provide them with skilled staff, and many use the scientific and technological literature to access research results for their own search activities, the extent to which they become directly involved in knowledge production processes in the public research system varies considerably. The public research system is here understood as the set of organizations whose employees are primarily engaged upon research for publication together with the institutional arrangements governing their funding, direction and evaluation (Whitley, 2000b; 2003b). Differences in the extent of such involvement obviously affect the speed with which companies are able to use new knowledge, as well as their ability to understand the relevance and implications of new research techniques and processes. The more dependent is technical development upon the knowledge and skills produced by the public sciences, the more significant these linkages become.

At least three forms of such connections can be distinguished. First, relatively passive and indirect forms of involvement in public science systems occur where innovative companies rely on universities and similar educational organizations to select and train scientists and technologists in particular skills and disciplines for initial employment, but do not actively participate in research development or recruit staff in mid-career. Any use of the knowledge and techniques produced by the public science system tends to be at arm's length and relatively remote, with a strong reliance on codified forms. While such firms may employ researchers as private consultants to deal with specific problems, they rarely seek to incorporate publicly oriented research projects and skills in their technological problem solving activities. Many large Japanese companies appear to prefer this autarkic mode of knowledge development with respect to the formal research system (Kneller, 2003), as do most artisanal companies.

Second, more direct and active engagement with formal knowledge production outside the firm is encouraged where state agencies and associations of companies support technologically focused research activities in public or semi-public institutions that are closely connected to current problems, products and markets. Here, both SMEs and large firms are encouraged to participate in co-funding and guiding knowledge production in public-private organizations, such as the German Fraunhofer Institutes, and often employ their staff on a part-time or full-time basis (Abramson et al., 1997). External knowledge production and skill development is thus linked to companies' learning and search activities, but these remain within current technological and market trajectories and so are continuous with existing competences rather than being radically different.

Third, even greater levels of active involvement in the production of new knowledge and techniques occur when companies develop close links with universities and other research organizations engaged upon the study of generic processes and phenomena. Perhaps the best known instance of such direct connections with the public sciences is in the biotechnology industry, but it has also occurred where other emerging technologies depended greatly on new knowledge and skills developed by academic scientists, such as the German dyestuffs industry towards the end of the nineteenth century and the US computer software industry.

Such involvement is more focused on the processes by which new knowledge is produced and problems are solved than the use of codified results, and so encompasses advanced training of researchers, co-development and management of research projects, recruitment of mid career scientists and technologists, as well as secondment of employees to academic posts and sharing facilities.

In addition to these differences in the extent to which firms obtain and use new knowledge from different kinds of sources, a third major contrast between innovation systems concerns the extent to which knowledge production, transfer, and use, and innovative activities in general, are coordinated through ad hoc, anonymous, market transactions or more continuous and cooperative relationships between economic actors governed by common authority commitments. Low levels of authoritative coordination of innovative activities occur where most transactions between companies and other actors are similar to those in spot markets and there is little continuous commitment to maintaining particular relationships between them. Learning across organizational boundaries here tends to be short term, ad hoc and built around individuals rather than being sustained, partner specific, and organized into routines.

Greater levels of authoritative integration of innovative activities occur in societies where there are stronger constraints on opportunistic behaviour and both public and private agencies are involved in generating and disseminating new technologies and techniques. Such integration can be achieved either through state commitment to, and support for, particular innovation goals and/or through inter-firm alliances, business groups and research consortia, often involving public research organizations. Sharing knowledge and collaborating in the development of innovations is easier and less risky in these kinds of economies than in more arm's length ones. However, such collaboration may inhibit more radical innovations that are discontinuous with, or disruptive for, established technologies and customers.

Combining these three broad dimensions of innovative firm characteristics and the coordination of their activities enables us to identify six ideal types of innovation systems that resemble many of the examples discussed in the literature. These types can be further distinguished in terms of three further dimensions: (a) the firm specificity of innovative capabilities, (b) their likelihood of producing radical, discontinuous innovations, and (c) their ability to generate systemic as opposed to modular innovations.

Two more combinations of different degrees of authority sharing, involvement in the public science system and non-market coordination of innovative activities could in theory become established. However, it seems unlikely that active involvement in the public science system will be combined with low levels of internal authority sharing since an openness to new formal knowledge and research skills implies a willingness and ability to deal with considerable technical uncertainty. This in turn encourages delegation of control to technologists who are most able to judge and make use of new knowledge. Authority thus has to be shared with qualified employees if innovations are to benefit from close links to the formal knowledge production system of a society.

Equally, the combination of high levels of authoritative integration, low authority sharing and passive involvement with the public science system seems improbable because alliance based knowledge sharing and coordination encourages employer–employee commitment by restricting economic opportunism. Where such coordination is more based upon state-led technology policies, it is likely to involve closer connections between the formal research system and companies, although probably limiting the level of delegation of authority within firms. The key features of the six more likely ideal types of innovation systems are summarized in Table 3.1 and will now be further discussed.

There are three distinct kinds of innovation systems with limited authoritative, non-market coordination of innovative activities between knowledge producers and users. First, those where learning and development of innovations take place largely within the upper echelons of managerial and technical hierarchies can be termed highly autarkic because they rely mostly on the internally generated knowledge produced by engineers and managers. Firms here do not make much use of either skilled workers' knowledge or research activities in the public science system. Collaboration and information sharing across formal authority boundaries is low in such systems and inter-firm relations are essentially adversarial and governed by short-term market logics. Authority sharing in general is limited in this kind of innovation system, as is the systemic integration of innovative activities across organizations.

Innovations are therefore quite firm specific, closely dependent on managers' and engineers' knowledge as well as on their ability and willingness to incorporate publicly available, codified knowledge into developmental activities. As technological 'paradigms' and innovative styles become institutionalized within large companies, their capacity for integrating different kinds of knowledge and pursuing novel kinds of innovations

Table 3.1. Characteristics of six ideal types of innovation systems

Characteristics	Type of Innovation System					
	Autarkic	Artisanal	Technological Teams	State-Led	Group-Based	Highly Collaborative
Authority sharing	Limited	Considerable	Considerable	Limited	Considerable	Considerable
Involvement with public science systems	Passive	Passive	Active	Active	Passive	Active
Authoritative coordination	Limited	Limited	Limited	Considerable	Considerable	Considerable
Firm-specificity of innovations	High	Limited	Limited	High	High	Considerable
Discontinuity of innovations	Limited	Limited	Potentially High	Varies	Limited	Limited
Systematic nature of innovations	Considerable	Low	Low	Considerable	Considerable	Considerable

that do not readily fit with them reduces. This means that learning new skills and ways of dealing with technical and market problems becomes difficult for such firms without substantial changes in personnel.

Second, where coordination of innovative activities across organizations remains predominantly market based through contracting and labour mobility, but owners and managers share considerable authority over problem definition, work organization and technical development with engineers and other experts inside companies, two distinct kinds of innovation systems can be distinguished. These can be termed technological team and artisanal systems of innovation.

In the former system of innovation, involvement with formal knowledge production in the public science system and rapid acquisition of new ideas and skills through buying firms and/or researchers is considerable. However, technology alliances or risk sharing agreements tend to be short term and limited for particular purposes. Commitments between investors, managers and workers are restricted in scope and time, but employee discretion over work performance and involvement in problem solving is much greater than in the previous type of innovation system, partly because of the considerable level of technical uncertainty. Innovations here are often quite radical in terms of technological or market discontinuities because of the rapid integration of new and different kinds of knowledge and skills, but are more modular than systemic because of the high levels of technical and market uncertainty involved and limited organizational coordination, as will be further discussed in Chapters 7 and 8.

Artisanal innovation systems combine similar levels of authority sharing inside companies with greater cooperation between firms in developing and applying new technologies and knowledge. Competition between companies is less adversarial and zero-sum than in the previous two cases, and supplier-customer relationships are more collaborative, often encouraged by local and regional governments, consulting agencies, banks and marketing cooperatives. However, direct involvement with research projects in the public science system tends to be relatively limited, and new formal knowledge that is both generic across technologies and product families and different from that currently being used rarely impinges upon firms' innovative activities. Innovation is here driven more by the incremental and separate improvements of relatively small companies in industrial districts than by systematically coordinated investments and developments across them. It is more continuous within current technological trajectories than radical and disruptive.

There are also three kinds of innovation systems that are more coordinated through non-market relationships. These vary in how such authoritative coordination is achieved, particularly whether this is primarily by the state or through inter-firm alliances, and in the extent to which companies are actively involved in the formal knowledge production system.

In state-led systems of innovation, authority sharing both within and between companies tends to be limited by the high level of dependence of many leading firms on state agencies, but central coordination encourages considerable integration of projects in the public research system with corporate innovation development. The risks involved in developing major systemic technological change are here shared between the state and private companies, often through the provision of cheap credit and state subsidized and/or conducted research. Innovations can be correspondingly large scale and complex in terms of the variety of scientific and technological knowledge involved, but are unlikely to rely extensively on skilled workers' contributions to the incremental improvement of operational procedures.

Greater levels of internal and external authority sharing occur in group based innovation systems. Here, large firms develop relatively stable networks of commitments and collaborations within and across sectoral boundaries to share knowledge and opportunities within distinct groups of companies. These are often cemented by mutual shareholdings, as in the Japanese inter-market groups and some vertical *Keiretsu*, as well as exchange of managers and common banking relationships (Gerlach, 1992; Westney, 2001a). Long-term employment commitments encourage firm-specific problem solving and competence building amongst the core workforce, so that organizational learning becomes continuous and broad in scope.

However, companies in these kinds of innovation systems tend to have rather passive connections with the formal research system, except through the recruitment of new graduates, and in that sense are relatively separate from generic knowledge production, as Kneller (2003) has claimed is the case for many large Japanese pharmaceutical companies. Innovations here build on continuous, group learning in and between network members, and so tend to follow particular technological trajectories that do not devalue current organizational capabilities.

Finally, there are highly collaborative innovation systems that combine considerable authority sharing within and between companies with more active involvement in the public science system, especially that part focused on the development of technologically and industrially specific knowledge. Innovations are here based on learning within the firm, within industry and trade associations and within research associations and similar public-private collaborative institutions connecting formal knowledge production with technical development. National and local state bodies are often directly involved in encouraging such links, through joint funding of projects and the establishment of public research organizations dedicated to technological innovation, such as the Fraunhofer institutes in Germany.

Insofar as new formal knowledge becomes integrated into firms' innovative activities, these may be less limited to firms' current knowledge and capabilities than are those in group based innovation systems, but the extensive cooperation within and between companies means that radically different innovations are unlikely to be a major feature of these kinds of innovation systems. In new industries, such as software and biotechnology, companies here tend to focus on more incremental and technologically continuous kinds of innovations, as will be shown in Chapter 7.

Institutional Conditions for the Establishment of Different Innovation Systems

Having distinguished six ideal types of innovation systems, I now consider the circumstances in which they are most likely to develop and become reproduced as distinct ways of generating new products, processes and services, particularly the role of different institutional regimes as outlined in the previous chapter. Different sets of institutions governing property rights, capital and labour markets lead owners and managers to delegate authority to skilled workers and involve them in collective learning to varying extents. Combined with different state science and technology policies and kinds of public science systems, variations in these sorts of societal institutions also lead to contrasting patterns of firm involvement in public research organizations and coordination of innovative activities (Whitley, 2003b).

Considering first the institutional arrangements affecting variations in authority sharing, which are outlined in more detail in Chapter 6, these include the norms governing trust and authority relationships in a society as well as the institutions encouraging commitment between economic actors. Trust in the formal institutions governing economic transactions, and economic activities more generally, is critical to investors and other economic actors delegating control over assets. In societies where it is low, owners are unlikely to share substantial amounts of authority with relative strangers with whom they do not have strong personal bonds of loyalty and reciprocity. Additionally, in highly paternalist political cultures that justify leadership more in terms of elites' superior abilities to look after the best interests of the population, owners tend to consider employees as unqualified to exercise discretion or contribute to problem solving.

In contrast, where the dominant institutions governing economic activities are more reliable and the norms justifying subordination to elites are less paternalistic, owners may well share authority with some employees and business partners and establish organizational careers. How much they do so, though, and with whom, varies considerably between market economies with different political, financial and labour market institutions affecting economic opportunism. In general, the more financiers, managers and skilled workers are locked-in to each other's destinies the less likely they are to act opportunistically and seek short-term advantages through changing business partners. Institutional frameworks that encourage such lock-in therefore reduce the risks associated with long-term commitments and so facilitate authority sharing.

Key institutional features that constrain short-term opportunism include: (a) coordinating and risk sharing state policies, (b) strong business associations and union federations—often encouraged by state corporatist policies—and (c) insider dominated financial systems. Where promotional states share some of the risks incurred by investing in new technologies and coordinate firms' innovation strategies, companies are more likely to work together and trust each other not to engage in highly opportunistic behaviour. Such collaboration and market stability in turn are likely to encourage firms to enter into relatively long-term commitments with many employees. However, states that pursue more directive innovation policies in which inter-firm collaboration is not encouraged may limit authority sharing within and between companies. In dominant developmental states as described in the previous chapter, firms develop closer connections to state policy makers than to each other, as the state tends to limit the establishment of independent collaborative organizations that could threaten their dominance of the political-economic system.

Where, in contrast, more arm's length states focus on establishing clear rules of the competitive game within which economic actors are free to pursue their objectives as they wish and to develop new technologies as separate, competing entities, incentives to share authority with employees and business partners tend to be fewer, as discussed in the pervious chapter. Such states often consider collaboration between companies in developing new technologies to be anti-competitive and it is discouraged, except in a few areas of direct state concern such as defence.

Second, strong business associations help to control opportunistic behaviour by member companies, and so encourage longer-term investments in developing new technologies and training employees. They also restrict employee opportunism, whether individual or collective through unions. Particularly if wage rates and other aspects of employment relationships are agreed centrally, either at the industry or national level, and firms are constrained from poaching skilled staff by offering higher wages, employers are encouraged to develop quite long-term commitments to employees. This is enhanced by strong regulatory frameworks governing employment relations in many of the more coordinated market economies of Continental Europe.

In addition to strong business associations affecting authority sharing between and within firms, powerful labour unions and federations are also important, especially when they collaborate with employers' groups in managing effective public training systems, as in the German 'skills machine' (Culpepper and Finegold, 1999). The more highly skilled is the workforce, particularly when employers recognize the high quality of these skills, and the greater is the bargaining power of unions, the more employers are encouraged to share authority with skilled workers, and involve them in problem solving activities.

Third, the nature of the financial system, especially whether it facilitates a strong market for corporate control, affects authority sharing both between companies and between employers and employees. Where capital markets are small and illiquid and shareholder control over large companies is relatively concentrated, it is difficult to transfer ownership through the market and large owners are often locked-in to particular companies, especially if significant proportions of firms' shares are held by strategic investors and/or are effectively controlled by top managers, as is the case in many European countries (Barca and Becht, 2001) and Japan (Lincoln and Gerlach, 2004; Sheard, 1994). This enables employers to make credible long-term commitments to skilled staff.

In contrast, the combination of liquid capital markets, legal and other restrictions on managers' ability to develop strong defensive measures against hostile takeovers, and fragmented shareholdings in more 'liberal' kinds of market economy can result in a strong market for corporate control that limits investor-manager commitments and reduces the credibility of long-term career incentives. While employers may delegate considerable autonomy over work procedures to skilled staff and be willing to enter into short-term alliances with other companies in such societies, long-term collaboration and organizational learning through continuing employee involvement in problem solving are inhibited by the ease and frequency of ownership changes.

These sorts of institutional differences also affect the extent and mode of authoritative coordination of innovative activities in an economy. Where the state is actively involved in coordinating economic development, whether directly or through business associations and other groupings, we would expect firms to cooperate more in achieving technological change than in societies where the state prohibits collaboration. Similarly, industry and trade associations that are accustomed to coordinating economic activities and resolving disputes seem likely to promote joint R&D projects, collective setting of technical standards and sharing of new knowledge. Promotional state policies, strong business associations and corporatist arrangements, then, should be associated with considerable non-market coordination of innovation, while societies with states pursuing arm's length regulatory policies and weak business associations will not.

Turning to consider next the institutional features influencing business involvement with the public research system, the role of the state is again critical, not least because most of these systems are funded and directly controlled by nation states. In the case of dominant developmental states, we would expect them to ensure that firms in favoured sectors were able to access the results of publicly supported research activities. These kinds of states are often associated with centralized academic systems, typically with strong hierarchies of prestige and resources, which limit organizational competition and pluralism. Active involvement in the public science system is here more facilitated and coordinated by state agencies around public objectives and missions than the result of strategic investments by autonomous companies. It will, therefore, tend to be restricted to particular areas of economic activities favoured by the state rather than generalized throughout the economy.

More collaborative state coordination of technological development with firms and industry associations can be expected to generate different kinds of company involvement in parts of the public science system. Where the state provides funding for a range of applied research organizations and encourages firms, both individually and collectively, to organize and fund research in them, as in Germany (Abramson *et al.*, 1997), companies often cooperate with public research organizations in developing and diffusing new technological knowledge. By underwriting much of the costs associated with technological research and involving industry associations in its management, states here facilitate both inter-firm cooperation and the widespread involvement of firms in part of the public science system. An important feature of such 'diffusion-oriented' technology policies is their involvement of small and medium-sized enterprises, as well as large ones, in technical improvements, and their extension over many sectors of the economy (Doremus *et al.*, 1998; Ergas, 1987; Morris-Suzuki, 1994).

This kind of involvement in publicly oriented research is, though, usually limited to work on technologies and materials that are closely connected to current problems and trajectories rather than with more generic research that could lead to quite different technologies. Because the primary goal is to enhance and improve existing industrial compe-tences, such state policies are unlikely to encourage strong connections with researchers engaged upon more remote topics intended to produce general explanations of phenomena, especially in academic systems that are strongly structured around discrete disciplines, and where the incen-tives for senior researchers to move into the private sector are restricted by employment regulations.

In addition, how the state and other actors organize the public research system greatly affects the degree and form of company involvement. Par-ticularly important in this respect is the extent to which formal research systems are organized into a strong and stable hierarchy of prestige and resources dominated by a small number of elite research organizations (Whitley, 2003b). In highly concentrated and hierarchical academic sys-tems, the best researchers are not only recruited and trained in the leading organizations but are also likely to remain in them for most of their careers because of their superior status and resources. More peripheral universities are rarely able to improve their standing through attracting leading scientists, or by acquiring better facilities through competitive processes. Open competition between research organizations in such soci-eties, therefore, is quite limited, as is mobility between employers in the course of scientific careers.

Where, in contrast, there are a number of competing research universi-ties that are funded in different ways by a variety of agencies pursuing dif-ferent objectives, together with different kinds of research organizations

71

also competing for scientific prestige, it will be more difficult for such groups to monopolize intellectual goals and standards. In the case of the postwar US research system for instance, the variety of state funding agencies, and of Congressional committees overseeing them, has probably encouraged intellectual competition and pluralism (Stokes, 1997). More generally, the variety of institutional forms, high level of decentralization and institutionalization of competition for prestige and resources in the US academic system have encouraged universities and colleges there to compete with leading institutions in a way that is unusual in much of Europe and Japan (Feller, 1999; Graham and Diamond, 1997).

Generally speaking, the greater the rate of competition between research organizations for prestige and resources, and the more mobile are scientists in seeking promotions, the more ideas and skills circulate between departments, and the more likely intellectual change and novelty will increase. Such mobility is affected by broader patterns of labour market organization that vary across market economies, as well as by the nature of competition between universities for leading researchers.

A second important feature of public research systems that affects their flexibility and pluralism is the organizational segmentation of goals, careers, and resources between different employment units. By this I mean the strength of the separation and division of labour between research universities, applied research institutes, technology transfer agencies, research association laboratories and private companies. Where these have quite distinct goals, funding arrangements and control procedures, so that researchers in them are: (a) trained in different ways, (b) do different kinds of work, and (c) have separate career paths, the degree of organizational segmentation is high. In such systems, researchers are discouraged from undertaking a wide variety of types of research, including that focused on technological and commercial objectives, within universities, and from moving between different kinds of employers without suffering a great loss of intellectual credibility.

Knowledge and skill transfer between types of research organizations will be relatively slow and difficult in highly segmented public science systems. Rapid technological responses to new research results are unlikely to occur here, and technological trajectories will continue to develop largely in isolation from radical intellectual innovations. For example, the separation of much biological research from medical schools and hospitals in France, Japan, and perhaps Germany, has been seen as inhibiting the development of biotechnology firms in these countries (Henderson *et al.*, 1999; Kneller, 1999; Thomas, 1994).

In contrast, where organizational segmentation is lower, research organizations have overlapping goals, contain a variety of kinds of research activity and have overlapping labour markets, funding arrangements and control procedures. As a result, knowledge and skills flow more easily between them and the development of joint projects between researchers from different employment units and fast adaptation to new knowledge is facilitated. Low segmentation can also allow academic scientists to pursue a variety of objectives more easily, and thus transfer their results directly to the development of new products and processes, than in more segmented environments. As Stokes (1997: 45) points out, it has long been a feature of the US research system that many organizations, such as research universities and Bell Labs, have provided a home for researchers pursuing both theoretical and applied goals. The founding and development of Genentech exemplify these low levels of organizational and goal segmentation in the emergence of the US biotechnology industry (McKelvey, 1996).

These features of public science systems affect the ease with which scientists and engineers are able to develop new intellectual goals, fields and approaches, such as software engineering and molecular biology. Where objective and strategies are varied and changeable, as distinct from being tightly integrated around established disciplinary goals, frameworks and expertise, it should be easier to extend and apply new ideas and techniques for technological purposes. The boundaries between theory-driven scientific research and more instrumental knowledge production are more fluid, permeable and overlapping in such public science systems than in those where intellectual, skill and organizational boundaries are structured around separate disciplines.

Here, firms should find it relatively easy to become involved in research networks that combine theory-driven research with more instrumental projects and organizations. Such fluidity and adaptability of intellectual goals and skills in public science systems also generates a high level of change in ideas and expertise, which in turn enables firms to hire new kinds of skills relatively easily, especially where research training is closely integrated with current projects. Because labour markets in such systems are typically not highly segmented around separate kinds of intellectual goals, employing organizations and performance standards, researchers are able to move relatively easily between universities, other research organizations, and private companies without losing status and long-term career opportunities.

Overall, then, more flexible and pluralistic public science systems should enable innovative firms to become more involved in research projects and incorporate new knowledge and skills into their developmental activities more rapidly than those organized into strong prestige hierarchies with stable disciplinary and organizational boundaries and separate labour markets. When combined with 'mission-oriented' state science and technology policies (Ergas, 1987), these kinds of research systems should encourage fluidity of research goals and skills as researchers adapt their projects to state priorities within the overall peer review system and facilitate close connections between firms and researchers in sectors favoured by such policies. Where research training is also tied to current research projects, firms are able to recruit highly skilled researchers in these areas, and so adapt rapidly to new knowledge and expertise.

These connections between authority sharing, involvement in the public research system and non-market coordination and institutional environments enable us to identify the key conditions in which the six ideal types of innovation systems are likely to occur and become institutionalized. These are summarized in Table 3.2 and will now be discussed.

Considering first innovation systems relying mostly on market forms of coordination of innovative activities, these will tend to develop in societies with fluid external labour markets, limited state coordination and promotion of industrial development, limited segmentation of product markets, relatively weak industry associations policing entry and exit and generally few constraints on economic opportunism, at least at the national level. In the case of autarkic innovation systems, these are particularly likely to become established where: (a) an arm's length state outlaws inter-firm cooperation, (b) liquid capital markets facilitate an active market in corporate control, and (c) there are few restrictions on hiring and firing employees. They additionally rely on an education and training system that provides relatively generic and codified skills for key roles, and sufficient organizational stability to encourage managerial staff to build firm-specific innovative capabilities.

Innovation systems relying on professional teams can also develop in such institutional environments, but usually depend on some state support for the development of new technologies, often through the funding of novel research skills and fields in universities, as in the case of computer science groups in the USA (Mowery, 1999), and some relaxation of anti-trust rules for pre-competitive collaboration. Strong technical communities facilitate the evaluation and improvement of technical skills in such systems, as well as reducing search costs for both employers and

Table 3.2. Institutional conditions encouraging the establishment and reproduction of different innovation systems

Institutional Conditions	Type of Innovation System					
	Autarkic	Artisanal	Technological Teams	State-Led	Group-based	Highly Collaborative
Type of State	Arm's length	Interdependent	Arm's Length	Dominant developmental	Business corporatist	Inclusive corporatist
State science and technology policy	Mission	Weak	Mission	Mission	Diffusion	Diffusion
Strength of independent business associations	Low	Some	Low	Low	Considerable	Considerable
Strength of independent labour unions	Low	Some	Low	Low	Some	Considerable
Financial system	Capital market	Local bank-based	Capital market	State-credit based	Credit based	Credit based
Scope and strength of collaborative public training system	Low	Considerable	Limited	Low	Limited	Considerable
Strength of prestige hierarchy of universities and research organization	Limited	Varies	Limited	Considerable	Considerable	Limited
Competitive and pluralist public science system	Varies	Varies	Yes	No	Limited	Some
Segmentation of research organizations and careers	Some	Varies	Limited	Some	Some	Some

employees. In addition, these kinds of innovation systems are helped by flexible and pluralistic public science systems that enable new fields and intellectual goals to become institutionalized in the academic system relatively quickly and new organizations to compete effectively with existing elite groups. Organizational segmentation and prestige hierarchies are thus not strong or stable in societies that encourage such innovation systems to become established and reproduced.

Artisanal innovation systems also rely on some institutional infrastructure to encourage inter-firm cooperation in improving technologies, exploring new markets and acquiring resources, albeit often at the local or regional levels of organization. Rather than arising in regulatory states that implement a firmly arm's length approach to economic development throughout the economy, however, these kinds of innovation systems seem more likely to become established in societies where the central state acts interdependently with strong business associations and unions who are able to exercise considerable influence on the development of distinctive rules of the game. Such interdependent states are not necessarily weak in the sense discussed by Migdal (1988) but rather have limited autonomy in organizing civil society.

In the case of countries like Denmark, major intermediary groups include local and national employers' associations, industry groups and craft associations (Karnoe, 1999; Kristensen, 1992; 2006; Pedersen, 2006). Such groups are also often involved in the establishment and running of technical schools and other support facilities that enable skilled staff to continue to improve their expertise without becoming tied to any particular employer. Strong technical communities, whether local, regional or national, provide the basis for effective reputational evaluation and control of expertise, as well as incentives to enhance technical competences, in these kinds of innovation systems (Kristensen, 1996; 1999).

A further important feature of the institutional environments of artisanal innovation systems is the lack of a strong market for corporate control, and a relatively decentralized banking system in which connections between local savings and municipal banks and SMEs are close (Hopner, 1999). Together these local and regional institutional arrangements facilitate the establishment of loosely cooperative networks between small firm owners and managers that enable learning to be continuous within and between them (Lundvall *et al.*, 2002).

The last three types of innovation system manifest greater reliance on non-market forms of coordination of innovative activities. In the case of state-led systems, this is mostly achieved through dominant developmental states coordinating investment strategies, risk sharing and technical problem solving, as well as often underwriting credit provision and guaranteeing sales. Such states typically pursue mission oriented science and technology policies with substantial funding and coordination of research supporting their developmental objectives, often in state laboratories attached to individual ministries as well as in universities. The ability of public research organizations to pursue independent strategies and obtain resources from different kinds of agencies and groups is often limited in such societies.

Group-based and highly collaborative innovation systems are also assisted by considerable state coordination, but usually this involves much greater reliance on business associations and decentralization of control over resources to scientific and technological elites. Such corporatist states seek to play a leading role in economic and technological development but in, and through, employers' groups, industry associations and, sometimes, with the support of unions and other representational groups (Crouch, 1999: Chapter 12; Streeck and Schmitter, 1985). They develop and implement diffusionist science and technology policies in collaboration with trade associations, often supporting their use of public research faculties to improve technologies and solve technical problems.

As discussed in the previous chapter, however, these kinds of states differ in their involvement of labour unions in economic policy making and implementation, in developing and managing public training systems and in the extent to which unions are able to play a coordinating role in technical change at local, regional and national levels. While business corporatist states collaborate with business associations and individual companies in developing new technologies and improving existing ones, they rarely encourage unions to become involved in such activities and typically do not establish national public skill formation and certification systems in collaboration with union federations.

Inclusive corporatist states, in contrast, encourage the development of more collaborative innovation systems by institutionalizing the role of national and regional union federations in economic policy making and implementation and establishing cooperative skill formation systems that encompass a wide range of skills with employers' groups and unions. The relatively important role of independent unions in these activities, and their continuing negotiations with employers' groups and other organizations in managing labour relations issues, encourage the development of more cooperative norms governing relations between economic actors and enables unions to coordinate technical improvements in some industries, as Herrigel and Wittke (2005) have shown in the German car industry.

Group-based innovation systems are additionally more likely to develop in societies with stable and strong prestige hierarchies of public science research organizations whose goals and labour markets are quite segmented. In these kinds of public science systems, firms are likely to find it difficult to gain access to current research projects and to influence their objectives. This is especially likely where academics are civil servants who are restricted in the kinds of external activities they may pursue, and cannot easily move between universities and private business without losing prestige and other benefits. In general, strongly hierarchical public science systems in which competition between universities and other research organizations is limited are likely to encourage autarkic innovation strategies (Kneller, 2003).

More collaborative innovation systems in which companies become more actively involved in the public science system are likely in countries where there is greater competition between research organizations and they are not ordered into a stable strong hierarchy of social and intellectual prestige. They will also be encouraged by the existence of different kinds of research laboratories with distinct goals and means of support, especially non-state ones, and the institutionalization of transorganizational career paths for researchers that enable them to move between these types without greatly losing status. Organizational pluralism, flexibility and permeability in terms of recruitment and cooperation are likely to encourage such innovation systems when combined with the other characteristics of coordinated market economies outlined above.

Institutional Conditions for the Construction of National Innovation Systems and the Consequences of Increasing Transnational Governance

Many of these conditions favouring the establishment of different kinds of innovation systems are nationally specific, which suggests that such distinctive types are most likely to become established and reproduced at the national, rather than sectoral, regional or transnational, level of collective organization. However, as with business systems, this does not necessarily mean that each nation state develops its own kind of innovation system, nor that distinctive systems cannot be established at regional, international or sectoral levels of collective organization. Both the national specificity and distinctiveness of these key institutions, and the extent to which they standardize the nature of economic actors and their strategies across industries and regions, differ between countries.

In particular, following the same logic as that outlined in the previous chapter, the development of nationally distinctive and homogenous innovation systems is contingent upon three key features of national institutional regimes. First, the strength of national institutions governing innovative economic activities relative to regional and international ones. Second, the extent to which they are complementary in reinforcing particular strategies and patterns of behaviour of leading firms and, third, the extent to which they standardize the organization of socio-economic groups, and the ways that they compete and cooperate, throughout the national economy.

Considering first the national strength of institutional arrangements, this reflects the relative importance of national 'rules of the game' governing innovative activities as compared to those operative regionally or across national borders or within particular industries. The more that national norms and regulations governing competition and cooperation, the constitution of economic actors and their access to key resources, and the organization of public science systems, dominate those at other levels, the more likely that patterns of innovation will vary between countries rather than between regions and sectors.

Second, institutional complementarity at the national level refers here to the extent to which national institutions governing different aspects of innovation systems encourage similar kinds of behaviour, or, on the other hand, conflict in their implications for actors' rationalities and strategies. For example, public science systems with fluid boundaries between different kinds of research organizations, high tolerance of varied intellectual goals and performance criteria in the higher education and research system, and high levels of competition within and between universities and similar organizations, can be said to be complementary to highly fluid labour markets with few constraints on employer and employee opportunism in their encouragement of labour mobility and the rapid transfer of new knowledge and skills between academia and business in research intensive industries.

On the other hand, highly segmented research organizations and strongly hierarchical higher education systems can be seen as complementary to relatively constrained labour markets that limit mobility between employers through their encouragement of firm specific innovation strategies and capabilities. To a considerable extent, this kind of complementarity has characterized much of the postwar Japanese economy (Kneller, 2003; Whitley, 2003b).

The more such complementarities between key institutions occur nationally rather than regionally or transnationally, the more likely that distinctly national innovation systems become established and reproduced. Where dominant national institutional regimes are complementary in encouraging particular patterns of: (a) authority sharing, (b) involvement in the public science system, and (c) overall coordination of innovative activities, innovation systems will tend to be nationally cohesive and distinctive rather than regional or sectoral. Where they are relatively weak and/or conflicting in their implications for economic actors, distinctive kinds of regional and/or industrial innovation systems may well develop.

Third, the more states, financial systems and labour market institutions standardize the rules of the game specifying appropriate actors and norms of economic behaviour throughout a country, the less likely will distinctive sectoral innovation systems become established around particular technological regimes (Malerba, 2002; Malerba and Orsenigo, 1993). In contrast, where such specification is restricted to the establishment of formal rules within which a variety of kinds of groups can pursue different strategies with different resources, and are able to shift direction relatively easily, the more sectoral and regional differences in innovation patterns will tend to become significant.

In a country like the USA, for instance, the combination of particular kinds of capital and labour market institutions, national state structures and policies and legal institutions has produced a distinctive framework for innovative activities that has encouraged the development of a particular kind of innovation system at the national level (Casper *et al.*, 1999; Hall and Soskice, 2001a). However, this framework does not greatly restrict the kinds of collective entities that can be constituted as economic actors and interest groups, how they are to be organized, or how they can acquire, dispose of, and reallocate key resources between activities and sectors. It therefore permits considerable variety of innovative actors and organizations. Within the broad set of capital and labour market institutions dominating the US economy, then, there is scope for regional and sectoral patterns of innovation and economic organization to vary considerably (Crouch, 2005; Jacoby, 2005).

Where, on the other hand, more corporatist states encourage firms to join business associations and to form federations that unite major interest groups, their organization tends to be more systematic and standardized across sectors. Additionally, the more inclusive corporatist states often encourage positive union attitudes and delegate certain welfare functions to them, as well as systematically organize labour representation at the national level. Some such states have also developed relatively homogenous skill formation systems that integrate state schools with employer provided training, usually with the active participation of labour unions and workplace representatives (Hinz, 1999). Such cooperation may limit the speed of response to market changes but does ensure rapid introduction of new standards and courses once they have been agreed.

Overall, then, the more inclusive corporatist is the political system, the more innovative activities are likely to be organized in similar ways and deal with each other according to relatively standardized procedures. Firms in highly corporatist environments will be more constrained to follow institutionalized conventions and should vary less in their innovation strategies than those in less organized societies. Sectoral, regional and size differences between companies should be less marked in these kinds of regimes than in other ones. Because the institutions governing labour and capital markets typically encompass small and medium-sized firms as well as large ones here, more companies are likely to follow similar policies and practices—and so develop similar kinds of organizational capabilities than where states focus on larger firms and do not establish stable mechanisms for managing labour relationships. The national specificity and cohesion of innovation systems should, then, be greatest in societies where the state takes a leading role in orchestrating economic development with systematically organized and standardized forms of interest group representation and bargaining on a continuing basis.

This analysis has emphasized the key role of the state and nationally specific institutions in constituting national innovation systems, which raises the question of how changing inter-state relations and the growth of multi-levelled governance (Bache and Flinders, 2004) can be expected to affect them. As in the case of business systems, such issues involve the comparison of the relative strength and complementarity of transnational institutions governing innovative activities across national boundaries with those established at national and regional levels.

In general terms, most transnational institutions are less sovereign and autonomous in terms of establishing their own competences and constitutional choice rules governing innovative activities than many, if not all, of the industrialized countries in the Organization for

Economic Cooperation and Development (OECD). For the EU to develop an effective pan-European innovation system, for instance, it would have to be able to establish distinctive transnational rules of the game for firms and other groups that dominated national ones. This would require, amongst other things, the support of key international actors, such as strong European industrial associations and research organizations, who could dominate national ones. Just as the weakness of employers' groups and unions in France contributed to the failure of the attempt to reshape existing patterns of skill formation around 'German' collaborative institutions in the 1980s (Culpepper, 1999; 2001; Hancke, 2002: 32; Hancke and Goyer, 2005), so too the lack of strong supporting groups at the European level limits the likely success of attempts at creating an effective technological development system across the EU.

Insofar as the European Commission (EC) has been able to pursue distinctive public policy 'missions' that involve substantial scientific and technological development, such as those in the IT industry, these have rarely been as substantial in terms of resources committed, or as centrally integrated and directed, as those implemented by some national governments, and their success may be questioned (Anderson and Braendgaard, 1992). Furthermore, much EU support for European research networks and collaborations appears to have reinforced existing national prestige hierarchies and 'short-term' objectives (Garcia-Fontes and Geuna, 1999; Geuna, 1999). This suggests that the ability of the EC to achieve long-term objectives involving the restructuring of national and international hierarchies is limited.

There is also little evidence that strong European institutions governing public science systems have become established. The funding, organization and control of universities and other research organizations remain concentrated in the hands of national and regional governments, with little pan-European regulation or specification of research roles, skills or authority structures. Research evaluation methods, strategies and outcomes, for example, vary considerably across national systems and are clearly developed and implemented in different ways by national governments (Geuna and Martin, 2003; Whitley and Glaser 2007). Despite the 'Bologna' agreement on degree courses—which seems likely to be implemented differently across Europe—the transnational harmonization of academic structures remains limited and few European institutions have become established that could greatly influence the organization of national systems.

Furthermore, as the evidence in Braithwaite and Drahos (2000) suggests, the prevalent pattern of transnational business governance is more arm's length than developmentalist or corporatist, and so is unlikely to encourage much standardization of innovative behaviour across national boundaries. This is additionally encouraged by the lack of democratic legitimacy of most transnational institutions, including those in the EU. Given the overwhelmingly national nature of political competition, parties and interest group organization, it is difficult to see how international organizations could implement active innovation policies in favour of specific sectors or projects and encourage inter-firm collaboration and/or monopolistic forms of interest group representation, especially in the face of resistance from nationally elected governments and groups supported by them. It is much easier for the EC and similar unelected agencies to legitimize liberalization of markets as a way of opening up opportunities for all European companies and reducing the influence of special interests than to segment markets, promote European champions and support particular groups amidst democratically elected governments.

Insofar as transnational institutions do establish a distinctive and complementary set of regulatory institutions and governance norms dealing with innovative activities, then, these tend to permit considerable variation in how innovation systems are organized, whether at the national, sectoral or regional levels. The standardization of a single 'European' type of innovation system, for example, is most improbable. However, the prevalence of an arm's length transnational regulatory approach may constrain the national specificity and homogeneity of state coordinated and collaborative kinds of innovation systems in some states, especially when combined with pressures from external investors.

In general, the impact of any transnational regulatory approach to innovative activities is going to be most evident when it coincides with, and complements, other efforts to restructure commitments between companies, employers and employees. It is probably too weak and contradictory to develop new kinds of innovation systems across national boundaries, but when combined with broader international, national and regional pressures to limit constraints on economic opportunism, it may well reduce the national specificity, complementarity and standardization of group-based and highly collaborative innovation systems in some countries. In so doing, it could encourage the strengthening of sectorally specific innovation systems around different technological regimes within national boundaries (Breschi and Malerba, 1997; Malerba, 2002). However, the continued diversity of labour market institutions, skill formation systems and public science systems will limit the extent to which these become established transnationally.

Concluding Remarks

In conclusion, it is perhaps worth emphasizing four main points arising from this discussion. First, the development and reproduction of particular ways of inventing and commercializing new processes, products and services as coherent systems of innovation depends greatly on the strength and complementarity of key institutions at particular organizational levels. Because of this institutional dependence, different kinds of learning, cooperation and competition take place in different institutional contexts. While many institutions governing innovative activities are associated with the nation state, not all are, and the extent to which they do indeed complement each other in encouraging particular logics of action varies considerably between countries and over historical periods. Insofar as we are in a post-Westphalian state era (Held *et al.*, 1999: 37–8; Schmidt, 2002: 17–57), the dominance of national institutions may be weakening and their construction of distinctively national innovation systems becoming less autarkic and cohesive, especially within the EU.

Second, the homogeneity and standardization of economic actors and other socio-economic groups, as well as of the norms governing their behaviour, within any particular set of complementary institutions varies according to the kind of institutions and organizations that dominate a given social system, and the policies that key agents, especially states, pursue. Insofar as technological regimes are significant in the construction of different kinds of sectoral innovation systems, these are more likely to become established in arm's length institutional environments than in highly corporatist ones in which interest groups, and the regulation of their interaction, are organized in similar ways across industries.

Given the considerable variety of institutions, agencies and policies between European countries, this means that innovative activities organized in different ways in different industries in one country may be less separately structured in other ones, so that pan-European sectoral innovation systems are relatively rare. British, German, and Swedish biotechnology firms, for instance, differ considerably in their competences and strategies as a result of major variations in state policies, financial systems and labour markets, as is shown in Chapter 8.

Third, the development of transnational rules of the competitive game and supranational forms of governance in some regimes, particularly in the EU, has created a new tier of institutional constraints and opportunities for innovative activities without necessarily leading to the demise of existing ones at national and regional levels. This is because of the limited ability of international organizations to act independently from national ones as authoritative agents in establishing constitutional choice rules, as well as the often contradictory policies followed in different areas. Additionally, political parties, interest groups and other socio-political actors remain more focused on national competitions, and these are quite heterogeneously organized.

Finally, insofar as this additional tier of governance has followed a particular approach to economic organization and behaviour in a consistent manner, it resembles the institutions and logic of liberal market economies rather than those of more coordinated ones, as is shown in more detail in Chapter 5. It therefore permits considerable variability in the kind of firms that compete in different markets, how they do so, and how they adapt to changing circumstances. It is unlikely, then, to encourage much transnational standardization of patterns of innovation, although it may reduce the level of homogeneity within some national innovation systems by providing alternative opportunities for strategic managers. Overall, then, while the strength and cohesion of collaborative innovation systems may decline in some states, and state-led ones seem unlikely to be viable, the variety of different ways of organizing innovative activities, and of the kinds of innovations successfully produced, seems likely to remain considerable, and perhaps to increase.

4

Changing Institutional Regimes and Business Systems: Endogenous and Exogenous Pressures on Postwar Systems of Economic Organization

Introduction

These accounts of the conditions under which different kinds of business systems and innovation systems become dominant in different nation states help to explain the development and persistence of nationally divergent patterns of economic organization in many OECD countries in the postwar period. They also suggest how we might begin to understand changes in these dominant forms as a result of both endogenous and exogenous shifts in key institutions and coalitions of interest groups. In particular, it is important to take account of how shifts in the relative cohesion and influence of the different kinds of socio-economic groups that support dominant institutional regimes and business systems in different societies, as well as the growth and organizational mobilization of new ones, generate significant changes in political economies.

As Amable suggests (2003: 68):

institutions reflect the socio-political equilibrium of a society, and the costs and benefits associated with political change affect individuals differently. A political coalition will seek to stay in power by finding support from the dominant social bloc, to that effect it will seek to implement those institutional changes that favour some or all of the socio-political groups that constitute the dominant bloc and try to prevent change that is detrimental to the bloc.

When analysing institutional and business system change, it is therefore important to consider which groups and interests constitute the dominant block in a society, how they are changing, and which other groups are becoming influential. In addition, such analysis has increasingly to incorporate changing international constraints and opportunities as economic actors, governance structures and socio-political groups operate across national political boundaries.

For any change in dominant business systems to be significant, it has to involve qualitative changes in: (a) the nature of leading firms, their priorities, governance and core competences, (b) the ways that they compete and cooperate, and (c) the nature of dominant groups. These may result from endogenous shifts in socio-political balances, such as the growth of an educated middle class in fast growing, state dominated economies, and/or from exogenous political and economic changes that affect dominant firms and elites, such as the collapse of the USSR and the internationalization of competition and capital flows. The task of understanding socio-economic change then becomes focused on how dominant actors, institutions and logics decline and alternative rules of the game, leading firms etc become established.

It is worth emphasizing that such change does not always, or indeed frequently, imply the wholesale replacement of one dominant cohesive and stable kind of business system by another equally cohesive and coherent one. In the case of France, for instance, the dominance of the postwar state developmentalist institutional regime may be much less than it was, and the independence of large firms from state tutelage correspondingly increased (Hancke, 2002; Hancke and Goyer, 2005), but the ties between the *grands corps*, political elites and strategic managers seem to remain quite strong, as does the common understanding of, and commitment to, the national political-economic interest (Levy, 2005; Loriaux, 2003; Schmidt, 2002). There is little sign of investor returns becoming more important than growth goals, or of increased authority sharing with employees, suppliers and customer on the part of top managers of leading French companies in the noble industries, who largely remain products of the *grandes écoles*.

This example suggests that some changes in prevailing governance relationships amongst leading firms, agencies and interest groups can occur without necessarily implying the radical transformation of dominant logics of action and elite connections. Similarly, it is possible to argue that the changes in US capital markets in the 1970s and 1980s led to increased investor constraints on top manager behaviour without fundamentally altering the prevalent nature of economic actors and relationships in that economy (Davis *et al.*, 1994; Lazonick and O'Sullivan, 1996). Indeed, they can be seen as intensifying economic opportunism and pressures to increase market power through growth by acquisition (Jacoby, 2005).

In general, given the diverse nature of the institutional regimes, business systems and key interest groups that dominated many OECD economies in the postwar period, both the kinds of influences that encouraged changes in them, and how they did so, can be expected to vary considerably between political economies. In considering how dominant patterns of economic organization have changed as a result of endogenous and exogenous developments, it is therefore crucial to identify: (a) the key features of the institutional regimes that encourage particular kinds of firms to dominate different economies, (b) the nature of the groups directing them and the prevalent logic guiding their actions, and (c) the broader political–economic groups they were supported and reproduced by, such as those discussed by Djelic and Quack (2005) in their account of changing German competition and banking regulation. It is changes in these actors and rationalities that can be expected to signify substantial shifts in the nature of political economies and in how firms develop distinctive organizational capabilities.

We can begin to analyse changes in the prevalent postwar business systems of many OECD economies by extending the analysis of the four ideal types of institutional regimes presented in Chapter 2 to incorporate two further features that affect the priorities and strategies of leading firms, and to identify the nature of the dominant coalitions that support these types. These features of institutional regimes and the key groups associated with them will be discussed in the next section of this chapter, together with their impact on prevalent growth strategies. In the following one, I consider the major endogenous and exogenous pressures for change that are most likely to have affected these features since the 1960s, and how they have had different consequences for different political economies.

Dominant Groups and Economic Logics in Different Institutional Regimes

One of the central distinguishing features of institutional regimes that affects the dominant economic logics underlying corporate decision making concerns how state agencies and dominant institutions specify, monitor and control the powers and responsibilities of private companies, especially their exercise of market power and ability to act opportunistically. These vary considerably between industrial capitalist societies, as well as over time (Dobbin, 1994; Milhaupt, 2003; Roy, 1997), in ways that generate major differences in firms' competitive behaviour. As the varieties of capitalism literature has emphasized (Hall and Soskice, 2001a), considerable differences in economic organization and outcomes result from the relative strength of institutions encouraging mutual dependence between investors, managers and workers, and the associated dominance of exit or voice logics of action (Nooteboom, 2000). These variations especially affect patterns of authority sharing and the generation of innovative competences in new industries, as is discussed in more detail in Part III of this book.

However, the simple contrast of liberal and coordinated market economies obscures important variations in the kinds of institutions and agencies that constrain market power and encourage commitment, and how they do so (Allen, 2004; Crouch 2005). National and local state regulatory regimes, the nature and role of business associations of large and small companies and of labour unions, the organization of skill formation systems and the nature of state technology policies, all vary across market economies and significantly affect competitive strategies within and across industrial sectors.

Another important feature of institutional regimes that affects dominant firms' growth strategies concerns the external provision of what Colin Crouch and his colleagues have termed 'collective competition goods' (Crouch et al., 2001). These include knowledge about new technologies and markets and support in accessing them, the availability of highly skilled workers of different kinds, the development and certification of quality and technological standards, the management of labour and other disputes, and access to capital on favourable terms (Le Gales and Voelzkow, 2001: 3). The more these are provided by domestic agencies and organizations and are governed by national institutions, the more embedded are companies in national and regional institutional contexts that help them to create distinctive organizational capabilities that provide competitive advantages in certain markets. As these change, so too we can expect firms' perceptions of opportunities and constraints in national and international economies to alter.

These two features of institutional regimes are sometimes positively correlated, as when the extra-firm provision of collective competition goods increases with external constraints on firm behaviour, but this is by no means always the case. Growing capital market pressures on publicly quoted firms' strategies, for instance, is rarely accompanied by significant assistance in achieving them, except perhaps through higher share prices facilitating takeovers. Insofar as powerful financial intermediaries such as fund managers do provide some assistance in capital market dominated financial systems (Zysman, 1983), it is typically at arm's length and for limited periods and purposes.

Equally, in some circumstances particular territorial communities and/or sectorally bounded groups and organizations may provide collective competition goods such as highly trained and skilled workers, entrepreneurial law firms and knowledgeable venture capitalists, without greatly constraining market power or economic opportunism. The Silicon Valley economy is perhaps the most well-known instance of this kind of phenomenon (Kenney, 2000; Lee, 2000). The combinations of these factors vary also between types of industrial districts, or local production systems (Crouch *et al.*, 2001).

In analysing changes in the major kinds of business systems that became established in many industrialized economies during the postwar growth period, I suggest that it is changes in these features of institutional regimes in conjunction with shifts in the dominant political-economic groups and alliances supporting them that are especially important. These interest groups are often summarized in terms of rather general categories such as investors, managers and workers, but the increased differentiation of socio-economic groups and organizations in the late twentieth century requires a more elaborate set of distinctions. Investors, for example, have become separated into the ultimate beneficiaries of shareholdings, on the one hand, and those organizations that control them on a day-to-day basis—institutional shareholders and fund managers—on the other hand.

Similarly, strategic or top managers of the larger companies have become separated in their remuneration patterns and socio-economic interests from other managers in a number of market economies, and skilled workers have become more differentiated with the expansion of higher education and increasing significance of research-led innovations in some industries. Additionally, of course, new social movements and pressure groups have become significant socio-political actors in several states, as well as forming international alliances that affect policy decisions and business strategies (Braithwaite and Drahos, 2000; McNichol and Bensedrine, 2003; Smith, 2005).

These features can be incorporated into the four major ideal types of institutional regimes discussed in Chapter 2 to suggest how particular kinds of firms and their strategic managers are encouraged to grow in varied ways and become dominant in differently organized economies.

These connections are summarized in Table 4.1 and will now be further discussed. Insofar as internationalization and more endogenous changes have resulted in significant institutional and business system change since the 1960s, this should be reflected in the relative decline in dominance of some of these features and/or the transformation of institutional regimes and dominant groups in ways that have affected the nature of leading firms, their priorities and growth patterns in different economies.

Arm's length institutional regimes have few constraints on economic opportunism and the exercise of market power. Capital and labour markets in these kinds of regimes are flexible, with few restraints from state agencies, business associations and unions on entries and exits. States are more 'custodial' than 'promotional', to use Evans' (1994) terminology, and do not seek to structure the decision rules of particular firms or most sectors. Business associations and labour unions are usually fragmented and weak, functioning more as lobbyists for special interests than as long-term partners in determining economic policy and its implementation. Given the largely regulatory state economic policies, there are relatively few externally provided collective competition goods in such regimes, and so most large firms internalize skills and technology development, as well as relying heavily on self-financing of investments.

Additionally, since there are few barriers to exercising market power, or on the ability of large companies to take over smaller ones, managers have every incentive to grow as quickly as possible, through acquisitions as well as organically, and across sectors as well as within them. This is especially the case in capital-intensive industries where complex and expensive technologies are developed and coordinated by technical specialists, and large firms are able to exert sufficient control over product markets to offer relatively stable organizational careers to managers and engineers. In such 'managerial' forms of capitalism (Lazonick, 1991), top managers tend to be internally promoted and identify their interests with those of their long-term employer and the growth of the firm as a whole, since its size and success usually determines their own status and rewards. This encourages incremental innovation and the accumulation of firm specific knowledge amongst managers and senior engineers, but can inhibit the development of radical innovations that could threaten current market positions.

However, such commitment and freedom from capital market pressures for increasing investor returns can decline in these economies when inflation reduces the real returns received by bondholders, collective ownership of equities by insurance companies, pension funds and other

Table 4.1. Key features of four ideal types of institutional regimes governing market economies

Key Features	Types of Institutional Regimes			
	Arm's Length	Dominant Developmentalist	Business Corporatist	Inclusive Corporatist
Constraints on economic opportunism and autonomy from:				
State elites	Limited	High	Considerable	Some
Business associations	Low	Low	High	High
Labour federations	Low	Low	Low	Considerable
SME associations	Low	Low	Low	Considerable
External provision of collective competition goods:				
Capital	Market-based	State subsidized for favoured firms	State and bank co-ordinated.	Bank-based
Labour (including skill formation and development)	Limited, generic	Limited, generic	Limited, except for general education	Considerable, sectorally based
Knowledge	Public policy focused	State provided for favoured firms and sectors	State assisted diffusion to larger firms	State assisted diffusion to large and small firms
Dominant coalitions	Strategic managers of large firms, sometimes with financial elites	State—big business owners—top managers	Bureaucratic elite and strategic managers of large firms	Peak associations of capital and labour
Prevalent goals and strategies	Growth and market power of individual firms through acquisitions, innovations and predatory pricing. Sometimes, investor returns.	Growth and economic dominance through obtaining state support and diversifying across sectors to limit risk	Growth through incremental innovation and diversification, risk sharing and joint development in business groups	Growth in niche markets through incremental innovation and diversification, sectoral technology development and customization

financial intermediaries grows significantly, and this increases the concentration of control over stocks and shares and changes the balance of power between large firms and the managers of shareholder funds. Unlike earlier portfolio investors who tended to be beneficial shareholders with relatively small proportions of issued share capital in any one company, and who traded relatively infrequently, these professional fund managers control much larger blocks of shares on behalf of ultimate beneficiaries. Because they compete for mandates as well as trading on their own account, fund managers focus on increasing the relative returns of the portfolios they manage and are much more willing to trade—with lower transaction costs—in order to demonstrate their short-term success. As a result, liquidity grows and the market for corporate control becomes intensified, especially when supported by political shifts, as in the USA in the 1980s (Davis *et al.*, 1994).

Strategic managers of large firms in this situation have to deal with financial market pressures to a greater extent and can come to see their interests aligned more with short-term shareholders than with the future growth of their current employer. This is especially likely if their own rewards come as much from shareownership as from straight salary, and they are able to become independently wealthy from such ownership. The top managers of the largest companies then join financial elites and large shareowners to constitute the dominant political economic block, separately from the other managerial and technical labour force of large firms.

The other three ideal types of institutional regimes to be considered here combine more extensive provision of collective competition goods with some constraints on the behaviour of strategic managers of leading firms. They differ, though, in the number and variety of agencies and organizations providing services for companies, and exercising constraints and guidance on their strategies, priorities and development. In dominant developmental state regimes, for example, the central state provides a variety of collective competition goods that are crucial for large firm survival and development, but intermediary associations, labour unions and other potential interest groups that could restrict favoured firms' independence of action are typically weak and/or repressed by state elites as possible threats to their supremacy. Political-bureaucratic elites dominate such regimes in alliance with the owner managers of large businesses, sometimes supported by military groups, as in South Korea after 1961 (Fields, 1995; Kim, 1997; Woo, 1991).

High levels of business dependence on state support here encourages owner managers to pursue strong growth goals while retaining personal and/or family control by funding expansion through subsidized credit. To meet state demands and limit political as well as commercial risks, firms typically try to control production chains through vertical integration and diversify across industries and markets, either through direct ownership or by forming large business groups, such as the Korean *chaebol*. Vertical dependence additionally limits authority sharing between companies as rivals compete for state support and the fate of companies is often dependent on personal relationships between owner-managers and state leaders as well as meeting state objectives.

Corporatist institutional regimes in contrast involve peak associations of different socio-economic interests in developing and implementing economic policies, usually in conjunction with promotional state agencies (Evans, 1994). These associations have strong de jure or de facto power over their members and so exert considerable constraints on individual firm or union behaviour. Corporatist regimes not only help to provide collective competition goods for companies, then, but also limit opportunism and 'free rider' forms of behaviour. They differ, however, in the range of interests that are represented in policy making and implementation as well as in the activities constrained by national or sectoral associations.

In business corporatist regimes, associations of large forms and business groups are much more organized and cohesive at the national level than are labour unions and small business groups. Partly because state elites find it easier to pursue developmentalist goals with groups of large firms than to involve large numbers of small- and medium-sized companies, especially in highly centralized political systems, and partly because of historical patterns of collaboration between leading firms during industrialization in many countries, big business here forms a strong socio-economic grouping together with bureaucratic and political elites pursuing economic development goals.

Financial organizations, especially banks, are more integrated into national policies of industrial growth in these kinds of regimes than they are in more arm's length ones, and more subordinated to the accomplishment of development goals than constituted as a separate sector with its own distinct interests. In contrast, labour management and skill formation issues are typically delegated to individual companies, sometimes with active state discouragement of national labour associations, as in postwar Japan (Garon, 1987).

Collective competition goods are here quite widely provided by associations and organizations external to the firm, often coordinated by state agencies and big business groups to pursue developmentalist objectives. While technology policies in these kinds of institutional regimes are more 'diffusion' than 'mission-oriented' (Ergas, 1987; Morris-Suzuki, 1994), and so support general technical improvements throughout favoured industries, SME development and protection from large firms is not a core priority of business corporatist societies. Occasionally, though, smaller firms are supported by local governments, as in the Japanese machine tool industry (Friedman, 1988), as well as by national political parties in particular electoral systems such as that of postwar Japan (Gao, 2001; Pempel, 1998). In such a system, there are strong incentives to grow since managers and employees benefit greatly from being part of larger organizations, and financial returns to investors are typically less important than increasing market share (Clark, 1979).

More inclusive corporatist institutional regimes extend involvement in economic policy development and implementation to labour union federations and smaller firms. Collective competition goods provided by extra-firm associations and organizations include skill formation and credentialing systems and wage and other reward bargaining support, as well as technology upgrading and marketing/distribution assistance for SMEs. Typically, these regimes help to organize SME interests and restrict large firms' ability to takeover or undercut smaller companies by encouraging industry associations to represent the concerns of smaller firms in their sector rather than just the largest ones.

As a result, firms are subject to more veto groups and institutionalized constraints on economic opportunism in these kinds of regimes than in the others discussed here. Cooperation between the strategic managers of large companies, their domestic competitors, customers, suppliers and union leaders is encouraged more than zero-sum competition, and dominant socio-economic groups include labour and SME representatives as well as those of large firms, banks and state agencies. Authority sharing between companies within sectors, and between employers and skilled employees, is also encouraged by strong business and union associations, and this furthers the development of firm-specific innovation capabilities based on employee commitment to problem solving, process improvements and meeting customer demands, as will be further discussed in Chapter 6.

These kinds of regimes tend to favour existing commitments and capabilities over new ones, so that radically new technologies that could threaten current coalitions, skills and markets are developed relatively slowly. While all key stakeholders favour growth goals over short-term investor returns, the relative protection and support provided for smaller companies here means that the pressures to grow fast and increase market share are less strong than in business corporatist regimes. Rather, growth is a more general priority for all firms in each sector than being a crucial goal for individual firms that involves losses for domestic competitors. The considerable sunk costs involved in developing sectoral growth and industry specific skills and knowledge also are likely to constrain diversification into unrelated technologies and markets, especially if strong union federations are predominantly organized on a sectoral basis and skill formation is likewise organized around existing industry boundaries.

Changes in Institutional Regimes and Business Systems

This summary of the key features of four ideal types of institutional regimes governing economic actors suggests that significant changes in these regimes involve qualitative shifts in: (a) the nature and degree of constraints on the economic opportunism of strategic managers, (b) their qualifications, experience, skills and resources, (c) the nature and source of collective competition goods, and (d) the cohesion and composition of dominant blocks. The nature of leading firms, their strategic priorities, capabilities and behaviour, is only likely to alter significantly, in this view, when such shifts in their environments occur.

Much of the recent literature on changing forms of capitalism and business systems has focused on the increasing internationalization of much economic activity, especially capital transfers and trade, especially after the breakdown of the Bretton Woods' regime in the 1970s. Without necessarily accepting all of the speculations of the 'globaloney' (Emmott, 1992: 29–40) literature, it is reasonable to suggest that the postwar growth in cross-border trade and investment, the expansion of international capital markets and increasing significance of international governance, with or without transnational government (Braithwaite and Drahos, 2000), have significantly affected the pre-eminently national character of the major institutions governing economic activities.

In particular, given the predominantly anomic character of the international business environment, with few strongly established institutions mitigating the direct use of market power and controlling economic opportunism, the increasing internationalization of economic activities seems likely to have reduced the strength of domestic institutional constraints on opportunistic behaviour of the largest companies in many countries, as well as weakening the cohesion of domestic associations and alliances. Additionally, the predominantly arm's length focus of much 'global business regulation' (Braithwaite and Drahos, 2000), including in the European Union, has limited many states' ability to provide direct support for domestic companies.

However, as Hirst and Thompson (1996) and others have emphasized, the nation state remains the pre-eminent unit of political mobilization and competition as well as being the key agency guaranteeing and policing private property rights, and many, if not most, of the key institutions governing economic activities remain nationally specific. Insofar as the dominant role of states and national institutional regimes in organizing economic affairs within their territorial boundaries has weakened since the 1960s, this may reflect greater willingness to share authority across national boundaries, as in the case of the European Union, and changes in how different states pursue promotional policies rather than radical shifts in political and economic arrangements, as discussed in more detail in many contributions to Weiss' *States in the Global Economy* (2003a).

In addition to economic internationalization and the limited expansion of transnational governance, though, many of the key features of the dominant institutional regimes that became established in the major industrial economies after the end of the Second World War have been affected by more endogenous changes. It is when these more internal changes complement shifts in the international environment that we can expect significant changes in the nature of dominant national institutional arrangements and patterns of economic organization to occur. Amongst these largely endogenous changes are: demographic movements, particularly urbanization and reductions in family size, the expansion of formal education and training, the growth of large companies and their rate of self-financing, decline of the primary sector and growth of the service sector, and changes in the structure of some financial systems, especially the management of investments. Additionally, many states have implemented significant changes in competition and anti-trust policies, as well as developing new kinds of science and technology policy and supporting innovation. In some cases, they have also shifted from direct support for particular firms and industries to a more indirect promotion of economic development through social protection and active labour market policies (Amable, 2003).

In broad terms, many of these endogenous and exogenous changes can be expected to weaken domestic institutional constraints on large-firm opportunism and to reduce the value of domestically provided external collective competition goods for the more internationalized companies. They may additionally reduce the cohesion of alliances between state elites and big business groups in some regimes, especially when educational expansion, urbanization and economic growth increase the size and influence of the middle class (Shiraishi, 2006). It also seems likely that they will mitigate the dependence of strategic managers of the largest firms on banks and industry associations, thus encouraging the differentiation of these firms' interests from those of their smaller and more domestically focused competitors.

Such differentiation of interest and priorities may also occur between labour organizations representing workers in sectors that vary in their exposure to foreign competition, and could further weaken the cohesion of national associations of employers and employees, and of corporatist arrangements more generally. At the same time, increasing emphasis on more indirect state-provided collective competition goods, such as investments in pre-competitive research, can encourage the growth of new research-based industries in some economies and further weaken current coalitions. Alliances between firms and between organized labour and business in these countries can become less effective as the fates on individual companies develop in contrasting ways and the homogeneity of relations between investors, intermediaries, managers, and employees declines. These expectations are summarized in Table 4.2.

As this table suggests, the nature and consequences of these kinds of change vary between types of institutional regimes and do not always have straightforward outcomes because of mediating factors. In particular, they depend on the following features of market economies: (a) the size and significance of domestic markets, (b) the extent to which key institutions are complementary in their consequences for economic actors—including gender roles and skill formation and certification systems—and their importance for the development and improvement of key organizational capabilities, (c) the extent and significance of foreign competition and investment, and (d) the strength of organized labour and its involvement in the publicly organized training systems.

In general, the larger the size of the domestic market and the more complementary are domestic institutions in helping leading firms to develop distinctive competitive competences, the less likely are they to support moves to change dominant arrangements. This is particularly probable when foreign competition and investment is relatively limited and labour unions are strong. Even in smaller and relatively open economies, such

Table 4.2. Likely effects of endogenous and exogenous changes on key features of institutional regimes

Endogenous and Exogenous changes	Features of Institutional Regimes		
	Constraints on economic opportunism	External provision of collective competition goals	Dominant political-economic blocks
Demographic shifts, economic growth and education expansion		Growth of educated labour force	Weakening of state big-business alliances, decline of rural groups, expansion of civil society
Increase in large firm self-financing Growth of institutional ownership and fund management, intensification of market for corporate control in some regimes	Reduced for big firms Reduced in some states	Less important for big firms Facilitation of entry and exit and of market for acquiring companies	Decline of bank-based business groups Detachment of top managers from other employees and firms, emergencies of coalition with financial elites
Expansion of mission-oriented technology policies and support for research-based innovations		Reduced risks for entrepreneurial technology firms, access to new knowledge and skills in favoured industries	Growth of new business elites in innovation-led industries
Internationalization of competition and investment	Reduced, especially for MNCs	Reduced significance for MNCs, reduced direct state support	Separation of MNCs, decline in cohesion of domestic associations and alliances
Growth of transnational governance especially in EU	Reduced	Reduction in direct state support for domestic firms, increase in indirect support through labour market and innovation policies	Weakening of domestic alliances, some transnational alliances and interest groups in EU

Depending on: Size and significance of domestic market

Complementarities of domestic institutions and their importance for developing key organizational capabilities

Openness to foreign competition and investment

Strength of labour organizations and their involvement in the training system as Denmark and Sweden, internationalization *per se* need not generate radical institutional or business system change when strong domestic institutions and interest groups such as employer and labour organizations remain effective in providing collective competition goods and maintaining constraints on short-term opportunism (Katzenstein, 2006; Kristensen, 2006; Swank, 2003).

The effects of endogenous and exogenous changes on: (a) established institutional constraints on economic opportunism, (b) the provision and importance of collective competition goods, and (c) dominant political-economic blocks should, then, vary considerably between economies dominated by different intuitional regimes, business systems and interest groups. I now turn to consider how these pressures are likely to affect business system characteristics in institutional regimes with different features in more detail.

(a) Arm's Length Regimes

Considering first the impact of endogenous and exogenous changes on the arm's length type of institutional regime, probably the most significant ones in the late twentieth century occurred in their capital market-based financial systems with the further fragmentation of beneficial shareholding and increasing concentration of fund management and financial intermediation in equity markets. Since the 1960s, relatively patient 'bondholder' capitalism has become replaced by impatient, often junk bond financed, restructuring of many of the largest companies in the USA, and increasing blocks of shares are controlled by large intermediaries and their agents intent on increasing investor returns. While these processes have varied between the predominantly arm's length economies (Tylecote and Conesa, 1999)—and the role of anti-trust and competition policy changes have also differed between states—there has clearly been a major shift in the control of capital resources towards institutional shareholders and fund managers, and a corresponding decline, at least in the USA, in the earlier considerable autonomy of strategic managers of large firms and their ability to pursue longer-term growth goals (Davis *et al.*, 1994; Lazonick and O'Sullivan, 1996).

This growing power of organized investors and intensification of the market for corporate control has been accompanied in many such economies by changes in the orientation, experience and interests of strategic managers themselves. Neil Fligstein (1990) has already documented the increasing importance of financial experts and the 'financial conception of control' in the top management of many US companies in the late 1950s and 1960s. Subsequent intensification of pressures from financial markets for continuing increases in investor returns further reinforced the view that companies were combinations of assets to be managed for maximum 'shareholder value' by 'leaders' who could be sacked if they failed to deliver. To ensure that such managers followed these imperatives, their rewards were increasingly tied to shareholder returns through varied and complex remuneration schemes devised by recruitment consultants that made the more successful ones—and sometimes those that were less successful—independently wealthy.

With the periodic booms in mergers and takeovers and increasing intensity of corporate restructuring in many of these kinds of economies, a growing number of top managers have become detached from the fates of the companies that employ them, as well as from other employees, and their interests have effectively become aligned with other wealth holders and financial organizations such as private equity firms. Within the increasingly opportunistic environment dominated by highly liquid capital markets and fund managers competing for mandates from institutional shareholders, strategic managers of the largest companies have combined with the leaders of the financial services industry to constitute a powerful socio-economic block pursuing relatively short-term investor returns.

Another important, largely endogenous, change in some arm's length economies concerns competition and innovation policies. Whereas antitrust regulations and policies had inhibited vertical and horizontal mergers within industries in some countries for much of the early postwar period, more liberal approaches in the 1980s relaxed many of these and, coupled with growing disenchantment with the performance of conglomerates, encouraged greater sectoral concentration of resources and control (Davies *et al.*, 1994; Fligstein, 1990). Additionally, increasing concern with national competitiveness in the face of growing East Asian success in both domestic and export markets led some states to encourage precompetitive cooperation between innovative firms in high technology industries and change the patent system to encourage academics and universities to become more proactive in the commercialization of the results of scientific research.

While the direct impact of some of this legislation, such as the Bayh–Dole Act of 1980, may have been modest (Mowery *et al.*, 1999, 2004), increasing state support for technological innovation based on academic research built on substantial local and national state investments in higher education and scientific research during the Cold War period. Many states in predominantly arm's length institutional regimes, notably the UK and USA, have developed mission oriented science and technology policies in which major resources were committed to achieving public policy goals, especially military and health related ones. While implemented in different ways in different countries (Doremus *et al.*, 1998; Ergas, 1987), these effectively provided extensive collective competition goods for innovative technology companies in related fields, including of course the development and subsequent commercialization of the Internet.

Such state support may not be sufficient to generate self-sustaining Silicon Valley types of innovative economic organization, especially in economies where it is not supported by the provision of other collective competition goods and services that encourage knowledge and risk sharing. As long, though, as innovators are able to produce enough new products and services in highly uncertain technologies faster than larger firms to attract venture capital funding, they may well survive as independent companies. In addition to risk capital and other business services, firms in these kinds of economies are critically dependent on the supply of highly skilled researchers, engineers and other development experts who are willing to invest their knowledge and energies in highly risky enterprises that may well fail.

As well as this implying the effective functioning of a research and training system producing a wide range of skills from technicians to post-doctoral researchers and mid-career engineers and scientists, it also requires the existence of a fluid labour market in which people are able and willing to move between the public and private sectors as opportunities change (Casper, 2003; Casper and Murray, 2005). Such labour markets in turn depend on flexible boundaries between different kinds of research organizations and the ability of engineers and scientists to pursue a variety of intellectual goals within universities and similar entities. Academic systems with high levels of segmentation of goals and career paths are unlikely then to support such forms of economic organization (Whitley, 2003b).

(b) Dominant Developmentalist Regimes

Turning now to consider the effects of these changes on institutional regimes that constrain economic opportunism to a greater extent, these shifts have often combined endogenous changes in socio-political blocks, and in the degree of large firm embeddedness in domestic institutional arrangements, with exogenous geo-political changes and the increasing internationalization of economic competition and coordination. Perhaps the most significant endogenous changes in the most rapidly expanding economies have stemmed from economic development and urbanization, which have altered socio-political balances and enabled some of the largest companies to become more financially self-sufficient.

In the case of the more successful dominant developmentalist states, these have generated a substantial urban educated middle class that often demands greater democracy and involvement in the political system, as well as pressures to reduce the power of the dominant state big-business group elite (Shiraishi, 2006). Together with the rise of organized labour and demands for increasing rewards for employees in some economies, these shifts also imply a decline in the direct state provision of collective competition goods for favoured firms, often reinforced by foreign pressures, and a general growth in large firm autonomy from the state, albeit from a low base. Such reductions in direct state coordination and support need not, though, preclude continued indirect support for economic development goals, such as the implementation of an active labour market policy and increases in social protection measures to facilitate labour market change, as has perhaps happened in France (Amable, 2003; Hancke, 2002; Levy, 2005).

Given the generally weak nature of intermediary associations in these kinds of regimes, and the limited development of capital markets and financial intermediaries that could constrain large firms' growth goals, these developments seem likely to reinforce owner-managers focus on corporate expansion as long as internally generated funds permit. Opportunism on the part of strategic managers and owners will become less constrained in these circumstances, especially when coupled with the increasing internationalization of capital and product markets. The general expansion of international trade and investment in the last twenty-five or so years supported large firm independence from domestic constraints and broadly reinforced market power as the key to economic dominance, but reliance on foreign debt or equity obviously brings its own constraints, as many South Korean companies have found out.

Another consequence of the increasing separation of large business groups from state tutelage and support in such regimes is the difficulty of combining fast growth with continued owner management as state subsidized credit is reduced. This seems likely to reduce direct owner management of the largest companies in the medium to long term, although the continued high level of ownership concentration in many large European firms indicates that this need not imply the fragmentation of shareownership (Barca and Becht, 2001). Additionally, business groups may become less diversified as they respond less directly to state demands and can no longer support failing subsidiaries in the absence of state subsidized credit.

Although the cohesion of the state big-business alliances may weaken in these circumstances, they seem unlikely to disappear altogether as a major socio-political force, especially when national interests are seen to be threatened. However, states may well replace direct support for favoured firms and groups by more indirect promotion of developmentalist strategies through, for instance, pursuing active technology policies and investment in the education and training system.

At least for the faster growing economies of the postwar period, then, these points suggest that this kind of institutional regime will undergo considerable modification as socio-political alliances alter and domestic insulation from international pressures declines. State restriction of large firm autonomy and opportunism will decline, as will its provision of collective competition goods and the close personal ties between owner-managers of the largest business groups and state elites. Large firms may well become less diversified across unrelated industries and markets, but seem likely to continue to pursue growth goals, albeit subject to more stringent funding constraints.

(c) Business Corporatist Regimes

Turning now to consider changes in more corporatist institutional regimes, these kinds of societies are often considered to have altered most as a result of what Streeck and Thelen (2005b) term the secular process of liberalization that has developed in the last few decades of the twentieth century, both within and between national economies. Considering first the more endogenous changes that have resulted from decades of continued economic growth, urbanization and deregulation of markets, especially financial ones, these have affected the autonomy of the largest firms from banks and other financial intermediaries, and from state agencies, as well as the strength of collective identities and cohesion among members of business groups and industry associations. They have additionally altered the nature and strength of dominant socio-political blocks and encouraged the creation of new interest groups that are challenging them, especially urban middle class ones that have quite distinct interests from rural and agricultural groups.

In the case of business corporatist regimes, the growth of large companies, particularly when they have substantial foreign sales and assets, is likely to weaken their attachment to, and dependence on, domestic institutional arrangements that constrain their opportunities. As well as reducing their dependence on bank financing and other bank-provided services, expansion in sales, profits and employment seems likely to accentuate the difference between the largest firms and others such that corporatist arrangements designed to mobilize employer and sectoral interests across a range of firms become increasingly conflict-ridden. Equally, as the largest firms grow even bigger, their strategic managers may see their interests being less tied to the political priorities of national politicians. This is of course more likely when they not only invest significant resources in different states, but additionally encourage key suppliers to do likewise, in the manner of many large Japanese assembly companies.

As well, then, as the strategic managers of larger firms, in general, becoming less dependent on obligational ties with banks and state elites as they are increasingly able to finance their expansion themselves and develop treasury capabilities, the more foreign market oriented ones are likely to develop distinctive identities and concerns from their domestically focused competitors. Together with other changes weakening business group and inter-firm cohesion, such as financial deregulation and international trade (Laurence, 2001), these differentiating developments reduce the strength of big business federations and their ability to police member firm behaviour.

The importance of the state in coordinating economic development is also reduced in the post high growth period of these kinds of economies, as firms become more able to access new technologies and markets themselves and bureaucratic-political elites become more differentiated. This decline in state cohesion is encouraged by changes in political coalitions resulting from urbanization and from the decline in the number and significance of traditional supporters of dominant blocks. Business corporatist alliances between big business and state elites that were focused on relatively long-term development goals and supported by conservative groups in rural society, as well as protected interest groups in the domestic economy, become weakened by large-scale movements to urban agglomerations, the decline of traditional industries, and the rise of new socio-economic groups with different allegiances and interest. In postwar Japan, for example, where the 'iron triangle' of mutual support and benefits between the *Keidanren*, the Liberal Democratic Party (LDP) and the leaders of the central state bureaucracy appeared to be so effective in generating continued high growth rates, these connections have become rather tarnished and rusty, especially since the collapse of the bubble economy in the early 1990s (Gao, 2001; Kelly and White, 2006; Pempel, 1998; 2006).

The reduced significance of state-provided collective competition goods, coordinated risk sharing and technology upgrading, at least for the largest companies, and has been further accentuated in many states by the growth of international governance without government and extension of 'global business regulation' (Braithwaite and Drahos, 2000). To the extent that such transnational developments have restricted the promotional activities of nation states, especially with regard to measures supportive of national business corporatist alliances and the importance of national companies at the expense of foreign ones, they reduce the cohesion of national business corporatist alliances and the importance of externally provided collective competition goods. Thus, the prevalent logics of action in such economies become more diverse between the more foreign focused largest firms, those less exposed to foreign markets and jurisdictions and competition, and other companies that remain embedded in existing institutional arrangements.

In the case of Japan, though, the sheer size of the domestic economy, the strong complementarities of the institutions governing capital and labour markets, including family structures and welfare policies, and the limited extent of inward FDI and competition, have limited the impact of outward investment on large firms' behaviour, including their separation from SMEs and decline in obligational contracting and business group cohesion. Although many of the largest Japanese companies have established substantial foreign operations and come to depend considerably on foreign sales, as in the vehicle and electronics sectors since the 1970s, most have continued to locate their core functions, particularly technology development, in Japan, which is where many strategic managers see their core strengths being created and renewed (Beechler and Bird, 1999; Doremus *et al.*, 1998; Lam, 2003). While the dominant institutional regime in postwar Japan may have become less integrated and homogenous than it was, the dominant logic governing firm behaviour and strategic managers' interests does not seem to have been radically altered in terms of constraints on economic opportunism, the provision of collective competition goods for most leading companies and the dominance of alliances between large firms and state elites.

(d) Inclusive Corporatist Regimes

Increased firm and sector differentiation can also be expected in economies dominated by more inclusive corporatist institutional arrangements as economic growth, sectoral shifts and internationalization have weakened the cohesion of key alliances and generate new kinds of socio-economic interests. However, the inclusion of organized labour associations and SME interests in economic policy making and implementation processes—in addition to their involvement in national skill formation systems and welfare administration in many European corporatist societies—is likely to reinforce inter-firm and state-based constraints on economic opportunism, as well as providing a wider range of external collective competition goods and so limit the degree and pace of change. While such support for coordinated economic actions within industries and regions may not greatly affect the growing independence of large firms from their house banks and other national financial institutions, it should restrict strategic managers' ability to act opportunistically in dealing with domestic suppliers, customers and employees, especially when they benefit from state supported technology development and diffusion policies.

Although, then, large firm self-financing and internationalization can be expected to increase these companies' autonomy from national institutional constraints in inclusive corporatist institutional regimes, the powerful role of labour associations will restrict this. Strong industrial unions are also likely to reinforce the cohesion and influence of employers' associations in order to ensure that they will enforce collective agreements and limit opportunism, as Thelen and Kume (2003) suggest is the case in Germany. Despite, then, some reduction in the degree of mutual dependence between large banks and the largest firms in corporatist societies in general, and some banks seeking greater financial deregulation to develop new arenas and opportunities for growth as profits from loans to their largest domestic customers decline, the strength and influence of large union federations in inclusive corporatist regimes is likely to restrict the decline of business associations' cohesion and strength, and hence the overall growth of economic opportunism relative to that in business corporatist ones.

However, just as internationalization can encourage the differentiation of interests between firms primarily dependent on the domestic market from those more involved with foreign ones, so too labour organizations can develop divergent interests as a result of different levels of export dependence and the ability of some employers to relocate key facilities elsewhere. Such sectoral differentiation can weaken the cohesion of labour federations as national peak associations and limit their ability to influence economic policies and employment regulations as well as to constrain employer opportunism. Indeed, the intensification of international competition may encourage greater cooperation between enterprise level labour representatives and management at the expense of sectoral and national solidarity amongst unions as works councils and similar groups focus on the immediate threats to their employment. The ability of national labour federations to discipline local unions and impose national wage bargaining agreements throughout an industry may well decline in the more internationalized sectors as enterprise cooperation becomes important, as seems to have happened in some European corporatist economies such as Germany and Sweden in the 1990s (Thelen, 2001; Thelen and Kume, 2003).

The growth of inward FDI and portfolio investment can also weaken corporatist arrangements of course, as foreign investors are less committed to nationally specific agreements and compromises, and may actively seek to change them. Whether acting as a collective pressure group, as some foreign firms have done in many former state socialist economies in Eastern Europe, or individually, extensive foreign investment in inclusive corporatist regimes seems likely to limit the scope of domestic constraints on economic opportunism and to fragment—or at least differentiate— interest groups and weaken dominant socio-political groupings. While some foreign companies may join trade associations and employers' groups, and implement national wage agreements, others may not, and in general such firms are more able to be independent of both business and labour associations than are their domestically based competitors. Especially when they have considerable market power relative to the size of the economy and leading domestic competitors, large scale external investments seem likely to weaken constraints on opportunism and generate more varied forms of interest representation. They also provide alternative employment opportunities and careers for managers and technical experts that may reduce their attachment to domestic institutions and groups, increasing the diversity of interest groups and separating them from other employees.

Corporatist dominated economies in Europe have additionally been affected by the policies and structures of the European Union, as will be discussed in more detail in the next chapter. While some of these have supported the involvement of labour organizations in economic policy development and implementation, as well as encouraging companies to take account of workforce interests, the prevailing approach to European integration has focused on the establishment of a pan-European market free from national barriers to entry and exit, and from 'market-distorting' national provision of collective competition goods.

This predilection for a liberal market regulatory regime, in which increasing product market competition and reducing the costs of transnational business activities have received greater priority than promoting European economic development through the coordination of business and labour interests, can be expected to weaken the ability of many European states to maintain corporatist policies and enhance the influence of large firms relative to labour organizations that are more nationally bounded. At least for the largest companies, then, the EU seems likely to reinforce their growing autonomy from national corporatist constraints and declining interest in nationally provided collective competition goods.

Overall, while we might expect the incorporation of labour organizations and smaller firms' interests into national policy making and implementation in these kinds of regimes to reduce the impact of internationalization and economic growth relative to more business corporatist regimes, the segmentation of sectoral interest groups, including unions, and EU promotion of arm's length regulations can increase large firm autonomy from domestic constraints and domestic business interests. If combined with increasing foreign ownership and listing on foreign stock markets, as well as transnational managerial careers, this could separate the perceived interests of the strategic managers of the largest companies from those of smaller and medium-sized ones, and encourage them to invest across sectoral and national boundaries, and further internationalize their supply chains.

However, these developments should be less likely in the larger economies where strong labour unions lay a significant role in administering parts of the welfare state. Additionally, the importance of corporatist arrangements in providing collective completion goods may well outweigh the possible advantages of detaching large firms from irksome constraints and restrict strategic managers' interest in transforming the dominant institutional regime. Authority sharing within and between companies can continue to be a major feature of such societies despite growing large firm autonomy from domestic institutions as long as it is thought to enhance their competitive competences.

For these kinds of institutional regime to change significantly, the cohesion and dominant position of alliances between business and labour organizations would have to weaken considerably such that the strategic managers of large companies would no longer feel constrained by them or value their provision of collective competition goods. Internal fragmentation of labour federations and employers' groups, increasing foreign ownership and outward FDI, weakening state cohesion and coordinating capacities, together with the demise of sectoral bargaining and skill formation systems, would all contribute to a substantial decline in the dominant role of these kinds of institutional regimes.

On its own, though, the loosening of ownership and business ties between banks and large companies—which in any case has not gone as far as complete separation in countries like Germany, Japan, and Sweden (Jackson, 2003)—is unlikely to herald qualitative shifts in dominant alliances and other features of inclusive corporatist regimes. It would need to be more far-reaching and combined with significant changes in the organization of labour and SME representation, as well as in state policies, for the dominant logic of economic action to alter greatly. As long as the key institutions governing labour markets, skill formation and knowledge production and dissemination in countries such as Germany do not change greatly, it is unlikely that Silicon Valley types of economic organization will become entrenched there, or that established firms will generate radical innovations or grow through predatory acquisitions and exploitation of smaller companies (Casper, 2000; Lehrer, 2000).

Conclusions

This discussion suggests four main conclusions for the analysis of institutional and business system change. Most obviously, it emphasizes that the nature and consequences of changes in national and international institutions and agencies, as well as in socio-economic structures more generally, vary significantly across types of institutional regimes and concrete societies. While this may be unsurprising to historically minded social scientists, many globalization cheerleaders presume that internationalization is the same phenomenon, and has the same results, in all the OECD countries. Similarly, some believers in efficient capital markets expect the growth of institutional shareownership to occur in the same way in all 'modern' economies, and to have similar outcomes, despite the significant differences between the UK and the USA in this respect

(Goshen, 2003; Tylecote and Conesa, 1999), let alone elsewhere (Aguilera and Jackson, 2003).

Second, insofar as there are general inferences that can validly be drawn about the impact of endogenous and exogenous changes on postwar institutional regimes and business systems, these suggest increasing differentiation of the interests and behaviour of economic actors between sectors and political-economic groups rather than wholesale transformations. The standardization and homogeneity of leading firms, those who control them, and the policies they pursue have probably declined in the last quarter or so of the twentieth century as internationalization, economic growth and demographic change have generated more varied interest groups and the cohesion of national coalitions has weakened.

Strategic managers of large firms have become more detached from other employees, especially in the more capital market dominated economies, and the ability of business associations and labour federations to police national agreements has declined in some corporatist economies. Enterprise level commitments and agreements between employers and employees are perhaps more significant in many inclusive corporatist regimes than they were, although the continued importance of sector-based collaborative skill formation and certification systems in countries like Germany (Culpepper and Finegold, 1999) will probably limit any tendency to move to more enterprise-based labour relations.

Third, while many states have reduced their direct control over, and responsibility for, economic and industrial development, few, if any, are willing to let global market forces rule unconstrained throughout national economies (Weiss, 2003a). Rather, indirect support for developing competitive competences through training and research funding, and other infrastructural improvements, seems to have become more widespread in many countries, and states are concerned to steer public facilities and activities—such as higher education—towards developmental purposes, especially in emerging technologies and industries. Additionally, some European states are encouraging greater flexibility in labour markets through pursuing active retraining policies and providing greater social protection for those made redundant. Externally provided competition goods remain significant in many countries, then, but their form and manner of provision have become more indirect and less targeted to specific companies.

Finally, the extent to which, and ways in which, dominant economic logics have altered as a result of endogenous and exogenous changes differ across institutional regimes. In the case of many arm's length regimes, for instance, the increased concentration of control over shareholdings by institutional investors and fund managers has resulted in many, if not most, large public companies increasing investor returns and focusing more on 'shareholder value' as their key concern. It has also encouraged a reduction in the extent of unrelated diversification and decline in the valuation of conglomerates, albeit less so for some of the very largest companies such as General Electric (Davis *et al.*, 1994). However, in terms of pursuing large size and market power through predatory tactics, hostile acquisitions and opportunistic strategies, it is not at all obvious that a great deal has changed in these kinds of economies, nor that major shifts should be expected in the absence of economic and financial collapse.

Greater change has perhaps occurred in some dominant developmentalist regimes as leading firms have become less dependent on state elites, and somewhat more dependent on international capital markets. Strategic managers of the largest companies are now less concerned to obtain political support and follow state guidance, and may reallocate resources away from loss-making subsidiaries thus reducing their overall degree of unrelated diversification. Additionally, the relative weakness of horizontal associations of businesses and organized labour in these societies means that constraints on opportunism remain rather limited in general, so that owners and manager are relatively free to pursue internally financed growth goals through acquisitions and predatory behaviour, albeit more subject to organized pressure groups than they were.

Large companies in business corporatist regimes are less likely to change their prevalent patterns of behaviour, especially when their domestic market is large, most key institutions are complementary in terms of encouraging incremental growth and diversification, and foreign competition and investment remains limited. While some of the larger MNCs from such regimes may attempt to diversify into quite new fields of activity, especially abroad, and pursue more radical innovation strategies, most seem unlikely to do so as long as their dominant competences and capabilities are domestically embedded. Furthermore, given the high level of interdependence and coordination between companies that is characteristic of this kind of economy, and their reliance on committed employees, they seem likely to experience some difficulty in developing novel kinds of competences in quite different environments, as demonstrated by many Japanese banks in London and New York, and some pharmaceutical companies, in the late 1980s and 1990s (Lam, 2003; Sakai, 2000).

Similar difficulties in adopting radically new strategies can be expected for leading firms from more inclusive corporatist regimes, at least in the short term. Growing differentiation of large firms from their domestically focused competitors and separation of the strategic managers of such firms from domestic alliances could lead them to pursue more discontinuous innovation policies and grow through acquisitions in foreign markets, as some European companies have tried to do in the USA. However, managing such hybrid organizations is not a straightforward matter, and while some MNCs from these kinds of institutional regimes have reduced their dependence on domestic partners, as well as limiting their susceptibility to institutional constraints, most have yet to change their prevalent growth strategy radically. Greater emphasis in firm-based bargaining, commitments and knowledge development, as well as greater willingness to use market power to influence suppliers and employees, need not—and largely so far do not seem to—imply the adoption of highly novel innovation and growth policies.

5

The Growth of International Governance and the Restructuring of Business Systems: The Effects of Multi-levelled Governance in Europe and Elsewhere

Introduction

Just as the impact of increasing economic internationalization on established business systems varies considerably between types of institutional regimes, so too we would expect the growth of transnational institutions governing economic activities to have quite different effects in different contexts. For instance, the impact of the increasing cross-national regulation of business activities in the EU is likely to depend greatly on the complementarity of such institutions with prevalent national ones, as well as on the cohesion and strength of interest groups supporting or opposing them (Majone, 2005; Schmidt, 2002). Furthermore, as Weiss (2003b) and others have emphasized, the expansion of cross-national regulation and economic coordination provides opportunities for different states and other national agencies to pursue diverse objectives, as well as constraining their freedom of action.

Together with the continuing importance of sub-national regional institutions and agencies in many countries, the development of these supranational rules of the game highlights the contingent nature of national institutional dominance and the growing complexity of multi-levelled governance of economic actors in many parts of the world (Bache and Flinders, 2004). Where transnational institutions have become established as distinct supranational influences on economic activity in a number of countries, their impact will vary according to the strength and type of domestic institutions as well as the preferences and capabilities of dominant socio-economic groups, just as the role of national governance norms depends on their relations with regional and sectoral institutions and groups, as in the case of postwar Italy.

In considering how growing international governance is likely to affect established business systems, it is therefore important to consider the following issues. First, what is the nature of such transnational institutions? Second, how much do they complement or conflict with each other in their implications for economic actors? Third, how are they related to the institutions established at national and regional levels, including of course their relative strength? Fourth, what roles have different national and international interest groups played in developing and supporting or opposing them?

Accordingly, in this chapter I first summarize the major principles of transnational business regulation that have become established since 1945. Next, I discuss their most likely and general implications for the organization of economic coordination and control systems before continuing to consider their likely impact on three ideal types of institutional regime, and on relationships between key actors in societies dominated by them. Finally I suggest how this general analysis could be applied to the developing institutions of the EU, which is the most elaborate and institutionally established example of transnational governance.

The Nature and Consequences of Growing Transnational Economic Governance

In analysing the nature and significance of increasing international economic governance, it is important to note that, although there is widespread agreement on the broad tendency of transnational institutions to encourage economic liberalization, much debate remains as to what exactly this liberalization consists of, and to what extent it heralds a developing liberal international economic order that will dominate national economies (see, e.g., Campbell and Pedersen, 2001; Levi-Faur and Jordana, 2005; Streeck and Thelen, 2005b). Most scholars, however, agree that the key phenomena include the deregulation of certain product markets and the liberalization of cross-border trade, as well as the internationalization of capital markets and their growing influence on state policies and firms' strategies (see, e.g., Djelic and Quack, 2003a; Morgan and Engwall, 1999; Ventresca *et al.*, 2003).

Recent accounts of such deregulation have also drawn attention to the parallel re-regulation of many aspects of business behaviour as market entry, exit and behaviour become less constrained by administrative regulation, especially in the financial services industry (Laurence, 2001; Menz, 2005; Morgan and Knights, 1997; Schmidt, 2002; Way, 2005). In Crouch's (2005) terminology, these changes can be seen as the replacement of much substantive national governance of economic activities by more procedural forms, especially at the international level.

Much of the expansion of transnational governance in the late twentieth century has been concerned to establish common rules of the competitive game for cross-border trade and investment and so international markets for most products and services, as exemplified by the European Union's institutionalization of the single European market (Fioretos, 2001; Majone, 2005). If we accept the wide-ranging and comprehensive synthesis of the increasing international regulation of business activities by Braithwaite and Drahos' *Global Business Regulation* (2000) as an accurate account of the major principles underlying such transnational governance, it is clear that most of these are concerned with breaking down regulatory barriers to cross-border trade and ensuring equal treatment for all participants in market economies. According to Majone (2005), it is this kind of negative integration that has been much more effective in creating transnational rules of the game in Europe than more 'positive' regulations intended to harmonize and raise all countries' standards (see, also, Knill and Lehmkuhl, 2002; Knill and Lenschow, 2005).

In particular, they see the international transparency of economic regulation as a, if not the, major principle of global business regulation, and claim that: 'transparency has been the one (principle) which has most consistently strengthened in importance.... Transparency is at its strongest in the domains of finance, corporations and securities' (Braithwaite and Drahos, 2000: 507). This norm of regulatory transparency has become 'an emergent property of globalization, a meta-principle in the sense of revealing the operation of all other principles' (*ibid*: 29).

It has been especially important in the regulation of companies and securities markets where it has formed a significant part of the process of transforming local insider network capitalism into 'global transparency capitalism' (*ibid*: 163) that depends on the value and risks of tradable assets being visible to the internal management of traders, their auditors, regulators, analysts, fund managers, ratings agencies and investment advisors. Driven by the interests of outside investors, investment banks and multinational companies seeking large, liquid and transparent capital markets, this focus on public and formalized regulatory procedures exemplifies central features of outsider-dominated financial markets and arm's length capitalism (Laurence, 2001; Lutz, 2004; Tylecote and Conesa, 1999).

Other principles governing business regulation that they consider to be strengthening cross-nationally include: the harmonization of regulatory norms, the mutual recognition of different states' regulatory regimes and the extension of national treatment of companies to foreign ones. Most of these are intended to ensure that national markets are open to foreign competition on equal terms. However, it is worth emphasizing that Braithwaite and Drahos also suggest that attempts to harmonize national systems of contract and securities law have not been successful so far, and that 'there have not been concerted attempts to harmonize competition law since the collapse of ITO ratification' (*ibid*: 212).

Furthermore, while much of the argument over trade principles in the General Agreement on Tariffs and Trade (GATT) and the World Trade Organization (WTO) has focused on extending the principles of most favoured nation and national treatment to all trading partners, many states have in practice continued to implement the principle of strategic trade, i.e. designing trade regulations in such a way as to advantage domestic companies (*ibid*. 512–14). Even the principle of deregulating state control over markets has only strengthened in 8 out of the 15 issue areas considered by Braithwaite and Drahos (2000: 508–15).

In banking, securities, nuclear safety and many other areas, efforts to deregulate control over economic activities have been weakened by safety and systemic risk concerns that have led to greater emphasis being placed on transparency, harmonization and mutual recognition of standards, often ratcheting these higher, as has also happened within the EU (Lutz, 2004). Additionally, the principle of implementing the world's best practice in an area of economic activity has become stronger in nine fields, despite the considerable costs involved for many actors. As they suggest (*ibid*. 519), this is an asset building principle that can enhance both corporate and national reputations in finance, securities, trade, the environment, pharmaceutical and many other fields.

This account of increasing transnational regulation of business activities in the last few decades of the twentieth century highlights both its multifaceted nature and the limited areas in which it has succeeded in establishing a distinctive international regulatory regime. Rather than manifesting an inexorable progress towards national deregulation and global standardization of market rules based on 'liberal' principles of economic governance, Braithwaite and Drahos portray a much more complex set of developments in which market opening and regulatory transparency principles have been combined with those raising quality and safety standards above those established in some domestic economies, and sometimes providing greater restrictions on what can be traded internationally. They also emphasize the varied nature of business interests in further deregulation, just as Fioretos (2001) and Herrmann (2005), amongst others, have recently argued that national political and economic elites have different interests in dealing with European liberalization attempts depending on the particular competences of leading firms and institutional legacies.

Furthermore, there is little indication that transnational business regulation is about to encompass the treatment of foreign investment, competition rules or corporate governance practices on a worldwide basis, despite various attempts being made to do so (Gordon, 2003; Goyer, 2003). As yet, there are no global rules standardizing shareownership rights and duties, even across the European Union, the nature of interfirm agreements including norms of fair dealing (Teubner, 1998), or state support for innovative investments and knowledge development. Despite the apparent success of the agreement on Trade-Related Aspects of Intellectual Property Rights (TRIPS) agreement in the WTO in establishing a global standard for intellectual property rights, it remains unclear whether this is a harbinger of greater global standardization of property rights or rather a one-off attempt to extend the US conception to other WTO members that remains highly contested.

If we summarize the key institutions governing economic activities in market economies as those dealing with: (a) product market entry and access to customers, (b) competitive behaviour, including anti-trust regulation, (c) access to capital and financial markets, (d) ownership and control, limited liability and the rights and duties of public companies, (e) the organization of labour markets, employment relations and bargaining, and (f) skill formation, evaluation and certification, then it is clear that effective transnational regulation has so far encompassed only a small number of these. Only with regard to the opening of markets to foreign competition and capital flows, and this last remains subject to considerable national regulation in many countries, and increasing transparency of corporate reporting and access to securities markets could it reasonably be claimed that international governance has become a significant force in firm behaviour that could dominate national institutions. As Perraton and Wells (2004: 193) suggest, the WTO is 'the only genuine institution of global governance'.

Overall, then, the bulk of global business regulation in the late twentieth and early twenty-first centuries remains focused on establishing common rules for international trade in goods and services, so that markets become more integrated across national borders. Additionally, the considerable deregulation of national markets—such as the removal of boundaries between segments of the financial services industry—has been accompanied by increasing reregulation of market participants and practices through procedural norms and arm's length agencies, at national and international levels. These agencies are both public and private and frequently overlap in their jurisdictions, extending governance vertically and horizontally (Bache and Flinders, 2004; Braithwaite and Drahos, 2000: 491–4; Laurence, 2001; Levi-Faur and Jordana, 2005; Schmidt, 2002: 94–104).

In Crouch's (2005: 100) terminology, much of the growing international regulation has tended to be: (a) exogenous to the activities being governed, (b) procedural rather than substantive, (c) signalling compliance and transgressions rather than engaging in dialogue, and (d) communicated vertically rather than horizontally. However, the strength and scope of rule enforcement vary, as does the ease of exit from regulatory control, and it provides both public and private collective competition goods. Many of these characteristics reflect arm's length relationships between governing institutions and economic actors. Given the limited democratic legitimacy of many transnational agencies and regulatory regimes, which limit their ability to undertake substantive interventions that might disadvantage particular interests (Majone, 2005), not to mention the leading role of the USA in establishing these in much of the twentieth century, this is not too surprising.

Turning now to discuss the major consequences for established patterns of economic organization that could follow from these kinds of transnational principles becoming strongly institutionalized, there are four very general ones that can be expected to have different effects on firms, markets and institutions in different kinds of institutional regimes. First, the reduction of trade barriers and opening of foreign markets to many goods and services should increase the potential size of markets for many companies and affect their degree of specialization. Second, this growth in foreign-based competition should increase the intensity of competitive pressures in domestic markets as well as uncertainty over the nature of present and future competitors. Third, active and direct state support for domestic companies and industries will become more difficult to justify and implement as transparency increases and Most Favoured Nation (MFN) treatment of foreign firms becomes the global norm. Fourth, both the facilitating of foreign entry to domestic markets and the reduction of barriers to foreign direct investment (FDI) can be expected to diminish the stability and homogeneity of firms involved in domestic markets. These general effects in turn should have five more specific consequences for firms and their institutional environments.

Considering first the probable effects of increasing potential market size, as Langlois (2003) has recently emphasized, market growth can be expected to increase firm specialization and vertical disintegration, especially where technical standards are highly codified and accepted throughout the global market. This is particularly likely where markets are 'thick' in the sense of having numerous potential suppliers, and common standards across the world enable companies to concentrate on innovating in one particular part of the sector's value chain, such as in the electronics industry (Sturgeon, 2002).

Transparency, liberalization and the growth of formally specified standards throughout an industry, such as the GSM one in mobile telephony, should, then, encourage leading firms to narrow the range of activities they undertake, *ceteris paribus*. On the other hand, such specialization is less likely in emerging industries, where technologies are less standardized, markets are thin and demand is highly uncertain (Langlois and Robertson, 1995). Overall, though, the expansion of markets for products and services cross-nationally, together with the increasing concentration of fund management in many capital markets and the transparency and standardization of financial accounts across national jurisdictions, can be expected to reduce the overall level of vertical integration and horizontal diversification of activities managed within large companies, especially where these businesses are 'unrelated' in technological and market terms. To some extent, we can see this in the opening up of international markets in telecommunications that both encouraged, and was encouraged by, the restructuring of national PTTs and the creation of national specialist telecommunications companies in Europe and elsewhere (Thatcher, 2004).

Secondly, opening domestic markets to foreign competition intensifies price competition as new entrants typically try to gain market share by undercutting domestic companies. This can be expected to weaken institutional constraints on opportunistic behaviour as foreign firms have few incentives to cooperate through collective agencies such as trade associations. By forcing firms to reduce costs, as in the German machine tool industry in the 1990s (Glassman, 2004), such international competition encourages many companies to subcontract the production of components and more routine processes to firms in lower cost locations, or to move a substantial part of their own activities abroad, while often retaining the key value added ones at home. In this way, the liberalization of trade can weaken long-standing linkages between companies within supply chains in the domestic economy, and focus customer-supplier relationships much more on price competition than may have been previously the case, as well as reducing domestic employer–employee interdependence.

However, such restructuring of supply chain and employment relations need not necessarily result in radical changes to domestic patterns of economic organization, particularly if companies are able to reduce their costs by transferring the more routine parts of their activities abroad while retaining the advantages of their home economy for more critical capabilities. According to Kristensen (2006), this is what many 'skill container' types of firms in Denmark are doing in order to avoid losing their highly skilled workers through giving them boring tasks. Such internationalization of production is obviously easier when work processes are decomposable and modular, as seems to be the case in the consumer electronics industry. As a result of liberalization, then, average firm size and vertical integration can be reduced, and cross-border modular production networks established (Sturgeon, 2002), but distinctive business systems remain entrenched in different institutional regimes, especially where these are seen as continuing to provide significant competitive advantages. Indeed, the intensification of competition could well encourage further differentiation of national and regional patterns of authoritative coordination and control of economic activities as actors organize themselves in particular ways, and specialize in specific activities, that are best supported by their institutional context (Herrmann; 2005; Vogel, 2001).

Thirdly, growing international regulation of state industrial policies, at least as they affect market access and direct support for firms, will limit substantive aid for national champions and the preferential provision of collective competition goods for domestic companies. This should reduce the differences between firms and sectors promoted by the state and those not so supported, as well as the national specificity of state risk sharing, market segmentation and regulation. However, it has not prevented considerable state investment in technology development related to public policy goals, as in the US health and defence sectors, or continuing national support for R&D, skill development and similar general collective goods in many countries (Armingeon, 2004; O'Riain, 2000).

Overall, while direct state subsidies for favoured national companies, and discriminatory policies against foreign takeovers and investments have become more difficult to implement in the EU and WTO, they remain significant in many countries, as the recent battles over bank takeovers in Italy and the French approach to strategic industries testify, and many state promotional policies have become more indirect and focused on improving the socio-economic infrastructure rather than being discarded altogether. State-business relations remain quite varied between national economies, albeit with a broad reduction in overt discrimination against foreign firms in many OECD economies (Schmidt, 2002).

Fourth, the growth of cross-border trade and investment, together with the deregulation of some markets in terms of entry and exit, can be expected to weaken the cohesion and authority of domestic business associations and employers' groups as market participants become more varied and changeable in terms of their ownership, control and interests (Schmitter, 1997). As more foreign firms become significantly involved in domestic markets, and some existing ones are taken over or decline in importance, the ability of formal associations to enforce collective decisions that primarily benefit domestic companies seems likely to be reduced. While some of them may be willing to join these associations, their interests may well diverge from those of their domestic competitors and so the ability of business groups to provide collective competition goods for all members of an industry at the national level should decline as foreign firms increase their market share. Equally, of course, as more domestic firms invest in reaching foreign markets, their interests may begin to diverge from domestically focused companies, and this may well also weaken the authority of national business associations. Overall, then, the degree of inter-firm cooperation and authority sharing between firms can be expected to decline as markets become more internationalized.

Fifth, the internationalization of capital markets and growing ability of large firms with foreign sales and subsidiaries to access them—which partly results from trade liberalization, harmonization and MFN principles—enables companies to circumvent domestic restrictions on financial policies, such as the Japanese foreign exchange controls and limitations on corporate bond issuance (Calder, 1993; Ramseyer, 1994), and, in some countries, reduce their dependence on national banks. In general, then, we would expect the level of domestic interdependence between large firms, state agencies and banks to decline as liberalization and deregulation of financial markets grow. In turn, this seems likely to weaken lock-in effects and commitments between major economic actors and groups at the national level and provide opportunities for powerful groups to pursue their own interests at the expense of domestic associates, as arguably has happened in the restructuring of financial markets in London, if not yet in Japan (Laurence, 2001).

The overall effects of such internationalization of trade, competition and investment are, then, to weaken the stability and cohesion of dominant national coalitions of interest groups and commitments between major companies, banks, state agencies and other economic actors. Large firms, in particular, seem likely to be able to pursue their own interests more autonomously from domestic constraints and associations, and often exert pressure for more liberalization and deregulation of domestic and foreign markets. However, the extent to which these consequences do in fact materialize and change established patterns of economic organization significantly will vary between market economies and their dominant institutional regimes, particularly of course the latter's nature and cohesion (Armingeon, 2004), as well as on the amount of foreign direct investment and willingness of foreign firms to try to challenge dominant domestic patterns of economic organization.

In general, we would expect these effects of international liberalization and deregulation to be more evident when the cohesion of domestic dominant coalitions of interests is weakening and new collective actors, such as consumer and environmental groups, as well as firms in emerging industries, are able to mobilize support for political-economic change. This in turn should be easier when the existing regime is seen to be failing to support economic growth and key groups—such as large companies— are seeking to change current institutional arrangements, as for instance after several years of low or no growth. Cohesion can also decline when some companies, such as the commercial banks of Germany, Japan and some other countries, experience declining profits in their traditional business activities and seek to enter new markets with new kinds of skills, creating conflicts with established partners.

In the case of the European telecommunications industry in the 1980s and 1990s, for instance, it was the combination of international economic pressures with major technological changes and shifts in domestic coalitions in many countries, together with EU regulatory changes, that seem to have been key to both institutional restructuring and the emergence of new competitors (Thatcher, 2004). In particular, both new entrants and established companies, as well as state elites, supported radical change in the new commercial and technological environment of the late 1980s, in many cases after having opposed it earlier.

On the other hand, if, as argued in the previous chapter, the domestic market is large and many large firms and key industries are primarily domestically focused, the effects of such growth in transnational governance may be more limited. This is especially probable if the amount of FDI is limited as a proportion of GDP and domestic patterns of inter-firm collaboration restrict the impact of market liberalization, as is arguably the case in Japan (Vogel, 2001). As long as the importance of international trade and investment for the economy as a whole remains limited and the dominant coalition of interests retains considerable support—perhaps by changing some of its policies and payoffs—these consequences will be slow in appearing.

Consequences of Expanding Regulatory Transnational Governance in Different Institutional Regimes

Considering next the likely impact of such trade and investment liberalization and deregulation on differently organized business systems and institutional regimes, this can perhaps best be explored by comparing their consequences in three of the major ideal types of institutional regimes discussed in previous chapters: arms' length, dominant developmental state and corporatist. The expected effects of this growing transnational governance on interest group organization, dominant firm strategies and market structure are summarized in Table 5.1 and will now be further discussed.

In the case of arm's length regimes, many of the predominant national institutions are quite similar to these transnational norms and predilections, such as market-based relations between owners, investors and the strategic managers of large companies, strong preferences for transparent financial accounts and protection for minority shareholders, fluid labour markets and easy entry to, and exit from, product markets. As pressures for cross-national liberalization and deregulation increase, not least of course as a result of political and economic lobbying and influence by many leading firms from these kinds of economies, they will tend to reinforce the dominant norms and conventions in these societies rather than conflict with them, although the continuing disputes in trade negotiations

Table 5.1. Likely effects of regulatory transnational governance on three different institutional regimes

Likely effects on:	Type of Institutional Regime		
	Arm's length	Dominant developmental state	Corporatist
Cohesion and authority of business associations	Further reduced	Limited	Reduced as largest firms internationalize and foreign firms invest
Cohesion and authority of union federations	Further reduced	Further reduced in private sector	Reduced at national and sectoral levels, increased differentials between internationalized firms and industries and others
Market segmentation	Reduced	Reduced where state withdraws from direct control	Reduced where domestic coalitions weakened
Investor-firm relations	Reduced commitments, growth of fund manager influence	Decline in state influence, growth of investor influence	Weakening of bank–firm ties in large firms
Diversification of large firms	Reduced	Reduced where state influence weakened	Reduced where foreign shareholders dominate
Inter-firm cooperation	Low, except for pre-competitive collaboration in public mission fields	Low, beyond business groups	Reduced where business union groups weakened
Constraints on short-term opportunism	Further weakened	Reduced where state influence weakened	Reduced for largest and most internationalized firms, especially where unions weakened

over state support for domestic industries, regional aid and other forms of national investment indicate the resilience of domestic interest groups and their ability to influence state policies in the most liberal market economies.

We would not, then, expect major changes in prevalent patterns of economic organization in arm's length regimes to result from this sort of growth in transnational governance. The general reliance on market-based forms of coordination should be reinforced, with exit being preferred to voice in inter-firm dealings and state opposition to cooperation between companies becoming stronger, except perhaps where it continues to provide major investments for technological development and seeks to coordinate private strategies for national public policy goals. Cost reduction strategies, price competition and labour market flexibility will also be further encouraged by such liberalization pressures. In the case of the UK, the combination of liberalization and intensification of international competition 'brought the system closer to the market capitalist ideal, with business relations more distant, government relations more arm's length, and labour relations more market-reliant' (Schmidt, 2002: 147).

On the other hand, where dominant national institutions, interest groups and patterns of economic organization conflict with these expected consequences of trade liberalization and transparency imperatives, outcomes are likely to be more varied. In the case of dominant developmental state regimes, for instance, the state executive and bureaucracy form a coherent elite that takes the leading role in coordinating—and sometimes directing—economic development, often through controlling bank credits, technology licensing, access to foreign exchange and market segmentation. Such state domination of the economy directly conflicts with many of the international rules of the game outlined above, and so both state and business elites in these kinds of institutional regimes can be expected to restrict their implementation.

This is especially likely when foreign trade and investment constitute a fairly small part of GDP and the owners of the largest firms are closely allied to state elites, with few being willing to forgo the advantages of state support for the benefits of easier access to capital markets and foreign opportunities. Extending the argument of the previous chapter, there are, though, a number of factors that might weaken the cohesion and strength of national institutions and actors in such a regime when dealing with external liberalization and transparency pressures.

Some of these result from the very success of state developmentalist policies that might otherwise seem to reinforce existing practices and norms. By achieving high rates of economic growth and the establishment of an educated urban middle class, for instance, these kinds of policies can lead to the growth of socio-economic groups that oppose authoritarian and centralized decision making, as well as the close relations between the state and big business typical of such regimes. These groups may support external pressures to increase the transparency of state regulation and resource allocation decisions in order to improve domestic political accountability and reduce the dominance of state supported companies. Where such groups are linked to entrepreneurs trying to establish new industries that are not supported by dominant alliances, they could also encourage economic liberalization and reduce the role of the state in directing the economy.

Furthermore, some owners and managers of the largest firms may also wish to reduce their dependence on state elites and political priorities as they become more involved in foreign economies and wish to enter new markets, such as Samsung producing cars in South Korea some years ago. They could use the international trade regime to put pressure on domestic state agencies and elites to deregulate markets at home and move to more indirect methods of support for their attempts to compete on a worldwide basis.

In addition, the economic and political costs of pursuing active promotional state policies on a stand alone basis may become too great in an increasingly interdependent political-economic environment, especially when these are combined with an expensive welfare state, as arguably happened in France in the 1980s (Levy, 2005; Schmidt, 2002: 187–200). More generally, external geo-political pressures can become more important in weakening such states' opposition to liberalization and deregulation as their dependence on export markets grows and importing countries are less willing to tolerate discriminatory support for domestic companies.

Insofar as these factors do reduce developmentalist states' active coordination and direction of investment and strategic priorities, we would expect the following five consequences to become apparent. First, as the degree of business dependence on the state and associated political risks diminish, owners may become more willing to delegate strategic control to non-family managers, especially where elite universities and colleges can be relied upon to select the best students and encourage them to act in the owners' interests.

Second, as investment strategies become less directly influenced by political objectives, large companies may sell peripheral activities where they have little or no perceived competitive advantage, and so reduce their degree of unrelated diversification. This will be encouraged by the growth of foreign shareholdings and associated pressure for greater transparency of corporate activities, as well of course as by the increasing size of product markets resulting from trade liberalization.

Third, the decline of direct state coordination of economic development and provision of collective competition goods for favoured firms, together with the relative weakness of business associations, labour unions and other collective intermediaries in these kinds of institutional regimes, considerably reduces the strength of external constraints on economic opportunism for larger companies and enlarges their scope for independent strategic action. However, this increased autonomy of large companies from the state could become counterbalanced by their dependence on private investors' willingness to fund growth plans, which is likely to make them more focused on profitability goals than unlimited expansion.

Fourth, where the state reduces its control over the banking system and direct intervention in the flow of credit to favoured companies and industries, banks and other financial intermediaries become more autonomous but also have to develop new organizational capabilities to deal with the different competitive environment. This takes time, and some may fail, as has happened in France (Salomon, 1999; 2000). Eventually, though, a more independent and significant financial services sector should develop (Kleiner, 2003), although its relationships with the largest firms may well vary between countries, as is shown by the different ways it has developed in France and South Korea.

Fifth, the traditionally strong ties between state elites and big business owners in these kinds of regimes may decline in intensity and significance as the largest companies internationalize some operations and become more independent of state tutelage. However, they seem unlikely to disappear overnight, especially where they are reproduced through common selection systems and institutionalized by intra-elite rotations between politicians, the central bureaucracy and leaders of the largest firms, as in France's *grands corps* (Reberioux, 2002; Schmidt, 2002). The growing separation of large firm interests from those of state elites may, then, weaken the cohesion of the dominant coalition of active promotional institutional regimes without necessarily leading to its demise and replacement by a completely different group of interests.

In summary, where such internal and external pressures do result in a significant reduction in direct state coordination and steering of the economy and increased liberalization, the dominant business system is likely to alter in the following respects. First, the unrelated horizontal diversification of dominant firms should decline, as should some degree of vertical integration. Second, control over the largest companies by the owning family and those with whom they have family-like connections can be expected to become more indirect. Third, growth strategies will be more constrained by profitability considerations, especially where foreign investors are major shareholders. On the other hand, alliances between companies, the degree of employer–employee interdependence and authority sharing more generally seem unlikely to grow greatly.

Considering next the ways in which more corporatist institutionalist regimes could be affected by the growth of international governance encouraging market liberalization and deregulation, these are particularly dependent on the complementarity and homogeneity of domestic institutions throughout the economy. In terms of their implications for the authoritative coordination of economic activities, strongly corporatist societies encourage high levels of non-market integration at the national and sectoral levels. While such extensive coordination of decision making in input markets is quite consonant with considerable competition in product markets, as Sorge (2005) has recently emphasized, it does inhibit zero-sum, spot market-based competition between isolated enterprises based solely on price because so much information, technological and skill development and generation of collective competition goods is shared between members of dominant business associations (Soskice, 1999).

Market liberalization pressures on their own need not, then, necessarily conflict with corporatist institutions, but where they lead to increasing heterogeneity of competing firms in terms of their governance, key capabilities and interests, through substantial FDI for instance, they may result in some weakening of nationally organized interest associations, as well as reducing the ability of the state to play a leading role in the improvement of national companies' competences. Together with the increasing internationalization of economic coordination and control, whether by MNCs or the growth of cross-border institutions, NGOs and social movements, such pressures will challenge nationally specific corporatist arrangements that are based on common commitments to the public interest in national polities. Because these are premised on collective identities and interests that are relatively homogenous within national jurisdictions, they could be threatened by the growing heterogeneity of market participants as internationalization grows apace.

These kinds of changes increase the heterogeneity of domestic interest groups and weaken the complementarity of dominant institutions governing capital and labour markets in strongly corporatist regimes. Sectoral variations and differences between the larger, more internationally focused, firms and many SMEs may well become more pronounced in these situations, so that nationally specific business system characteristics decline in their homogeneity and generality across industries and firm sizes. Depending on the level of foreign investment, the size and significance of the domestic market for large firms, and the variety of competences needed in different industries, these regimes could develop a number of hybrid business systems in which some characteristics remain relatively homogenous throughout the economy while others vary significantly between sectors and firms.

In Germany, for example, many large firms have developed new kinds of links with banks and capital markets while smaller ones on the whole have not, but most of the corporatist arrangements governing skill formation, wage bargaining and other employer–employee relationships remain quite standardized across sectors and firm-size classes (Deeg, 2005a; 2005b; Schmidt, 2002: 175–82). Equally, although some firms may seek to decentralize wage bargaining and other aspects of employment relations to the enterprise level, others may prefer to maintain or reinforce national and sectoral coordination institutions in order to manage international threats and increase the predictability of the domestic environment (Crouch, 1999: 355–61). As Vogel (2001: 1109) suggests: 'German firms tend to adjust to shocks through internal labo(u)r market flexibility. . . . (and). . . . rely more on cooperative relations with labo(u)r' than on hiring and firing as the business cycle changes, although this may be less so for companies in more labour intensive sectors that compete more on price than quality (Thelen and Wijnbergen, 2003).

The most general consequence of these sorts of changes in the institutional environment for business system characteristics in corporatist societies, then, is likely to be increased differentiation of interests and patterns of economic coordination and control at the national level as institutions and actors become less standardized and homogenous across the economy. Patterns of ownership and control will become more varied as close bank–firm connections are weakened for many large firms and foreign shareholders are able to take significant stakes in some of these, such as Nokia. However, as long as the market for corporate control remains weak and hostile takeovers are not encouraged—which remains the case in most insider-dominated financial systems (Gordon, 2003; Goyer, 2003; Tylecote and Conesa, 1999)—this need not necessarily lead to radically changed priorities in these firms. Indeed, for ownership relationships in the largest companies in corporatist regimes to become generally transformed, the whole financial services sector would probably need to separate from, and come to dominate, the rest of the economy, as in the UK, with investment banks and similar intermediaries forming major blocks in leading political-economic coalitions.

Similarly, the impact of external pressures to reduce vertical integration and change supplier relationships, as a result of increased competition, market expansion and the increasing influence of outside investors, may well be limited by strongly corporatist institutions and their supporting interest groups, especially in industries where technological processes and organizational competences are not readily decomposable (Vogel, 2001). Where foreign suppliers are used by large firms in such regimes, these are often subsidiaries of domestic business partners, as in the case of many Japanese companies in China, and obligational contracting remains considerable (Ernst, 2006).

Equally, the strongly entrenched vertical and horizontal alliances and collaboration between competitors characteristic of corporatist dominated economies seem unlikely to be transformed radically as a result of external pressures from transnational institutions as long as: (a) business and employer groups retain considerable collective authority, (b) the state continues to encourage their involvement in economic policy making and implementation, and (c) firms cooperate in developing and applying new technologies, working with unions and state agencies in skill formation, and in negotiating with employees over working conditions. In the case of Japan for instance, the size of the domestic economy, limited amounts of FDI, continuing collaboration between state, the *keidanren* and other business associations, and the flexibility and commitment afforded by inter-firm networks have restricted changes to 'alliance capitalism' despite over 10 years of near recession, political and bureaucratic scandals and considerable restructuring of many industries, especially banking (Lincoln and Gerlach, 2004; Pempel, 2006; Vogel, 2001).

While the growing heterogeneity of employers and competitive pressures to reduce costs by moving some production abroad and/or outsourcing to foreign-based subcontractors resulting from internationalization could reduce employer–employee interdependence and commitment in corporatist societies, strong union and industrial relations institutions should limit this. Especially where the skill formation system is built around long-term cooperation between employers and unions, and is regarded by most firms as an important contributor to competitive advantage, continuing collaboration with unions and works councils seems likely. Even in economies where highly coordinated financial systems are weakening, institutionalized cooperation between employers' groups and union federations often remains considerable, as in many European societies. However, in some this cooperation has become more decentralized as firms and works councils reach agreement on restructuring initiatives that transcend the official negotiating arrangements and weaken their overall authority. This pattern can increase employer–employee interdependence at the enterprise level while reducing it nationally (Pontusson and Swenson, 1996).

Such attenuation of the national and sectoral corporatist arrangements for dealing with wage bargaining and other industrial relations issues is likely to increase the heterogeneity of employment relations within such societies. This, in turn, may enable firms in different industries and locations to develop different ways of managing their staff and so reduce the general cohesion of corporatist institutions and constraints on short-term opportunism. Where this decentralization of bargaining becomes institutionalized, then, the prevalent pattern of collaboration between companies within and between supply chains may well be weakened by the effects of international liberalization and cross-border investments on corporatist arrangements.

Multi-Level Governance in Europe: The Effects of 'More Europe' on Institutional Regimes and Business Systems in the European Union

These expectations of how growing international governance is likely to affect different kinds of institutional regimes and business systems can be helpful in analysing the emerging system of multi-level governance in Europe, which has received much attention from political scientists and others (see, e.g. Bache and Flinders, 2004; Gilardi, 2005; Hayward and Menon, 2003; Pierson, 1996; Majone, 2005). The EU is probably the most developed form of transnational governance that became established in the twentieth century, and so its regulations and institutions should have had the most visible impact on nationally distinct business systems, especially since it bundles together a number of policy competences into a general purpose jurisdiction (Marks and Hooghe, 2004).

Whereas most international governance regimes focus on particular issues and problems with intersecting memberships and overlapping jurisdictions, and are relatively limited in duration, the EU integrates governance over a considerable range of issues and claims substantial supranational authority over its member states in these areas on a long-term basis. It is therefore more likely to affect established systems of economic coordination and control as a whole than are more specialized forms of international governance. The combined effect of increasing EU governance and decentralization could, then, considerably reduce the national specificity of European institutional regimes, business systems and innovation systems, and possibly result in the establishment of novel forms of economic organization at different territorial levels and in different economic sectors.

To evaluate such possibilities, we need to clarify the nature of the distinctive supranational institutions in Europe and their implications for economic activities, their relative strength in influencing economic actors compared to national and regional ones, and the circumstances in which they are likely to change the nature and behaviour of leading firms, dominant socio-economic coalitions, and key institutional arrangements in differently organized European countries. Considering first the predominant features of EU institutions as they have developed since the foundation of the European Coal and Steel Community (ECSC) in 1951, these have primarily focused on the establishment of a single market in which people, capital, goods and services could move freely across national borders and progressively removed barriers to such mobility (Majone, 2005).

While the EU has additionally developed a number of initiatives and many regulations to harmonize standards and generate more 'positive' forms of European integration in the areas of health, safety and the environment, its most notable successes have tended to support more negative forms by removing national restrictions to free movement of the factors of production, limiting monopolies, protecting consumer interests and opposing discrimination against foreign firms (Knill and Lenschow, 2005; Knill and Lehmkuhl, 2002; Majone, 2005: 151–61). As Majone suggests, this is partly because most active forms of positive integration require considerable resources and implementation capacities that most EU institutions do not have. It is easier to demolish barriers and forbid discriminatory behaviour, and monitor compliance, than to ensure positive improvements in, say, water quality, across the EU when this would require substantial investments and active intervention in national economies.

Simplifying considerably, then, we can suggest that the most effective EU rules and regulations for much of the past fifty or so years have been concerned to liberalize trade and investment between member states and remove national regulations that protected domestic companies and related interests. Although the intensity and efficacy of EU attempts at integrating European economies have varied over this period—as have other aspects of EU policy making (Jessop, 2004)—they were greatly reinvigorated by the passage of the Single European Act of 1986 that 'conferred new powers on the EU in the areas of social policy, economic and social cohesion, research and technological developments, and environmental protection' (Majone, 2005: 11), as well as introducing qualified majority voting on a number of issues in the European Council.

This Act, and the subsequent Treaty on European Union signed in Maastricht in 1992, laid the foundation for Economic and Monetary Union that eventually produced the Eurozone in 1999 as the strongest form of economic integration achieved in Europe to date (Tsoukalis, 2003). While seen by some as a Trojan horse that could lead to greater political integration, the relative success of the EU in creating a single European market for most goods and some services through liberalization and deregulation has not been matched by equivalent progress in establishing common social policies and political institutions such as Europe-wide political parties and electoral competition (Majone, 2005). In general, as Amable (2003: 228–30) suggests, the neo-liberal quest for the single market has dominated alternative visions of a more 'social' Europe in which capitalism would be regulated by federal institutions, although Reberioux (2002) claims that the new European company statute governing *Societas Europeae* reflects the latter approach.

It does need to be borne in mind, though, that the European Commission (EC) has at times encouraged Europe-wide coordination of economic and industrial policies through the involvement of transnational interest groups, such as UNICE and labour union federations, and supported the foundation of the EUROFER steel cartel in 1976 that negotiated restrictions on price competition across Europe and established supply quotas. While this cartel collapsed after the second oil price shock in 1979, *dirigiste* market regulation at the European level continued under the terms of the 1951 ECSC Treaty until the mid-1980s (Voelzkow, 2004: 133–4). However, such coordination was probably easier to justify and implement when most member states shared a belief in the benefits of recession cartels and similar approaches to managing economic development, and has become less likely in an EU with 27 members that have very different industrial and social structures.

In general, although both the Commission and transnational interest groups may have a common interest in working together at the EU level, such relationships are rarely as close and effective in coordinating policy development and implementation as those within the more corporatist EU states, not least because the organization of interest groups varies so much between EU member states and the EC has no state-like powers to organize them into powerful units of authoritative coordination across the EU (Crouch, 2003; Mazey and Richardson, 2003). Furthermore, despite the growth of lobby groups and trade association agents in Brussels over the past few decades, there are few if any European peak associations that can: (a) credibly act as central bargaining organizations on behalf of all major companies throughout Western Europe, (b) resolve disputes between members, and (c) constrain opportunism and sanction deviance.

For instance, as Plehwe and Vescovi (2003) point out, European market integration in the transport industry has led to considerable fragmentation and polarization of interest group representation at the transnational level, and many associations have opened separate offices in Brussels to lobby for their sectional goals. In this field, 'supranational and national public authorities are confronted and cooperate with a growing number of competing business associations' (Plehwe and Vescovi, 2003: 211), although in some other industries companies have been more successful in developing 'interface actor associations'.

Similarly, labour organization and representation at the European level tends to be more a matter of coordinating national groups than integrating them into a cohesive transnational association that could negotiate centrally (Bieler, 2005). As Amable suggests (2003: 253): 'the ETUC (European Trade Unions Confederation) has no power over its national union members and must rely on their voluntarism and their active participation... voluntarism is in fact a more general problem for Continental Europe. Its generalization leads to the spread of the "contract culture"... and collective bargaining runs the risk of turning into... a vehicle for market coordination and competition'.

Overall, then, the EU-interest groups' interrelationships seem to be closer to the US pattern of sponsored pluralism than the many varieties of national corporatism in Europe (Crouch, 1999; Streeck and Schmitter, 1985). As Schmidt (2002: 246) puts it: 'a wide range of policy actors, governmental as well as non-governmental, negotiate the construction of policy programmes through an elaborate coordinative discourse... negotiations involve a complex system of Commission-organized discussion among experts, interest groups, governmental representatives, lobbyists and the like.' Even though such groups have developed distinctive epistemic communities in some sectors, with European coordinating discourses, they often have little legitimacy at the national level (Schmidt, 2002: 248).

Turning now to consider the strength of EU institutions and agencies relative to national ones, this has been the subject of extensive debates in the political science literature (see, for example, George, 2004; Majone, 2005; Sandholtz and Stone Sweet, 1998), often in terms of the ability of the European Commission (EC) and related agencies such as the European Court of Justice (ECJ) to act autonomously in establishing and implementing EU-wide rules of the game. The conflicts between 'intergovernmentalists' and 'supranationalists' concerning the powers and purposes of European supranational organizations have usually focused on the relative independence of their goals and strategies from national governments, and their capacity to exert autonomous causal influence on policy outcomes (Pierson, 1996; Pollack, 1998; Schmidt, 2002: 52–7).

Relying on rational choice models drawn from principal-agency theory to explain the varied influence of the EC on different policy issues, Pollack (1998), for instance, has suggested that four factors are critical: (a) the distribution of preferences between national governments and such agents, (b) the nature of the institutional decision rules governing the delegation of powers, (c) the distribution of information, and (d) their ability to mobilize transnational constituencies in support of their policies. Variations in these help to explain differences in the success of the EC and other agencies in creating 'more Europe' in different areas. While he concludes that the 'Commission enjoys considerable autonomy and influence on its implementation of Commission policies' (1998: 248), he also suggests that this should not be overstated and it depends very much on the preferences and coordination of member states, the behaviour of the ECJ and the interests of associated transnational actors in different issue areas.

From a rather different perspective, Majone (2005) has emphasized that the EU has few, if any, of the conditions necessary to form a distinct supranational political entity, especially the existence of a common European political identity that could provide legitimacy for an EU government. Europeans are members of the EU through their national citizenships, not as members of a separate European polity governed by an EU citizenship law that is superior to national ones (Majone, 2005: 25). Furthermore, EU institutions are only able to exercise the powers granted to them by member states, and in particular are unable as sovereign authorities to define the limits to their own competences, the so-called 'Kompetenz-Kompetenz' (Majone, 2005: 205).

As part of a multi-tiered governance structure, then, the EU is less sovereign and autonomous in terms of establishing its own 'constitutional choice' rules that affect who determines, and how they do, the 'collective choice' and 'operational' rules governing innovative activities in Amable's

(2003: 68) hierarchy of institutions, than most, if not all, European governments, and is more subject to lower level rules and agreements. Despite the emergent powers and path dependent competences of many supranational agencies arising from the combination of large fixed costs, learning effects, coordination effects and adaptive expectations (Pierson, 1996), they remain relatively weak in this sense.

In sum, much of what the EU has achieved in the past fifty or so years in terms of economic regulation has been concentrated on the liberalization of trade and investment. As such, it could be expected to complement the international trend towards liberalization and deregulation and so reinforce the consequences discussed above (Schmidt, 2002: 41–52). Additionally, despite many attempts by the EC to establish Europe-wide institutions governing economic activities and complete the single European market, few have materialized. For example, most EU attempts at standardizing shareholder rights and duties and the organization and governance of financial markets across Europe have failed, as has recently (2006) been exemplified by the difficulties of agreeing the takeover directive and the varied responses by many member states to its provisions. According to the *Financial Times* of 2 March 2006, five states have signalled that they intend to opt out of Article 9 of this directive, eight intend to opt out of Article 11 and over four will opt out of Article 12.

Furthermore, although competition law has been seen as central to the EU since the Treaty of Rome, the European model was only incorporated into domestic legislation in Germany and the UK in 1998 and has been implemented in quite different ways by different administrative systems so that national practices remain heterogeneous (Page, 2003). Most of the key institutions governing economic activities in Europe are not, then, homogenous across member states and, where EU institutions have become strongly established, these depend greatly on national implementation, which can vary considerably, as the conflicts over the liberalization of service provision exemplify (Menz, 2005). The institutionalization of a distinctively European pattern of economic organization seems highly improbable, especially as EU decisions and trade-offs become more politicized as they move into more sensitive areas (Hurrell and Menon, 2003) and member states become more heterogeneous with the EU's expansion eastwards.

Bearing these points in mind, it is nonetheless worth considering how the development of the Single European Market and similar liberalization agreements have affected the different kinds of institutional regimes and business systems that have become dominant in various member states.

One of the more obvious consequences of adopting such measures has been the move to more 'regulatory' types of state management of economic development as direct state support for domestic companies and industries has become outlawed, albeit in different ways and to varying degrees (Gilardi, 2005; Majone, 2003; 2005). State subsidies have now to be justified to the EC, and are often forbidden, so that the more *dirigiste* states have turned to more indirect methods of managing change (Schmidt, 2002: 198–200).

In the case of France, this has involved considerable expenditure on encouraging early retirement, social protection and other labour market adjustment policies, as well as on promoting small and medium-sized businesses in what Levy (2005) terms the social anaesthesia state. As he and others have pointed out, the dismantling of the instruments of direct coordination of industrial development has granted the largest French companies considerable autonomy in the absence of strong intermediary organizations and collective actors, especially labour unions (Goyer, 2003; Hancke, 2002; Reberioux, 2002; Schmidt, 2002: 124).

While maintaining the traditionally close relationships between business, bureaucratic and political elites through the *grands corps*, strategic managers have been able to engage in major restructuring of their companies, especially narrowing their range of business activities and reducing employment, at greater distance from state objectives. Together with reduced state control over the financial system and the breaking down of barriers between different financial markets, these changes have considerably increased the autonomy of firms' top managers and encouraged a focus on profitability (Hancke and Goyer, 2005). But, as Schmidt (2002: 137–43) has suggested, while France may have moved from a state-directed form of capitalism to more of a state-enabled form, it still exemplifies a variant of state capitalism in terms of the central role of the state in the economy.

Turning to consider the likely effects of EU liberalization on the more corporatist institutional regimes in Europe, we would expect these to become less homogenous and standardized across sectors, regions and firm sizes as firms from different kinds of regimes increase their market share in these countries and domestic companies invest abroad. As Schmitter (1997) has suggested, the larger firms in highly corporatist regimes develop different interests from domestic competitors and collaborators as they internationalize their operations and are able to lobby the EC and other EU institutions directly, and so may become less willing to share authority with domestic business associations. Insofar as they additionally encourage the decentralization of national negotiating institutions to local bargaining, and are successful in this, the strength of national corporatist institutions should decline (Pontusson and Swenson, 1996; Thelen and Wijnbergen, 2003). Such weakening of the national cohesion, coverage and standardization of such regimes will obviously be more likely where the cohesion and strength of labour union federations also declines.

While, then, many national corporatist regimes in Europe may be changing for a number of different reasons, the effects of EU liberalization can be expected to reinforce their differentiation and declining strength, although some states may try to reinvigorate them to deal with international competition and potential economic decline, as Crouch (2003) has suggested. Such attempts seem most likely to be successful where the labour movement is cohesive and powerful across sectors, and inclusive corporatist arrangements are strongly entrenched throughout the economy, as in many Scandinavian countries (Bowman, 2002). In the case of Germany, Schmidt (2002: 141–5) has suggested that prevalent patterns of business relations, the role of the state and the organization of labour relations continue to exemplify managed capitalism, despite some erosion of inter-firm commitments and changing bank-firm relationships. In contrast, business corporatist arrangements that exclude organized labour from the development and implementation of national economic and social policies may be more affected by liberalization and deregulation.

This weakening of national corporatist regimes in many EU countries as a result of liberalization and fragmentation of business interests—and sometimes of labour interests in different sectors and types of firm (Pontusson and Swenson, 1996; Thelen and Wijnbergen, 2003; Vogel, 2001)— is likely to be echoed by changes in dominant socio-economic coalitions. This is especially probable where such coalitions were based on the state's provision of collective competition goods that are now outlawed and business elites were closely allied to political and bureaucratic ones.

To the extent that the EU, and more general transnational regulation, reduces large firm dependence on national states, the cohesion and integration of such alliances can be expected to decline as their owners and strategic managers seek more autonomy from state direction, access international capital markets and pursue links with other groups at home and abroad. Even in France, where ties remain close, there seems to be an increasing willingness of the top managers of some firms to speak out against state policies and seek more autonomy. Similarly, the liberalization of financial markets, where it does occur, can, together with the growth of MNCs in Europe, encourage new interest groups to become influential at the national and European level, such as investment banks and fund managers (Laurence, 2001).

The institutionalization of the EU as a distinct supranational legislative arena may have encouraged some interest groups to weaken dominant national institutions and coalitions by influencing European policies and regulations directly (Mazey and Richardson, 2003), but, as Crouch (2003) has pointed out, lobbying governments at different territorial levels is not necessarily a zero-sum game, and successful groups typically enlist national state support as well as EU backing in seeking to achieve their goals. In particular, large firms often lobby the EC, the European Parliament and other bodies, singly and collectively, as well as their 'home' state agencies, and are more effective in doing so than groups that rely on the goodwill of the EC to promote their cause. It is also worth noting that the EC itself is highly internally differentiated, with each Directorate fighting its own corner and limited overall coordination (Majone, 2005), so that gaining consistent EC support for particular policies over a period of time requires substantial resources and commitment, thus limiting the ability of nationally disadvantaged interest groups to use 'Brussels' as a means of attacking domestic dominant coalitions.

One group that probably has lost some of its political and economic influence in many EU states as liberalization weakens the cohesion and homogeneity of national corporatist institutions is, of course, organized labour, although how much of the general decline in union power in many European states can be attributed to the EU and other liberalizing agencies is difficult to determine. Furthermore, some of the apparent decline in national union power in some member states seems to have been offset by the growing influence of works councils and enterprise level bargaining as employers and employees align their interests around individual firms rather than domestic sectors or national economies. This has been encouraged by the weakening of some employers' associations following the divergence of interests between MNCs and more domestically focused smaller companies. As Thelen and Kume (2003) and others have emphasized, in Germany it is very much in the interests of national union groups to have a strong employers' group with whom to strike agreements so that they can restrict the growth of opportunistic behaviour on the part of member unions. To the extent that such attempts have failed, we can say that national and sectoral authority sharing between firms and their associations and between employers' groups and workers' federations may be declining, yet at the firm level employer authority sharing may continue or even increase.

Where, on the other hand, labour unions and their federations remain strong and cohesive at the national level, we would not expect large firms to restructure their operations very radically or quickly, as Goyer (2003) indicates was the case in Germany for much of the 1990s. Nor are they likely to forgo the advantages of corporatist arrangements in a hurry where these continue to provide important collective competition goods for all firms in particular industries. As long as the dominant institutions governing labour markets and skill formation processes are nationally standardized and encourage inter-firm cooperation, authority sharing between firms and within them seems likely to remain a significant phenomenon in corporatist societies despite liberalization and increasing competitive pressures.

Overall, then, while some differentiation between the largest and most internationalized companies and other firms, and between sectors dominated by different kinds of companies, has taken place in corporatist regimes as a result of EU liberalization, its extent will be limited by nationally cohesive and integrated institutions governing labour markets and the need to act collectively in dealing with powerful unions. In these circumstances, the coordination and control of economic activities seems likely to remain characterized by quite high levels of authority sharing between owners, managers and employees as well as between companies.

Concluding Remarks

This discussion has highlighted four main points about the growth and impact of transnational governance. First, the scope of economic activities and relationships effectively subject to international institutions is limited. On the whole, most of these transnational institutions have dealt with issues of market liberalization, competition regulation and discriminatory state support for domestic companies. They have not standardized the rules governing limited liability, the rights and responsibilities of private companies, relationships between owners, managers, and employees, mergers and acquisitions, let alone those dealing with skill formation, specification and control. Insofar as, then, they have had a significant effect on established patterns of economic organization, this is largely restricted to the internationalization of markets for some, but by no means all, goods and services.

Second, the impact of these cross-national institutions on economic actors and relationships depends greatly on other changes in national and international political economies. As the case of the European telecommunications industry exemplifies, changing the international regulatory environment is both encouraged by, and itself encourages, major shifts in the national and international opportunity structure for key members of domestic coalitions and for potentially powerful outsiders. Such shifts can result from novel technologies and emerging industries, but also from changes in financial flows and the organization of financial and other markets. It is difficult, then, to separate the consequences of increasing international regulation from other aspects of economic internationalization that have developed interdependently with it. As Djelic and Quack (2003b) have emphasized, transnational institution building involves both top down and bottom up processes with many different kinds of actors organized at different levels. Equally, its outcomes depend on the interests and actions of national and international groups and organizations, as well as conflicting and complementary institutional arrangements.

Third, when combined with increasing international competition, the expansion of MNCs and the internationalization of financial flows, the main consequences of the growth of transnational governance on established institutional regimes and business systems have been: (a) to reduce direct state management of the economy and business dependence of state elites, and (b) to encourage the differentiation of actors and their interests in the most homogenous regimes, and (c) to weaken the cohesion and scope of their dominant institutions. This latter effect has, however, been mitigated by strong national labour movements in some European countries that seek to maintain national bargaining systems and other institutions governing labour markets.

Finally, the growth of EU regulation and supranational authority has had most impact on economic liberalization and moves towards, but not yet achieved, the single European market, especially when combined with complementary pressures for change from national and international interest groups. There is little evidence for dominant EU institutions governing other aspects of market economies becoming established, let alone increasing homogeneity of business system characteristics throughout the EU. Furthermore, as Majone (2005) has emphasized, the lack of common European identities, political parties and a European constitutional demos by whose ultimate authority pan-European constitutional arrangements could be established make it most unlikely that a distinct and dominant set of European political institutions will become institutionalized. Indeed, continuing enlargement and increasing macro-economic and institutional heterogeneity coupled with the declining role of the EC and use of the community method to reach agreement on EU policies suggest that the development of homogenous Europe-wide institutions governing economic activities remains improbable.

Part III

Constructing Organizational Capabilities in Different Institutional Regimes

6

The Institutional Structuring of Organizational Capabilities: Variations in Authority Sharing and Organizational Careers

Introduction

A central concern in the analysis of competing capitalisms is to understand how different institutional arrangements and rules of the competitive game generate different patterns of economic organization and behaviour that in turn lead to variations in economic outcomes across market economies. What are the crucial social processes, or 'mechanisms' (Boudon, 1998, 2003; Bunge, 2004), through which variations in governing institutions generate varied economic results? In particular, how do the distinctive logics of economic action implied by different institutional regimes and associated dominant coalitions become translated into distinctive patterns of authoritative coordination and control such that they lead to contrasting sectoral structures and performances?

A useful way of dealing with this issue is to develop the competence or 'dynamic capabilities' (Dosi *et al.*, 2000) theory of the firm, which builds on the seminal contribution of Penrose (1959) in emphasizing the organizational nature of competitive advantages and the critical role of managerial routines in transforming human and material resources into productive services (Foss and Knudsen, 1996; Lazonick and West, 1998; Teece and Pisano, 1994). By coordinating and directing particular inputs systematically through firm-specific rules and procedures, managers generate idiosyncratic organizational capabilities that provide unique competitive advantages. Such capabilities vary in their flexibility and adaptability from those largely concerned with coordination and control of business activities, through the ability to improve products and processes incrementally by individual and collective learning to those more 'reconfigurational' ones that enable firms to transform their competences and knowledge quite radically (Teece *et al.*, 2000).

By developing different kinds of organizational capabilities, companies become more or less able to compete successfully in different markets and technologies. The types of competences that managers seek to specialize in thus affect their likely effectiveness in different industries, and so market economies dominated by particular institutional regimes that encourage firms to focus on specific kinds of capabilities are likely to become more specialized in these sectors. In this sense, the ways in which leading firms in an economy develop particular kinds of organizational capabilities constitute the crucial mediating mechanisms between institutional regimes and economic outcomes. Different sets of dominant institutions and interest groups enable and guide leading firms in differently organized economies to develop particular kinds of collective competences that, in turn, lead to relative success in particular kinds of competitive markets.

How, then, do firms in different economies develop different kinds of capabilities? As many discussions have emphasized, the key feature of firms is the use of authority, or subordination to legitimate superiors, to direct and control economic activities in a variety of ways. Hamilton and Feenstra (1997: 56), for instance, claim that firms, and economic organizations in general, are 'above all authoritative organizations that structure relationships according to established rules of conduct' in which participants recognize that they are bound to the authoritative norms of the organization, and there are coercive means to enforce collective rules.

The ability to direct employees to undertake specific tasks through delegated authority from private property rights' holders is crucial to the organizational development of distinctive collective competences, not least because the flexibility that employment agreements provide enables managers to organize economic activities in different ways for varied purposes, and to change these to suit altered circumstances (Richardson, 1998). This flexibility enables authority hierarchies to manage increasingly complex and uncertain activities, particularly innovation. As Lazonick (1991; Lazonick and West, 1998) and others have suggested, the planned coordination of a specialized division of labour has enabled firms to build distinctive organizational capabilities for developing process and product innovations on a continuing basis.

Central to the development of distinctive organizational capabilities is the willingness of employees to commit themselves to joint problem solving and the improvement of employer-specific knowledge and skills, sometimes at the expense of enhancing their own individual competences and value on external labour markets. The more complex and risky are problem-solving activities, and the more they involve the coordination of complementary activities and types of knowledge, the more important such commitment becomes. Two major means of developing continuing employee commitment to collective problem solving and enhancing firm specific competences are authority sharing and organizational careers.

Authority sharing here involves owners and top managers delegating considerable discretion over task performance—and sometimes task organization—to skilled employees, and encouraging them to contribute to product and process improvements. It varies in the degree of such delegation, i.e. the amount of discretion exercised by subordinates, and its scope, i.e. the range of activities and decisions over which discretion is exercised. While these aspects are often positively correlated, it is clearly possible for managers to delegate high levels of discretion over specific, narrowly defined, tasks without extending it to more general features of the work situation.

Such intra-organizational delegation of discretion to employees is sometimes complemented by external authority sharing with suppliers, customers and competitors in varied inter-firm networks, especially when there are strong constraints on short-term opportunism. In both instances, firms are thereby enabled, in principle, to learn from the knowledge and experiences of their employees and business partners. On the whole, then, the greater is the degree and scope of such authority sharing, the more firms should be able to integrate different kinds of activities and types of knowledge in dealing with complex problems, and to develop new routines and knowledge.

Similarly, providing long-term organizational careers to key groups of employees, as exemplified by many large Japanese companies in the post-war period, encourages them to contribute to the development of collective firm-specific capabilities through extensive collaboration within and across departmental boundaries. By tying personal futures to the growth of the employing organization, and making credible commitments to maintain employment across the business cycle, such careers intensify employee commitment to the improvement of collective competences, even if that limits their visibility on external labour markets.

Authority sharing and organizational careers are interrelated in the sense that providing the latter for some employees involves a considerable amount of the former. It seems most unlikely that owners would offer relatively long-term commitments for managers and skilled workers if they were not prepared to delegate substantial levels of task autonomy to them. While, then, firms that do not provide long-term careers for employees can vary in the degree of authority sharing they implement, between for instance isolated autocracies in many developing economies and project-based firms in Silicon Valley (Bahrami and Evans, 1995), those that do offer organizational careers for at least some groups of staff are also likely to delegate considerable task autonomy to them.

Variations in authority sharing and organizational careers help to explain differences in the kinds of collective capabilities that companies develop, especially those involving extensive collaboration and sharing of knowledge and expertise. The willingness of owners and managers to share authority with different groups and offer organizational careers is, in turn, greatly affected by societal institutions, especially those governing trust relations and skill formation and control. As a result, economies dominated by different institutional regimes vary significantly in the concentration or dispersion of authority over various kinds of decisions in work groups, organizational divisions, firms and business associations, as well as the significance of organizational careers, and these differences affect the sorts of collective capabilities that leading firms and other strategic actors are able to generate in them. In turn, such distinct competences enable companies to be more or less effective in dealing with particular kinds of problems and innovating in different ways. Consequently, market economies with contrasting institutional arrangements tend to display different kinds of economic development and specialization.

In this chapter I explore these relationships in more detail through an analysis of how institutional frameworks are connected to variations in authority sharing and organizational careers such that firms in contrasting institutional contexts are encouraged to develop different kinds of capabilities. Initially, I summarize the ways in which authority sharing and delegation affect the kinds of competences that firms develop, and then consider how these latter are connected to the institutionalization of careers within and between companies. In the following section, I explore the key features of different institutional frameworks that encourage divergent patterns of authority sharing and career development, and help to explain how different countries and regions generate contrasting types of firms and organizational capabilities.

Authority Sharing and Organizational Capabilities

In analysing the connections between variations in authority sharing, organizational careers and the sorts of capability that are developed by different kinds of firms, it is useful to follow Teece and Pisano (1994) and Teece *et al.* (2000) in distinguishing three kinds of collective capabilities that may be particularly effective in different technological and market situations. These vary in their ability to adapt to changing circumstances. First, coordinating capabilities involve the development of integrative routines that, for example, gather and process information about internal and external processes, connect customer experiences with engineering design choices and link production facilities with suppliers. In Chandler's (1990) account of the rise of large companies, these were key to the realization of economies of scale and scope through managerial hierarchies.

Second, organizational learning capabilities involve joint problem solving and improvement of production and related processes, both through continuing work experience and the execution of specific projects, as well as continually developing the firm's understanding of business partners and other external agents. Firms with strong learning skills rapidly codify, diffuse, and apply throughout the organization new knowledge that is developed by individuals and groups, so that routines and procedures are continuously being updated in a process of cumulative improvement. This ability to incorporate new knowledge into organizational procedures on a continuous basis has been seen as key to the success of many large Japanese companies, such as Toyota (Fujimoto, 2000; Nonaka and Takeuchi, 1995).

Third, reconfigurational capabilities involve the transformation of organizational resources and skills to deal with rapidly changing technologies and markets. They enable companies to restructure their operations and routines quite radically as knowledge changes, often by acquiring new skills and competences through hiring on external labour markets or buying newly formed firms, as in the case of Cisco (Lee, 2000). Such transformations can destroy existing routines and competences, as arguably happened with the changes in drug discovery methods and skills following the molecular biology revolution (Casper and Matraves, 2003; Zucker and Darby, 1997).

Differences in the degree of authority sharing and provision of organizational careers are associated with variations in the development of these organizational capabilities. We can consider how differences in authority sharing impinge upon the development of collective competences by

Table 6.1. Varieties of authority sharing and competence development

Characteristics	Authority Distribution in Different Types of Firms		
	Isolated Autocracies	Managerially Coordinated	Cooperative Hierarchies
Extent of internal authority sharing	Low	Limited to managerial hierarchy	Extended to skilled staff
Extent of external authority sharing	Low	Limited and highly specific	Considerable and wide-ranging
Key developer of competitive competences	Owner-manager	Managerial hierarchy	Organization of skilled staff
Ability to integrate varied knowledge and problem-solving skills systematically	Low	Restricted to managerial hierarchy	Considerable
Focus of competence development	Flexibility, responsiveness to short-term market changes	Managerial integration and routinization	Collective development of new skills, products and processes

contrasting three ideal types of firms in terms of how much authority over economic decisions, organizational issues and work performance is shared by owners with managers and skilled staff. The key attributes and capabilities of these types are summarized in Table 6.1 and will now be discussed.

First, in what might be termed isolated autocracies, authority is highly concentrated in the hands of owner managers, delegation of discretion to managers and skilled employees is usually very limited, and authority sharing restricted to close family members. Second, there are managerially coordinated companies where considerable authority is delegated to a managerial hierarchy, sometimes including senior technical staff, but not to the bulk of the labour force. Third, more cooperative hierarchies share considerable authority with technical staff and skilled workers, especially over task performance and perhaps work organization and direction. In some European countries such authority sharing is enshrined in legal regulations and extended to broader issues.

Isolated autocracies are typically owner-controlled firms in economies where formal institutions for generating and reproducing trust between economic actors are weakly established. Usually funded from family resources, and often operating in environments that are unsupportive of privately generated and controlled concentrations of wealth, owner-managers find it difficult to share authority beyond those with whom family-like connections have been established. Delegated discretion tends to be limited to a relatively narrow range of activities whose outputs can be easily monitored, as in many businesses in Taiwan, Hong Kong and other parts of Pacific-Asia (Hamilton, 1997; Hamilton and Kao, 1990; Redding, 1990).

Such high levels of centralized authority enable firms to make decisions rapidly, and to alter key features of the business, such as the products and services offered and the markets served, as exemplified by small firms in Hong Kong that switched from making plastic flowers, to wigs, to toys etc in very brief time spans (Enright et al., 1997; Redding, 1990). They do not, though, encourage the long-term development of organizational capabilities, since commitments by employees tend to be limited—or highly personal—and turnover among the more skilled and competent is often high as they leave to start their own businesses.

Competitive competences accordingly are more dependent on the personal qualities of the owner-manager and his or her close associates rather than on the planned coordination of different kinds of skills and knowledge. Flexibility and responsiveness to market changes are more important to these kinds of firms than the systematic and continuous improvement of products and processes. They do not, then, readily develop strong coordinating capabilities through systematic routines and organization-specific knowledge. As a result, isolated autocracies tend not to be highly effective in managing complex technologies and introducing innovations that need highly skilled staff to be motivated and coordinated to work together for substantial periods. Although highly responsive to changes in market demand, their organizational ability to mobilize new skills and knowledge for dealing with uncertain and risky problems is limited by their reluctance to delegate and involve specialist staff in joint problem solving.

In more predictable and rule-governed environments, owners are usually willing to delegate authority to salaried managers who establish routines and formal procedures for coordinating and controlling work and skills. However, in institutional regimes favouring exit over voice (Nooteboom, 2000) this kind of delegation is often limited to the managerial hierarchy and rarely extended to skilled workers or business partners. According to Lazonick (1990) such 'Chandlerian' firms in the USA developed distinctive organizational capabilities by taking control of production operations away from manual employees and codifying work procedures in formal routines and managerial control systems. As Chandler himself (1990: 36) puts it: 'The combined capabilities of top and middle management can be considered the skills of the organization itself. These skills were the most valuable of all those that made up the *organizational capabilities* of the new modern industrial enterprise' (italics in original). If firms are constituted by their distinctive knowledge and problem solving capabilities (Kogut and Zander, 1992), this means that most employees are not really full members of such companies.

Organizational competences are here embodied in managerial procedures that do not depend greatly on the skills and knowledge of individual employees below the management group and senior technical staff, or on their long-term commitment to this particular organization. Consequently, most staff, including some technical experts, have little incentive to contribute to the development of firm-specific competences at the expense of developing their own skills, and will need considerable persuasion to commit large amounts of time and energy in resolving problems that require organizational cooperation and collaboration across functional boundaries. Innovations, and organizational improvements more generally, that depend on such commitment for their effective development and implementation are therefore not likely to be rapidly realized.

Rather, significant process and product changes will probably be decided by unilateral authority and coordinated managerially, and may well involve changing the skills of employees by hiring and firing or acquiring new businesses with the desired skills, instead of developing those of current staff. The limited extent of authority sharing and cooperation with suppliers and customers likewise restricts the flow of new information and problem-solving routines from outside these kinds of firms, and discourages investment in customer-specific innovations. The variety of information and knowledge coordinated through such managerial hierarchies is therefore limited in these kinds of organizations.

While the managerial coordinating capabilities of such firms may be quite considerable, they usually do not involve much cooperation between skilled workers or direct connections between operators, suppliers, and customers. Organizational learning tends likewise to be restricted to the managerial hierarchy and focused more on what Lazonick (1991: 199) terms adaptive rather than on innovative strategies. These kinds of strategies concentrate on improving the efficiency with which material and human resources are used as opposed to investing in the development of novel capabilities for producing new goods and services at reduced costs. As Lazonick (1991: 200) puts it: 'the adaptive organization chooses to avoid productive uncertainty by investing only in those process and product technologies for which the required productive capabilities are known'. This suggests that the transformation of assets and resources in these kinds of firms will be infrequent and disruptive, and may well involve destroying current competences and routines. Reconfigurational capabilities depend considerably here on the ability of senior managers to implement such restructuring without radically reducing managerial commitments.

Third, where collaboration between economic actors is more encouraged by dominant institutions, owners and managers are more likely to delegate authority to skilled technical and manual workers. These cooperative hierarchies also tend to develop closer relationships with customers and suppliers, and cooperate with competitors in setting technical standards, deciding skill definitions and managing union negotiations. This is partly because they are more able to rely on employees and business partners in adjusting to external changes and integrating information from a wide variety of sources than in more adversarial environments. Commitment to dealing with organizational problems across skill boundaries is likely to be easier to elicit in these contexts, and, once change has been agreed, it should be introduced faster and more effectively than elsewhere.

Many such firms incorporate individual learning and skill development into organizational routines. Typically, this involves engaging core employees in continuous improvement activities and codifying their suggestions so that these can be systematically incorporated into work processes throughout the organization—including suppliers and customers where appropriate, as in Toyota (Fujimoto, 2000). In other words, organizational learning can occur on a much broader scale in cooperative hierarchies because it builds on the contributions of all long-term employees and closely allied business partners, and is diffused to a much wider range of groups within and beyond the formal boundaries of the firm. Whereas the US Chandlerian enterprise typically restricts learning to the problem solving activities of the narrowly circumscribed managerial hierarchy, and modifying work routines within the formal organization accordingly, here the organization incorporates most long-term employees, business partners and competitors into a collective endeavour in such as way that the whole ensemble 'learns' by integrating new knowledge and skills into codified routines and problem solving practices.

In principle, then, these kinds of companies should be able to learn faster and more effectively from a wider range of sources and activities than more isolated managerial hierarchies. Authority sharing—while varying in degree and scope between different groups within and between formal organizational boundaries—here facilitates coordination of knowledge and skills by encouraging joint commitments to growth through continual improvements of processes and products as employees and business partners become locked-in to the authoritative organization's development of distinctive collective competences. This lock-in leads to joint investments in enhancing firm-specific capabilities rather than individual and group skills and reputations.

Consequently, innovations produced by such firms tend to be relatively incremental in that they build on existing skills and knowledge. Where inter-firm cooperation throughout industrial sectors—as distinct from supplier networks—is considerable, product development also tends to focus on particular kinds of customers rather than being generic across a mass market. Competition between firms here is based more on quality and differentiating products and markets than on price and cost reduction (Soskice, 1997). As a result, both coordinating and learning capabilities of these kinds of firms are considerable, but their ability to restructure operations and competences radically is restricted by these lock-ins.

Organizational Careers and the Development of Organizational Capabilities

This kind of employer–employee interdependence is greatly enhanced by the provision of long-term organizational careers for those who demonstrate commitment to, and success in, organizational problem solving and collaboration. Given the risks of being fired and/or having employment conditions unilaterally changed in many market economies, employees seem likely to prefer to demonstrate their prowess in using generally applicable skills to deal with specialist problems than to focus on improving employer-specific capabilities. Organizational careers therefore have to be relatively stable over business cycles to convince staff that it is worth taking these risks by improving their internal organizational reputations (Marsden, 1999; Miller, 1992).

Where such internal careers are highly significant, employees are encouraged to demonstrate their commitment to organizational goals and contribution to company success through, for example, working effectively in cross-functional teams and welcoming rotations across departments and divisions. Knowledge of organization-specific activities, skills, technologies, and markets—including major customers—will be highly valued by employees in such situations, and they will focus on improving their internal reputations for effective organizational problem solving rather than enhancing their external visibility. Firms that create such strong organizational careers for skilled staff encourage long-term commitments to organizational problem solving, and are more likely to develop distinctive and effective collective learning capabilities, than are those that do not do so.

However, just as the level of authority sharing varies between firms, so too do the extent and scope of organizational careers. In uncertain and low trust institutional environments, for instance, most isolated autocracies tend to restrict long-term commitments to members of their immediate family and those partners with whom they have established close personal connections. Business careers in these kinds of society are more often built around a succession of new firm start-ups than being organizational specific. A similar limitation of long-term organizational careers exists in more predictable contexts where many small firms are too vulnerable and lack a hierarchy of positions that could reward organizational success through promotion. In addition, the structure of organizational careers varies as firms organize their hierarchies in different ways, especially in terms of the importance of functional departments and publicly certified expertise.

We can, then, distinguish between types of organizational careers in terms of three characteristics. First, the longevity of commitments between employers and employees, and in particular the willingness of companies to establish long-term careers for those who demonstrate high levels of organizational commitment. Second, the range of staff covered by such careers, especially their extension to skilled workers beyond the managerial hierarchy. Third, the functional specificity of organizational careers in terms of how far up the formal hierarchy of managerial positions successful staff remain in the same broad functional field of expertise. At least four distinct types of skilled employees' careers that help to develop distinctive organizational capabilities can be distinguished in terms of these dimensions. In order of increasing organizational commitment, these can be described as, first, professional team careers, second, managerial careers, third, functionally specialized careers, and, fourth, organizational generalist careers. Their key characteristics are summarized in Table 6.2 and will now be discussed.

Considering first professional team careers, these consist of a series of memberships in teams of specialists with varied skills tackling complex and often highly uncertain problems. Successful careers of this kind

Table 6.2. Organizational careers and organizational capabilities

Characteristics	Types of Organizational Careers			
	Professional Team Careers	Managerial Careers	Functionally Specialized Careers	Organizational Generalist Careers
Organizational longevity	Low	Considerable	Considerable	High
Range of employees covered	Most skilled staff, but for short periods	Limited to managers and senior experts	Considerable	High
Functional specificity	Technically specialized careers	Limited to roles within profit centres	High, up to senior management	Limited
Associated organizational capabilities				
Coordinating	Limited to teams	Considerable	Considerable	High
Collective learning	Limited to teams	Limited to managerial hierarchy	Considerable within functional departments	High within and across departments
Reconfigurational	High	Limited by managerial routines	Considerable within current competences, low beyond these	Considerable within current competences, low beyond these

depend on reputations in both employing organizations and external technical communities for dealing with more and more complex and difficult problems, often under tight time constraints. As well as being able to demonstrate high levels of technical excellence, an additional important requirement for such careers is the ability to work together with other specialists in teams to achieve visible success in complex problem solving. Because of the highly risky and uncertain nature of many projects undertaken by such teams, these kinds of careers do not usually involve lengthy commitments to particular employers, especially in emerging industries where new technologies are being developed. Labour mobility is typically quite high, although often territorially restricted, as in Hollywood and Silicon Valley (Almeida and Kogut, 1999; DeFillippi and Arthur, 1998; Marsden, 1999: 238–41; Storper, 1989).

Even where engineers are locked-in to individual firms through programmes of rolling share options and bonuses, as at Intel (Jackson, 1997), organizational careers are frequently structured around a series of relatively discrete projects in which specialist staff compete to demonstrate their technical excellence and contribution to collective success. Project team membership and success is often more important for employees in this situation than building company-wide organizational capabilities. As a result, the development of coordination and learning competences at the organizational level can be limited by individual and group mobility where labour markets are highly fluid and structured around publicly certified skills, as discussed in Chapter 9.

Firms that are dependent on the success of such teams often limit the provision of long-term organizational careers when high levels of technical and market uncertainty restrict financial and employment commitments, and results have to be achieved relatively quickly. Competitive advantages and competences here derive from flexible and speedy responses to new knowledge and skills, and the ability to integrate new kinds of information and expertise to generate disruptive products and processes, especially in winner-takes-all competitions where network externalities and economies of scale of demand are high (Shapiro and Varian, 1999).

More managerial careers consist of a series of hierarchical positions within a company based upon success in dealing with significant organizational problems. They are, then, more firm specific than professional team careers, and usually involve greater employer commitment to key staff. However, these careers are usually restricted to managers, engineers and other technical experts who demonstrated success in dealing with organization-specific problems and were willing to acquire knowledge of different functions and activities through job rotation and management development programmes (Lazonick and West, 1998; Lazonick and O'Sullivan, 1997). In particular, they typically have not been available to non-college educated staff in the USA and elsewhere, and have also been subject to corporate restructuring, especially since the 1970s (Jacoby, 2005).

As a result, organization-specific knowledge development and learning in these kinds of firms tend to be limited to the managerial hierarchy and reified in formal procedures and routines that often limit flexibility and adaptiveness to changing technologies and markets. Although these kinds of organizational careers are often available for specialist staff within functional departments, they can involve relatively early moves from such functional fields to more general managerial posts that integrate a number of complementary activities and skills in distinct profit centres, especially in multidivisional companies that decentralize such general profit responsibility below top management. Demonstrating a commitment to developing general managerial competences across fields of functional specialization is thus an important requirement for success in such careers.

Companies where these career types dominate are able to generate strong coordinating capabilities, particularly of different functions and expertise, but tend to be less effective in learning how to implement continuous improvements to work processes, especially when that involves the skilled labour force. The restriction of organizational careers and commitments to managers and potential managers seems likely to discourage many employees from making great efforts to improve firm-specific knowledge and skills, and so limits organizational learning capabilities. It may, though, enable such firms to restructure resources and activities by changing personnel, depending on the rigidity of their managerial routines and their ability to gain the commitment of new staff to contribute to organizational objectives.

Functionally specialized careers extend further down organizational hierarchies to encompass many skilled employees, and so encourage widespread commitment to joint problem solving and organization-specific knowledge development. Such a broadening of long-term commitments to non-managerial groups enables firms that establish these kinds of careers to improve product functions and production processes through continuous cumulative innovations by gaining the active cooperation of core employees in coordinating complementary activities and enhancing collective organizational capabilities (Lazonick, 1991; Soskice, 1999; Streeck, 1992).

However, by structuring organizational careers largely around functional departments, at least up to senior management levels as in many German companies (Stewart *et al.*, 1994), success may be based as much on contributions to departmental problem solving activities as on those to more general organizational issues. Skilled workers, technical experts and managers may accordingly develop quite strong departmental loyalties that can inhibit cross-functional cooperation and the development of organization-wide collective capabilities, as Herrigel and Sabel (1999) have suggested happens in parts of Germany. Coordinating and learning capabilities are likely to be quite strong here, then, but organization-wide learning may be restricted by departmental boundaries. While innovation capabilities within existing technological trajectories and skill bases can be quite considerable, more radical transformations of resources and activities are unlikely in firms with these kinds of careers because of the long-term commitments to existing skills and competences.

More generalist organizational careers encourage greater mobility across functions and departments, and reward employees who learn new organization-specific knowledge and skills in a variety of jobs over the course of their working lifetime. Comparing engineers' more generalist careers in Japanese firms with those in German firms, for instance, Sorge (1996: 82) suggests that: 'The Japanese engineer is more of a multi-specialist, the German engineer a specialist who extends his domain into other specialisms'.

Success in companies with more generalist careers depends on demonstrating significant contributions to organizational problem solving in different teams and different fields. Flexibility and continuous learning are therefore key qualities for ambitious employees, as well, of course, as dedication to their employer's growth and success. Because staff are strongly locked-in to the long-term fate of their employer through the firm-specificity of their knowledge and skills, they are highly committed to improving organizational problem solving capabilities, including knowledge of key customers' processes and needs. Additionally, the generalist nature of organizational careers here facilitates the development and introduction of new products as employees rotate between departments. As a result, such companies are able to develop very effective coordination and learning capabilities within the enterprise.

However, this focus on continuously improving organization-specific knowledge and skills can inhibit learning from external sources, especially if those are organizationally and cognitively remote such as some academic science or radically new industries. While absorption of new information and skills in areas close to current activities and competences is likely to be straightforward in such companies, greater difficulty may be involved in searching for and using effectively knowledge and expertise that is more distant, as has arguably been the case for many firms in the Japanese pharmaceutical industry (Kneller, 2003; Thomas, 2001; see also Nooteboom, 2000).

These different degrees of authority sharing and types of organizational careers are encouraged to develop and be reproduced by varied institutional frameworks. Where the dominant institutions governing authority and trust, the allocation of capital, and the development and organization of skills, as well as state structures and policies, differ significantly, owners and managers are likely to adopt varying degrees of authority sharing and investment in organizational careers.

Institutional Frameworks, Authority Sharing, and Organizational Careers

As emphasized in earlier chapters, one of the most important factors affecting owners' willingness to share authority in market economies is the extent to which they trust the formal institutions governing economic transactions, and economic activities more generally. Where this is so low that they feel unable to rely on the legal system, accounting conventions and formal systems for assessing competence and contractual compliance to control the behaviour of customers, suppliers and employees in predictable ways, they are less likely to delegate substantial amounts of authority to relative strangers with whom they do not have strong personal bonds of loyalty and reciprocity. Additionally, in paternalist political cultures that justify leadership more in terms of elites' superior abilities to look after the best interests of the population than through their formally credentialed expertise or by success in formally governed electoral competitions (Beetham, 1991), owners tend to consider employees as unqualified to exercise discretion.

Such low levels of trust in formal institutions are often associated with predatory states and unpredictable financial systems. Where state elites are unwilling to allow the growth of large concentrations of privately controlled capital and/or seek to extract substantial amounts of surplus for their own benefit, owners are faced with a highly uncertain political and economic context in which personal connections are often the only reliable means of ensuring trust and predictable behaviour. The legal system in such countries is either very limited in its ability to resolve disputes, or liable to render capricious and unpredictable judgements.

Many industrializing countries, and those undergoing radical institutional change such as the former state socialist societies of Eastern Europe in the early 1990s, exemplify this kind of institutional context (Fafchamps, 1996; Humphrey and Schmitz, 1998; Menkhoff, 1992; Whitley and Czaban, 1998; Whitley *et al.*, 1996). When business owners do develop alliances and partnerships in such economies, these are usually based on personal ties, and are family-like if not actually based on close kinship links, as in Taiwan and other Pacific-Asian societies (Gates, 1996; Hamilton, 1997; Hamilton and Kao, 1990). They also tend to be quite limited in scope, so that owner-managers are not exposed to high levels of risk by such shared commitments.

In these relatively particularistic business environments, authority tends to remain highly concentrated and personal, and commitments to impersonal collective enterprises very limited. Organizational structures are usually fluid, without a stable set of positions that could constitute a career for ambitious skilled workers and managers, and highly dependent on the personal decisions and judgements of the owner-manager, as in many Chinese family businesses (see, e.g. Redding, 1990; Silin, 1976). Incentives for long-term organizational commitment are dependent on personal ties and often restricted to the immediate family or those with whom family-like connections have been developed. Collective problem solving is therefore dependent on the direct authority of the owner-manager, and limited to a small proportion of the workforce. Firms are often organized as isolated autocracies in such market economies.

In contrast, where the dominant institutions governing economic activities are more reliable and patterns of authority are less paternalistic, owners may well feel able to share authority with some employees and business partners and establish organizational careers. However, how much they do so, and with whom, varies considerably between market economies with different political, financial and labour market institutions. As a result, the sorts of organizations and the nature of their capabilities that become established in societies with contrasting institutional regimes vary considerably.

The key features of institutional regimes that affect variations in authority sharing and organizational careers concern the support they provide for firms to enter into continued commitments with business partners, including employees, and their limitation of rapid exit from them. In general, the more financiers, managers, and skilled workers are locked-in to each others' destinies the less likely they are to act opportunistically and seek short-term advantages through changing business partners. Institutional frameworks that encourage such lock-in therefore reduce the risks associated with long-term commitments and so facilitate both authority sharing and the development of organizational careers. They can also, though, inhibit firms' ability to adapt to radical technological and market change.

Extending the analysis presented in earlier chapters, four main features of institutional regimes that help to explain variations in authority sharing and organizational careers across industrialized market economies can be identified. First, the extent and nature of the state's provision of collective competition goods and concern to constrain short-term economic opportunism. Second, the cohesion and organizational basis of business associations. Third, the strength of the market for corporate control. Fourth, the organization and effectiveness of the skill formation system and its links to labour market institutions.

Since the provision of organizational careers for key employees typically involves delegating considerable task autonomy to them, we can explore how these institutional features affect employers' willingness to delegate discretion to different groups of employees and to develop long-term organizational careers for them by combining these two organizational characteristics. In addition to the low levels of authority sharing and provision of organizational careers characteristic of particularistic business environments, there are at least four distinct combinations of some authority sharing and careers that can be readily identified. The first combines high levels of discretion over task organization and performance with professional careers that limit the extent of organizational commitment. The second restricts delegation and long-term organizational careers to managerial and expert employees, while the other two extend both discretion and careers to skilled employees, but organize careers differently. The expected connections between these four types and the four key features of institutional regimes are summarized in Table 6.3 and will now be discussed.

Considering first the role of the state in supporting economic development and limiting opportunism, as described earlier this can vary considerably across market economies in ways that affect the extent of cooperation between firms and their ability to share risks, both with

Table 6.3. Connections between institutional features, authority sharing, and types of organizational careers

Institutional features	Types of Authority Sharing and Careers				
	High delegation and professional team careers	Considerable delegation and organizational careers limited to managers	Considerable delegation to skilled staff and functionally specialized careers	Considerable delegation to skilled staff and generalist organizational careers
State support for coordinated development and limits on opportunism	Negative or neutral	Varies	Positive	Positive
Strength of business and employers' associations	Negative	Negative or neutral	Positive	Positive
Strength of market for corporate control	Positive	Positive	Negative	Negative
Strength of professions and public education system for certified skills	Positive	Positive	Varies	Negative
Effectiveness of employer–union controlled public training system	Negative	Negative	Positive	Negative
Segmented, enterprise-based unions and training	Negative	Negative	Varies	Positive

state agencies and with each other. In particular, an important aspect of such state support is the implementation of what Ergas (1987) has termed 'diffusion' technology policies that encourage widespread diffusion of new knowledge and practices throughout an industry so that all firms can engage in technological upgrading. Through state support for collaborative research projects, subsidy of public and quasi-public laboratories, joint setting of technical standards and the dissemination of new information, such policies attempt to improve the general standard of technological competence rather than leaving it to individual firms to develop new knowledge and appropriate rewards as separate entities. Sometimes, states delegate considerable authority to business associations to organize research projects and gain access to public support for technology development on behalf of their members, as in Germany (Abramson *et al.*, 1997).

In general, the more that states provide these kinds of collective competition goods and limit short-term opportunism, the more firms are likely to work together in developing new technologies and opportunities and to plan long-term investments. Owners and managers thus share more authority between themselves and reduce risks of opportunistic behaviour in economies with coordinating states. This provides a relatively stable basis for establishing organizational careers for skilled staff and investing in their training. Because the state here encourages cooperation and mutual commitment between firms, they are more likely to feel able to enter into commitments with many employees than in societies where the state operates more at arms' length from companies and opportunistic behaviour remains considerable.

State encouragement of national business associations to collaborate in policy development and implementation is an important factor in the institutionalization of strong business and employer associations. These are a significant feature of the business environment that encourages employer–employee commitment by restricting opportunistic behaviour by both member companies and employees. Particularly if wage rates and other aspects of employment relationships are agreed centrally, either at the industry or national level, and firms are constrained from poaching skilled staff by offering higher wages, employers are encouraged to develop quite long-term commitments to employees. This is enhanced by strong regulatory frameworks governing employment relations in many of the more coordinated market economies of Continental Europe. In contrast, economies with weak employers' groups and fragmented bargaining practices have few institutional constraints on employer or employee opportunism and so do not encourage long-term commitments between them.

Additionally, where there are strong legal restraints on unilateral employer actions and strategies, such as the Works Constitution Acts in Germany and European legislation on works councils' rights, employees are more likely to believe in employers' commitments and themselves engage in long-term joint problem solving and firm-specific knowledge development. According to Streeck (1992), the expansion of co-determination in Germany has encouraged continuous retraining and redeployment of the labour force as both managers and workers become more committed to the success of the firm and internal labour markets dominate external ones. In his words (1992: 163): 'Acceptance by the workforce of rapid technological change, flexible work organization and high internal mobility is required to ensure the competitive edge and the economic success of the enterprise on which, in the last instance, the realization of the employment guarantee depends.' The importance of organizational careers for most employees has hence been increased by the expansion of such formal joint governance structures.

The third feature of institutional frameworks that is likely to affect authority sharing and employer–employee commitments is the nature of the financial system and in particular whether it facilitates a strong market for corporate control. The combination of liquid capital markets, legal and other restrictions on managers' ability to develop strong defensive measures against hostile takeovers, and fragmented shareholdings in outsider-based financial systems results in a strong market for corporate control that limits investor-manager commitments and reduces the credibility of long-term career incentives (Tylecote and Conesa, 1999). Where capital is impatient and volatile it is difficult to convince skilled employees to become committed to the long-term development of a particular firm's organizational capabilities.

In contrast, insider-based financial systems are characterized by relatively small and illiquid capital markets and much greater concentrations of shareholder control over large companies. Here it is much more difficult to transfer ownership and change direction radically, especially if significant proportions of firms' shares are held by strategic investors and/or are effectively controlled by top managers, as is the case in many European countries (Barca and Becht, 2001) and Japan (Sheard, 1994). Such stability encourages longer-term employer–employee commitments, and indeed other long-term strategies. In general, where firms are committed to long-term alliances with suppliers, customers and other members of enterprise groups through mutual shareholdings, links with banks and other financial institutions, and regular exchanges of information and personnel, as in the alliance capitalism of Japan (Gerlach, 1992; Lincoln and Gerlach, 2004), they are more likely to make credible long-term commitments to employees. Such alliances additionally of course facilitate collective control of labour markets and restrict employee opportunism.

Lastly, the skill formation systems of market economies vary considerably in ways that, together with labour market institutions, affect the kinds of skills developed, social identities and organizational commitments. At least three distinct kinds of education and training systems can be distinguished that encourage increasing levels of employer–employee commitment in conjunction with other features of labour market control. First, the relatively unstandardized and variously controlled skill development and certification system found in many liberal or arms' length societies. Second, the much more standardized and wide-ranging public training systems of many continental European societies, which often involve highly influential labour unions, and third the highly selective educational system and 'segmented', employer-based training practices developed in Japan and some other countries (Crouch *et al.*, 1999; Finegold and Wagner, 1999; Thelen and Kume, 2001).

In the first kind of skill formation system, general educational success is more valued than the acquisition of practical skills, which are developed and controlled by a variety of public and private agencies including professional elites. Certified practical skills tend to be 'owned' and developed by individuals who invest in particular training programmes provided by relatively autonomous educational institutions without much involvement of employers or unions. Skills are often generic across firms, and sometimes industries, as in the case of accountancy and some other business services, and are rarely tied to specific organizational arrangements. In terms of the problems they deal with, though, they can be quite specialized, especially when controlled by practitioners. In such cases, workers identify strongly with their professional expertise, particularly when occupational associations combine trade union functions with those of technical societies, as in the UK.

As a result, managers can find it difficult to develop cooperation across functional boundaries tied to such skills, and to develop organizational career paths (Child *et al.*, 1983). Because most skilled staff in these sorts of economies owe their primary loyalty to their profession, they will be reluctant to invest in developing firm-specific skills and acquiring firm-specific knowledge. Even when employers establish internal labour markets and organizational careers, many may prefer to remain technical specialists if such careers require professionals to abandon their technical identity in favour of a more managerial one, as did some British engineers (Watson, 1976). Such attitudes and behaviour limit employers' willingness to share authority with professional employees, which of course further restricts the latters' commitment to develop firm-specific knowledge and skills, as well as other staff. While innovative firms rely on the specialist skills of these staff to develop new products and improve process technologies, they cannot assume that professionals will readily transfer across functions and dilute their specialist skills by working in cross-functional teams to deal with organization-specific problems.

Second, in more solidaristic training systems, such as that developed in Germany (Thelen, 2004; Thelen and Kume, 2001), employers, unions, and state agencies together organize and control strong skill formation systems that develop highly valued standardized skills for a majority of the labour force. These form the basis for strong occupational identities in both large and small companies. Here, pride in one's publicly certified expertise is considerable, and encourages loyalty as much to horizontally defined occupational groups as to vertical authority hierarchies constituting firms. Such skills additionally facilitate mobility between companies and the institutionalization of active labour markets within particular occupational boundaries (Hinz, 1999). However, in many continental European countries this mobility is restrained by strong employers' associations and centralized wage bargaining organized on a sectoral basis, as well as by legal constraints on unilateral employer actions.

Overall, the systematic involvement of sectorally based employers in the standardized system of skill formation here ensures that skills are valued by firms and fit into their particular systems for organizing and coordinating work. Consequently, firms should find it easier to use and coordinate specialist skills in such economies than when they are controlled solely by state agencies or practitioner elites. Together with regulatory barriers to firing staff in market turndowns, and industry wide barriers to hiring new skills from competitors, these factors mean that both firms and workers in these kinds of societies have strong incentives to improve individual and collective skills within current technological trajectories and industry boundaries. Organizational careers are here encouraged by extensive employer–union collaboration within each industry that ties firms and workers into a common destiny.

Employers in these circumstances are encouraged to establish organizational career paths for skilled employees to advance along, so contributing to the development of firm-specific knowledge and skills on top of their standardized expertise. Careers and identities are accordingly structured by both certificated skills and organizational hierarchies. Because of the widespread diffusion of new knowledge, technologies and skills throughout each sector, firms in these kinds of coordinated market economies seek to differentiate themselves in terms of products and market niches, and to construct distinctive competences through the organizational coordination and development of skilled staff. They therefore invest considerably in developing skilled workers' commitments to construct such capabilities, but the strong commitment to certified professional expertise in these societies often restricts the amount of job rotation across major departments and cross–functional integration that can be implemented easily.

While gaining commitment to solving complex, organization-specific problems should be easier in such environments than in arm's length ones, skilled workers may well resist transfers across occupational labour markets. Accordingly, developing highly firm-specific capabilities on a long-term basis that threaten established occupational identities will be difficult in such societies. As Herrigel and Sabel (1999: 93) suggest in the case of Germany:

the craft system itself involves hierarchy and fragmentation: divisions between separate *Berufe* are considered to be virtually natural division within the production process and in the system of social differentiation in society. Masters, moreover, are the superiors of apprentices and of newer and younger skilled workers within their *Beruf*.

Similarly, Crouch *et al.* (1999: 148) suggest that: 'today ... the training which equips workers with this kind of occupational identity is providing a static concept of the occupation that can run counter to the flexibility required of new firms'. However, some German firms faced with intense foreign competition and technological change have managed, with considerable difficulty, to break down these kinds of boundaries (see also Finegold and Wagner, 1999).

Third, in market economies where the educational system strongly selects children and young adults for different positions in the labour market through academic examinations, and the public training system is relatively poorly developed and/or low in prestige, skill-based occupational identities are weaker (Marsden, 1999: 121–38). Firms here rely on the educational system to select and train workers in general competences that they can build upon during the course of a working lifetime. Because the strong business associations characteristic of many such societies restrict poaching and limit free riders' ability to appropriate skills developed by competitors, both employers and employees make considerable investments in collective competence development through organizational careers, especially in the larger firms. Authority sharing in the larger firms in these kinds of collaborative institutional frameworks is often considerable because both managers and workers are highly dependent on the growth of the firm, and jointly develop distinctive competitive capabilities. Such interdependence tends, however, to be lower in smaller firms where labour turnover is greater and skills less organization specific.

The lack of strong horizontal occupational identities based on certified expertise and reinforced by skill-based unions here facilitates job rotation across functional groups, as well as cooperation between them, so that innovation development and implementation are, in principle, faster and more effective than where functional boundaries are reinforced by publicly standardized skills. Expertise therefore becomes highly firm specific in large companies in such economies as both managers and core workers invest in the long-term development and improvement of distinctive organizational capabilities. Firms thereby establish strong organizational cultures, but may also share authority with long-term business partners to ensure continuous acquisition and use of new knowledge and cooperation with firms possessing complementary capabilities.

Conclusions: Institutional Frameworks and Organizational Capabilities

This analysis suggests that market economies with different combinations of these institutional features will encourage firms to share authority and develop organizational careers to varied extents, and so generate different kinds of organizational capabilities that are likely to be more or less effective in different kinds of industries. For example, firms with strong competences in the integration of complex forms of knowledge and advanced skills to develop and commercialize systemic technologies are unlikely to be successfully established in societies where trust in formal institutions is low and the state is antagonistic to independent control of major economic activities. Rather, companies in these sorts of contexts are more likely to compete by being highly flexible to be able to deal with an uncertain environment, and responding rapidly to changing customer requirements through centralized decision making. In particular, they will be reluctant to make substantial investments in developing organizational competences through long-term commitments to skilled staff, or to institutionalize managerial routines that might inhibit flexibility.

More systematic coordinating capabilities are more likely to be developed by firms in arms' length institutional regimes that combine regulatory states with liquid capital markets. These features encourage owners to delegate some authority to salaried managers by providing a more predictable environment for investments than where the legal system is unreliable and/or corrupt, as well as an educational system that identifies the more academically able and offers a range of publicly certified skills. However, the weak business associations and strong market for corporate control often found in these kinds of market economy provide few incentives for long-term inter-firm cooperation or widespread investment in developing firm-specific problem solving skills and knowledge. The largely adversarial and fragmented relationships between economic actors typical of such societies prevent lock-in effects and limit the effectiveness of attempts to sanction opportunistic behaviour. In particular, the focus on professional careers and low institutional support for long-term employer–employee commitment here limit professionals' willingness to subsume their specialist identities under more organizationally specific groupings and activities.

The limited authority sharing characteristic of these kinds of market economy restricts skilled workers' contributions to problem solving and hence the ease of developing continual improvements to production processes and innovating by upgrading products on a continuing basis. The Chandlerian firm is a typical product of such an environment in which coordination of specialists takes place through the managerial hierarchy and its routines, rather than at the project level, and unilateral decision making is more common than joint problem solving and development. Accordingly, the ability of firms to develop strong organizational learning capabilities is often quite restricted by this kind of business environment.

However, the strong market for corporate control here enables firms to buy and sell units relatively easily, and the fluid labour markets pose few restrictions on managers hiring and firing people to change their skills and capabilities. Depending on the rigidity of managerial routines and procedures, as well as the significance of managerial loyalties, then, this kind of institutional framework can facilitate considerable restructuring of firms' assets and resources, although these obviously take some time to generate novel organization-specific capabilities. These kinds of institutional frameworks also enable firms to develop radical, transformative innovations and technologies when the state and other agencies, such as universities, invest in producing new technological knowledge and research skills on a large scale. In the case of the US biotechnology and computer hardware and software industries, direct and indirect state support was critical to their rapid development (see, e.g., Kenney, 1986; Langlois and Mowery, 1996; Leslie, 2000; McKelvey, 1996; Saxenian, 1994).

More coordinated institutional frameworks restrict opportunism to a greater extent and encourage higher levels of authority sharing within and between companies. As a result, owners, managers and skilled employees become more willing to invest in the relatively long-term development of organization-specific problem solving skills and knowledge. In these circumstances skilled workers are more likely to pursue organization-specific careers than to concentrate on enhancing individual expertise for external labour markets because employers are more inhibited from adopting very short-term labour management strategies. Coordinated market economies with these kinds of institutions, coupled with credit-based financial systems that encourage close ties between capital providers and users as well as supportive state policies, therefore tend to develop collaborative types of large firms that have strong coordinating and learning capabilities. Such firms are likely to be quite effective in sectors where the precise coordination of complementary activities and the continuous improvement of production and development processes are crucial to their competitive success, as in the car assembly industry.

Firms in these sorts of societies, however, are less likely to be effective where technical and market uncertainty are high, so that neither the outcomes of development projects, nor the nature of skills required to undertake them, can be reliably predicted in advance, because their ability to reconfigure their skills radically is restricted. As a result, many companies in countries such as Germany focus on developing incremental, cumulative innovations that depend on employee commitment and firm-specific knowledge in new industries such as biotechnology and internet software (Casper, 2000; Casper and Glimstedt, 2001).

Variations in skill formation and certification systems between these kinds of coordinated market economies affect the strength of occupational identities and the institutionalization of occupational labour markets. Consequently, the ease of obtaining skilled workers' commitment to collective competence development that threatens such identities as well as reputations for high levels of individual expertise is likely to be lower in countries with strong public training systems and powerful expertise-based unions. This may affect the speed with which knowledge, skills and activities can be integrated across functional departments, and so the rate of new product development and introduction.

Continuing job rotation across functions and use of cross-functional problem solving teams to build firm-specific knowledge and capabilities should be more straightforward in societies where practical skills are largely developed inside companies and unions are either weak or predominantly based on enterprises, as in postwar Japan. If individuals have few externally certified skills that are generic across employers, they become highly dependent upon the growth of their firm and so are much more willing to invest in gaining knowledge of all a company's operations and contributing across specialist boundaries in order to progress. However, such generalist organizational careers may inhibit the acquisition and use of new knowledge and skills from cognitively distant sources.

In summary, variations in authority sharing and organizational careers connect differences in institutional frameworks to the generation of distinct kinds of organizational capabilities. These capabilities in turn affect firms' competitive effectiveness in different sub-sectors, especially their ability to develop cumulative or radical innovations, such that economies with contrasting institutional arrangements develop relative strengths and weaknesses in different kinds of industries. In particular, employers' establishment of distinctive types of organizational careers in variously coordinated market economies influence employees' willingness to commit themselves to the continuous improvement of firms' knowledge and collective problem solving capacities, and hence enhance companies' learning capabilities. These relationships will now be explored in more detail through an analysis of how different kinds of firms develop innovative organizational capabilities in different institutional environments, and so affect patterns of technological and sectoral specialization in differently organized market economies.

7

Developing Innovative Competences in Different Institutional Frameworks

Introduction

This analysis of how key features of dominant institutional regimes encourage owners and managers of leading firms to develop different kinds of organizational capabilities can be integrated with the account of innovation systems presented in Chapter 3 to help explain how different institutional frameworks lead to contrasting patterns of technological development through their structuring of firms' innovation strategies and competences. While the connections between institutions, firms and innovation patterns have been explored in a number of papers contrasting the technological and sectoral specialization of Germany, the USA and some other countries in the last few decades of the twentieth century (see, e.g. Casper, 2000; Culpepper, 2001; Soskice, 1999), these have tended to rely on an overly stylized contrast of coordinated and liberal market economies (Crouch, 2005).

Additionally, as the literature on national innovation systems has emphasized, the increasing importance of academic research skills and knowledge in the development of new industries (see, e.g. Cohen *et al.*, 2003; Mansfield, 1995; Narin *et al.*, 1997) means that variations in the dominant institutions governing the development and use of research skills also have significant consequences for the rate and type of technical changes in different market economies. Differences in the rate of movement of scientists and engineers between the public research system and private firms, and between firms, also affect the flow of knowledge and skills throughout the economy (Riccaboni *et al.*, 2003). These variations are especially important in industries where product and process changes are dependent upon the integration of knowledge from different scientific fields, as they seem to be in many of the newer sectors (Brown and Duguid, 2000; Cohen and Fields, 2000; Gambardella, 1995).

In this chapter I suggest how we can extend and integrate the analysis of innovation systems presented in Chapter 3 and the account of how different firms develop different kinds of organizational capabilities outlined in the previous chapter to explain how leading firms in differently organized market economies develop distinctive innovative competences and strategies. Differences in these strategies reflect the pressures and possibilities of different institutional environments, especially constraints on opportunism, the nature of the public training system and a number of features of the public science system.

Initially, I shall discuss four major differences in how innovating firms develop distinctive competences. These are connected to variations in the kinds of innovations developed by different types of firms, particularly their cumulativeness and customization. The following section suggests how key features of the institutional frameworks governing labour and capital markets, as well as public science systems, encourage firms to develop innovative competences in contrasting ways, and so generate different patterns of technical change in different societies.

The Development of Innovative Competences

In comparing innovative firms across market economies, key differences between, say, new technology based firms, large integrated mass production companies and firms enmeshed in business associations, concern the ways in which they develop innovative competences. These vary considerably in terms of their relative dependence on knowledge generated internally as distinct from that obtained externally, on the one hand, and in their ability to adapt to radical technological and market change by changing organizational competences, on the other hand. These differences can be summarized in terms of four sets of choices that help to distinguish the innovation strategies of leading German, Japanese, US, and other firms in the post-Second-World-War period.

The first key choice concerns whether firms concentrate on developing innovative competences internally, keeping knowledge production and skill development in house, or prefer to develop them in cooperation with external agencies and business partners. Second, if external partners are involved in developing innovative capabilities, are these to be the organizations and personnel working in the public science system, or those in the same industry and using similar technologies, or both? A third major choice concerns how much innovative firms invest in the development of firm-specific organizational capabilities and problem-solving routines, as distinct from relying upon more individual specialist skills that are generic across companies. Fourth, how flexible are firms in responding to new knowledge and techniques, and how able and willing are they to change technological trajectories in the short to medium term?

Considering first the decision about whether to develop knowledge production and technical problem-solving competences internally, or to involve other organizations and groups on a continuing basis, firms that rely primarily upon their own organizational resources ensure that ownership is secured and spillover risks are minimized. In theory, such internal development also facilitates the integration of varied skills and competences through a unified authority structure based on ownership. It does, though, limit access to, and integration of, new knowledge and skills that do not easily fit into the firm specific technological framework, as well as restricting learning from suppliers and customers. As a result, firms that focus on developing innovation capabilities internally are more likely to have difficulties in incorporating varied kinds of new knowledge, and to produce generic rather than customer-specific products and services. Such isolation from business partners and public researchers can be particularly disadvantageous in sectors where the rate of technical change is high and dependent on a wide variety of knowledges from different fields produced with different research skills. In newly emerging industries especially, reliance on external sources of knowledge and research skills is often considerable, as is perhaps most clearly seen in the development of biotechnology firms (Kenney, 1986; McKelvey et al., 2004).

For firms that do decide to develop innovative competences in cooperation with external partners, there are important differences between types of such partners that affect how these relationships are managed and the sorts of innovations that they generate. In particular, there are significant contrasts in how firms cooperate with agencies in the public science system, on the one hand, and with organizations in the same industry, on the other hand. These reflect major contrasts in research objectives and the types of knowledge produced. In considering how companies cooperate with external agencies, then, it is important to distinguish between cooperation with researchers in the public science system and that with industry partners.

The principal differences between involvement with the public science system and with business partners derive from the quite different institutional frameworks governing priorities and rewards in research oriented towards publication and that focused on private use. In very broad terms, the public sciences are primarily reputational work organizations in which researchers compete with specialist colleagues around the world to make significant contributions to the collective intellectual goals of their specialism or discipline (Whitley, 2000b). This encourages them to focus on theoretically significant intellectual problems dealing with general phenomena because these have more impact on the work of colleague/competitors. As a consequence, the results, techniques and intellectual approaches involved in current research in the public sciences tend to be more generic than specific to particular materials, phenomena and technologies, and are often remote from current industrial concerns and practices. Firms wishing to access and use them have to make considerable investments in what Cohen and Levinthal (1990) term 'absorptive capacity', typically by hiring trained researchers and conducting more generic research than is required for current technological problem-solving activities.

The extent to which this idealized contrast between theory-driven generic research in the public sciences, and proprietary technological development in firms and business association laboratories, is institutionalized in practice varies across historical periods and countries. For example, in countries that pursue what Ergas (1987) has labelled 'diffusion-oriented' science and technology policies, there are a considerable number of public and semi-public organizations that focus more on technologically and industry specific research than on theory-driven topics (Abramson *et al.*, 1997). Firms can be involved in the former without being closely connected to the latter, as are many German firms that have close ties to applied research and technology transfer institutes (Herrigel, 1993; Soskice, 1997).

Similarly, in some countries the postwar separation of theory-driven public science from commercially driven private research has weakened in the last few decades of the twentieth century. Changes in patent law, state funding policies and university structures have encouraged some companies in emerging industries to become more closely involved with theoretically focused research in academic laboratories. As well as hiring trained researchers from universities, these firms increasingly rely on the latest generic knowledge produced by academics to develop new products and services, especially in the US biotechnology industry (Gambardella, 1995; Henderson *et al.*, 1999; Kenney, 1986; McKelvey, 1996). In this industry, the key research remains largely conducted in university laboratories but has been used to found new firms, often by the academics themselves, and knowledge of general biological phenomena has had direct commercial utility (McKelvey *et al.*, 2004).

In considering how firms develop different kinds of innovative competences, it is useful to elaborate the distinction between passive and active involvement in public science systems drawn in Chapter 3 by distinguishing between two levels of active involvement in terms of the degree of companies' use of current research skills and knowledge of generic phenomena and processes. We can therefore identify three patterns of firms' involvement in academic research.

First, there are firms that have only a minimal, rather passive, involvement with current research, relying essentially on scanning the published journal and patent literature for obtaining relevant scientific and technological knowledge. Many large Japanese companies seem to have followed this pattern, especially in the pharmaceutical industry (Coleman, 1999; Kneller, 1999; 2003; Westney, 1993b). Second, other firms may be more actively engaged with researchers and organizations in the public and quasi-public research system, but these are usually working on particular technologies and materials that are most relevant to firms in specific industries. A third group of firms is more directly involved in current research on generic phenomena and processes. They are concerned to access relatively general and abstract knowledge, especially the skills for producing it, to develop key competitive competences. Especially in the pharmaceutical industry, it has become increasingly important for firms to gain first mover advantages through their employees being part of the recognized network of competent contributors to general public scientific knowledge, and so to be much closer collaborators of academic scientists than hitherto (Gambardella, 1995).

These three varieties of involvement in the public science system can be termed passive, industry and technology specific, and complementary. They vary in the extent to which: (a) firms recruit trained researchers, (b) fund and participate in generic academic research, and (c) actively recruit leading engineers and scientists from the public science system. Companies that have an essentially passive involvement, for instance, tend to recruit graduates with BSc and MSc degrees rather than PhDs and post-doctoral researchers, limit financial support of academic research to consultancy payments, and rarely, if ever, hire academics in mid-career. In contrast, those that invest in complementary involvement with the public science system recruit both highly trained researchers and leading scientists, as well as funding significant research projects into the study of both generic processes and technologically focused ones. Generally, the more firms are involved in such research networks, the more they should be able to search effectively for, and use appropriately, new knowledge and skills from a wide variety of fields and disciplines (Gambardella, 1995). This obviously has implications for the sorts of innovations that they develop, the kinds of resources they use, and the risks that are involved in doing so.

Considering next the development of innovative competences in cooperation with business partners, innovating firms often gain considerable knowledge about new technologies, markets and process improvements from trade associations, industry groupings, suppliers and customers (Cohen *et al.*, 2003). Firms vary greatly, though, in the extent to which they share knowledge with business partners through membership of industry associations. In countries like Germany and Japan, for example, business groups, industry associations and similar networks often engage in joint standards setting, knowledge diffusion and technical development, as well as establishing and policing norms of appropriate firm behaviour (Culpepper, 2001; Morris-Suzuki, 1994; Odagiri and Goto, 1996; Soskice, 1997; Tate, 2001). Their members are accordingly able to access new knowledge and information more quickly than those not involved in such groupings, which can be especially advantageous to small and medium-sized companies (Herrigel, 1993).

This kind of knowledge sharing with suppliers, competitors and customers can be termed the degree of involvement in industrial collaborations. When this involvement is considerable and continuing, it encourages firms to invest more in the development of customer-specific knowledge and skills than when inter-firm relationships are more adversarial. Through such stable connections and authority sharing, firms are also likely to develop strong competences in integrating information from a variety of industry sources, and in developing innovations that are more customized than generic. Equally, though, the mutual commitments developed in industry networks will typically limit the degree of technological change undertaken by firms since radical, transformative innovations threaten current organizational competences (Christensen, 1997; Tushman and Anderson, 1986). High levels of industry network involvement, then, tend to be associated with relatively incremental innovation strategies in the sense of developing existing technological knowledge and skills.

The third aspect of competence development considered here concerns the extent to which firms rely more on the specialist skills of individuals that are generic across organizations as opposed to developing distinctly organizational capabilities based on a stable group of core employees. As discussed in the previous chapter, while all companies develop collective competences as emergent properties of each organization, the degree to which these depend on individuals' specialist expertise varies considerably. The ability of Toyota to improve production processes continuously through the results of employee commitment to joint problem solving being codified and disseminated throughout the organization represents an extreme case of core workers investing in the development of collective firm-specific knowledge and skills (Fujimoto, 2000). Elsewhere, staff are more concerned to enhance the value of their own expertise on external labour markets and so firms are here less able to build collective capabilities separately from individual skills.

For instance, the role of new firms founded by highly trained and experienced engineers and scientists in the development of the US biotechnology and computer industries has shown how relatively small and quickly formed organizations of specialist researchers and designers can play a major role in developing significant innovations. Under particular conditions, that is, the ability to create firms that integrate high level skills around specific goals can generate competitive advantages in industries undergoing high rates of technical change. Such firms depend greatly upon the skills and knowledge of project leaders and their teams of specialist staff to develop innovations, as distinct from developing distinctive collective competences that are more organizational and institutionalized into managerial routines.

Among the important conditions that encourage such reliance on individually owned and controlled specialist skills are the ease of appropriating profits from innovations, for example through patenting in the pharmaceutical industry (Gambardella, 1995), and the existence of open standards facilitating the development of modular innovations (Langlois and Robertson, 1995; Langlois and Mowery, 1996; Sturgeon, 2002). High levels of appropriability and modularity of innovations facilitate the specialization of firms in product design and development without having to invest in complementary assets in marketing and distribution (Teece, 1986).

Coordination of innovative activities in such circumstances can thus be carried out by project groups of specialist experts rather than needing extensive organizational routines and procedures. They organize their activities around teams of highly qualified specialized engineers and scientists focused on short- to medium-term innovation goals because the high levels of market and technical uncertainty in emerging industries, where such firms play a major role, limit financial and employment commitments and results have to be achieved relatively quickly. Competitive advantages and competences here derive from flexible and speedy responses to new knowledge and skills, and the ability to integrate new kinds of information and expertise to generate disruptive products and processes, especially in winner-takes-all competitions where network externalities and economies of scale of demand are high (Shapiro and Varian, 1999).

Conversely, where appropriability is difficult and/or technological change is systemic rather than modular, innovating firms tend to coordinate product development with production, marketing and other complementary activities to protect their assets and integrate components of technological systems. Such coordination usually involves the construction of formal organizations with collective capabilities because spillover risks and technical uncertainty inhibit contracting for specialist services. Knowledge production and problem-solving skills are here more organizational than individually owned and developed.

Firms in many assembly and machinery industries, for instance, typically coordinate technological and market knowledge from different sources, both within and outside the organization, to develop and commercialize innovations, and establish organizational routines to do so. Distinctive firm-specific skills develop as a result that are not tied to particular individuals' skills and contributions. These skills become entrenched in distinctive technological paradigms that guide development trajectories and how engineers tackle problems in, say, car design and aircraft development. While all work organizations, then, generate particular kinds of competences by coordinating and controlling work in a systematic manner, the extent to which these capabilities depend on the generic skills of specific individuals, as opposed to collective, organizational competences, varies considerably. This aspect of innovating firms' competences can be characterized as their dependence on the specialist skills of individuals.

The fourth aspect of competence development to be considered here concerns the speed with which, and degree to which, firms are able and willing to change their innovative capabilities and competitive competences. Many companies, for instance, diversify into new technologies and markets through developing new skills and abilities incrementally, building on existing ones, as emphasized by the dynamic capabilities approach to firm behaviour. In contrast, others are able to change their core competences more radically by hiring new staff with quite different skills, as in the case of some US pharmaceutical firms developing biological research skills (Zucker and Darby, 1997), or by acquiring companies with expertise in new technologies such as biotechnology and software start-ups. Depending on the modularity of technological systems, such acquisitions may involve quite radical changes to firms' competences and the overall architecture of their technologies.

This contrast reflects the level of firms' commitments to staff and business partners, as well as their specialization in particular technologies and industrial sectors. The more they develop distinctive competences through investments in employee training and customer-specific knowledge, the more difficult they will find it to develop radically new capabilities, and to be successful in novel and discrete technologies in emerging sectors, as argued by Rosenbloom and Christensen (1998). Technological changes made by such firms will, then, tend to be incremental and customer-focused rather than generic and transformational. This aspect of innovative competence development can be described as the rapidity of competence transformation.

Some of these alternative modes of developing innovative competences are mutually independent. For example, involvement in public science networks can be combined with varying degrees of involvement in industry associations. Firms can develop close connections with public and private research organizations, hire PhDs and participate actively in scientific and technological conferences and technical exchanges, and yet fail to form powerful industry associations or long-term ties with customers and suppliers. Many firms in the US computer hardware and software, and biotechnology, industries seem to combine such considerable technical involvement in the research community with largely adversarial and autarchic inter-firm relationships (Chesbrough, 1999).

Similarly, high levels of industry embeddedness and inter-firm dependence, as in many Japanese industries in the postwar period, can be combined with largely autonomous knowledge development in relative isolation from the public science system. Most large Japanese firms, for instance, have restricted their academic contacts to hiring engineers and scientists with MScs rather than PhDs and informal research support for individual professors on a relatively small scale (Coleman, 1999; Kneller, 1999; Westney, 1993b; Yoshihara and Tamai, 1999). On the other hand, many German firms in the chemical and engineering industries seem to combine strongly coordinated technical exchanges within industry sectors with close connections to applied research organizations such as the Fraunhofer Gesellschaft laboratories and technical schools (Herrigel, 1993; Lehrer, 2000).

Other choices, however, are more interconnected. High levels of involvement in industry collaborations, for instance, tend to lock firms into current technological trajectories and sectoral boundaries. This is because firms that share information and risks with industry partners need to be fairly sure that business partners are equally committed to the industry and improving current technologies, so that opportunistic use of such information and resources can be meaningfully sanctioned by loss of reputation. Where companies restrict such commitments, and can change their competences quite radically through hiring and firing, other firms will not be willing to share important resources with them. Strong and continuing collaborations with industry partners, then, encourage relatively cumulative development of innovative competences within firms, and not the introduction of competence-destroying innovations. This limits their ability to change innovative competences radically, as well as inhibiting their capacity to absorb quite different forms of new knowledge.

Equally, firms able and willing to transform their capabilities radically are unlikely to invest greatly in developing strong collective competences through organizational routines, unless perhaps they change the nature of the firm through buying and selling whole businesses. This suggests that companies that institutionalize career paths for core employees, such as managers and senior technical experts, as a way of gaining their commitment to developing firm-specific knowledge and capabilities that are not dependent on individual skills, will not usually radically transform their competences.

On the other hand, those pursuing incremental innovation strategies that build on current skills can either rely heavily on the specialist knowledge of individuals or on more collective competences, depending on their ability to access complementary assets and the modularity of their innovations. Similarly, small firms that depend on the specialist skills of their employees can develop either incremental or radical innovations in different situations, as the comparison of craft-based businesses in Italy and Denmark with Silicon Valley-type firms shows.

Given these interconnections between some of the choices that firms make in developing innovative competences, four major combinations of involvement in public science and industry networks with varying reliance on individuals' generic skills and ability to transform competences can be distinguished, as summarized in Table 7.1. These are ideal

Table 7.1. Approaches to developing innovative competences

Characteristics of Competence Development	Isolated Hierarchy	Flexible Teams	Cumulative Commitment	Highly Collaborative
Involvement in public science networks	Passive	Complementary	Passive	Technologically specific
Involvement in industry networks	Low	Low	High	High
Dependence on specialist skills of individuals	Limited	High	Low	Low
Rapidity of competence transformation	Limited, but potentially considerable through acquisitions	High	Low	Low
Innovation pattern	Cumulative, generic, except when restructuring organization	Transformative, generic, modular	Cumulative, market-driven	Cumulative, building on new technologically specific knowledge, customer-focused

types of strategies for developing innovative competences that are encouraged to varying degrees by different institutional frameworks. In practice, of course, individual firms can follow different combinations, but the ones discussed here do reflect four particular approaches to technical change that seem prevalent in different kinds of market economy such as those of postwar Germany, Japan and contrasting sectors in the USA (Casper, 2000; Coleman, 1999; Kenney and Florida, 2000; Kneller, 2003; Soskice, 1997).

First, the type of approach that focuses on largely internal innovation development with little continuing involvement with either the public science system or industry partners can be termed the isolated hierarchy mode of developing innovative competences.

Second, the flexible team approach adopted by many project-based firms in new industries combines complementary forms of involvement with public research institutions with arms' length relations with suppliers, customers and competitors, and short-term commitments between employers and employees.

In contrast, the third, cumulative commitment, approach to developing innovative competences combines close relationships with industry partners, and high levels of employer–employee commitment, with little involvement with current research projects and teams in the public science system. A variant of this combination occurs in coordinated industrial districts where smaller firms both cooperate and compete with each other, and rely on a range of territorially specific agencies for general services, but do not usually develop close links with public researchers, or offer long-term careers to skilled employees. Finally, the approach that involves the greatest cooperation with external partners, both in the more technologically and industry specific parts of the public science system and in their industrial sectors, can be termed highly collaborative. This also involves substantial employer–employee commitment.

The isolated hierarchy approach to developing distinctive innovative competences relies heavily upon internal resources and so produces highly firm-specific knowledge and skills, often codified into managerial routines. Organizational boundaries are here quite strong and relatively impermeable. Problem-solving competences and procedures in these kinds of firms are usually strongly institutionalized, with limited openness to new knowledge and skills from outside. They thus develop collective technological approaches and frameworks that depend relatively little upon the skills and knowledge of individuals. In principle, though, their isolation from business partners enables them to change technologies quite radically by acquiring new skills and/or businesses if the institutions governing capital and labour markets facilitate such restructuring, as in the UK and the USA.

The predominantly internal focus of knowledge production and innovation development in isolated hierarchies means that their ability to integrate quite different kinds of knowledge and research skills is limited, with new recruits usually being expected to fit into the dominant way of thinking. Except when top managers deliberately restructure the technological paradigm by acquiring new organizations and skills and selling or sacking current ones, then, such firms tend to limit the variety and novelty of new knowledge that is integrated into development programmes. Similarly, their relative lack of close involvement with the public science system restricts their ability to develop innovations on the basis of new generic knowledge and skills, at least before it has been published, as well as their capacity to take advantage of new techniques and skills.

Additionally, their low level of commitment to suppliers and customers limits their investment in customer-specific knowledge and technologies, and implies a preference for more generic innovations. As Chesbrough (1999) has pointed out, the reluctance of IBM to become dependent on particular suppliers of disk drive storage products, and its willingness to change them if others offered better technical specifications and/or lower prices, discouraged firms such as Seagate from investing substantial sums in technical research to meet IBM's needs. Clearly, there is little incentive for them to develop customer-specific innovations if customers are likely to switch suppliers abruptly.

Flexible team approaches, on the other hand, focus on producing quite novel innovations, which are often disruptive, in rapidly emerging technologies and industries. They combine complementary involvement in public science research networks with a willingness to change key skills and knowledge bases at short notice to deal with high levels of technical uncertainty. This implies a low level of commitment to current industry partners. Such uncertainty also means that investment in developing distinctly organizational capabilities over the medium to long term would be highly risky for these firms. Instead, they rely on specialist experts to work together in project teams to develop generic products for largely anonymous markets, often with relatively high-powered incentives, as in many project-based firms in Silicon Valley and elsewhere (Ferguson, 1999; Kenney and Florida, 2000).

As Angel (2000:128) suggests: 'The ease with which firms in Silicon Valley are able to assemble and reassemble teams of highly skilled engineers and technical workers, and the knowledge and experience they embody, are central to the technological dynamics and commercial success of the region.' Because the risk of project failure is high in such emerging industries, employees have little incentive to commit themselves to developing firm-specific skills, and both firms and staff have a common interest in developing and improving more generic skills that can be readily recognized and traded in fluid external labour markets.

This kind of approach has been facilitated by the growing importance of generic knowledge of general processes and phenomena that can be applied to a range of materials. Gambardella (1995), for example, sees the growing use of molecular biology and genetic engineering in pharmaceutical R&D as increasing the dependence of drug discovery on generic sources of knowledge that are quite codified and can be traded between firms. In these circumstances, research-focused firms are likely to be more closely involved in public research networks than innovative firms relying more on specific forms of knowledge, especially where the public science system is relatively organizationally fluid and technical labour markets are well established.

Although generic knowledge is often more codified and formalized than specific understandings of process technologies and applications, the skills that produce it are usually quite tacit, as the process of engineering human growth hormone illustrates (McKelvey, 1996). This means that the more firms rely on new generic knowledge of fundamental processes— i.e. unpublished and in process—the more they will either conduct such research themselves, or develop close alliances with research teams in the public science system. As innovations become more closely dependent on generic knowledge, then, firms can no longer rely on remote and formal access to the scientific and technological literature, but have to become more involved in acquiring and managing the relevant skills themselves.

The cumulative commitment approach, in contrast, combines extensive involvement in industry networks with the development of strong collective and organization-specific skills to produce technologically cumulative innovations. This emphasis on the rapid development of new products through integrated research, development, manufacturing and marketing activities at the expense of developing more generic specialist research skills, as in many large Japanese companies (Westney, 1993b), may well prevent firms from gaining close access to current research and skills in the public science system. This is because careers and other rewards in such firms are more tied to long-term investment in firm-specific knowledge and organizational skills than to competence in producing generic knowledge and collaborating with university researchers. Firms adopting this approach apply formal scientific and technological knowledge that is already in the public domain to achieve product development goals, and rely on organizationally-specific knowledge and skills to bring new products to market faster than their competitors.

This concentration on competence coordination within the firm and group, often through quasi-lifetime employment for core staff, little or no mid-career recruitment, and systematic rotation of researchers and engineers through the major technologies and functions, and sometime affiliated companies, provides the basis for integrating development projects effectively, as in many large Japanese companies (Chesbrough, 1999; Kneller, 2003; Westney, 1993b). Together with their embeddedness in industry networks, it also encourages them to invest in customer-specific knowledge and enables them to develop technologies that meet their needs. These practices do, though, limit the development of highly specialized research skills and make it difficult to adopt radically new ideas and skills, as well as to change current technological paradigms that are entrenched in organizational routines, careers and cooperative agreements, in the short to medium term. It is important to note, however, that long-term strategic shifts can be implemented by such companies, as many Japanese firms demonstrated in the development of the optoelectronics industry (Miyazaki, 1995).

The more extensive highly collaborative approaches to innovative competence development adopted by absorptive hierarchies, on the other hand, combine technologically specific knowledge from the public science system with their own research and with knowledge from industry collaborations to develop new products and processes within current technological trajectories. They invest in the development of strong organizational competences and firm-specific skills to carry out this coordination, which typically restricts their ability to transform key skills quickly. Building on current competences and expertise to innovate incrementally, they have a deep organizational understanding of the dominant technology in the industry that is often remote from the intellectual approaches and concerns of more theoretically directed research in the public science system.

This involvement in both kinds of networks, together with substantial commitments to the core labour force, limits their capacity to transform their core competences radically, as well as sometimes creating coordination difficulties within the enterprise. Membership of business groups, industry associations and networks of mutually interdependent suppliers and customers helps to share risks and knowledge, but it also locks firms into current trajectories and competences, and restricts the ease with which absorptive hierarchies are able to reshape radically their organizational capabilities around highly novel skills and ideas. Similarly, their dependence on organizational routines and collective competences to develop innovations with firm-specific skills based on long-term employer–employee commitments means that such innovations will be competence enhancing rather than destroying.

Innovative Competence Development in Different Institutional Frameworks

Firms are encouraged to adopt some of these alternative ways of developing innovations, and discouraged from pursuing other ones, by particular combinations of dominant institutions in different kinds of market economies. The critical features of institutional frameworks considered here are those encouraging 'voice' rather than 'exit' modes of behaviour (Nooteboom, 2000), especially information and risk sharing between firms in developing innovations, as well as those facilitating the generation and transfer of formal and tacit knowledge of generic processes between the public research system and private enterprises.

Since the general institutional arrangements structuring economic behaviour have been extensively discussed in previous chapters, I shall here focus on two major features that directly affect inter-organizational relationships and constraints on short-term opportunism: the strength of business associations and the organization of financial flows. Then the key relationships between the organization of scientists' training and careers, the flexibility and pluralism of the sciences, and the nature of state technology policies and firms' prevalent strategies for developing innovative competences will be outlined. The links between these features of institutional frameworks and the approaches that firms adopt in different market economies are summarized in Table 7.2 and will now be further discussed. Particular kinds of institutions are listed in this table to highlight relationships between institutional arrangements and patterns of innovative competence development.

Beginning with the general features of market economies that encourage firms to develop innovative competences in different ways, as

Table 7.2. Associations between institutional features and approaches to developing innovative competences

Institutional Framework	Approach to Developing Innovative Competences			
	Isolated Hierarchy	Flexible Teams	Cumulative Commitment	Highly Collaborative
Strength of business associations and involvement in strong public training systems	Negative	Negative	Positive	Positive
Insider-dominated financial system	Negative	Negative	Positive	Positive
Size of research training system and its integration with current research	Positive	Positive	Negative	Positive
Flexibility and pluralism of public science systems	Weakly positive	Positive	Unconnected	Positive
Dominance of professional researcher role model	Positive	Positive	Negative	Somewhat negative
Strong diffusion-oriented science and technology institutions	Negative	Negative	Positive	Positive

emphasized in earlier chapters powerful business associations can play important roles in constraining short-term opportunism as well as in diffusing new technologies, establishing technical standards and generally facilitating cooperation in particular kinds of 'industrial orders' (Herrigel, 1994; 1996). In some European economies where employers' associations are also directly involved in the public skill formation system, often in collaboration with unions and state agencies, companies cooperate with each other in defining, developing and assessing publicly certified expertise on a continuing basis.

Given the limits on individual wage bargaining and restrictions on poaching in many economies that have such strong business associations, mobility between employers tends to be lower than in more arm's length market economies, and skilled workers have strong incentives to invest in enhancing their firm-specific skills (Culpepper, 2001). Equally, employers have considerable incentives to integrate workers' skills and knowledge into product and process improvements since they are unable to change them easily and, in effect, much of the labour force in countries like Germany and Japan is a fixed cost in the medium term for large firms. Labour mobility of technical staff between employers does not appear to be nearly as great in these countries as in the UK and USA, not least because the risks of changing organization are higher and the rewards less obvious (Casper, 2000; Streeck, 1997).

Likewise, employers are often constrained in many of the more coordinated market economies from rapidly changing the nature of scientific and engineering skills through hiring and firing by legal rules, works councils pressure, strong unions and collective bargaining conventions (Soskice, 1997; 1999). This means that new technologies and capabilities are built more on existing ones, and the ability of companies to access and integrate radically novel knowledge that differs strongly from existing skills will be limited in such economies.

Conversely, more arm's length institutional regimes that have a relatively weak education and training system, in the sense that it does not provide most of the population with valuable qualification and skills, encourage the academically successful to invest in skills that are generic across firms and sectors. They also lead to considerable mobility between employers. As a result, skills are more individually owned and traded in these kinds of market economies. Depending on the particular structure of higher education and the organization of professional expertise, such skills can be rather remote from employers' collective views of what is needed, and so may be differently valued by different firms. Given the greater tendency to hire and fire in these kinds of economy, this further encourages skilled staff to invest in qualifications that are generic across a range of firms and industries, such as the MBA.

In broad terms, then, firms in economies with strong trade, industry and employers' associations will be deeply embedded in industry networks that facilitate collective standards setting, joint research activities and cooperation on a range of issues. Skills in such societies are as much organizational as individual. They are also difficult to change radically in the short to medium term, although continual incremental improvement will be the norm as both employers and employees seek growth opportunities through innovations in technologically and market-related activities. This contrast in institutional arrangements can be summarized as the strength of business associations and their involvement with strong public training systems. Where this is high, firms are more likely to find it easier to share information and risks in developing innovations than in economies where such associations are fragmented and weak. Accordingly, they are more likely to adopt highly collaborative and cumulative commitment approaches to innovative competence development than flexible team and isolated hierarchy ones.

The second major institutional feature that directly affects firms' preferences for adopting different ways of developing innovative competences is the type of financial system. In general, insider-based financial systems in which major investors are locked-in to the fates of individual firms favour innovating firms that build long-term organizational competences with business partners and employees to develop new products and technologies within existing technological trajectories. Majority owners here develop detailed knowledge of each firm they control and their industry in order to evaluate risks and opportunities adequately to deal with their greater exposure. They are therefore able to judge innovation strategies and competences within established industries in a more informed way than are investors in outsider-dominated financial systems, who operate more at arm's length from individual companies. This means that they can evaluate and support incremental and long-term technological developments relatively effectively.

As Tylecote and Conesa (1999) suggest, such insider-dominated financial systems should, then, be more competitive in industries where innovations are jointly developed by employers, employees, suppliers and customers and appropriability risks are reduced by long-term alliances between key actors. Conversely, outsider-dominated ones find it easier to develop radically novel generic innovations that are competence destroying because they facilitate rapid restructuring of assets and skills, often through venture capital firms that provide high-risk capital for start-ups in industries where the returns to successful innovations are high and can be appropriated by the innovating firm and its shareholders (Kenney and Florida, 2000). They therefore are more associated with flexible team and isolated hierarchy approaches rather than highly collaborative and cumulative commitment ones.

Turning now to consider how differences in the organization and control of the public science system affect firms' approaches to developing innovative competences, a crucial feature concerns the amount and type of research training. Where this is integrated with research projects and is carried out on a large scale, as in the postwar US biomedical sciences, it reduces the costs of undertaking research and encourages the rapid diffusion of new research skills throughout the economy (Riccaboni *et al.*, 2003). As Feller (1999: 83) suggests:

Students also are a means by which new scientific findings and technologically relevant knowledge are transferred from the campus to the firm. Indeed, as new technologically relevant research findings become more embedded in the tacit know-how of students regarding laboratory procedures and software, their importance as technology transfer agents is likely to increase.

The more that research training is integrated with the production of new knowledge, and is supported on a large scale, then, the more firms are likely to acquire novel research skills and be able to change their knowledge producing and using capabilities relatively quickly. Depending on the extent to which academically constituted identities are preferred by engineers and scientists to organizational ones, such integration may additionally encourage the development of strong specialist skills that inhibit the establishment of more organizational capabilities. Conversely, in economies where either research is not integrated with training and/or the public science base is limited in size and scope, firms will find it more difficult to change their innovative competences substantially—at least in the short to medium term.

This is especially so when the number of PhD students is lower than those undertaking masters' degrees, as in Japan for much of the postwar period (Coleman, 1999; Ogura and Kotake, 1999). Despite the expansion of graduate schools at many state universities in Japan since the 1960s, most of their students have left with MScs rather than PhDs. This is because firms rarely preferred to recruit PhDs, regarding them as being too specialized and remote from commercial concerns (Westney, 1993b). In fact, not only did PhDs not receive more pay than MScs in most firms, but often they were paid less because they had less seniority with the company (Sienko, 1997; Yamamoto, 1997). Together with the limited expansion of universities and other public sector research organizations in the 1970s and 1980s, this discouraging labour market for researchers in Japan has considerably restricted the output of knowledge producers, and so the availability of novel kinds of research skills for Japanese firms.

On the whole, then, integrating research and training through doctoral programmes that are well funded facilitates involvement in public science research networks, and the development of innovation strategies based on rapid access to new knowledge and skills. Flexible team and highly collaborative approaches are therefore encouraged by such arrangements. They also provide a substantial pool of skilled researchers that can be drawn upon by isolated hierarchies, even if these firms are not concerned to become closely dependent on new knowledge generated by the public science system.

The second major feature of public science systems concerns the ease and frequency with which research scientists and engineers in the public science system are able to develop new intellectual goals, fields, and approaches, such as software engineering and molecular biology (Whitley, 2003b). Where research objectives and strategies are varied and changeable, as distinct from being tightly integrated around established disciplinary goals, frameworks and expertise, it should be easier to extend and apply new ideas and techniques for technological purposes, and to develop new areas of research with new skills. The boundaries between theory-driven scientific research and more instrumental knowledge production are more fluid, permeable and overlapping in such public science systems than in those where intellectual, skill and organizational boundaries are structured around separate disciplines.

In the more flexible research systems that have relatively low levels of organizational segmentation, firms find it easier to become involved in research networks that combine theory-driven research with more instrumental projects and organizations than they would in more stable, discipline-bound research systems. Such fluidity and adaptability of intellectual goals and skills in public science systems also generates a high level of change in ideas and expertise, which in turn enables firms to hire new kinds of skills relatively easily. Because labour markets in such systems are typically not highly separated around distinctive goals, performance standards and career paths, researchers move across employment organization boundaries fairly often, and can trade their specialist expertise between a variety of employers.

The intellectual and organizational flexibility of national research systems is additionally affected by the nature of the employment system in universities and allied organizations (Whitley, 2003b). Where individual heads of departments and research institutes exercise considerable control over resources and careers, the rate of change and variety of intellectual approaches and skills is likely to be less than in employment systems where there is greater pluralism of power and authority within administrative units.

The US, and to some extent UK, pattern of locating a number of research groups within relatively large university departments permits greater intellectual pluralism of projects than the German and Japanese pattern of individual research groups and institutes controlled by a single or couple of professors who combine scientific leadership with administrative responsibility (Clark, 1995). When this separation of intellectual production units from administrative ones is combined with extensive reliance on external funding of research projects, the power of institute heads to direct research programmes is greatly reduced and competition between groups within departments encouraged. Diversity of research goals and approaches is therefore greater in such employment systems than where control over research programmes is more centralized.

This flexibility and pluralism of national research systems affect the ease with which firms are able to develop innovation strategies based on rapid access to new knowledge and skills produced by public science systems. *Ceteris paribus,* flexible team and highly collaborative approaches to innovative competence development are more readily adopted when the organization of intellectual goals, identities, and boundaries is flexible rather than when it is structured around distinct, separate theoretical objectives that segment labour markets and administrative units. Firms that are not so concerned with integrating new generic knowledge and research skills into their development programmes are less affected by this factor, although flexible and pluralist research systems may well generate new skills that isolated hierarchies will find useful when seeking to change their competences.

A further feature of public science systems that affects the ways firms develop innovative competences concerns the extent to which professional researcher roles and identities are institutionalized. These cosmopolitan role models focus on the development of highly specialized skills that are generic across employers, and limit researchers' commitment to organizational goals. Where these models are strongly established, typically in societies with fluid external labour markets, firms find it more difficult to develop collective innovative competences on a long-term basis than in societies with stronger organizational than professional identities, such as Japan (Westney, 1993b). They are associated with the establishment of a professional labour market that enables firms to access new specialist skills and techniques, and so to develop new innovative competences and access the public science system quickly. Flexible team and isolated hierarchy approaches, then, are more likely to be adopted in societies dominated by the professional scientist model than are highly collaborative and cumulative commitment ones.

One example of a research system that combines this role model with considerable organizational flexibility is biomedical research in the late twentieth-century USA. Here, the fluidity and pluralism of employment units and funding arrangements are reinforced by the provision of considerable research resources by the state and other organizations, as well as by the NIH laboratories that provide alternative sources of employment and elite hierarchies to the leading research universities. As a result, constraints on intellectual novelty are relatively low in US biomedical fields, but the high rate of competition for scientific reputations—enhanced by substantial state delegation of control to practising scientists and by the high number of qualified researchers produced by the graduate schools

(Feller, 1999)—ensures considerable coordination of research results and a willingness to take intellectual risks.

Where the knowledge produced by this kind of research system is directly relevant to R&D activities in firms, as in biotechnology, this combination of novelty and competition in the public sciences generates a continuous stream of potentially useful research results that innovative companies have to keep up with, and hence need to be involved with research networks. They also have to be flexible and able to adapt to changes in the public knowledge base, typically by changing their skill mix and reorganizing R&D projects, as new knowledge becomes available (Casper and Kettler, 2001).

Flexible team approaches adopted by project-based firms are particularly well suited to such an environment. Indeed they are themselves more likely to develop in countries with these kinds of public science systems since the combination of intense competition for funds and reputations in pluralist intellectual and employment environments generates intellectual entrepreneurs who rapidly incorporate new results and ideas in pursuing their distinctive research agendas. Such entrepreneurs are skilled at recognizing intellectual opportunities, and combining different expertises and knowledges in the pursuit of potentially highly rewarding research goals.

National research systems that encourage intellectual competition without strong disciplinary ties and boundaries are, then, favourable to the adoption of flexible team approaches to developing innovative competences, especially when combined with fluid labour markets (Casper and Murray, 2005). Equally, those that are less competitive, and/or more constrained in the degree of intellectual change and novelty they encourage, develop different kinds of research skills and attitudes that are less flexible and adaptable. Strong disciplinary control, for example, encourages theoretical integration and highly coordinated research programmes, but inhibits interdisciplinary cooperation in project teams. Scientists trained in national research systems dominated by such control are unlikely, then, to find it as easy to work with colleagues from other fields as their counterparts trained in more fluid intellectual and organizational environments.

However, strong disciplinary control enhanced by hierarchical determination of research programmes and approaches within departments and institutes can be combined with elaborate applied research facilities and technology transfer arrangements in countries with 'diffusion-oriented' state science and technology policies, such as Germany (Abramson *et al.*,

1997). The highly collaborative approaches adopted by absorptive hierarchies here link firms to the more applied or instrumental research networks quite easily, but connections to the more generic and theoretically focused academic system are often more remote. Depending on the degree of segmentation of organizations and labour markets, this sort of system can be quite effective at rapidly diffusing new knowledge and technologies within established industrial boundaries. It is, though, less effective at coordinating the flow of knowledge and skills across such boundaries, and linking academic research goals with product development opportunities.

This highlights the importance of different state science and technology policies in the development of distinctive innovative competences. Although the contrast between 'diffusion' and 'mission' oriented state science and technology policies and practices is too simple to describe the variety of institutional arrangements and goals that states have established in the late twentieth century to manage public research, it does highlight important differences between them (Doremus *et al.*, 1998; Ergas, 1987). As emphasized in Chapter 3, a key feature of the diffusion oriented policy style is the strong collaboration between firms, business associations, state agencies and both public and private research organizations in developing and diffusing new technological knowledge. By underwriting much of the costs associated with technological research, and involving industry associations in its management, states here encourage firm involvement in the public science system.

Such involvement, however, is usually limited to work on technologies and materials that are connected to current problems and trajectories rather than with more generic research that could lead to quite different technologies. Because the primary goal here is to enhance and improve current industrial competences, diffusion oriented policies are unlikely to encourage close links with researchers engaged on more remote topics intended to produce general explanations of phenomena, especially in academic systems that are strongly structured around discrete disciplines. Since such policies are typically implemented with the help of industry associations and inter-firm alliances, they additionally reinforce firms' embeddedness in industry networks.

On the other hand, they limit the rate of change of technological competences and skills by focusing on the continual improvement of current capabilities within existing technological paradigms. Acquiring radically novel skills and knowledge to develop new products and processes in newly emerging technologies will be difficult for most firms in states pursuing such policies because they are locked into cooperative relationships with suppliers, customers, and core employees based upon the incremental upgrading of current ones. Strong 'diffusion-oriented' state science and technology policies, then, are linked to the adoption of highly collaborative and cumulative commitment approaches, as in Germany and Japan, rather than of flexible team and isolated hierarchy ones.

More 'mission-oriented' science and technology policies, conversely, encourage greater technological diversity across sectors as states invest in particular developments for public policy goals. When combined with high levels of intellectual competition, such policies increase the fluidity of research goals and skills as scientists adapt their projects to state priorities within the overall peer review system. If research additionally involves training, mission oriented policies generate large numbers of highly skilled researchers in the favoured fields who can be recruited by firms investing in developing new competences based on such knowledge.

Conclusions: Institutional Complementarities and Patterns of Technological Development

This analysis suggests how different features of institutional frameworks encourage firms to adopt distinctive approaches to developing innovative competences. As discussed in Chapters 2 and 3, some of these features are themselves interrelated to constitute distinctive institutional regimes that help to explain how particular kinds of market economies are associated with contrasting patterns of technical change and sectoral specialization.

For example, many, if not most, market economies dominated by arm's length institutional regimes establish quite strong professional researcher role models and labour markets. Together with liquid capital markets and fluid markets for corporate control, the lack of strong business and employers' associations in such economies discourages firms from sharing risks and knowledge with suppliers and customers, and from developing long-term commitments with technical employees. As a consequence, there is little incentive for engineers and scientists to invest in firm-specific skills, but considerable encouragement for them to improve specialist skills that are generic across organizations. Since such societies are often characterized by strong professional identities and conceptions of high-level expertise based on generic knowledge that are credentialed and controlled by professional associations independent of the state, the professional researcher model usually dominates that of the organizational researcher here.

Additionally, diffusion-oriented state science and technology policies and institutions are often associated with strong industrial associations as the state typically involves them in diffusing technological knowledge, developing research programmes and establishing standards. Mission-oriented policies and agencies, on the other hand, can encourage flexibility in public science systems when combined with decentralization of resource allocation decisions through a peer review system, but need not always do so, as the case of France indicates. These sorts of science and technology policies are, then, quite consonant with different types of financial systems and labour market institutions, as the comparison of Britain, France, and the USA demonstrates.

The implications of these interconnections can be summarized by considering three particular combinations of institutional arrangements that lead to firms adopting contrasting ways of developing innovative competences: arm's length with strong mission-oriented science and technology policies, coordinated knowledge production and coordinated knowledge acquisition institutional frameworks. These highlight many of the key features of the postwar market economies of the USA, Germany and Japan. The first combines weak forms of market organization, outsider-dominated financial systems, and strong professional researcher role models with relatively flexible public science systems, and large-scale publicly supported research programmes. These features of the institutional environment encourage firms to adopt the following forms of competence development.

First, in fields where the state has provided considerable support and/or risk sharing for knowledge production that is critical for innovation development they will become quite highly involved in public research networks. Second, by generating large numbers of highly skilled engineers and scientists who seek to update and improve their expertise, such societies encourage firms to rely on the specialized expertise of individuals who can be acquired through fluid labour markets to change their competences rapidly. Such radical shifts in organizational capabilities are also assisted through the active market in corporate control in these kinds of economies. Finally, these institutional features discourage extensive and long-term involvement in industry networks and hence limit investment in customer-specific knowledge and innovations.

In sectors where appropriability and modularity are high, they therefore encourage project-based firms to adopt flexible team approaches in developing major innovations with generic, codified knowledge from a variety of fields and novel skills. In other sectors where these conditions are not present and the state does not fund large-scale research programmes, however, this combination of institutional features encourages different kinds of approaches for developing innovative competences, particularly those associated with isolated hierarchies. Focused on developing new products and processes in house, but with limited investment in firm-specific skills, firms in these industries recruit staff with generic skills that can be integrated through authority hierarchies to achieve development goals. Both labour market institutions and the educational system encourage individuals to identify more with their specialist expertise than with particular employers in such economies, so that firms can readily acquire new skills and knowledge through the labour market. This does, however, make coordination across skill areas and functions more difficult, and can slow down the development of new products.

In contrast, societies dominated by coordinated knowledge production institutions combine strong business associations and diffusion-oriented state science and technology policies with large, integrated research training systems and substantial segmented public science systems. In these environments, firms are also likely to become involved in public research networks, albeit more technologically focused ones than in the previous case. They also will tend to be supportive of specialist researchers developing generic skills and researching topics not directly tied to current development projects. Such absorptive hierarchies integrate knowledge and skills from the applied sciences and industry networks to improve products and processes largely within current technological trajectories, but with the capability to absorb new kinds of knowledge and technologies in the longer term.

Finally, coordinated market economies with strong business associations can be combined with diffusion-oriented policies but weak research training and relatively low mobility between public science and industry, as is arguably the case in postwar Japan. Firms here have used the public research system more to find information to solve specific problems than to develop more generic knowledge that could be used for a range of new products and technologies. Social identities and loyalties are not so tied to specialist scientific expertise as they are where the role model of the academic researcher is well established and prestigious, and so graduates will be more amenable to developing careers and skills within organizations in these kinds of societies.

Together with strong diffusion-oriented science and technology policies, these features encourage firms to focus on developing new products and processes with general, firm-specific skills that facilitate organizational integration, rather than relying on more specialist research skills that could coordinate public knowledge production with corporate purposes. Typically sharing risks and knowledge with suppliers and customers, these kinds of firms are embedded in industry networks that encourage alliances and partnerships. Strong industry associations and insider-dominated financial systems support such long-term commitments and facilitate the speedy development of new products with a flexible, stable workforce.

These interconnections suggest that, while public science systems can and do vary considerably in some respects between market economies, their general organizational pattern, and consequent effects on the development of innovative competences, reflect broader institutional frameworks and priorities. In Japan, for instance, the long-standing concern with economic and technological catching up with Western Europe and the USA led to the development of a predominantly diffusion-oriented science and technology system (Ergas, 1987; Morris-Suzuki, 1994; Odagiri and Goto, 1996), and an educational system that focused on developing knowledge acquisition skills as much as advanced knowledge production. It is, then, the combination of general institutional arrangements governing capital and labour markets with particular features of public science systems that encourage firms to develop innovative competences in different ways, and so follow distinctive innovation strategies.

In sum, firms have a number of choices in developing innovative competences and selecting innovation strategies that are guided by dominant institutions. These institutions include those governing the development of skills and labour markets, capital markets and inter-firm relationships as well as the organization and conduct of research in the public sciences. As a result, societies with distinctive institutional frameworks encourage the development of particular kinds of innovative capabilities, and so manifest contrasting types of technological development and sectoral specialization, as the examples of late twentieth century Germany, Japan, and the USA illustrate. These interconnections will now be further explored by considering how entrepreneurial technology companies in two different kinds of industries develop competences and manage risks in contrasting kinds of institutional environments in three European countries.

8

Constructing Capabilities in Entrepreneurial Technology Firms: A Comparative Institutional Analysis of Germany, Sweden, and the UK

with Steven Casper

Introduction

In explaining how institutional frameworks generate distinctive innovative strategies that are effective in different kinds of industries, it is important to understand the varied nature of technological and market risks in different subsectors, especially in emerging industries. Because key kinds of risks, such as appropriability and competence destruction, differ between subsectors of new industries, we would expect entrepreneurial technology companies in these subsectors to develop different types of capabilities. Their ability to do so is strongly affected by the nature of the dominant institutions governing economic activities, and so the relative success of entrepreneurial technology firms in different kinds of subsectors can be expected to vary between countries dominated by contrasting institutional frameworks.

In this chapter we explore these processes through a comparison of how the institutional frameworks of Germany, Sweden and the United Kingdom have affected strategies for dealing with two major kinds of organizational problems that firms have to manage in developing new technologies in different subsectors of the biotechnology and software industries. In particular, we focus on the role of different kinds of skill formation systems and labour market institutions in encouraging the development of contrasting kinds of organizational capabilities. While the predominantly arm's length institutions in countries such as the USA or UK are conducive to the development of project-based entrepreneurial technology start-ups focusing on discontinuous radical innovations (Soskice, 1999), there are other subsectors of these industries where more complex and stable organizations are effective. Success in such segments is strongly advantaged by institutional structures that encourage competence enhancing human resource strategies (Casper, 2000).

The more coordinated market economies of postwar Germany and Sweden have dominant institutional frameworks that encourage these kinds of collaborative enterprises and have emerged as leaders within Europe in developing them. However, in the case of the development of middleware software in Sweden, a subsector in which external coordination across firms is especially important, the activities of large firms appear to have altered 'normal' institutional incentives. As a result, a considerable number of software firms with high levels of technical intensity became established there in the late 1990s.

We discuss this case in some detail in the last section of this chapter. The first section focuses on two key issues faced by entrepreneurial technology firms in different subsectors of the biotechnology and computer software industries, while the second suggests how these are connected to varied institutional arrangements. The third section provides evidence on patterns of specialization across different subsectors of the biotechnology and software industries within Germany, Sweden, and the UK, while the fourth considers the German case in more detail. Finally, we examine the development of middleware software firms in Sweden.

Key Management Issues Facing Entrepreneurial Technology Firms

In seeking to explain variations in patterns of development of entrepreneurial technology companies in different subsectors, it is useful to distinguish two kinds of technological risks that affect managerial priorities and the kinds of organizational capabilities firms need to develop (Breschi and Malerba, 1997; Dosi, 1988; Malerba and Orsenigo, 1993). First, appropriability risks reflect the ease with which competitors can imitate innovations. They are typically managed either through patent and copyright protection or through controlling complementary assets, as discussed by Teece (1986). In the pharmaceutical industry, for example, patent protection is relatively effective because minor changes in the structure of therapeutic drugs can have major consequences for their operation in the human body (Gambardella, 1995). As a result, drug discovery firms are able to specialize in highly risky activities without needing to develop complementary assets to protect their innovations.

Second, competence destruction risks reflect the volatility and uncertainty of technical development that vary greatly between technologies, both in terms of the technological trajectories being followed and market acceptance. Where technological uncertainty is high, it is difficult to predict which investments and skills will be effective and innovative firms have to be able to change direction at short notice. Consequently, the managers of firms attempting to develop radically discontinuous innovations are faced with the need to attract and motivate expert staff to work on complex problems when unpredictable outcomes may involve dismissal and/or organizational failure.

To offset high technical or market uncertainty, most firms competing to create radical innovations in markets where the winners of innovation races can expect to capture a relatively large share of emerging markets focus on technology areas in which appropriability regimes through copyright and patent protection are quite strong. When appropriability risks are relatively low, management can focus primarily on R&D activities. This minimizes organizational complexity, allowing a coherent focus on core milestones needed to develop a new product or technology. Such radically innovative firms are typically project-based organizations (Hobday, 2000) where managers organize highly skilled staff into a series of teams focused on solving complex problems under very tight time constraints. They often employ strong performance-based incentive schemes and employee ownership plans to induce employees to work very intensively to solve organizational problems.

These two kinds of technological risk tend to be inversely related. Investments in developing highly uncertain technologies are usually undertaken when appropriability risks are limited, while firms developing innovations that are more open to such risks focus on more cumulative and predictable technologies. Companies racing to produce highly radical, discontinuous innovations have to be flexible in their use of key resources such as highly expert technologists and in changing direction, while those developing more imitable technologies usually develop complementary competences and integrate them through organizational routines. By making innovations more customer specific and bundling additional services with them, as in the postwar German plastics industry

(Streb, 2003), such companies increase their organizational specificity and limit the ease with which they can be imitated and/or supplied more cheaply. However, these kinds of entrepreneurial technology firms are more organizationally complex than radically innovative companies and have to develop stronger coordinating organizational capabilities. We now discuss how companies deal with these different kinds of risks in different subsectors in a little more detail.

(a) Subsectors with High Competence Destruction Risks but Limited Appropriability Risks

Considering first the key issues faced by firms in subsectors that combine high levels of technical uncertainty with low appropriability risks, a critical organizational capability here involves being able to change the direction of research and development activities quickly. As this often means acquiring new skills, companies need rapid access to a pool of scientists, technicians, and other specialists with known reputations in particular areas (Bahrami and Evans, 1995). If there is a cultural stigma attached to failing or changing jobs regularly, then engineers and managers may choose not to join firms with high-risk research projects, for fear that if the project fails, the value of his or her engineering and/or management expertise could significantly decline. Furthermore, high levels of competence destruction create knowledge investment problems. Employees have an incentive not to invest in large amounts of firm-specific knowledge, such as proprietary software languages, when there is a strong probability that their employment tenure at the firm will be low, or that the firm could quickly fail.

Many subsectors of the biotechnology and computer software industries share these characteristics, as listed in Table 8.1. One is standard (or application-based) software created for large homogenous markets where demand for customization is low. Examples include graphic application software (e.g. CAD/CAM), multimedia and computer entertainment software, and a variety of application software used to run computer networks (e.g. e-mail, FTP, groupware, and document management programs). Most companies developing such standard software are project-based firms with relatively simple organizational structures, as will be discussed further in the next chapter.

Low customization and high-scale economies here lead to intense competitive races to establish dominant designs and introduce new features (or 'functionality') to software products through periodic upgrades. Such

Table 8.1. Technological risks of biotechnology and computer software subsectors

	Examples	Appropriability Risks	Competence-Destruction Risks
Biotechnology			
Platform, enabling technologies	DNA purification kits, Compound screening apparatus	High	Limited
Therapeutic technologies	Alzheimer's disease therapies	Low	High
Computer Software			
Enterprise software	ERP, CRM	Considerable	Limited
Standard, applications-based software	CAD/CAM, Computer games, e-mail	Limited	High
Middleware software	Secure payments systems, search engines	Limited	High

competition creates high competence destruction within the software industry and the failure of small development houses. Since it is relatively easy to protect standard software products through a combination of: (a) patent/copyright protection, (b) secrecy over a program's so-called source-code, or (c) 'lock-in' effects once a product becomes successful and a customer base develops (Shapiro and Varian, 1999), these firms do not usually need to integrate R&D with other activities. Knowledge properties across standard software firms are relatively standardized or industry-specific. While software developers and engineers working within the firm often have advanced graduate training, their skill-sets are relatively generic across employers and customers, including industry-wide computer languages and analytical training.

Therapeutics-based biotechnology is a second common example of a subsector populated by radically innovative technology start-ups. A defining feature of therapeutics research is its very high scientific intensity in the sense of being closely dependent upon new scientific knowledge of generic biological phenomena and processes. Firms often are constituted on the basis of scientific expertise in particular biomedical research areas, and then develop or acquire any number of more specific application technologies needed to pursue projects as research progresses. Uncertainty regarding the success of basic scientific research creates relatively high technological volatility for start-up therapeutic firms. Ethnographic accounts consistently document the widely changing course of therapeutic firm research activities over time, which often leads to repeated changes in the competence structure of the firm (e.g., Rabinow, 1996;

Werth, 1994). More generally, failure rates are high and time horizons are relatively long throughout the drug development process (Henderson *et al.* 1999). A study of research dynamics within the area of Alzheimer's disease, for example, noted over twenty discrete networks of firm/lab combinations conducting competitive research (Penan, 1996).

A final example of a radically innovative subsector is middleware software. Firms in this market compete to develop new interface technologies that are used to link the basic architecture of digital communication networks to standard application software. The subsector's growth has been strongly affected by the development of the Internet. Typical middleware products include secure payment systems used in Internet banking and e-commerce, software that transforms the content of web servers into a format that can be used in small mobile telephones or Palm Pilot devices, and search engines that are used for navigation on the World Wide Web. Most firms in middleware software race to create new technologies with superior functionality or speed to market (Glimstedt and Zander, 2003).

However, in comparison with standard software and therapeutics-based biotechnology firms they have to deal with an additional coordination problem. Because successful innovations in this subsector are developed with a variety of different kinds of knowledge that are interdependent, technical standards, design interfaces and other product architecture-related issues have to be integrated if firms are to have a high probability of success (see, generally, Kitschelt, 1991). For middleware firms, low technological cumulativeness and the need for coordination across groups of firms in complementary markets create considerable standards-related risks (Arthur, 1994). To succeed firms must coordinate technical specifications or designs with other firms in a technology area.

(b) Subsectors with Limited Competence Destruction Risks but Considerable Appropriability Risks

Turning now to consider firms operating in subsectors that combine lower levels of technological uncertainty with greater appropriability risks, they are likely to attempt to integrate new technologies with other assets that generate firm-specific advantages (Teece, 1986). For example, companies facing appropriability risks often develop specialized assets in sales, distribution or a variety of technical implementation and consulting activities that are relatively customer-specific. Development work therefore becomes more complex, involving cross-functional team-organized projects in which R&D personnel work with consultants, marketing personnel, and implementation technicians to customize technology platforms for clients. In these kinds of subsectors firms attempt to develop learning economies or create tacit knowledge embedded within project teams that are difficult for other firms to mimic.

These kinds of complex, multi-functional firms coordinate more varied skills and activities through the managerial authority hierarchy than most project-based firms, and so develop distinctive coordination capabilities. Such organizational complexity affects employment policies due to the existence of considerable tacit and often firm-specific knowledge developed across functional teams within the firm (see, generally, Miller, 1992). While this firm-specific knowledge is valuable to the firm, it is often hard to sell on external labour markets or markets for technology. As a result, firm-specific knowledge investments, once made, could lead to opportunistic demands by employers. Employees might hesitate making such investments without a credible commitment from management that they will not be exploited. Moreover, tacit knowledge can easily lead to information asymmetries between the management and employees of a firm, creating potential difficulties for management to monitor and appropriately reward work, particularly across members of project teams. The management of skilled staff in such situations involves, then, quite different issues from those faced by radical innovation firms. In particular, owners and managers need to encourage employees to collaborate in developing organization-specific capabilities, often through long-term employment and generally consultative workplace arrangements as argued in Chapter 6, in order to exploit tacit knowledge within the firm.

Such competence-enhancing human resource policies are far more feasible when institutional constraints on hiring and firing exist and the expectations of scientists, engineers, and technicians are focused on long-term employment and consultative workplaces. These conditions should enable the rapid formation of complex organizational structures and associated knowledge investment patterns within groups of entrepreneurial start-ups. Where, in contrast, employee poaching is an accepted and common practice within a community of firms, then employees will naturally gravitate towards skill development strategies centred on generic and publicly visible skills that are easily saleable on such labour markets.

Entrepreneurial firms in the enterprise software and platform biotechnologies subsectors exemplify this constellation of organizational competences. In contrast to standard software, enterprise software consists of software platforms or modules that are extensively customized for individual clients (Lehrer, 2006). Firms in this category include those developing enterprise resource planning (ERP), customer relationship management (CRM), groupware and systems integration products as well as a number of firms creating sector-specific enterprise tools (e.g. logistics and supply chain management tools).

Companies developing platform biotechnologies share a similar pattern of business organization. They create enabling technologies that are sold to other research labs. Products include consumable kits used to rationalize common molecular biology lab processes, such as the purification of DNA and cloning of DNA segments. Platform technology firms have also developed a number of engineering and information technology-based applications that have been used to automate many aspects of the discovery process within therapeutics. Examples include high-throughput 'combinatorial chemistry' applications to aid the screening of potential therapeutic compounds and the development of genetic sequencing and modelling techniques.

In both subsectors, technologies tend to have high appropriability risks created by relatively weak intellectual property regimes. While patents for particular technologies exist, 'work-arounds' are relatively common once initial innovators establish proof of principle. As a result, entry is relatively easy, and dozens of firms exist in most enterprise software and platform biotechnology segments. Highly competitive enterprise software markets include enterprise resource planning and, more recently, Internet software to run e-commerce. Numerous firms also compete in most platform technology markets, such as nucleic acid filtration or amplification (PCR) or information technology rich areas such as DNA sequencing and bioinformatics. Within these markets, companies generally create complementary organizational capabilities that can be protected by the firm. These include assets needed to customize general technology platforms for specialized product niches. Doing so creates larger, more complex organizational structures than those seen at entrepreneurial technology firms focused more on the management of competence destruction risks.

Institutional Frameworks and Competence Development

The ways that managers deal with these problems in entrepreneurial technology firms vary between market economies with different institutional frameworks, as discussed in previous chapters. The preceding analysis suggests that project-based entrepreneurial technology firms faced with high competence destruction risks develop quite different managerial practices to those adopted by more collaborative firms attempting to govern complex organizational structures. These latter companies encourage competence-enhancing patterns of work organization, while the ability to hire and fire employees rapidly is important for firms facing competence destruction. These different kinds of practices are greatly influenced by the skill formation and labour market institutions of different countries, in addition to their financial and political systems.

Institutional frameworks within the more coordinated market economies, for instance, strongly favour the development of managerial commitments needed for employees to make firm-specific knowledge investments that are not easily saleable on open labour markets. Such arrangements tend to 'lock-in' owners, managers, and skilled employees into long-term, organized relationships. Strong norms and legal obstacles to 'hire and fire' combined with a long-standing tradition, reinforced by co-determination laws in countries such as Germany, of consultative patterns of work organization, favour competence-enhancing human resource policies. In terms of encouraging different kinds of entrepreneurial technology firms, this analysis suggests that these kinds of economies have a comparative institutional advantage in creating clusters of organizationally complex collaborative firms developing firm-specific competences in cumulative technologies. In contrast, they have a comparative institutional disadvantage in the governance of radically innovative project-based firms focused on developing competence-destroying technologies with high failure risks.

On the other hand, companies in more arm's length institutional regimes face far less institutionalized 'lock-in' regarding employees or other stakeholders to the company. Hire-and-fire, when embraced by most companies within a sector, can be used to create large external labour markets for most skills. However, employees facing this pattern of labour market organization will be extremely reluctant to invest in the development of firm-specific skills that are needed to support high organizational complexity. Consequently, such low commitment economies have a comparative institutional advantage in creating clusters of radically innovative project-based firms, but have a comparative institutional disadvantage in the governance of entrepreneurial firms where continuing organizational commitment is needed.

In the light of this analysis we now examine the performance of three European economies in three radically innovative subsectors (standard software, therapeutics biotechnology, middleware software) and two more organizationally complex subsectors (enterprise software and

211

platform biotechnologies). Two economies are governed by institutions that encourage high levels of non-market economic coordination, Germany and Sweden, while the third, the United Kingdom, most resembles the stereotyped liberal market economy.

Germany and Sweden are paradigmatic examples of coordinated political economies (Pontusson and Swenson, 1996; Swank, 2003; Thelen, 2004). In both countries non-market forms of business coordination are facilitated by the embeddedness of large firms within networks of powerful trade and industry associations, as well as a similar, often legally mandated, organization of labour and other interest organizations within para-public institutions (Crouch, 1999). Businesses and other social actors engage in these associations to create important non-market collective competition goods, such as the apprenticeship system or networks of collaborative technology transfer institutes. Public policy in both countries focuses on neo-corporatist bargaining environments through the legal delegation of specific bargaining rights to unions and other stakeholders within firms (Streeck, 1984). Industrial relations institutions in both countries lock managers and employees into long-term relationships, promoting competence-enhancing human resource development within firms. These institutions should advantage the governance of organizationally complex collaborative firms.

In strong contrast, the UK has developed largely arm's length institutions. The financial system is strongly capital market-based, with total market capitalization as a percentage of GDP at the end of 1997 at 151 per cent exceeding the United States (121 per cent) and far ahead of Germany's still predominately bank-centred system (26 per cent) (*Deutsche Bundesbank*, 1998). Financial and labour markets are largely deregulated, facilitating rapid 'hire and fire', while corporate law is primarily enabling in nature and focused on shareholder primacy (Monks and Minow, 1995). Particularly through the 1980s and 90s, the UK dramatically deregulated markets and weakened the power of collective actors within society, above all unions. This liberal market orientation should enable the development of radically innovative project-based firms.

All three countries have strong research capabilities in the life and computer sciences. These include departments and laboratories associated with Oxford and Cambridge Universities in the UK, the Karolinska Institute in Sweden, and several large Max Planck Institutes specializing in the life sciences in Germany. A large number of companies have been commercialized from these and other academic institutes in each country (see Ernst and Young 2001 and Casper and Murray 2004 for Germany/UK comparisons). Large pharmaceutical companies also exist in each country, such as Bayer and BASF in Germany, GlaxoSmithKline in the UK, and Astra (now merged with the UK firm Zeneca) in Sweden.

Similarly, leading universities in each country have large computer science departments, generating an ample supply of skilled computer scientists in each country. These include the Royal Institute of Technology in Sweden, Oxford and Cambridge in the UK, and several large public universities in Germany, most notably the University of Munich. In each country large downstream markets exist in several areas that could plausibly drive the creation of software companies. In addition to general business service markets, these include London and Frankfurt's large financial services markets. Each country has also historically been home to large telecommunication manufacturers (Ericsson, Siemens, Marconi), companies that could plausibly influence the creation of middleware software companies.

Given our characterization of the different technological and market risks faced by firms in the five dynamic subsectors discussed above, we would expect the success of project-based and collaborative entrepreneurial technology firms in each to vary considerably between Germany, Sweden, and the United Kingdom. In particular, while the first two countries should evince greater success in platform biotechnology and enterprise software, they are likely to be less successful in the other three subsectors. These expectations are summarized in Table 8.2.

Subsectoral Distribution of Biotechnology and Software Companies in Germany, Sweden, and the UK

To assess the validity of these expectations, we examined the distribution of publicly quoted companies in the biotechnology and software industries in these three countries across subsectors with different kinds of risks.

Table 8.2. Expected success of three European economies in five technologically dynamic subsectors

	Germany	Sweden	United Kingdom
Platform biotechnology	Successful	Successful	Unsuccessful
Enterprise software	Successful	Successful	Unsuccessful
Standard software	Unsuccessful	Unsuccessful	Successful
Therapeutics biotechnology	Unsuccessful	Unsuccessful	Successful
Middleware software	Unsuccessful	Unsuccessful	Successful

While the ability of a company to take a stock exchange listing does not necessarily imply long-term success, it is a good comparative indicator of relative growth. It suggests that a company has performed well enough during its initial start-up phase for investment banks and private investors to invest in their further growth through initial public offerings on the stock market and so reflects their relative success.

One potential criticism of using the number of public companies in a subsector as an indicator of success is that the UK has historically had stronger capital markets, which might more easily fund higher-risk 'radically innovative' companies than those in Sweden or Germany. However, during the late 1990s a large number of technology-oriented companies were able to pursue initial public offerings in these countries. While Germany and Sweden historically have not enjoyed venture capital (VC) industries, the sector boomed in each country in this period. Available VC funding rose in Sweden from $2 billion in 1996 to $25 billion in 2001 (Glimstedt and Zander, 2003: 144) and in Germany from $4 billion to $17 billion during the 1996–2000 period.

Technology-oriented stock markets also grew dramatically in each country. By early 2001 the German *Neuer Markt* had over 270 listed companies (Casper, 2003: 246), while in Sweden the technology-oriented OM Stockholm Stock Exchange had 311 listed companies (Glimstedt and Zander, 2003: 146). Given the strength of both venture capital and IPO markets for technology companies in Germany and Sweden during the late 1990s, the comparison of these countries with the UK can be considered reasonably representative. We suggest, then, that if a country has a high number of public firms specialized in a particular subsector, this is a good indicator that competences associated with that subsector can be effectively developed in its particular institutional framework.

We used the following procedures to classify the subsector specialization of companies. The primary business of each company was determined through an analysis of their web pages. We also drew upon company summaries and subsector classifications published on the Internet by financial service companies to verify our classifications. All biotechnology and software firms listed on technology-oriented stock markets in the UK, Germany, and Sweden were included. As our theoretical analysis rests largely on nation-specific institutional effects on the organization of firms, we checked to ensure that all companies included in our analysis had corporate headquarters in Germany, Sweden, or the UK. This led to the removal of three companies listed on the German *Neuer Markt* that had headquarters outside Germany.

For many biotechnology companies, determining whether the primary orientation was towards development of platform technology or therapeutic products was quite straightforward. Therapeutic companies presented themselves as specialists within particular therapeutic areas, such as immunology or cardiovascular diseases, and had extensive internal expertise in disease-specific areas. Platform technology companies focused extensively on their technological competencies that are usually presented as applicable across a wide array of therapeutic research areas. However, some companies, particularly in the genomics area, develop technology platforms that can then be used to generate therapeutic targets (so-called 'gene to lead' strategies). For these companies, we examined whether the primary technological orientation was towards the improvement of a general purpose technological platform and its licensing to other firms, or towards in-house therapeutic development.

Classifying the software firms was also straightforward in most cases. Middleware software firms usually identified themselves by this product category, and were focused on the development of software to improve the efficiency with which different computing systems interfaced within communications networks. To differentiate standard and enterprise software vendors we focused first on well-known standard and enterprise software categories (e.g. enterprise resource planning and customer relationship management products are well-known enterprise software segments, while multi-media, entertainment, and graphics software are well-known standard software segments).

For all other firms, we examined the degree by which the company offers to customize its software for clients. Companies offering extensive consulting, implementation, or systems integration services were classified as enterprise software firms. Standard software companies, on the other hand, generally licensed software 'as is' to clients and did not engage in extensive consultancy-related services. These classifications were, when possible, verified by gathering data on the percentage of a company's earnings generated through software licensing, which is high for most standard software companies and low for enterprise software vendors (available for about half the firms in our database).

While for most cases subsectoral classification was not difficult, the problem with investigator bias remains inherent in this type of analysis. Future research could reduce it through identifying structural characteristics of firms within particular subsectors that could be captured through more quantitative data, such as those used by Casper and Vitols (2006). As our purpose within the present analysis is to capture broad trends at

Table 8.3. Subsector distribution of publicly quoted biotechnology companies

	Germany		United Kingdom		Sweden	
	Number	Percent	Number	Percent	Number	Percent
Platform biotechnologies	13	81	6	15	8	73
Therapeutics/product-based biotechnologies	3	19	34	85	3	27
Total	16	100	40	100	11	100

Source: classification by authors based on company web pages, annual reports, and IPO prospectuses.

a macro-level, the more puzzling or interesting of which can then be explored in more detail, we believe simple investigator-led classifications are sufficient. Furthermore, adopting a multiple-method approach should help minimize the bias and classification error issues; supplementary data will be used to verify these macro-results for some cases.

Considering first the distribution of biotechnology firms in Germany, Sweden and the UK, summarized in Table 8.3, we can see that the United Kingdom was the only one of these three countries with a well-developed concentration of public therapeutics biotechnology firms (34). These data support a number of consulting reports and previous academic studies concluding that the UK had Europe's strongest biotechnology sector (e.g. Casper and Kettler, 2001; Cooke, 1999; Ernst and Young, 1999, 2006; Senker, 1996).

Neither the German nor Swedish sectors had a critical mass of therapeutics biotechnology firms (only three in each country), while each had a larger number of platform biotechnology firms. While supporting our expectations, these results could not be considered conclusive due to the small number of public biotechnology firms existing in Sweden and Germany, despite considerable state encouragement in both countries. We therefore discuss the German biotechnology case in more detail below, drawing on a range of supplementary statistics that strongly suggest that firms in this country had a comparative institutional advantage in platform biotechnologies.

Turning to the software cases summarized in Table 8.4, the German evidence strongly supported our predictions. While a relatively large number of German software firms were traded on the German stock market for growth companies, ninety per cent of firms (54 in total) were in enterprise software, while there were only three firms in either standard software or middleware. The UK data were also supportive. The UK had the largest software industry in Europe and 74 per cent of these firms were

Table 8.4. Subsector distribution of publicly quoted software companies

	Germany		United Kingdom		Sweden	
	Number	%	Number	%	Number	%
Enterprise software	54	90	23	26	20	44
Standard software	3	5	58	66	16	34
Middleware software	3	5	7	8	10	22
Total	60	100	88	100	46	100

Source: classification by authors based on company web pages, annual reports, and IPO prospectuses.

in 'radically innovative' segments, standard software or middleware. This combined with the smaller number of enterprise software firms generally supports our predictions. However, the UK case is puzzling in another respect. Why were most of the UK software firms in standard software, with so few in middleware software?

The pattern of Swedish software firm specialization, on the other hand, is less straightforward. While a large number of enterprise software firms existed (20, or 44 per cent of the total), over half of the Swedish software firms were in radically innovative areas, and Sweden had Europe's largest concentration of publicly listed middleware firms. As we will discuss in more detail below, the 10 publicly listed middleware firms represented only a small percentage of a much larger population of recent start-ups in this area. The Swedish concentration of middleware software firms poses a strong challenge to the theoretical predictions of this chapter; such a highly coordinated market economy should not have a comparative institutional advantage in this area.

Overall, these statistical data, despite limitations, provide good support for our theoretical analysis. Of the fifteen cases, twelve could be interpreted as confirming our expectations (UK middleware, Swedish middleware and standard software being problematic). For these three European economies, the claim that national institutional frameworks influence patterns of competitive advantage, and specialization, should be taken seriously. To show how some changes in the institutional framework, especially state policies, have had some effect on entrepreneurial technology firms but in directions encouraged by other institutional features, particularly those governing labour markets, and also to investigate the problematic middleware software case, the remainder of the chapter considers two areas in more detail.

First, we examine developments in Germany where the state has developed an array of technology policies designed to spur German industry into the types of entrepreneurial technology start-ups discussed here. These policies, while generally successful in promoting entrepreneurial start-ups, have led to the development of relatively few successful firms in 'radically innovative' market segments characterized by project-based firms. We examine this case in more detail, providing richer evidence that successful German entrepreneurial technology firms were almost exclusively clustered in subsectors characterized by collaborative firms with more cumulative technological orientations.

Second, we examine the middleware software case in more detail, focusing on the Swedish case but with comparisons to Germany and the UK. The activities of large firms capable of developing useful technical standards for firms active in the sector were crucial in this case and help to explain how Swedish firms became more successful in the middleware software sector than UK ones. We use this case to examine the process by which radically innovative technology start-ups have become sustainable within a coordinated market economy.

Germany's Engagement with the 'New Economy'

Beginning in the mid 1990s the German government introduced a range of new technology policies designed to create clusters of entrepreneurial start-up firms. Starting in 1996 the government decided to provide 'public venture capital' in the form of 'sleeping' or silent equity partnerships from federal sources (Adelberger, 2000). In the five years to 2001 well over one billion DM was channelled into such investments, with over half of the new firms specializing in information technology, communications, or biotechnology. German public officials have crafted a dense network of support policies for university-centred spin-offs. This includes funding the creation of several technology parks and incubator labs, hiring of consultants to persuade university professors or their students to commercialize their research findings and help them design viable business plans, subsidies to help defray the costs of patenting their intellectual property, and the provision of management consulting and partnering activities once new firms are founded. These programmes originally concentrated on biotechnology, but were later extended into other sectors including software (Lehrer, 2000).

Given the relative ease of obtaining VC finance and, particularly for biotechnology firms, fairly sophisticated infrastructure support within low-rent start-up incubators, it is not surprising that hundreds of new

Table 8.5. Therapeutic compounds pipelines of German and UK biotech companies

	Preclinical	Phase I	Phase II	Phase III	Total
United Kingdom (public companies (n = 40)*	32	37	46	13	128
Germany (public companies (n = 16))	2	2	1	1	6
Germany (45 university spin-offs)**	19	10	2	1	32

*Source: Ernst and Young (2001): **Source: Casper and Murray (2004).

start-up firms have been founded in Germany. Evidence on the activities of these companies strongly supports our expectation that German companies focused in the platform biotechnology and enterprise software segments will outperform those in more radically innovative segments. We briefly support this with more detailed evidence from the German biotechnology and software sectors.

Turning first to biotechnology, most of the leading German companies are in the platform technology area. These firms include Qiagen, a leading supplier of consumable lab kits, Lion Biosciences, a bioinformatics software supplier, and Evotec, a leading supplier of high-throughput assay technology. On the other hand, very few German companies focused on therapeutic companies have found sustained success. One way to measure this is to examine the ability of firms to develop and test compounds through clinical trials processes. Table 8.5 summarizes data compiled by Ernst and Young on public biotechnology companies, complemented by data on German university spin-offs collected by Casper and Murray. These figures dramatically illustrate the superior ability of UK biotechnology companies to develop and commercialize therapeutic discoveries. Despite an increase of German companies pursuing therapeutic strategies in the early 2000s, the latest Ernst and Young survey (2006) reports their continued greater involvement and success in platform technologies, as well as the UK having 40 per cent of all European publicly quoted biotechnology companies.

A second way to examine the technological intensity of companies is through patent analysis. Figure 8.1 examines the average number of scientific journals referenced in German and US patents from 1985 until 1998. This is a rough indicator of technical cumulativeness—the greater the number of basic research citations in a patent application, the 'newer' or less cumulative on previous discoveries the innovation may be presumed to be. These figures show that the average number of US scientific references in 1998 (about 24) is about three times as many in Germany (about 8), with the gap widening substantially over

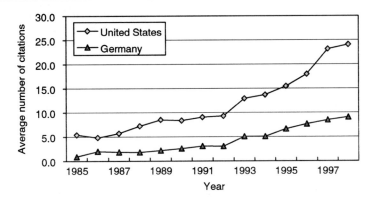

Figure 8.1. Scientific intensity of biotechnology patents, 1985–1998
Source: US patent data.

the 1990s. This finding suggests that firms that successfully innovated—seen through the successful patenting of ideas—do so in subsectors of biotechnology firms with technological characteristics that are generally more cumulative in nature. Both the pipeline and patenting findings are consistent with the argument that German biotechnology firms share a comparative institutional advantage in platform biotechnologies.

Turning to the software industry, German companies are more specialized in enterprise software markets than in standard software ones. A closer analysis of the sixty publicly listed German software firms supports this claim (Casper 2003; Lehrer, 2006). Most German software firms were founded during the 1980s to help fuel the corporate enterprise software markets; the average age across the sixty public firms is 15.3 years. Examples of prominent segments include enterprise resource planning (four of the publicly listed firms), customer relationship management (five firms), systems integration (seven firms), and a variety of sector-specific enterprise tools in areas such as logistics and supply chain management (nine firms).

There is only one cluster of German publicly traded software firms that is relatively young—a group of seven firms active in the e-commerce software field (average age 7.4 years as of May 2000). This group of firms has received substantial private venture capital funding, facilitating much faster growth before initial public offerings. Rather than relying on 'organic' driven growth based on earnings, they have had the opportunity to invest lavishly to create large organizational structures in an attempt to grab substantial market shares quickly. E-commerce software is one of the core Internet infrastructure areas in which German firms have established substantial market share in non-German language markets. While American firms dominate several segments, particularly in the provision of software for 'business to business' transactions, German firms are internationally competitive in the provision of software to facilitate on-line retailing ('business to consumer' e-commerce) and are also strong in creating secure-transaction software for financial services (Casper, 2003).

Business concepts underlying e-commerce software resemble those pioneered by the German firm SAP to create the Enterprise Resource Planning market. E-commerce software firms develop customizable software modules designed to help client firms organize e-commerce platforms. The business model involves the creation and updating of a kernel of e-commerce applications—inventory tracking, accounting, order completion, as well as the creation of visual web-interfaces used by customers—which are typically installed and extensively customized by the software provider or third-party software consultancies.

While e-commerce software firms may compete to introduce software with enhanced functionality, especially in the 'ease of use' area, the software itself is relatively generic. E-commerce software platforms are proprietary systems completely owned and maintained by the developer. Patenting over core e-commerce processes appears weak; dozens of e-commerce software firms exist, most of which offer relatively similar technologies. To reduce these appropriability concerns, firms invest in a core proprietary library of programs that are then customized for clients during extensive implementation programs. Doing so creates a lock-in effect for the software vendor, and can also help capture rents from periodic 'up-grade' cycles as the software is improved.

Germany's e-commerce software specialists resemble most German firms in developing human resource policies that are broadly competence-enhancing in nature. Firms usually organize a group of programmers with advanced degrees who update the core software platform, together with a much larger group of trained technicians and consultants involved in implementation and service issues. Proprietary programming environments tend to keep competence destruction low—new programmers may be added to accommodate inevitable 'feature creep', but existing staff have high job security due to the periodic need to update the code. Relatively complex coordination across teams of programmers and technicians involved in customization and implementation work is key to competitive success.

Sweden's Strong Performance in Middleware Software

The technological characteristics of middleware software are more complex than standard software, due to the importance of technical standard coordination across firms. This depends upon the resolution of collective action dilemmas that are difficult for numerous small firms to resolve, particularly when distributive issues hinge on the particular constellation of technical knowledge chosen (Shapiro and Varian, 1999). In addition to human resource policy risks created by high competence destruction, then, middleware software firms, face the additional coordination risk created by uncertainty about which emerging standards in a firm's chosen technical field will succeed.

Though governments have at times played important roles within telecommunication standards (Glimstedt, 2001), within much of the middleware software sector most firms are dependent upon large corporations, typically telecommunication equipment manufacturers and established companies active in network intensive standard software products, for the provision of standards to help products become interoperable (Casper and Glimstedt, 2001). Examples of the former include large network equipment manufacturers such as Cisco Systems, Lucent, or Ericsson, while Microsoft, Sun, or Oracle exemplify the latter. Each of these firms has been involved in the creation of technology platforms for emerging network communication markets that function as 'club goods' to middleware software companies, encouraging them to develop a variety of follow-on technologies for creating new software platforms. Large firms are self-interested when providing these standards since they hope to secure large markets for equipment and software using the standards by controlling emerging network communication protocols.

As a result, middleware software firms are most likely to exist within technology clusters dominated by large companies that can entice them to commit to a technical standard, either through a reputation of past success and/or through financial incentives or technical support. Through locating within regional economies dominated by such firms, middleware firms can plausibly hope to insert their software engineers into the emerging technical communities surrounding new platforms. Privileged access to such communities can provide a competitive advantage for middleware firms, through, for example, supplementing codified technical knowledge (protocols, languages) with tacit knowledge about their efficiency.

In sum, the existence of a firm that can credibly coordinate technical standards can help to reduce risks, though high levels of technical and market uncertainty remain. This suggests that middleware firms in liberal market economies that are home to dominant technology firms should excel in creating clusters of companies producing such software. The United States, for example, is a clear example of a country that has both. Large concentrations of middleware firms exist in the Silicon Valley and New Jersey areas, in part due to the existence of several firms dominant in setting network infrastructure standards (e.g. Lucent and Cisco in the telecommunications area, Microsoft, Sun, and Oracle in the network services area).

Of the three European economies examined here, the UK is not home to a dominant network technology firm. This helps to explain why so few UK firms are in middleware technology, but are more successful in standard software. The UK is home to technology clusters that are embedded within the type of labour markets needed to facilitate flexible forms of human resource coordination but does not have a hegemonic network communications player capable of sponsoring emerging middleware software standards. UK software firms have instead gravitated to standard software segments, for which technical intensity remains high but inter-firm coordination is low.

Germany is a clearer case. It is also not home to a dominant technology provider in this sector. Siemens is strong in some equipment markets, but is not a leader in promoting new telecommunications standards. Furthermore, most of its investments in Internet-related telecommunications technologies have been channelled into the United States (Casper, 2003). As discussed above, Germany also does not have a business system conducive to the creation of flexible labour markets. For these reasons, it is overdetermined that the governance of middleware software firms should be difficult, as our data on public firms suggest.

In the case of Sweden, which has quite strong non-market forms of coordination as well as dominant technology firms in this industry, Ericsson's leadership in third generation wireless technologies helped to create a technology hub in the Stockholm area that has a technological intensity similar to that in Silicon Valley (Casper and Glimstedt, 2003; Glimstedt and Zander, 2003). Ericsson has become the dominant provider of end-to-end wireless communication systems, and currently has about

40 per cent of all orders for third generation wireless equipment. Other major telecommunications equipment players such as Nokia have set up development centres in Stockholm, and Microsoft recently opened a R&D centre for wireless software there. Hundreds of software firms focusing primarily on wireless Internet technologies have developed in the Stockholm area of Sweden, most in technically intensive middleware technologies (Glimstedt and Zander, 2003: 128–34).

The key issue exemplified by this case is: what constellation of policies must the large firm take to induce engineers, managers, and financiers to make commitments to projects that are normally extremely risky within their societal contexts? Can dominant actors take actions to 'tip' labour market institutions in a direction contrary to 'normal' institutional incentives within an economy? We focus here on two factors: (a) the influence of technology standards in fostering a switch from firm specific to more generic, industry-specific technical skill-sets among software engineers, and (b) initiatives taken by Ericsson to foster entrepreneurialism surrounding technologies it is sponsoring. From the perspective of human resource coordination, these factors have reduced the career risk of working in a radically innovative technology start-up, and through doing so allowed competence-destroying firm strategies to become sustainable.

Ericsson through the 1980s and early 1990s in many ways resembled Siemens, Alcatel, and other European telecommunication equipment manufacturers. Operating as a quasi-monopoly equipment provider in a highly regulated domestic telecommunications market, it developed large systems integration capabilities needed to design early digital switching technologies designed primarily for voice-traffic. As the only significant telecommunications equipment manufacturer in Sweden, it could attract the country's best engineering graduates, who were then offered stable, long-term careers in Ericsson. The company developed proprietary protocols and systems integration languages. The core of Ericsson's programming staff, for example, were experts in Ericsson's in-house systems integration language, Plex, a computer language used nowhere else. While the convergence of data-communication and voice-based digital communication technology has forced Ericsson to adopt new languages for its next generation telecommunications gear, several thousand employees have been retained for their expertise in Plex, which is still used to update legacy equipment.

During the late 1990s data-communication networking devices have begun to converge with traditional telecommunication switching equipment. The increased use of Internet Protocol based switching has forced firms like Ericsson to increasingly adopt connectivity standards developed for data-communications networks. An issue for such firms is how this influences internal product development. In designing switching equipment, base tower systems, and related capabilities for its Internet-compatible wireless equipment, a small group of systems engineers within Ericsson developed a new systems integration language, called Erlang. As with Plex, Ericsson's initial strategy was to make this technology proprietary. However, unlike Plex, Erlang is a systems development language based on standardized object-oriented programming tools with the potential to help firms in a number of industries develop software to manage complex technological systems. Upset at Ericsson's move to keep Erlang proprietary, the chief developer of Erlang along with a group of systems programmers left Ericsson in 1999 to form an independent start-up software company (Glimstedt and Zander, 2003).

Around the same time as this personnel crisis, Ericsson faced important strategic decisions regarding its sponsorship of wireless connectivity standards. Through its strong advocacy of the GSM standard, Ericsson management learned that, in relatively open data-communication network architectures, network externalities play a crucial role in determining which network standards become dominant (Glimstedt, 2001). Ericsson was a major sponsor and developer of two important new web-based wireless connectivity standards, WAP and Bluetooth. The firm realized that if these standards were to succeed, dozens of other firms would have to work with these standards, creating unique applications software and middleware technology. Through creating marketplaces for various wireless applications, demand for Ericsson's end-to-end wireless systems technology would increase. Nurturing nascent wireless technology start-ups in the Stockholm area would promote Ericsson's favoured technologies.

To help promote technology spillovers into the Stockholm economy, Ericsson made two strategic moves. First, in deciding to make Erlang an 'open source' development language, it allowed the founders of Bluetail as well as other firms to use Erlang as a development tool. In this case, using open source development protocols ensures that enhancements to Erlang by third parties would flow back into Ericsson. More importantly, however, it helped to create industry-specific rather than firm-specific skills among engineers involved in large-scale systems integration. Sponsorship of emerging wireless connectivity standards, such as Bluetooth and WAP, or widely used mobile scripting languages like UML, produces a similar effect. Standardization of development tools, protocols, and connectivity standards dramatically increases the portability of skills across local firms working in wireless technology areas.

Second, Ericsson has changed its personnel policy towards engineers who leave to work in start-up firms. It had formerly strongly shunned engineers leaving long-term careers at Ericsson to work elsewhere, signalling that they would not be re-employed by Ericsson in the future. Through creating a corporate venture capital program, it now allows engineers leaving Ericsson to try their hand at technology entrepreneurialism. Given that most wireless start-ups within the Stockholm area are involved in the development of Ericsson-sponsored standards, and in many cases are using its core systems development language, local start-up ventures are working primarily to develop technologies compatible with Ericsson's next generation wireless technologies. If individual firms fail, their managers can now easily return to work within Ericsson, perhaps having developed new managerial skills or career perspectives through working in a start-up. If start-up firms are successful, Ericsson benefits through its sponsorship of key technologies and has close links with the management of the new companies.

Conclusions

By focusing on the characteristics of different subsectors in this chapter, we have been able to explore the mechanisms linking dominant institutions to distinctive business competences and relative success in some detail. As a result, it is clear that the more coordinated European economies can perform well in emerging technology industries, such as biotechnology and software, by seeking sub-segments within these sectors in which firms can embrace long-standing comparative institutional advantage rather than by radically altering institutional frameworks to mimic the US liberal economy model. Evidence presented in this chapter has documented the existence of important subsectors, such as high quality platform biotechnologies and enterprise software, in which patterns of company organization and related business strategy need to develop complex organizational structures focused on competence-enhancing human resource management. Firms in Germany or Sweden have specialized in these technologies not as a 'second best' solution, but because the institutional organization of these business systems create institutional advantages in resolving the key managerial dilemmas in these subsectors.

An implication of this analysis is that there are important trade-offs in designing policies intended to foster entrepreneurial technology firms. Because different types of technology firms vary in the nature of their core organizational competences, their optimal governance requires their embeddedness in differently organized innovation systems. While the US has a large lead in fostering new technology firms, as key technological forces diffuse through the international economy, one can expect that a division of innovative labour will emerge cross-nationally between countries dominated by different institutions and interest groups.

The focus on subsectors also sheds light on the organization of more 'radically innovative' technological segments such as therapeutics biotechnology, standard software, and middleware software. Our analysis complements a number of important studies of the institutional organization of high-technology regions such as Silicon Valley (Almeida and Kogut, 1999; Kenney, 2000;). We share with these studies the suggestion that low technological cumulativeness and resulting competence destruction across clusters of new technology start-ups can be facilitated by the creation of extremely fluid local labour markets. While most studies of technology clusters have a regional focus, we focus primarily on broader national institutional frameworks that structure patterns of coordination across particular sectors and regions within the economy. Doing so helps explain broad differences in technological specialization across economies, but cannot explain the relatively rare development of regional economies capable of fostering high levels of technological intensity across start-up firms within particular economies.

9

Project-Based Firms: New Organizational Form or Variations on a Theme?

Introduction

The important role of project-based modes of organizing and controlling work in new industries, such as the biotechnology and software sectors considered in the previous chapter, together with their increasing use in more established sectors, have been seen by some as heralding the development of a new 'logic of organizing' in market economies (Powell, 1996: 1; see also, DeFillippi and Arthur, 1998; Eckstedt et al., 1999). According to Powell (2001), this involves the flattening of organizational hierarchies, the weakening of firms' boundaries in favour of networks of collaborations, and the restructuring of competition between firms within and across industries. Both the nature of the firm as a hierarchically controlled system of work organization combining legal personality, centralized authority, investor ownership and transferability of shares (Kraakman, 2001), and the arm's length, adversarial nature of inter-firm relations in markets, are, in this view, becoming transformed into more fluid, overlapping organizational arrangements in which both internal and external boundaries are breaking down and cooperation between firms is growing (Jones et al., 1997).

Additionally, entire companies are becoming structured around distinct projects in which people with different skills are brought together to develop innovative products and services within fixed periods of time, and business functions become embodied in project teams (Prencipe and Tell, 2001; Sydow et al., 2004). As Hobday emphasizes (2000: 874–5), in such project-based organizations (PBOs), 'the knowledge, capabilities, and

228

resources of the firm are built up through the execution of major projects'. These kinds of organizations differ from other ways of organizing highly skilled workers in their focus on: (a) creating novel outputs by, (b) integrating varied forms of expertise in, (c) fixed time periods.

A similar contrast is expressed by Mintzberg in his comparison of the 'Adhocratic' organizational form, which is similar to the PBO in its emphasis on novelty, with the professional bureaucratic one. As he suggests (1983: 255–6): 'the Adhocracy must treat existing knowledge and skills merely as bases on which to build new ones. Moreover, the building of new knowledge and skills requires the combination of different bodies of existing ones... Thus, whereas each professional of the Professional Bureaucracy can operate on his own, in the Adhocracy the professionals must amalgamate their efforts... in multidisciplinary teams, each formed around a specific project of innovation.' Task coordination here requires much more face-to-face mutual adjustment than in professional bureaucracies, which rely predominantly on standardized skills for doing so.

In addition to the growing use of projects as coordinating mechanisms, project-based firms (PBFs) in which the company as a legal and financial entity becomes project specific seem to be spreading from the feature film and other entertainment industries to new media and similarly highly dynamic sectors such as computer software development (Grabher, 2002c; DeFillippi and Arthur, 1998; Sydow et al., 2004). Vermeer Technologies, for example, was specifically established as a separate firm to develop a software package for Internet websites that became FrontPage, and was subsequently sold to Microsoft with most of its technologists (Ferguson, 1999). The legal entity controlling property rights was here principally a means of mobilizing a project team to create a new product in a highly competitive and risky environment.

Not only, then, are project-based methods of organizing work in general becoming more noticeable in a range of industries, especially perhaps in the USA (Christopherson, 2002a), but temporary and limited purpose project-based firms (PBFs) seem to be critical agents in the development of new industries, particularly those producing highly innovative products and services. Furthermore, as technologies and markets develop, such PBFs often remain significant actors rather than being replaced by larger, more stable, oligopolistic enterprises. Relatively small, entrepreneurial firms continue to play important roles in the biotechnology industry, for example, instead of being swallowed up by the established pharmaceutical companies, especially in its highly risky therapeutic subsectors (Casper, 2000; McKelvey et al., 2004; Powell et al., 1996).

In their combination of rapid entry and exit, high flexibility and focus on developing major innovations involving discontinuous learning, these kinds of PBFs are distinct from many other kinds of project-based organizations that undertake a number of projects with more cumulative learning and greater continuity of employment, as in the Munich software industry (Grabher, 2004b; Ibert, 2004). Insofar as they play a leading and continuing role in the development of a number of industries, they raise questions about the nature of firms as learning organizations specializing in the creation and transfer of knowledge, especially how firm-specific problem-solving capabilities can be developed if skilled staff have only very short-term and temporary commitments to particular companies (Grabher, 2002a; Kogut and Zander, 1993; 1996; Teece *et al.*, 1994; 2000). As DeFillippi and Arthur (1998: 125) put it: 'How can project-based enterprises create competitive advantage when its knowledge-based resources are embodied in highly mobile project participants?'

If organizational learning is indeed key to the development of innovations and effective dynamic capabilities, and 'the firm creates its distinctive signature by coordinating the internal division of labour and . . . by transforming the knowledge and skills of the individual members into a collective unitary capability' (Metcalfe and James, 2000: 42–3), in what sense can single-project firms be considered viable enterprises? They may constitute distinct legal and financial entities yet fail to develop organizational capabilities that are firm specific. Insofar as major new industries, and some more established ones in the Italian industrial districts and Denmark, are dominated by such project-based enterprises, how and where does learning take place, and how is it incorporated into new routines and procedures (Andersen and Christensen, 1999; Gann and Salter, 2000; 2003; Hobday, 2000; Kristensen, 2006; Prencipe and Tell, 2001)?

In attempting to deal with these sorts of questions, it is important to distinguish between the considerable varieties of different kinds of PBFs. While they all: (a) organize work around relatively discrete projects that, (b) bring particular groups of skilled staff together to work on, (c) complex, innovative tasks for, (d) a variety of clients and purposes, they vary in the number and variety of projects they undertake, the customization and market uncertainty of their outputs, and the technical uncertainty involved in achieving their purposes (Grabher, 2002a; 2004b; Jones *et al.*, 1997). These kinds of differences are related to appropriability regimes and patterns of technological cumulativeness (Malerba and Orsenigo, 1993; Breschi and Malerba, 1997), as well as affecting the ease of gaining investor and worker commitment in contrasting institutional environments. In turn, differences between sectors and institutions help to explain variations in the prevalence of different kinds of PBFs in different industries, regions, and countries.

As a preliminary contribution to understanding how and why different kinds of PBFs seem likely to play a leading role in the development of particular industries in particular institutional contexts, this chapter outlines a way of distinguishing them as distinctive kinds of economic actors that can be expected to vary in their significance between societal environments. I separate PBFs from the more general project coordination and control of work by emphasizing their roles as economic actors with distinct legal and financial powers and responsibilities. Project-based firms are here understood as legally constituted collective actors that control property rights and exercise formal authority over task organization and performance through employment contracts. Some, but not all, types of PBFs are able to develop firm-specific capabilities and knowledge through the management of a succession of projects and employment of skilled staff.

In contrast, more general project forms of work organization are particular ways of coordinating tasks and skills that can be established both within individual firms and between them in various inter-firm networks and consortia (Jones *et al.*, 1997; Powell *et al.*, 1996; 2002). Thus, large firms may organize some of their activities around projects without thereby becoming PBFs, and people from different companies may work together on specific projects without becoming employees of a distinct and separate firm, although in practice it is not always straightforward to draw this distinction sharply, especially where activities are being outsourced and employees are 'lent' to sub-contractors (Grimshaw and Miozzo, 2006; Miozzo and Grimshaw, 2006).

To distinguish between kinds of PBF that are more or less likely to become significant in different industries and societies, I first outline two summary dimensions and identify the key characteristics of four ideal types. Next, I suggest how these different types can be expected to become prevalent in sectors with particular characteristics, notably the strength of appropriability conditions, the modularity of outputs and visibility of processes, the extent of client involvement in project development, and the degree of technological cumulativeness. I then consider the institutional conditions that seem likely to encourage the establishment of these different kinds of PBFs though their facilitation of investor and employee commitment. This analysis implies that highly flexible enterprises developing radical innovations are only likely to become dominant kinds of firms in a limited number of industries in particular institutional regimes. Insofar as they do represent the key economic actor in Silicon Valley (Bahrami and Evans, 1995) and similar innovative regions, this suggests that such socio-economic systems of innovation are not likely to become widely established.

Characteristics and Types of Project-Based Firms

Project-based firms vary considerably in the kinds of products and services they produce, the level of market and technical uncertainty they have to deal with, and their organizational complexity. Project outcomes, for example, can differ in terms of their customization, ambiguity of specification and extent to which clients co-produce them. They are also more or less discrete, tradable, predictable, competence destructive and technologically continuous (Breschi and Malerba, 1997; Tushman and Anderson, 1986). Such variations have significant implications for the management of PBFs and their ability to generate distinctive collective capabilities and knowledge, as discussed in the previous chapter. Additionally, the variety, interdependence and stability of knowledge and skills differ considerably between PBFs, as does the uncertainty of their work environments. These kinds of variations affect the complexity of project organization and coordination costs. In considering which characteristics of PBFs are likely to lead to particular kinds of them being significant economic actors in different industries and environments, two underlying dimensions dealing with learning and the development of firm-specific knowledge seem especially important.

These concern: (a) the extent to which firms focus on developing unusual, sometimes one-off, products and services for varied, and often uncertain, markets, and b) the extent to which the organization of expertise, tasks and roles is predictable and stable over projects. The first differentiating dimension of PBFs can be termed the singularity of their goals and outputs because it contrasts those producing a single or small number of quite different kinds of results for different customers or markets from those conducting a series of related projects producing similar kinds of outcomes. The more singular are outputs, the more likely that organizations will have to deal with exceptions to their routines and adjust to variations in materials and the work environment.

Highly singular PBFs carry out a limited number, sometimes only one, of quite different projects with varied participants and outputs. The novel, atypical and substantially inimitable nature of their products and services means that the development of market and technological knowledge is unlikely to be cumulative within the firm, although it might be at the individual level of analysis (Malerba and Orsenigo, 1993). In much feature film production, for instance, especially since the decline of the studio system in the USA (Christopherson, 2002b; DeFillippi and Arthur, 1998; Zuckerman, 2004), and many complex construction projects, a considerable number of technically qualified experts are contracted to work together on producing one or a small number of particular kinds of products, whose specification may be open to interpretation and change over the course of the project. The 'firm' coordinating such projects and employing these staff is often just a legal vehicle, or 'administrative convenience' (DeFillippi and Arthur, 1998: 137), for paying wages, acquiring other resources and owning property rights over the final product. Once the film or building is completed, such firms cease to exist, except perhaps as a paper entity with one or two principals controlling property rights (Davenport, 2005; Davenport and Czaban, 2005).

In contrast, what Grabher (2002a, 2004a) terms 'agency' businesses, such as those in the London advertising industry, undertake a series of similar projects, many continuing at the same time, with a core group of employees who work together over a period of time and develop collective routines for managing such activities. Although many staff are often quite mobile, changing employers, for instance, on average every two or so years in the London advertising labour market (Grabher, 2002b), they are more stable organizational members than freelancers, and the firms develop distinctive capabilities and reputations as a result of their collective learning. These kinds of PBFs, then, organize work around recurrent projects, and often rely on outsiders for completing individual tasks, but retain a core group of employees for initiating, organizing and conducting separate projects. Knowledge development is here more likely to be cumulative at the firm level than in highly singular PBFs.

The singularity of outputs is an important differentiating characteristic of PBFs because it distinguishes firms that are little more than a set of contracts, or 'hollow' companies in the terminology of Teece *et al.* (1994: 20), from those that are able to develop economies of recombination and repetition through learning from a series of relatively short-term and similar kinds of projects (Davies and Brady, 2000; Grabher, 2002c). Highly singular PBFs often contract specialists to work together as a team to achieve a specific objective, and neither party has any expectation of continued employment or cooperation after the successful completion of that goal (see, e.g., Almeida and Kogut, 1999; Angel, 2000; Eckstedt *et al.*, 1999: 210–16). While such flexibility enables companies to change direction rapidly as knowledge and markets alter, it limits the development of shared identities and firm-specific capabilities through collective learning (Kogut and Zander, 1996). Commitments and identities in these kinds of industries are as likely to be focused on professional communities and project teams as on such flexible firms, and so their ability to develop firm-specific knowledge over a succession of projects will be limited (Bresnen *et al.*, 2004; Prencipe and Tell, 2001).

Less singular PBFs, on the other hand, employ skilled staff to work in a number of teams on a succession of similar kinds of outputs. Although their labour turnover may be considerable, where projects are similar in the type of problems they generate, and perhaps in the sorts of customers they serve, teams and employers are more able to learn across projects and to develop distinctive routines that could form the basis of firm-specific capabilities. In Perrow's (1967) terminology, they have to deal with fewer exceptions and are able to use more standardized techniques to deal with problems. In principle, then, the less varied are project customers, goals and problems, the more PBFs may be able to generate distinctive, organization-specific competences, as in the case of some 'systems integrators' such as W. S. Atkins (Davies, 2003).

The second differentiating feature of PBFs considered here concerns the distinctiveness and stability of work roles, professional identities and skills within project teams and over the course of several projects, and so the continuity of patterns of work coordination and control across projects. In some craft-dominated sectors, such as the feature film industry (Christopherson, 2002a; 2002b; Davenport, 2005), roles and skills are clearly separated throughout projects, and skill-based identities remain stable over a succession of projects, if not indeed entire working lifetimes. This enables project teams to be quickly assembled and to work effectively together at short notice (Jones, C, 1996). Detailed coordination of tasks can be delegated to teams of specialists without needing to establish an elaborate control system with formal, organization-specific procedures governing work activities as long as task uncertainty and complexity remain limited. Learning in these kinds of PBFs tends to occur within established skills and roles rather than between them, and innovations, or 'freshness' (Grabher, 2004b), are often developed more through changing team members than through developing new ways of working together and combining expertise in novel groupings.

In other kinds of PBFs, such as those in the Munich enterprise software industry (Grabher, 2004b; Ibert, 2004), workers adopt different roles over the course of projects and in different project teams, and the division of labour is not so strongly structured around previously codified skills. The mutability of task organization and expertise means that staff are often required to adapt their roles and knowledge to changing circumstances, and so a capacity for developing new competences together becomes as, if not more, important as formally certified skills. Learning and new knowledge development are here more team and organization specific than individual, with greater emphasis on cumulative improvements in collective capabilities than on individual skill enhancement. Coordination of tasks and skills is more complex in these kinds of PBFs, but their greater organizational flexibility enables them to change work processes more readily. This distinguishing feature of PBFs can be termed the degree of role separation and stability because it concerns the flexibility and distinctiveness of their system of work organization and control.

This characteristic differentiates PBFs that organize task and skills in novel, fluid and firm-specific ways from those that rely more on pre-established competences, identities and routines for working together. The former types are more likely to develop distinctive kinds of organizational capabilities and learning through establishing and changing patterns of work organization and division of tasks and skills that are specific to each company. In contrast, the latter kinds of PBF tend not to invest significant organizational resources in managing teams and developing novel forms of the division of labour. Learning here tends to be more specific to each individual and role than collective and organizational.

In principle, these two dimensions are orthogonal in that projects with varying degrees of singularity can be accomplished with different degrees of role separation and stability, as comparisons of the Munich enterprise software and London advertising industries indicate (e.g. Grabher, 2004a; 2004b). Highly singular PBFs can operate with contrasting levels of organizational flexibility, as in many feature film and internet software companies such as Vermeer Technologies (Ferguson, 1999), and multiple project enterprises can exhibit different rates of change of key expertise and organizational structures (Christopherson, 2002b). This means that we can distinguish four ideal types of PBFs that have contrasting levels of commitment between investors, managers and employees, and varying organizational complexity and fluidity. These are summarized in Table 9.1 and will now be discussed further.

Table 9.1. Types of project-based firms

Singularity of Goals and Outputs

		Low	High
Separation and Stability of Work Roles	Low	*Organizational* PBFs producing multiple and varied outputs with different and changeable skills and roles. e.g. strategic consultancy, enterprise software, innovative business services.	*Precarious* PBFs producing risky, unusual outputs with varied and changeable skills and roles. e.g. some dedicated biotechnology firms, internet software firms such as Vermeer Technologies, many Silicon Valley companies.
	High	*Craft* PBFs producing multiple, incrementally related outputs with distinct and stable roles and skills. e.g. some business and professional services including London advertising firms, Danish furniture and machinery firms, some IT consulting.	*Hollow* PBFs producing single outputs and coordinating tasks through standardized, separate and stable roles and skills. e.g. complex construction projects, many feature films in the UK and USA.

The first, which could perhaps be labelled the hollow (Teece *et al.*, 1994: 20) or contractual PBF, combines a focus on one or a small number of different kinds of projects with a reliance on relatively distinct and stable skills and work roles. The types of knowledge and expertise required are here fairly predictable and can be decided in advance, as can when they will be needed. While goals and performance standards may be subject to change as projects develop, authority to decide their nature and resolve disputes can be allocated beforehand and procedures established to manage on-site contingencies. Coordination occurs through generic and standardized skills that define roles in a relatively stable division of labour, sometimes reinforced by union agreements, as well as through temporary authority hierarchies and contracts. Many companies established to make feature films in the UK and USA and undertake complex construction projects resemble these kinds of PBFs (Christopherson, 2002b; Davenport and Czaban, 2005).

Second, there are multiple project firms carrying out a number of similar projects with relatively stable and codified skills that structure the definition and allocation of tasks. Such craft PBFs resemble the artisanal small companies found in industrial districts (Crouch *et al.*, 2001), but also provide some business and professional services where teams of diversely skilled staff are constructed to generate innovative solutions for complex problems. Such innovation, though, is typically incremental and client specific. It does not usually result in major modification of occupational skills or the division of labour in project teams, it is competence enhancing or extending rather than destructive. Expertise and roles in these kinds of PBFs remain, then, quite stable over a series of projects.

Employees in craft PBFs owe their primary loyalty to their craft and occupational identity rather than to their current employer, as illustrated by Kristensen's (1996; 2006) account of Danish 'project coordinator' firms. Employment commitments are correspondingly limited, with many employees leaving to establish their own firms, and boundaries between owners, managers and workers being fluid. Firms are here built around the skilled workforce rather than being separate, autonomous managerially dominated organizations with distinctive administrative routines and capabilities (Karnoe, 1999).

The major difference between these kinds of PBFs and the third type to be considered here lies in the latter's greater fluidity and variability of knowledge, skills and the division of labour. In these organizational PBFs, expertise, work roles and coordination mechanisms are much more changeable, both within and across projects. Coordination costs are correspondingly greater since skills are only weakly standardized and do not structure work routines to a great extent. This means that cross-project learning has to be more formally organized than in craft PBFs, as is emphasized by Grabher (2000a; 2004b) in his contrast of the Munich enterprise software industry with the London advertising industry. Many business services, such as strategic consultancy, seem to be performed by these kinds of PBFs, although some consulting companies do use more distinct and stable skills sets and systems of work roles, as in certain information technology fields (Creplet et al., 2001; Werr, 2002).

Such PBFs often develop systematic procedures for managing workflows, allocating skills and monitoring progress. They also sometimes establish formal systems for codifying and storing project team 'knowledge' and training staff in the firm's collective expertise. Despite quite high levels of turnover, as in many management consultancies, such procedures and the development of a core group of employees who make their careers within these PBFs enable them to generate distinctive organization specific capabilities and cumulative knowledge development. They become the basis for the firm's reputation and competitive advantages.

Finally, firms contracting skilled staff to work on highly uncertain and singular projects can be characterized as precarious PBFs. Here, the inherent difficulty in gaining investor and employee commitment to temporary organizations producing unique outputs is exacerbated by the high risk of failure and difficulty of knowing which knowledge and skills will be needed as the project proceeds. The combination of singular goals and short-term commitments with complex and dynamic coordination needs makes such PBFs unstable and unlikely to become the dominant kind of economic actor in many industries, except in certain 'project ecologies' such as that surrounding many firms in Silicon Valley (Bahrami and Evans, 1995; cf. Grabher, 2002b; 2004b).

Coordination of workflows and knowledge in these kinds of PBFs is usually achieved through project teams in which roles and skills are highly fluid and changeable, as at Vermeer Technologies (Ferguson, 1999). Organizational procedures tend to be informal and project specific, as project failure is common and the firm cannot afford to establish more stable ones. The division of labour and expertise can become quite volatile in precarious PBFs as the organization is (re-) built around each major project and commitment is focused on accomplishing project objectives rather than being restricted to carrying out technically complex but recurrent tasks. Clearly, such commitment is difficult to develop, both for business partners and highly trained and skilled staff, and often depends on equity stakes and similar high-powered incentives, as in the case of Vermeer Technologies and many Silicon Valley firms (Bahrami and Evans, 1995; Ferguson, 1999).

Risk, Commitment, and Institutional Frameworks in the Development of Project-Based Firms

The economic significance of these four ideal types of PBFs can be expected to vary considerably between different kinds of industries and market economies. This is principally because of variations in: (a) the extent and kinds of risks involved in undertaking different kinds of projects in contrasting industries and, (b) the kinds of institutions governing the commitment of capital and labour power. I suggest that these differences are likely to encourage particular kinds of PBFs to become prevalent in particular kinds of sectors and societies, and discourage other types. For example, the widespread development, and continued significance, of precarious PBFs in new industries in particular geographical areas depends on the combination of specific circumstances that are difficult to replicate elsewhere, despite numerous attempts to encourage the growth of new Silicon Valleys in quite different contexts (Bahrami and Evans, 1995; Casper et al., 1999; Casper, 2000).

In this section, I outline the major factors that are likely to affect the prevalence and continued significance of PBFs with varied singularity of goals and outputs and stability of roles. Particularly important are: (a) the nature of project outputs and processes, including appropriability conditions, client involvement and levels of market and technical uncertainty (Malerba and Orsenigo, 1993; Jones *et al.*, 1997) and (b) the nature of institutions governing capital and labour markets (Hollingsworth and Boyer, 1997; Whitley, 1999). I first consider the conditions in which PBFs producing highly singular outputs are likely to become significant economic actors in an industry, and then those affecting role separation and stability, before suggesting how these factors can be expected to influence the kinds of PBF that become prevalent.

A key concern for PBFs producing highly singular outputs is to gain commitments from investors and skilled staff to time delimited organizations whose products and services are difficult to value. This is especially difficult when: (a) both market and technical uncertainty are high and the risks of project failure considerable, as in many emerging industries, and (b) when project outcomes are intangible and hard to trade, as in many business services. Ease of exercising property rights and ability to assess their value are key characteristics of project outputs that affect commitment and organizational form in such fields as software, therapeutic drugs, strategic consultancy, public relations, and investment advice, as discussed in the previous chapter (see, also, Clark and Fincham, 2002; Grabher, 2002a; Kipping and Engwall, 2002).

Very broadly, the more project outputs are discrete and identifiable as separate entities, and the more straightforward it is to realize their value through trading property rights over them, the easier it should be to gain support for PBFs producing singular products and services. Conversely, the more the nature and performance of project outcomes depend on the context in which they are produced, for instance because clients become involved in project development as in some new media fields (Christopherson, 2002b; Grabher, 2002c), and the more difficult it is to appropriate their value as separate entities, the less likely are singular PBFs to be widespread in an industry. We can summarize these factors in terms of the strength of appropriability conditions that enable firms to protect innovations against imitation and extract profits from their innovative activities (Malerba and Orsenigo, 1993: 48).

This dependence of PBFs producing singular outputs on strong appropriability conditions reflects the difficulty of assessing the value of highly distinctive and one-off products as opposed to those that are more similar to existing ones that have already been traded. Investors of capital and skilled labour are unlikely to become committed to a highly singular PBF unless they believe that it will produce a specific output whose distinctive value can be realized on external markets. The less tangible, visible and easy to trade are project outcomes, the more investors are likely to prefer PBFs that undertake a sequence of relatively short-term and similar projects. The risks associated with highly singular outputs also imply that investors will be more willing to support PBFs producing these in industries where there are common technical standards governing product specifications and their interoperability. Such standards enable firms to specialize in making modular innovations rather than producing whole technological systems, and thereby limit the risks of undertaking projects.

A further critical feature of highly singular projects that is needed to ensure continued financial commitment, especially for outside investors, is the visibility of milestones or indicators of significant progress being made (Tylecote and Conesa, 1999). Especially where failure risks are high, such visibility is likely to be essential for PBFs producing singular outputs to be established, and many venture capitalists insist upon obtaining board membership and regular progress reports as a condition of support for such enterprises (Ferguson, 1999; Kenney and Florida, 2000; Lewis, 1999). This often, in turn, means that investors have to be knowledgeable about the technological processes involved and market opportunities, as is the case with many Silicon Valley venture capitalists (Bahrami and Evans, 1995; Hellmann, 2000; Kenney and Florida, 2000). PBFs pursuing distinctive and unusual projects are, therefore, more likely to be supported in regional and national economies that have informed and risk taking venture capitalists, particularly where the rate of technical change is high.

Such venture capitalists often rely on capital markets to provide exit opportunities through public flotations or trade sales for their successful investments, especially where the firm has valuable innovative capabilities. These enable them to commit resources to a portfolio of projects that have considerable, but varying degrees of, risk and uncertainty. Without liquid capital markets that facilitate the trading of ownership cheaply, they are less likely to tolerate high levels of risk and to commit significant financial resources to funding PBFs producing unusual and uncertain outputs. Where, in contrast, capital is largely allocated through banks and similar financial intermediaries and capital markets are illiquid, investors and companies are more locked into each other's destinies (Tylecote and Conesa, 1999). As a result, financiers tend to be more risk averse and reluctant to fund uncertain projects that have few, if any, assets to back them. PBFs producing highly singular outputs are accordingly less likely to be widely established in such financial systems.

Considerable singularity in the goals and results of PBFs additionally depend on the institutionalization of fluid labour markets where requisite skills and knowledge are readily available (Almeida and Kogut, 1999; Bahrami and Evans, 1995). To construct single project firms to carry out complex and varied tasks requires a pool of skilled labour that can be hired at relatively short notice, and whose expertise can be readily assessed. In addition to low commitment employment relationships, this implies the institutionalization of a signalling system whereby employers can advertise opportunities and skilled workers can display their technical knowledge and ability to work effectively in project teams.

While technical expertise can often be signalled through formal qualifications, these may not always communicate critical practical competences, especially where such skills involve working with a range of diversely qualified people. In the case of some media industries, achievements are signalled through formal credits (Faulkner and Anderson, 1987; Hirsch, 1972; Jones, C, 1996), but personal networks in technical, industrial and geographical communities are often the primary means of generating reputations for competence and effectiveness (Jones, 2002). Crucial to the organization of production and distribution of products and services around highly singular PBFs, then, are fluid labour markets and effective signalling systems through, for instance, reputational networks.

Turning now to consider the conditions encouraging the prevalence of PBFs with considerable role separation and stability, there are three factors that are critical. First, the extent to which new products and processes in an industry build on current knowledge and technologies, or are technologically discontinuous, and so likely to be competence destructive as discussed in the previous chapter. Second, the degree to which clients become involved in developing the product or service. Third, the strength of skill formation systems and the extent to which labour markets are structured around certified expertise.

PBFs with a stable division of labour between skills and considerable continuity of professional identities within and across projects seem more likely to become established in industries where technical change is cumulative than where new knowledge, whether developed within or outside projects, frequently and radically alters the evaluation and use of skills. If technical change is rapid and disruptive to existing competences (Christensen, 1997), companies cannot easily plan work around existing established roles and expertise. Flexibility in changing direction, reorganizing skills and developing new knowledge and expertise become critical to PBF survival in such situations, either through rapid learning and altering roles by current employees, and/or by hiring other specialists.

Internal flexibility and restructuring of roles and skills are also important for PBFs in industries where project goals are liable to change as a result of client learning or market changes, as in many business services and new media sectors (Christopherson, 2002b). The more that clients are involved in the production and use of project outputs, as opposed to setting functionality targets and overall goals at arm's length from PBFs, the less likely are roles and skills to remain fixed over the course of projects, especially where these are long term and organization specific. Major consultancy projects that involve staff working intensively with particular firms over long periods to accomplish ambiguous and changeable goals will be difficult for PBFs to conduct successfully if they organize tasks around distinct, separate and stable roles and expertise. Many enterprise software companies that work closely with customers, for instance, encourage fluid roles and a flexible division of labour between technical specialists (Grabher, 2004a; Ibert, 2004).

High levels of role stability and separation within PBFs are additionally encouraged by the institutionalization of a strong public training system that standardizes skills throughout an industry and structures labour markets. The German 'skills machine' (Culpepper and Finegold, 1999) has of course been celebrated by many as critical to the effective production of standardized expertise that is both advanced and effectively signalled to employers. Countries without such an effective skill formation and credentialing system involving both unions and employers are unlikely to produce nationally standardized skills that employers feel able to rely upon in constructing project teams.

However, such standardized initial training is often followed by more idiosyncratic learning and development within companies as employees work on a series of problems with organizational colleagues. Depending on the system of labour market regulation within particular industries and nationally, practical skills become more or less firm-specific and tradable upon external labour markets as people: (a) remain working within a single organization, or (b) seek to enhance their specialist expertise and value in particular technical fields by working in a number of different companies. Where strong sectorally based unions and employers' associations establish industry wide wage rates and restrict poaching of skilled staff, as in Germany (Crouch *et al.*, 1999; Hinz, 1999; Streeck, 1992;

Thelen and Kume, 2003), mobility based on occupational identities is likely to be less frequent than in more liberal market economies. As a result, initially quite standardized expertise becomes less so as workers develop organizational, rather than occupational, identities.

Conversely, in industries and societies that regulate employment relations through intermediary associations based on skills, as in the US film industry (Christopherson, 2002a; 2002b) and Denmark (Pedersen, 2006), identities and roles remain tied to expertise and are more generic across employers. Although working careers in a number of different companies and projects incrementally develop such skills, and in the case of Denmark skill enhancements are often credentialed by various training schools so that they become more personally idiosyncratic (Kristensen, 1999), expertise in these kinds of regulated labour markets remains technically specialized and tradable across organizations. Consequently, they facilitate the development of PBFs dependent on the ability to mobilize teams of specialists with particular, known skills to deal with complex problems, and arguably the institutionalization of 'project container' firms as the prevalent type of firm in a country (Kristensen, 1996; 2006).

These relationships suggest that different types of PBFs are likely to become more significant kinds of economic actors in industries with specific characteristics, and in countries dominated by different kinds of institutional regimes as outlined in earlier chapters. The key connections between characteristics of project products and processes, on the one hand, and of institutional frameworks, on the other hand, in relation to the four types of PBFs discussed above are summarized in Table 9.2. Here, a plus sign indicates that a positive relationship can be expected between a particular characteristic of projects or institutional feature and the likelihood that a particular kind of PBF will become a significant economic actor, and a minus sign the reverse. The combination of both signs indicates an indeterminate connection.

Considering hollow PBFs first, this analysis suggests that they are particularly likely to be significant economic actors in industries with strong appropriability conditions, visible milestones and cumulative technological change. Where the value of project outputs is uncertain, as in much feature film production, they will also be encouraged by flexible capital markets that can facilitate the packaging of projects into risk diversified portfolios. Fluid, dynamic external labour markets structured around relatively standardized practical skills, often regulated by intermediary associations such as unions, are also important features of the institutional environments of these kinds of firms. Additionally, integrated technical

Table 9.2. Project characteristics and institutional frameworks favouring the establishment of different types of project-based firms

	Type of PBF			
	Hollow	Craft	Organizational	Precarious
Characteristics of project outputs and processes				
Strong appropriability conditions	+	+/−	−	+
Modular outputs and visible milestones	+	+/−	−	+
High client involvement	−	−	+	−
Low technical cumulativeness	−	−	+	+
Characteristics of institutional frameworks				
Liquid, transparent capital markets	+	+/−	+/−	+
Knowledgeable venture capitalists	+/−	+/−	+/−	+
Fluid, dynamic external labour markets with effective signalling systems	+	+	+/−	+
Highly standardized expertise structuring labour markets	+	+	−	−
Integrated technical, sectoral and geographical reputational networks	+	−	−	+
Overlapping academic and business labour markets	+/−	+/−	+	+

and industry reputational networks improve signalling processes between temporary employers and employees and reduce transaction costs for these types of PBF (Jones, 2002).

Craft PBFs are also likely to become widely established in industries where technical change is incremental and client involvement in project processes is limited. Additionally, most of the projects that they undertake are relatively short term and outputs are sufficiently similar in kind to enable learning across them. They will be more prevalent in societies where standardized skills and strong professional associations institutionalize relatively stable work roles and structure labour markets. These reduce coordination costs within companies by enabling them to rely on relatively stable and reliable expertise that can be signalled effectively within occupational communities. They also need to be able to mobilize teams of specialized experts to deal with clients' problems at short notice and so fluid labour markets are important to their success.

Organizational PBFs, on the other hand, are more likely to play significant roles in industries where appropriability risks are considerable and the provision of customized services integrates production of problem solutions and knowledge with close customer contact and delivery. Project teams of specialists are here coordinated by managers who ensure that their knowledge is directed to solving the clients' problems and providing customer specific outputs, as in much of the enterprise software industry (Lehrer, 2006). As argued in the previous chapter, while this means that such firms are quite complex in terms of combining different roles and competences, and have to invest in systematic forms of coordination and control, it also ensures that ideas and solutions remain relatively proprietary and are not easy for competitors to imitate.

Precarious PBFs dedicated to producing singular products in situations of high uncertainty, such as Vermeer Technologies in the mid-1990s (Ferguson, 1999), are most likely to play a prominent role in industries with strong appropriability conditions, visible milestones, and innovations are modular rather than systemic. They also depend on highly fluid labour markets in which skilled staff are willing to take high risks for potentially high rewards. Clearly, societies with high levels of employment protection and employer–employee commitment will not be conducive to the widespread formation of precarious PBFs, nor will they encourage highly trained workers to forgo employment in established organizations to join new firms in emerging industries. Equally, as many studies of Silicon Valley have suggested, the continued development of these temporary firms in emerging technologies and markets depends on a socio-economic infrastructure of knowledgeable venture capitalists, lawyers and other providers of business services who are willing to share some of the risks involved by taking equity stakes and managing these commitments as a portfolio of activities (Bahrami and Evans, 1995; Kenney and Florida, 2000; Lee, 2000; Suchman, 2000).

Given the limited stability of teams and work roles in such dynamic industries, and the need to attract new skills at short notice, precarious PBFs additionally depend extensively on reputational networks to find and attract skilled staff. Such networks are often, though not always, based on particular geographical localities where 'learning by monitoring' (Sabel, 1994) is relatively easy to practice and distinctive technical communities form. Effective signalling of relevant technical and social competences, as well as new job opportunities, becomes especially important in these circumstances, and is assisted by the institutionalization of reputational networks that integrate technical communities with industrial and territorial ones.

Furthermore, in industries where skills change rapidly because of new formal knowledge being produced, especially from universities and similar research organizations, the prevalence of precarious PBFs depends upon the boundaries between academia and business being quite permeable, with considerable mobility between universities and industrial enterprises (Whitley, 2003b). This, in turn, implies that labour markets for researchers are not strongly segmented between universities and companies and so movement from one to the other does not usually suggest scientific inferiority or typically prevent reverse transitions, as in the US biotechnology industry (Casper and Murray, 2005; Higgins, 2005).

These points suggest that the widespread establishment of these kinds of PBFs as prevalent units of economic action in a sector will be limited to a few industries and institutional environments, rather than heralding a distinctly new logic of organizing economic activities that can be expected to dominate the development of new industries in most advanced market economies. In particular, contrary to much of the hype surrounding discussions of Silicon Valley and the new economy, precarious types of PBFs are only likely to become significant economic actors in sectors and societies that have the following six characteristics.

Three of these concern business sectors. First, critical technical skills and knowledge are rapidly changing, second, innovations can be effectively protected through copyright and/or patents, and third, technical standards governing the interoperability of components are widely agreed. The other three features reflect the nature of the business environment. First, there is a large pool of highly trained skilled workers who are willing to take risks, together with, second, a 'project ecology' (Grabher, 2002b, 2002c) of supportive and knowledgeable agents and organizations, and, third, research organizations that are relatively open to varied intellectual goals and career patterns.

Concluding Remarks

This discussion of project-based firms has emphasized their considerable variety and lack of convergence to a single form. Rather than temporary systems of work organization and employment becoming the paradigmatic replacement for the Chandlerian company in twenty-first century capitalism, as some have suggested, they differ in a number of key respects that affect the kinds of industries and societies in which they become significant economic actors. In particular, the innovative, highly flexible PBF celebrated in many accounts of the growth of Silicon Valley is only one variant of such companies that differs in important respects from those prevalent in the construction, business services, entertainment and other industries.

Project-based firms vary significantly in how they elicit commitment from investors and workers, and how they coordinate their activities—both internally and externally—as a result of the variable singularity of their goals and outputs, and contrasts in the degree of distinctiveness and stability of the skills they use and how they organize work roles. These differences are important for distinguishing between the quite distinct kinds of PBFs found in a variety of industries and locations such as Silicon Valley, Silicon Alley, the Italian industrial districts, and Denmark. They also suggest a number of reasons why different types of such firms appear to be more or less significant in the development of these industries, and occur with varying frequency in differently organized institutional contexts.

The extent to which PBFs develop distinctive, firm specific organizational capabilities, and of what kind, depends on their longevity, singularity of outputs and coordination procedures. Where firms are established to create a single or very small number of discrete, separate kinds of products and services, and employment contracts are highly project specific, the firm as such is too temporary an organization to develop any distinctive organizational or technical competences. Insofar as learning does occur in the course of the project, it will be largely accomplished and appropriated by individuals and small teams.

Similarly, where skilled workers coordinate their activities directly, as in many craft PBFs in industrial district types of business system and professional service sectors, without much reliance on managerial routines or organizational procedures, learning remains primarily individual or team based. Employees here may improve their technical and team-working skills during each project, but such incremental growth in problem-solving capacities remains largely the property of the individuals involved, not codified into organizational procedures and practices.

It is when the PBF undertakes a series of similar kinds of projects with a core group of employees who remain with the firm for some time that distinctive organizational identities, knowledge and capabilities may be developed and provide competitive advantages. By establishing managerial routines for coordinating and directing teams of specialists to accomplish innovative goals, some PBFs are able to generate firm-specific problem-solving capabilities, including learning from project experiences, both at the individual level and in terms of organizing teams more effectively for dealing with novel problems (Scarborough *et al.*, 2004). Many such PBFs invest in knowledge management systems and related procedures for codifying, combining and disseminating project-based knowledge that enables the organization as a whole to develop distinctive organizational competences. This involves employers being able to offer both short-term incentives and credible long-term organizational career commitments to key staff to encourage them both to build such capabilities and to be flexible in the kinds of expertise and roles they perform within the organization. Organizational PBFs, then, are more likely to develop firm-specific collective unitary capabilities in the sense used by Metcalfe and James (2000) than are other types.

By focusing in this chapter on the singularity of PBF goals and outputs and the separation and stability of skills as critical features of PBFs, I have suggested a way of distinguishing them that might help to explain their varied importance in different kinds of industries and societies. Insofar as success in developing particular technologies and markets is associated with these sorts of companies—and dealing effectively with their commitment and coordination problems—these remarks should also contribute to our understanding of how and why countries and regions with contrasting institutional frameworks specialize to varying extents in such developments.

Part IV

**Internationalization and the
Development of Transnational
Organizational Capabilities**

10

Divergent Multinational Firms: Home and Host Economy Effects on Internationalization Strategies and Organizational Capabilities

Introduction

As discussed in Chapter 4, one of the major changes in the postwar global economy that has affected the cohesion and nature of many postwar business systems has been the growing internationalization of managerial coordination and control through the expansion of multi-national companies (MNCs). The expansion of MNCs in the last two or three decades of the twentieth century is often viewed as particularly significant for international economic coordination because many are more organizationally integrated as cross-national strategic actors than were earlier international firms (Hedlund and Ridderstrale, 1998; Jones, 2005; Wilkins, 2001). Furthermore, some appear to have been able to develop distinctive organizational capabilities that are 'transnational' rather than just being applications of domestically generated ones to foreign units (see, e.g. Bartlett and Ghoshal, 1989; Ghoshal and Westney, 1993).

Multinationals can be seen, then, as the extension of the visible hand of managerial coordination across national political borders. Potentially, they herald the emergence of a new kind of firm because of their management of significant operations in diverse national territories governed by different institutions. Whether such firms are really 'global corporations' (Doremus *et al.*, 1998)—however that is understood—is less significant for the understanding of contemporary capitalism than the possibility that growing managerial co-ordination across borders could generate novel forms of organization and competitive capabilities that are distinct from more nationally focused companies.

From this point of view, late twentieth-century MNCs could be crucial agents in the development of a more global and supranational system of capitalism insofar as they become different kinds of organizations as a result of operating across markets and societies. If new organizational properties and capabilities are being developed by such firms as a direct consequences of their authoritative coordination of economic activities across territorial boundaries and societies, then the increasing number and significance of MNCs in the world economy could represent a qualitative shift in the organization of economic activities throughout the world (Dicken, 1998; Dicken *et al.*, 1994; Whitley, 1998). Where, though, they remain largely national firms with international operations (Hu, 1992), as perhaps has been the case throughout most of the twentieth century, they are unlikely to change radically established patterns of economic organization or to lead to the establishment of a new global business system.

A particularly important factor here is the organizational impact of coordinating economic activities in a variety of business environments with different kinds of business partners. MNCs, that is, are of interest as distinctive organizational entities insofar as they authoritatively integrate economic resources and activities in quite different locations that involve managing contrasting kinds of employees and competing and cooperating with varied sorts of firms in differently organized markets. It is the coordination of major activities across significantly different institutional contexts through organizational routines that potentially makes MNCs distinctive kinds of organizations. The greater diversity of the environments, markets and personnel they have to manage within firms' boundaries suggests that they become more complex organizations than more domestically focused firms and may develop distinctive routines and capabilities as a result.

The extent to which they do indeed develop greater complexity and distinctive organizational routines depends on the following three factors. First, the degree of managerial commitment to different kinds of market economy, second, how much MNCs innovate organizationally in different business units as the result of such commitments, and, third, the extent to which they then institutionalize new ways of doing things across the organization. In general terms, MNCs are more likely to become distinctive kinds of organization when they locate major proportions of key assets and activities in quite different kinds of business systems, allow foreign subsidiaries to adapt to local conventions, and 'learn' from these novel developments by adapting and integrating them through organization-wide routines and procedures. It is the combination of variety of markets, employees, business partners and institutions with organizational integration within ownership-based boundaries that makes MNCs potentially significant different kinds of strategic actors.

It follows from this characterization of MNCs as distinctive organizations that only some types of them have innovative consequences for economic coordination and control systems (Whitley, 1998). It is when they integrate major operations located in quite distinctive and strongly isomorphic institutional contexts and business systems through organization-wide routines and procedures that MNCs are likely to develop novel and distinctive characteristics as a result of internationalization (Westney, 1999). In contrast, where: (a) the commitment of economic resources and activities to different kinds of business environments is limited, (b) subsidiary autonomy is low, and/or (c) foreign subsidiaries are managed at arm's length, so that any organizational innovations in host economies are limited to those units, the firm is unlikely to change its basic nature. Many Japanese MNCs have behaved in this way, and so have developed few new organizational capabilities as a result of operating abroad, as will be discussed further in Chapter 12 (see, also, Beechler and Bird, 1999; Ernst, 2006).

For high contextual variety to be significant in affecting the nature and behaviour of MNCs, then, they have to invest major assets in different kinds of business system and be strongly influenced by dominant institutions in these societies. Variety, in other words, is only meaningful for organizational change when it implies considerable pressure to do things differently for an important part of the business. It is not just a matter of geographical dispersion (Porter, 1986).

Multinational companies vary considerably in the extent to which they invest key resources in different kinds of market economy and encourage learning from these diverse environments. They therefore differ greatly in the level of organizational innovation and change they undergo as the result of internationalization, and in their development of novel and distinctive characteristics. These variations stem from both the governance and capabilities of the firms concerned, which in turn are connected to their dominant domestic business system characteristics and institutional pressures, and the nature of the business systems to which they commit significant resources.

In order to explore these connections in more detail and show how companies from different kinds of economies are likely to internationalize their activities in different ways, the next section of this chapter considers how three very different ideal types of firms are likely to follow contrasting internationalization strategies. The extent of subsequent organizational change, and development of novel capabilities, will also be affected by the nature of the host economies to which firms commit major resources, and how different kinds of MNCs manage their subsidiaries in these. At least three quite distinct ideal types of host economy business environments can be identified and likely patterns of subsidiary management by MNCs in these are discussed in the following section.

Internationalization Strategies of Three Ideal Types of Firms

Given the considerable variety of business systems, dominant strategic actors and institutional regimes in postwar market economies, we would expect both the nature of internationalization strategies, and their consequences for MNC characteristics, to differ greatly between firms from different types of home economy (Doremus *et al.*, 1998; Ruigrok and van Tulder, 1995; Sally, 1995). Rather, then, than seeking to identify how internationalization, per se, affects the nature of firms in general, we need to consider how different firms from contrasting business systems are likely to invest in varied kinds of market economies with different results in terms of organizational change and the development of new kinds of capabilities. To keep the logic of the analysis as clear as possible, I here concentrate on the probable internationalization strategies of the three very different ideal types of company described in Chapter 6, which differ considerably in their authority relationships and dominant kinds of organizational capabilities.

Beginning with the highly centralized isolated autocracies, these kinds of firms are often products of adversarial, unpredictable and highly uncertain business environments. Trust and commitment between groups are difficult to establish in such societies, except on a highly personal basis, and firms rarely develop complex and stable organizational capabilities and routines for managing activities and resources across geographical and temporal boundaries. Rather, authority and co-ordination are highly personal, centralized and non-routinized. Flexibility and responsiveness are key competitive strategies, as these firms have to be adept at adjusting to unpredictable environmental changes and typically limit commitments to any one technology, product or industry. This kind of firm shares many characteristics with the stereotypical Chinese family business in states that provide few collective competition goods for private companies (Gates, 1996; Hamilton, 1997; Redding, 1990).

Managerially coordinated kinds of companies and cooperative hierarchies, on the other hand, develop in more institutionalized business environments that permit strategic decisions to be made with a reasonable expectation that the outcomes of major investments can be rationally calculated. The established rules of the competitive game are here sufficiently institutionalized and stable for owners to delegate some authority to salaried managers and enter into long-term commitments with business partners on a continuing basis. As a result, distinctive organizational competences can be developed in these business environments and firms take on many attributes of Penrosian administrative structures (Penrose, 1959).

These two ideal types differ, however, in respect of the ability and willingness of owners and top managers to collaborate with employees and business partners. While skilled manual workers are typically integrated into the organization as core 'members' in cooperative hierarchies, as in the white collarization of many Japanese workers in large firms in the postwar period (Koike, 1987; Jacoby, 2005), this is rarely the case in managerially coordinated firms. In these types of companies, the 'firm' as an organization consists largely of the managerial and administrative apparatus, excluding most technical and manual employees who are not integrated into it.

Additionally, cooperative hierarchies are more used to collaborating with suppliers, customers and competitors than are managerially coordinated firms, usually through strong industry and trade associations as discussed in Chapter 2. In these business environments, lock-in effects between banks, employers, employees and business partners in general are quite strong, so that interests are shared rather than adversarial and organizational competences are often developed in conjunction with business partners.

In considering how these different ideal types of firms can be expected to internationalize their operations, it is worth pointing out that the relatively low degree of institutionalization of transnational regulatory norms means that established domestic patterns of economic coordination dominate international ones and many firms extend domestic patterns of business unit control to their foreign subsidiaries at first. The weak standardization of international coordination forms, in other words, encourages a plurality of integration patterns of foreign subsidiaries such that different kinds of firms will follow quite contrasting internationalization styles, once they go beyond simple one-off transactions.

These patterns of internationalization vary on a considerable number of dimensions, as the extensive literature on FDI management illustrates (see, for example, Bartlett *et al.*, 1990; Doremus *et al.*, 1998; Dicken *et al.*, 1994; Hennart, 2001; Jones, 2005; Porter, 1986; Sally, 1995). Most of these focus on the significance of FDI as a proportion of total investment, the reasons for FDI, parent-subsidiary relationships, and patterns of subsidiary development. Since I am here concerned with how FDI might generate significantly different kinds of organizations, I shall concentrate on three major aspects of internationalization. First, its strategic significance, rationale and location. Second, how firms manage the risks associated with FDI and their foreign subsidiaries. Third, the nature of subsidiaries' adaptation to, and integration with, local host economies. These can be divided into seven more specific characteristics of internationalization patterns that vary considerably between the three ideal types of firm.

Considering first the extent to which firms commit major resources to foreign locations that are quite different in key respects from their domestic business system and its associated institutions, this continues to vary between, say, British, German and Japanese companies (Doremus *et al.*, 1998; Ernst, 2006; Lane, 2001; Hirst and Thompson, 1996; Ruigrok and van Tulder, 1995). A major contrast here is between firms that have preferred to export to foreign markets for some time before making strategic FDI in quite different kinds of market economies later, and those that have invested significant resources directly in those markets. Second, the importance of firm-specific competitive advantages that can be transferred to foreign subsidiaries varies considerably between firms making foreign investments. While much US internationalization in the 1960s and 1970s, and Japanese manufacturing FDI in the 1980s and 1990s, was seen as gaining market share through exporting distinctive organizational capabilities that were superior to their host economy rivals, more recent FDI has often been focused on gaining access to foreign technologies and innovative capacities, especially that in the USA.

Third, the considerable risks involved in FDI in the relatively weakly institutionalized international business environment can be managed in a number of different ways that reflect firms' experience of risk management in their domestic business systems. This is linked to, fourth, the extent of parental control over major foreign subsidiaries, as well as, fifth, the dominant mode through which this control is exercised. Sixth, foreign subsidiaries vary greatly in their integration into local host economies with regard to technology and product development/modification, components and materials supplies, distribution and marketing. Allied to this is, seventh, their adaptation to local business conventions and practices that lead to major foreign units developing distinctive organizational capabilities. The ways that isolated autocracies, managerially coordinated firms and cooperative hierarchies can be expected to vary on these seven dimensions are summarized in Table 10.1 and will now be further discussed.

There are two key characteristics of these kinds of firms that strongly affect these seven dimensions of their internationalization. First, the extent and nature of their organizational capabilities, and their

Table 10.1. Firm Type and Patterns of Internationalization

Patterns of Internationalization	Firm Type		
	Isolated Autocracy	Cooperative Hierarchy	Managerially Coordinated
Willingness to transfer/ invest major resources in different kinds of business system	Limited	Limited initially	Considerable
Transferability of firm-specific competitive advantages to foreign subsidiaries	Limited	Limited in isolation	High
Prevalent risk management strategies	Flexibility and personal obligation networks	Transfer domestic alliances and market power	Market power and firm-specific advantages
Central control of subsidiaries and integration with parent operations	High	Considerable	Considerable, except where foreign units are large and successful
Prevalent control mode	Direct supervision	Access to strategic resources	Formal procedures
Integration of subsidiaries into local economies	Variable and *ad hoc*	Limited initially	Potentially considerable when large and successful
Subsidiary development of distinct organizational capabilities	Low	Limited, except when acquired for strategic assets	Potentially considerable when large and successful

organization-specific competitive advantages based on such competences, greatly influence both their ability to coordinate operations across borders and how they do so. Second, the prevalent mode of owner control and authority sharing affects how firms manage foreign subsidiaries and deal with uncertainty in different business environments.

Considering first isolated autocracies, these have few organization-specific competitive advantages based on standardized routines and procedures that coordinate complex activities and skills. Accordingly, these kinds of enterprises will gain relatively little from extending their organizational co-ordination of economic activities to overseas locations. Additionally, since owner control tends to be direct and personal in such companies, FDI will be limited to those operations that can be controlled by top management. In general, this concern with direct owner control is likely to restrict the amount and significance of their FDI since such investment increases the already considerable level of uncertainty and distrust between business partners by locating major commitments in new and relatively unknown contexts.

This uncertainty may be mitigated to some extent by such firms locating FDI in geographically or culturally proximate territories, where owner-managers are able to maintain close supervision and/or rely on common sets of expectations and conventions that permit the use of domestic control practices to govern behaviour in foreign subsidiaries. This is arguably what has happened in much Taiwanese investment in China and Malaysia. Thus, we would not expect these kinds of firms to transfer major resources and key value-added activities away from their domestic economies, and, when significant amounts of FDI did occur, this would probably be located in similar sorts of environments and, at least initially, be restricted to relatively easily controlled, routinized activities using cheap, semi-skilled labour (Yeung and Olds, 2000).

As in their domestic contexts, such firms are likely to limit commitments to employees, business partners and markets in foreign locations, and to emphasize flexibility over the long-term development of organizational capabilities in and between subsidiaries. These foreign units would, then, be subject to tight central control. Any integration of such subsidiaries into host economies is, consequently, likely to be short term and ad hoc, such that they will not readily adopt local conventions and routines, or develop distinctive organizational capabilities. Overall, then, isolated autocracies are likely to limit major amounts of FDI to business environments where they feel able to control activities through similar routines to those used domestically and/or through market power, and will strongly integrate foreign subsidiaries' operations with domestic ones.

Both cooperative and managerially coordinated hierarchies, on the other hand, do have some firm-specific competitive advantages that could, in principle, be transferred to foreign subsidiaries. However, as emphasized above, they differ in the extent to which these depend on, and are shared with, employees and business partners. The boundaries of the firm with such advantages are much broader in cooperative hierarchies than they are in more isolated ones. While the former typically include their core skilled workforce, first tier suppliers, lead banks and so on, the latter are largely constituted as distinct organizations by the routines and knowledge of the managerial hierarchy and key professional experts. Their competitive advantages are therefore the property of a more limited and more authoritatively integrated set of people and groups than are those of cooperative hierarchies. As a result, their willingness and ability to invest major resources across borders varies considerably, as does the predominant manner in which they do so.

Cooperative hierarchies develop much of their organizational capabilities and competitive advantage through cooperation with banks, suppliers, customers, and competitors. Because they are strongly embedded in a network of mutual obligations and commitments, their ability to implement radical strategic decisions that would dramatically change the nature of their business and key resources is quite limited in the short term. Change in these firms tends to be incremental, continuous and interdependent with major business partners. As a result, they find it difficult to shift key activities and significant resources rapidly to foreign locations, and moreover are unlikely to see the need for such investment as long as their domestic location and commitments are viewed as providing major advantages. FDI by cooperative hierarchies, then, is likely to take place incrementally, be subsequent to exporting and establishing sales offices, and will not typically involve transferring central activities that are closely linked to domestic partners and agencies.

Furthermore, since these kinds of firms have had limited experience of managing major facilities in adversarial, weakly institutionalized environments, they will find it difficult and time consuming to develop new ways of operating in the relatively anomic international business environment. This will reinforce their reluctance to commit large-scale resources to radically different foreign environments without substantial previous experience of them, through, for example, first establishing distribution and product modification units there.

One way of managing the risks and difficulties faced by cooperative hierarchies investing abroad, especially those from highly coordinated business systems, is to persuade suppliers and other business partners to move as well. This has been a common pattern among large Japanese firms in the postwar period, and also occurred among some European groups before the First World War (Jones, G, 1996: 33–40). Indeed, an important motive for many service companies, such as banks, to establish foreign subsidiaries has been to maintain their close connections with major customers who have undertaken significant FDI. This pattern replicates many key characteristics of the domestic business system in foreign locations and typically reinforces the strong and detailed central control of subsidiaries that these kinds of firms tend to exercise when establishing units in unfamiliar and sometimes threatening business environments.

Because their organizational capabilities are so embedded in particular relationships and contexts, managing major subsidiaries in different locations where partners, employees and institutions are new requires these kinds of firms to develop new competences, and that takes time. At least initially, then, most foreign subsidiaries of any significance will tend to be quite closely supervised and integrated into the parent activities of cooperative hierarchies, as Lane (1998; 2001) suggests has largely been the case for major German companies for many decades since the end of the Second World War. This close supervision of key functions, together with the highly domestically embedded nature of these kinds of firms and their competitive competences, limit the integration of foreign subsidiaries into host economies and their development of distinctive organizational capabilities (Doremus *et al.*, 1998), at least until they gain considerable experience and understanding of novel environments.

In summary, then, cooperative hierarchies are likely to limit the size and centrality of their initial FDI, and confine it to locations that are already familiar and easy to control, as many Continental European firms have done in the twentieth century by concentrating their major foreign investments within Europe (Hirst and Thompson, 1996; Ruigrok and van Tulder, 1995; Sally, 1995). Foreign subsidiaries of these kinds of firms are typically quite closely integrated with parent company operations and will often be linked to host economy units of their domestic business partners. Where the export of such relationships and risk sharing arrangements to foreign locations is feasible, as in, for instance, pluralist, arm's length environments, cooperative hierarchies may well be more willing to invest in these different kinds of business systems, as many Japanese firms have done in the UK and USA. In other words, the reluctance of these kinds of firms in general to commit major resources to quite contrasting economic coordination and control systems, can be mitigated, if not completely overcome, by sharing the risks involved with domestic partners and limiting subsidiary autonomy.

In contrast, managerially coordinated types of firms develop their organizational capabilities and advantages without much authority sharing with the bulk of their labour force and business partners. Competences are here more firm specific and exclusive to individual managerial hierarchies, rarely depending on alliances or cooperation between firms in trade associations and similar groupings, at least over the medium term, or involving non-managerial staff. Units of financial control are coterminous with units of authoritative integration such that authority and ownership are combined in relatively self-contained and discrete entities. As a result, these kinds of firms are much more able to move resources and subunits across borders without being greatly constrained by obligational ties to business partners, including employees. Since their competitive advantages over foreign firms are also more self contained and less dependent on links with domestic partners, they will be more willing and able to invest major resources abroad. Such investments will not typically be associated with suppliers and customers also moving to foreign locations.

In general, managerially coordinated hierarchies are more able to undertake major switches of financial and other resources into novel sectors that are unrelated to their core technologies and markets than are cooperative hierarchies. They also have more need to do so, since they cannot rely on business partners to manage sector risks on a joint, cooperative basis. We would expect, then, these more autarkic firms to be more prone to change technologies and markets discontinuously, and so reconfigure the company over relatively short time periods.

Successful experience of managing these shifts domestically seems likely to encourage top managers to believe that they can equally effectively integrate operations in novel foreign locations by extending their domestically developed practices and procedures to new subsidiaries, especially when these are small relative to their home operations, as in many of the US firms studied by Ferner *et al.* (2006). In such cases, head office control will probably be quite strong as the MNC tries to reap the benefits of applying its firm-specific managerial competences abroad. Additionally, it seems unlikely that they will be eager to adopt new practices from overseas appendages, particularly in areas deemed to be central to the firms' future such as managerial training and succession planning (Butler *et al.*, 2006; Edwards *et al.*, 2006).

However, where foreign subsidiaries are quite large and successful, and foreign operations as a whole constitute a significant proportion of the company's total activities, such central control may become more procedural than substantive and home country managers more willing to learn from abroad. As long as financial targets are met, and formal reporting procedures followed, subsidiaries may be able to exercise some operational independence, especially if they were acquired rather than being the result of greenfield investment, as Kristensen and Zeitlin's (2005) account of APV illustrates.

This emphasizes a more general characteristic of managerially coordinated firms that become established in arm's length institutional regimes, their considerable scope for pursuing varied and changeable strategies as a result of the limited institutional homogenization of their domestic environment. Because these kinds of firms are more able to develop idiosyncratic practices in many areas of their operations—such as employment policies and practices—than those in more standardized and 'thick' institutional environments (Hollingsworth and Streeck, 1994), they are more likely to differ in some aspects of their internationalization strategies and how they manage subsidiaries. They are also more likely to change such patterns quite sharply when market conditions alter and top personnel move, as noted by many of the European subsidiary managers of US companies interviewed by Ferner *et al.* (2006). Insofar as some such MNCs do delegate considerable operational autonomy to some foreign units, and these are integrated into their host economies with substantial local sourcing and product adaptation to local market conditions, we would expect them to develop distinctive capabilities that might contribute to other parts of the international organization.

Internationalization and Organizational Change

The extent to which, and likely ways in which, these three types of firms do change as a result of investing major resources in foreign locations are also affected by the sorts of business environments in which they establish subsidiaries. How firms from contrasting business systems are likely to manage their FDI in societies dominated by three quite different institutional regimes, particularistic, collaborative and arms' length, are summarized in Table 10.2 and will now be discussed. Their main features

Table 10.2. Firm type, foreign business environments, and management of FDI

Management of FDI by Different Firm Types	Types of Foreign Business Environments		
	Particularistic	Collaborative	Arms' Length
Significance of FDI			
Isolated autocracy	Low	Low	Low
Cooperative hierarchies	Low	Limited	Some
Managerially coordinated	Low	Variable	Considerable
Prevalent Risk Management Strategies			
Isolated Autocracy	Flexibility, personal networks	Personal networks	Personal networks
Cooperative hierarchies	Market power	Market power and incremental alliances	Transfer domestic alliances and market power
Managerially coordinated	Market power	Market power and short-term alliances	Market power and firm-specific advantages
Extent and Mode of Parent Control of Major Subsidiaries			
Isolated Autocracy	High, direct, personal	High, personal	High, personal
Cooperative hierarchies	High, direct, resource access	Considerable, resource access	Considerable, resource access
Managerially coordinated	High, resource control and targets	Considerable when relatively small, formal procedures	Considerable when relatively small, formal procedures
Extent of Subsidiary Integration into Local Economy			
Isolated Autocracy	Limited, *ad hoc* and short term	Limited and *ad hoc*	Limited and *ad hoc*
Cooperative hierarchies	Limited and *ad hoc*	Limited, incremental	Limited
Managerially coordinated	Some but short term	Potentially considerable	Potentially considerable
Subsidiary Development of Distinctive Capabilities			
Isolated Autocracy	Low	Low	Low
Cooperative hierarchies	Low	Limited	Limited
Managerially coordinated	Low	Potentially considerable for large acquisitions	Potentially considerable for large acquisitions
Extent of Organizational Learning and Change from FDI			
Isolated Autocracy	Low	Limited	Limited
Cooperative hierarchies	Low	Limited, but more complex	Limited, but more complex
Managerially coordinated	Low	Limited, but more complex	Potentially some, increased complexity

can be analysed along similar lines to the patterns of internationalization discussed above, beginning with the extent of FDI and the management of risks and control modes, then dealing with subsidiary characteristics and the extent of organizational learning that is likely to take place.

Considering first investment in particularistic environments, it seems unlikely that any of these kinds of firms will commit a large proportion of their key resources on a long-term basis to countries where there is great uncertainty over property rights and the reliability of formal institutions. As one Japanese top manager put it when asked about investment in China in the early 1990s: 'we rent space there', rather than making irreversible commitments to such an environment. It might be thought that many isolated autocracies would find it easier to manage subsidiaries in these kinds of societies because they are more used to dealing with highly uncertain and unpredictable contexts and their domestic control procedures may be generalizable to similar kinds of cultures and political economies. However, their general unwillingness to make irreversible and long-term commitments of substantial resources make it unlikely that they would do so in foreign countries anymore than they do at home.

When FDI in such locations does take place, typically because of the large potential market and/or major cost reductions, such firms seem likely to follow the same strategy for managing risks as they do at home, i.e. maximizing flexibility, minimizing commitment and developing close personal connections to those in power. This seems to be the dominant pattern reported by many authors in Yeung and Olds' *Globalization of Chinese Business Firms* (2000). Cooperative hierarchies and managerially coordinated types of firms, on the other hand, are likely to be much larger and be able to exert considerable market power over local business partners and state agencies. Since institutional regulation of economic relationships is weak in these environments, relying primarily on economic dominance and straightforward short-term advantages seems more probable than developing long-term collaborations or formal structures.

Similarly, the high level of uncertainty encourages strong parental control of subsidiaries in such economies, especially when these conduct significant operations and property rights are only weakly upheld. As a result, their adaptation to local norms and practices will be limited to the minimum necessary to ensure efficient operations in a similar manner to that practised in the home country. The combination of limited commitment, strong central control and considerable technology and product dependence on the parent company limits the likelihood that subsidiaries in particularistic environments will develop distinctive organizational competences or become highly integrated into local economies. Equally, few MNCs are likely to change their organizational routines much as a result of investing in such societies.

Collaborative business environments, on the other hand, are more predictable and co-ordinated social systems that encourage longer-term commitments and cooperation. They are, therefore, less risky sites for FDI than particularistic ones. However, foreign firms may find it difficult to gain access to the established networks and alliances that dominate such economies, at least initially. They also have to adapt to prevailing norms and practices that are quite strongly institutionalized in these societies. Since dominant business practices typically involve considerable authority sharing and mutual commitments, isolated autocracies seem unlikely to make major investments in them.

Cooperative hierarchies, in contrast, are used to these sorts of arrangements, but of course are embedded in different alliances in their home economies. They will therefore limit their commitments to new partnerships initially and proceed incrementally. Given the coordinated nature of these host economies, and the strength of institutional arrangements, the likelihood that cooperative firms could rapidly extend their domestic network to such foreign locations is low. As a result, when they do invest in such environments, these kinds of companies are likely to integrate their subsidiaries quite strongly into their parent firm's operations and only slowly develop local linkages.

Managerially coordinated firms have less close links with domestic business partners and institutions, but are also less familiar with the benefits that cooperation can bring and less willing to invest in the development of long-term linkages. It seems probable, then, that their commitments to collaborative environments will have shorter time horizons than those of cooperative hierarchies, but may be quite sizeable where market opportunities and technological learning possibilities seem attractive. The extent of their FDI in these kinds of locations, then, is variable.

The risks of FDI in these contexts are likely to be managed differently by these three types of firms. Isolated autocracies have few organizational capabilities and are unwilling to enter into long-term commitments, so alliances and partnerships remain unusual for these sorts of companies. Cooperative hierarchies, on the other hand, will probably try to develop such linkages, but slowly and incrementally as they learn about the new environment and adapt to it. This is especially likely when the host market is large and wealthy and its institutions are strong, as in postwar Japan.

Managerially coordinated companies may also adapt to dominant mores, but are perhaps more likely to rely on market power to short-circuit the process of building alliances, as well as on their firm-specific competitive advantages to attract local business partners. Where they do pursue local partnerships and adapt to local practices, as some US firms have done in Japan, they often find it difficult to integrate such subsidiaries into the global organization. This suggests that MNCs with major subsidiaries in a variety of strong collaborative environments will be limited in the extent of their organizational integration.

While these environments are not as uncertain and threatening as particularistic ones are, and so do not encourage high levels of direct control by the parent company, the pervasiveness of nationally based networks and alliances, and the generally uneven 'playing field', increase subsidiary dependence on the parent company, except of course for those taken over. Isolated autocracies will, in any case, continue to exercise strong direct control over foreign subsidiaries as they do at home as long as their domestic environment remains unpredictable and particularistic. Cooperative hierarchies might be more willing to allow subsidiaries to 'learn' about their novel environment and adopt new ways of doing things, at least as long as they have not committed major resources to it, but are likely to try to control them through access to key resources.

Managerially coordinated firms, on the other hand, are more used to relying on formal control systems, and are also more confident of their ability to manage diverse activities in varied environments through such mechanisms. Granting considerable autonomy to units in collaborative environments that are seen as 'different', as long as they meet financial and other targets, may therefore seem quite reasonable to these kinds of firms. Later on, of course, global integration could become more pressing as companies try to build on and extend their firm-specific advantages across major markets, but this will not be easy where foreign subsidiaries have successfully adapted to various kinds of business environments.

This willingness to tolerate some subsidiary autonomy means that local units of managerially coordinated types of firms will be more likely to adapt to collaborative host economy conventions and practices than those of cooperative and isolated autocracies. Additionally, because these norms are more organized and institutionalized in these kinds of business environments than those of particularistic ones, they will have more sustained impact, albeit incremental, on foreign subsidiaries of both cooperative and managerially coordinated hierarchies. Both German and US firms, for example, can be expected to adapt more over time to Japanese practices and institutionalized expectations than they would in China and similar contexts. Both kinds of environments encourage accommodating behaviour to dominant conventions, but the more systemic and strongly institutionalized Japanese environment is more likely to lead subsidiaries to adopt organizational routines that fit local norms as major components of their organization and strategies than is the less systematically integrated and more volatile and diverse Chinese one.

The greater autonomy of many managerially coordinated firms' subsidiaries should enable them to develop distinctive organizational capabilities at an earlier stage than foreign units of cooperative hierarchies or isolated autocracies, especially if they have been acquired. As subsidiaries of cooperative companies become more integrated into host economies, they develop particular routines and linkages to local partners that differ from those of their parent and are more isomorphic with the host economy than those of managerially coordinated hierarchies. However, this seems likely to take quite a time for new business units. Similarly, where subsidiaries of managerially coordinated MNCs are more independent, they can be expected to source more of their inputs from local suppliers, including technological services, as well as relying on local distribution channels. Those from cooperative hierarchies will rely more on products and technologies from the parent, or they may seek to reproduce domestic partnerships and connections with local subsidiaries of domestic allies. Isolated autocracies are likely to be governed by short-term price considerations in deciding where to buy supplies, and perhaps also by personal ties.

Overall, then, isolated autocracies seem least likely to adopt new routines and practices as a result of investing in collaborative environments. They are unlikely to commit major resources to such economies and equally unwilling to enter into collaborative, reciprocal linkages with business partners, including workers. Cooperative hierarchies are also unlikely to commit substantial investments to such economies in the early stages of their internationalization, and will 'learn' only incrementally when they do so invest. Once established, and if subsidiaries do become integrated into the host economy, however, their tendency to integrate units across borders may well generate some more significant changes in routines than occurs in isolated firms.

Managerially coordinated firms are the most probable to undertake major investments in these kinds of economies, often through acquisitions, and to grant subsidiaries some autonomy to develop their own ways of dealing with the local conventions. However, if these subsidiaries do become distinctive kinds of organizations with routines that are different from those of the parent company, it will be difficult to integrate these more collaborative ways of coordinating economic activities with the whole enterprise because both their domestic context and the international business environment are antagonistic to such patterns. It seems unlikely therefore that such firms which have invested extensively in collaborative business environments and developed subsidiaries that are successful in them will radically change the basic characteristics of the whole organization. Learning in the sense of institutionalizing new routines based on these foreign subsidiaries, then, is unlikely to be highly significant in such firms (Edwards *et al.*, 2006).

Arm's length business environments are perhaps the most open to FDI because formal regulatory norms are quite institutionalized and, in theory, equally applicable to all enterprises. To a considerable extent, then, foreign firms compete on a 'level playing field' with local ones. Neither particularistic connections nor membership of local networks grant host economy firms especially strong competitive advantages in these kinds of economies—or at least not as major ones as they do in the other two contexts just considered. Isolated autocracies, though, are no more likely to commit major resources to them than to other ones because of their anxiety about control and flexibility. While some may invest in leading economies to obtain access to new technologies and markets, the ways they have managed the unsupportive, if not antagonistic, environment at home will limit the size and centrality of FDI.

Cooperative and managerially coordinated hierarchies, on the other hand, have considerable organizational competencies for coordinating economic activities and experience of making large-scale commitments. However, the former have less familiarity with adversarial environments and fewer firm-specific advantages that can be detached and transferred from their domestic environment. They are therefore unlikely to make major investments in these sorts of economies without gaining prior experience of their dominant conventions, and so will proceed cautiously. Managers in the latter type of firm, on the other hand, will be more confident of managing significant activities in these kinds of contexts effectively and so be more willing to make substantial commitments.

Risk management strategies and parent control practices in arm's length environments often follow the logic of firms' domestic economies since local institutional pressures to conform to a single dominant set of business practices in all functional areas are weak. The formality and pluralism of dominant governance mechanisms in such societies permit more variation across such areas than they do in more integrated environments, so that incoming investors have some scope for introducing their own practices in particular fields (Rosenzweig and Nohria, 1994).

Thus, isolated autocracies can be expected to develop personal networks, often amongst similar ethnic groups, while cooperative hierarchies may well encourage domestic partners to establish subsidiaries in the same locations so that they can share risks with them and rely on established relationships to reduce uncertainty in the new environment. This, of course, implies that such firms reproduce domestic connections in the major overseas subsidiaries and maintain a high level of international integration. Their involvement in local host economies remains relatively low, as does their adaptation to local practices and conventions in many functional areas. As a result, subsidiaries' development of distinctive organizational characteristics and capabilities is limited. The many studies of Japanese subsidiaries in the UK and USA illustrate such behaviours (see, for example, Elger and Smith, 1994; Kenney and Florida, 1993, as well as Chapter 12).

Managerially coordinated firms, on the other hand, are used to managing risks internally and have competitive advantages that are more firm specific than shared with business partners. They are therefore likely to manage risks in foreign locations in much the same way as they do domestically, through their market power and organizational skills, and rely on standard control procedures to integrate foreign units. Since these environments are similar to their domestic one, these kinds of firms may well consider that their domestic routines should simply be applied to foreign units, especially where these are relatively small.

In terms of organizational learning from establishing subsidiaries in arm's length environments, this is clearly going to be limited in the case of isolated autocracies, both because they are not likely to make major investments and because, when they do set up subsidiaries, these will have limited autonomy and organizational capabilities. Cooperative hierarchies also limit their subsidiaries' adaptation to local norms and integration into host economies, but as they learn more about operating in adversarial environments and integrating operations across borders they may well develop more novel routines and adapt to host contexts. Especially in internationally competitive economies where they can obtain access to new technologies and markets, such firms attempt to develop new competitive advantages that will be firm specific, and so can be generalized throughout the whole organization.

An example of this kind of learning—or intention to acquire new knowledge and organizational capabilities—is provided by the investments by some German chemical and pharmaceuticals companies in US medical research organizations and bio-technology companies, and, to a much lesser extent, by some Japanese banks' investments in London and New York (see, for instance, Sakai, 2000 and the discussion in Chapter 12). Partly for regulatory reasons and partly because these locations were seen to possess advantages that could not be accessed domestically, firms from collaborative environments made substantial commitments to the Anglo-American economies in the 1980s. More recently, other German firms in different industries have begun to seek NYSE listings and acquisitions in the USA as a way of gaining more autonomy from domestic institutional pressures, especially labour management restrictions, and to develop new capabilities that, in principle, could be repatriated (Lane, 1998; 2001; Mueller, 1996; Mueller and Loveridge, 1997).

Although these companies have deliberately focused on acquiring new knowledge and skills from a different environment, they have adapted to the changed nature of the pharmaceuticals industry by differentiating locations and functions in the production chain, rather than radically changing the nature of their domestic organization and governance structure. This separation of activities across environments is facilitated by the highly codified nature of the knowledge involved, much more so than development and manufacturing know-how. As Kogut and Zander (1993) have emphasized, high levels of codification and teachability of knowledge enable technologies to be more easily transferred between firms than when they are highly dependent on tacit knowledge, and this contrast affects the degree of internal integration of activities within firms as well (Howells, 1998).

Similarly, the German car companies that sought to use the greater scope of the arm's length business environment by developing novel managerial and organizational practices and routines have yet to demonstrate that these are compatible with their traditional strengths in making high-value and innovative products (Lane, 1998; 2001). While, then, it may be possible in the longer term for cooperative hierarchies to learn from adversarial environments and then generalize their lessons to the whole organization, the strength of domestic institutions and continued ties to business partners will constrain the extent of such changes in the short to medium term.

In the case of many Japanese banks, while they may have learnt how to participate in international financial markets it seems that they largely bought market share in the late 1980s and 1990s by financing bond issues and similar instruments at a loss, and most focused the bulk of their activities on servicing their traditional Japanese customers (Sakai, 2000). Indeed, according to Sakai, these companies continued to regard international activities and the people who managed these as less important than domestic ones, so that they were not really interested in 'learning' from their London and New York subsidiaries. This may, however, be changing for some, as the result of the restructuring of Japanese banks, and the financial system in general, at the end of the 1990s (Morgan *et al.*, 2003). In the case of much Japanese manufacturing FDI, many business partners in the USA and UK are Japanese rather than local ones, and knowledge transfer has tended to be from the new investors to local firms rather than the converse.

Many managerially coordinated companies operating subsidiaries in arm's length environments are likely to assume that their firm-specific competitive advantages can be equally successful abroad as at home, and may be unwilling to 'learn' from foreign experiences, as illustrated by Ford in Britain before the Second World War (Tolliday, 2000). As they adapt to local conditions, though, subsidiaries will develop different routines and practices that, if effective, will lead to distinctive organizational competences. Since these are firm specific and not closely tied to particular links with local business partners and institutions they could in principle be appropriated by the whole organization. Whether they will be depends, *inter alia*, on the strength of the domestic business—and so the perceived need to change—and the extent to which the new practices would replace strongly entrenched practices that are closely tied to major domestic institutions such as the financial and legal systems. Just as learning from foreign firms investing in one's home economy is affected by the centrality of the practices concerned and their interdependent institutions, so too is learning from a firm's own foreign subsidiaries.

Conclusions

This discussion of how different kinds of firms from different business systems and institutional contexts are likely to conduct their FDI in contrasting business environments emphasizes the continuing importance of their domestic institutions and established ways of coordinating economic activities in their home economies. When these are cohesive and highly integrated, they have considerable impact on: (a) the amount and type of FDI undertaken, (b) how much autonomy subsidiaries are allowed, (c) how much they become integrated into host economies, and (d) how much impact their learning from host economies has upon domestic routines.

Even when MNCs deliberately undertake major FDI in quite different business environments to gain knowledge and learn from contrasting ways of organizing economic activities, as in the case of the German pharmaceutical investments in US biotechnology research, it seems that this encourages organizational differentiation rather than significant restructuring and innovation in domestic routines. The home economy institutions and practices remain largely in place despite a considerable amount of research now being located in the USA and managed in line with US practices. This is an example of MNCs encouraging considerable learning at the local subsidiary level but separating these organizational innovations from their domestic operations, and so reducing the degree of integration in the firm as a whole. While the highly codified nature of much of the knowledge presumably means that such differentiation does not prevent its effective transfer between research and development, production and marketing—and so is a feasible strategy in this industry at a time of radical change—it remains to be seen how viable it would be in other circumstances.

In any event, this case suggests that when cooperative hierarchies do invest major resources in arm's length business environments and adapt to the conventions and practices of such environments, they may prefer to manage the subsequent organizational innovations by differentiating units and functions rather than by incorporating them into the parent organization and so radically transforming it. This is especially so where their domestic operations remain effective in key value-added functions and strong institutional pressures reproduce established routines.

Such a combination of segmented functions in varied business environments with some organizational integration is highly dependent on the outputs from upstream units being sufficiently codified that they can be transferred effectively to downstream ones across major institutional boundaries without incurring high transaction costs. While, then, codification and teachability of knowledge in general facilitate technological transfers across firm boundaries, in this case they enable cooperative hierarchies to operate major facilities in quite diverse environments without having to change domestic routines radically. Ownership integration here presumably enables sufficient control to ensure effective coordination and low spillover dangers, while differentiation across environments limits organizational upheavals and conflicts with key institutions and agencies.

A more common pattern of internationalization for firms in highly coordinated home economies is to rely initially on exports because of their dependence on business partners and employees for competitive advantages, and hence the limited extent to which the managerial hierarchy can appropriate and transfer such advantages abroad. Additionally, their initial lack of experience of coordinating economic activities in anomic and adversarial environments inhibits managers in these firms from readily making major investments in distant foreign locations. When they do undertake significant FDI, the nature of the domestic business system and its associated institutions encourages risk sharing with home country partners and close integration of foreign subsidiaries with parent operations. In general, then, subsidiaries of cooperative hierarchies located abroad tend to be only weakly integrated into host economies and to limit organizational innovations based on adaptation to local norms. In sum, without substantial changes in domestic institutions, these kinds of firms are unlikely to change their governance characteristics or organizational capabilities as a result of FDI, but may become more varied, differentiated and complex organizations.

The influence of the home business system and institutional environment on FDI management and its consequences are equally important for isolated autocracies. As long as the domestic business environment remains highly particularistic and discourages long-term investments in building organizational capabilities and authority sharing, FDI by these kinds of firms will be limited to relatively peripheral activities with short-term pay back periods. Additionally, these activities will be located predominantly in environments where personal networks and common conventions facilitate high levels of direct control. When these firms invest in different kinds of business systems, such as the compartmentalized one that develops in arm's length institutional contexts, any learning that does take place in subsidiaries is unlikely to impinge greatly upon the domestic organization because the institutional supports for predictable, formal procedures and control systems to manage activities are absent in the home economy. The transformation of Chinese family businesses in Pacific-Asia into Anglo-Saxon corporations as a result of investments in the USA is, then, improbable, and their key characteristics are unlikely to change significantly (Yeung and Olds, 2000).

273

It is interesting to note in this connection that the developing linkages between Silicon Valley and firms in the Hsinchu Science Park in Taiwan are quite personal and particularistic according to Saxenian (2000). These Taiwanese firms have benefited considerably from state support and, in some cases, the personal patronage of leading figures in the political elite (Hung and Whittington, 1997), and so have had a much greater public profile than the typical small firm in the export sector (see, for example, Hamilton 1997; Shieh, 1992). Their owners have therefore felt more able to share risks and develop their own brands, as well as undertaking investments beyond the Asian region. Unlike many Japanese and Korean investors in North America, however, they have preferred to keep links with US firms flexible and tied to personal networks rather than hierarchically integrating them as directly controlled subsidiaries. Where a few Taiwanese firms have made relatively large-scale commitments to wholly owned subsidiaries in the US—and in the UK—they have not been very successful. In other words, a major part of the success of this trans-Pacific integration of economic activities seems to be due to its consonance with the traditional Taiwanese way of managing transactions, although Saxenian also suggests that these science park firms have become partly 'Americanized' as a result of recruiting US trained and experienced engineers and managers.

In the case of managerially coordinated types of firms, their foreign subsidiaries are more likely to adapt to local ways of doing things and be relatively integrated into their local economies. These firms, then, become more complex and differentiated organizations as the result of investing considerable resources in different kinds of business systems. However, the impact of such local learning on the basic governance and capabilities characteristics of the parent firms will be restricted by the weakly institutionalized international business environment and the largely arm's length domestic institutional context.

If, for instance, a US firm invests significant resources in Japan, and even makes that subsidiary the leading one for product development in a particular area, as Proctor and Gamble did for babies' nappies, the cohesion of the host business system and strength of its institutions will encourage the Japanese subsidiary to manage its internal and external relationships in different ways to those current at home. However, the transferability of such practices and routines to other subsidiaries, or to the parent company, will be discouraged by the varied labour market institutions, state structures and policies, and financial systems in different societies, and the difficulty of generalizing business partner commitments across institutional contexts.

To change the US firms' governance characteristics and capabilities significantly as a result of such investment would require substantial changes in domestic institutions, and probably the importation of its Japanese business partners to the USA in a similar manner to the Japanese transplants. This is not to say that no transfer of managerial technologies can occur, but to emphasize that these will be relatively codified and context independent.

The overall conclusion to be drawn from this analysis, then, is that MNCs from distinctive and cohesive business systems with strong associated institutions governing economic activities may well become more complex and differentiated as a result of FDI—and so encourage novel forms of coordination to develop—but are unlikely to change their fundamental characteristics. Isolated autocracies are less likely to make significant foreign commitments in the first place, and so will change to an even lesser extent. The key variables here are the strength, cohesion and integration of domestic institutions and their associated systems of economic coordination and control. As long as these domestic business environments remain distinctive and cohesive, and the international business environment is relatively anomic with weakly institutionalized norms and procedures governing business practices, FDI is likely to increase the organizational complexity of MNCs without changing the nature of the firms engaging in it.

11

Developing Transnational Organizational Capabilities in Multinational Companies: The Role of Cross-National Authority Sharing and Organizational Careers

Introduction

This analysis of the likely internationalization strategies of three very different ideal types of firm highlights the limited development of transnational organizational capabilities in many companies that operate across national borders, as well as the important influences of both home and host economy institutions on such processes. In particular, it is worth emphasizing that the integrated ownership and control of economic activities across political boundaries does not, in and of itself, generate distinctive competences and new kinds of organizations. For MNCs to become novel kinds of strategic actors with distinctive transnational capabilities, they would have to encourage substantial and continuing commitment to developing firm-specific knowledge by staff in different national subsidiaries (Kogut and Zander, 1993).

As suggested in Chapter 6, this would require owners and managers in the parent company to share some authority with employees in foreign subsidiaries, to involve them in joint problem solving and strategic development on a continuing basis and, sometimes, to establish transnational organizational careers. As we have seen, such authority sharing and career provision is closely dependent on the nature of dominant institutional regimes and interest groups in a society. The extent to which, and ways in which, international companies do indeed develop distinctive kinds of transnational organizational capabilities that differentiate them from more nationally specific firms therefore vary greatly, depending on their governance structures and the nature of dominant institutions in their home and host economies.

This variability in kinds of MNCs and their transnational organizational capabilities suggest it would be useful to consider in more detail how firms from different institutional frameworks are likely to develop particular competitive competences through encouraging cross-national commitment to firm-specific problem solving and knowledge generation. These relationships are central to MNCs becoming international learning systems with distinctive kinds of expertise through subsidiaries' contributions to their global competences and knowledge (Birkinshaw and Hood, 1998; Hedlund, 1993; Holm and Pedersen, 2000; Nohria and Ghoshal, 1997). A key question here is: to what extent, and how, do different kinds of MNCs generate firm-specific organizational capabilities through long-term employee commitments? Given the considerable variety of institutional arrangements governing economic activities in market economies, that is, how do international employers develop distinctive transnational competences through employee contributions to long-term cross-national skill and knowledge development when the organization of labour markets and skill formation systems vary significantly?

As Solvell and Zander (1998) have pointed out, the ability of such firms to integrate new knowledge and skills across national subsidiaries is often assumed rather than demonstrated (see also, Arvidsson, 1999; Szulanski, 1996), and there are significant difficulties in transferring situationally specific innovation capabilities between countries with contrasting institutional frameworks. Especially important in this regard are labour market institutions that encourage varied levels of commitment to employers and to the development of organization-specific knowledge. Where these institutions differ significantly, as in postwar Germany, Japan, and the USA, generating similar levels of commitment to long-term organizational problem solving and developing international capabilities across subsidiaries will be difficult, particularly from middle and lower level staff.

Even within a single national culture, such as that of the USA, ensuring sufficient positive commitment to organizational problem solving amongst a relatively small group of senior managers to achieve innovation and growth goals is difficult enough, as Freeland's (2001) study of General Motors illustrates. When institutional contexts diverge as much as they do in many MNCs, such active consent to formal managerial authority cannot be assumed, and nor can MNCs' ability to develop distinctive cross-national capabilities on the basis of this commitment. Rather, the extents to which they attempt to do so, and are successful, remain variable (Zander and Solvell, 2002).

Accordingly, in this chapter I suggest how the framework exploring the connections between dominant institutions and the development of distinctive organizational capabilities outlined in earlier chapters could be extended to MNCs by analysing how international companies from different kinds of market economy are likely to develop varied patterns of employer–employee commitment across national institutional regimes, and so generate different cross-border capabilities. I first consider how MNCs from four ideal types of institutional regimes are likely to share authority with, and provide organizational careers for, foreign managerial and skilled employees in the relatively weakly institutionalized international business environment. In the subsequent section, I suggest how different kinds of MNC that combine different degrees of transnational authority sharing and organizational careers can be expected to develop different types of transnational organizational capabilities.

The Impact of Institutional Regimes on Cross-National Authority Sharing and Organizational Careers in MNCs

The connections between home and host economy institutions and likely MNC control patterns discussed in the previous chapter, together with the more general linkages between institutional regimes and levels of employer–employee commitment outlined in Chapter 6, suggest a number of points about MNCs that are worth summarizing. First, MNCs with major facilities in different kinds of market economy are likely to develop varying forms of authority sharing and careers across their different subsidiaries. As a result, second, the kinds of collective capabilities they develop at different levels of the organization can differ greatly, and may well conflict in their basic principles, as highlighted by Kristensen and Zeitlin (2005) in their study of APV.

Third, MNCs will also vary in the extent to which they share authority with, and establish cross-national careers for, foreign employees as a result of variations in their domestic institutional environment as well as in those of their major subsidiaries. Thus, fourth, they differ in the extent to which they develop distinctive international organizational capabilities. Additionally, the dominant institutional features of the international business environment can be expected to impinge upon the extent to which MNCs are willing to delegate discretion to foreign employees and gain their commitment through providing organizational careers, as well as affecting such employees' responses to these opportunities.

While the role of different institutional environments in developing varied subsidiary competences in MNCs has become more widely discussed in recent years (see, e.g., Birkinshaw, 2001; Westney, 1993a), rather less attention has been paid to how national and international institutions affect the development of cross-national capabilities, especially through their impact on employment relations. Considering first the nature and influence of the international business environment on employment relations, it is important to recall that, as discussed in Chapter 5, most transnational institutions governing economic activities resemble regulatory institutions in arm's length regimes. Few, if any, encourage investment in employer–employee commitment on a long-term basis. Constraints on both employer and employee opportunism are typically lower across national borders than within most OECD countries, and hence the extent and longevity of employee commitments to MNC corporate goals and success are likely to be less than those to their national subsidiaries that employ them directly, especially amongst middle managers and professionals.

Pressures from international institutions, then, are unlikely to lead many MNCs to engage in the sorts of extensive authority sharing with, and long-term career commitments to, foreign employees that firms in collaborative market economies often develop with their home economy staff. As British employees of Japanese banks found out in the 1990s, the norm of long-term employment for male Japanese staff did not apply to them (Sakai, 2000, see also Chapter 12 in this book). In general, then, the lack of strong international institutions encouraging long-term loyalties between business partners suggests that the degree and scope of cross-national authority sharing and organizational careers within MNCs will not be particularly high, and usually less than occurs in their home organizations.

There remain, however, considerable differences between MNCs in their patterns of authority sharing and career commitments across national borders. As discussed in the previous chapter, these tend to reflect domestic and host economy institutional differences, particularly when dominant institutions are as contrasting as those in postwar Japan and USA (see, e.g., Beechler and Bird, 1999; Dunning, 1993; Ernst, 2006; Tolliday, 2000). In Kogut's terms (1993: 137): 'Even as the firm internationalizes, it remains imprinted by its early developmental history and domestic

Table 11.1. International authority sharing and careers in MNCs from different institutional regimes

International authority sharing and organizational careers	Home Economy Institutional Regime			
	Particularistic	Arm's Length	Business Corporatist	Inclusive Corporatist
Extent of cross-border authority sharing	Low	Varies, but rarely extended beyond managers and experts with codified skills	Some, but limited to managers and experts with codified skills	Limited
Longevity and scope of cross-national organizational careers	Low	Varies, but long-term career opportunities rarely extended beyond managers in most MNCs	Limited	Low

environment', especially how it learns and innovates (cf. Doremus *et al.*, 1998).

Additionally, as some MNCs invest more in foreign environments to acquire strategic assets and skills, rather than simply to reduce costs and access markets (Rugman and Verbeke, 2001), they can be expected to share authority more with foreign employees, especially in dealing with complex problems across borders, and try to elicit their commitment on a longer-term basis. Such attempts are clearly going to be affected by the nature of host economy institutions, particularly those governing skill formation and labour markets, and will vary considerably between subsidiaries, as has been emphasized by Nohria and Ghoshal (1997).

Extending the arguments presented in earlier chapters suggesting how firms from different institutional regimes are likely to encourage varying degrees of employee commitment to MNCs employing substantial numbers of people in differently organized market economies, we can summarize the expected connections between firms based in four kinds of institutional regimes and patterns of transnational authority sharing and organizational careers as in Table 11.1. In this table, the collaborative type of business environment is divided into two in order to take account of the important differences between labour market institutions and skill formation systems in business corporatist and inclusive corporatist institutional regimes as discussed in Chapter 2.

I first consider the probable patterns of international authority sharing and careers of firms from particularistic business environments. As suggested in the previous chapter, since owners in these kinds of market economies remain reluctant to share authority with employees in their domestic location because of unreliable formal institutions and an unpredictable political environment, they seem unlikely to trust foreign employees a great deal, and so delegate much discretion to them, The combination of a low trust home economy with weak transnational institutions is unlikely to encourage much authority sharing with foreign managers and staff.

Equally, the common restriction of long-term career opportunities to relatives and others with whom family-like relationships have been developed in these frameworks suggests that few firms will offer organizational careers to foreign employees. As a result, hardly any subsidiary staff are likely to become so committed to the parent company that they will invest their energies in improving firm-specific knowledge and skills on a medium- to long-term basis. This means that enterprises from such environments are unlikely to develop strong international organizational capabilities, as distinct from those based on predominantly individual relationships and qualities.

In contrast, owners of firms from more arms' length market economies that share authority with, and develop organizational careers for, senior managers and some professional staff domestically could be expected to delegate rather more discretion to those in charge of foreign subsidiaries where formal institutions are considered reliable. They may also involve foreign managers and professional staff in cross-national problem-solving teams when their specialist expertise is highly valued. This is especially likely when dealing with complex problems that require knowledge of different business environments, as in many professional service companies such as those discussed by Morgan and Quack (2005).

Authority sharing with foreign professionals will depend on MNC managers' knowledge of their expertise and the reputation of national skill formation systems. Given the importance of technical knowledge and specialist skills in dealing with complex and uncertain tasks, domestic managers of MNCs are unlikely to share much authority with foreigners unless they are convinced that they are highly skilled and able to contribute to current problems. This will be greatly facilitated by skills being standardized through professional associations that operate in similar ways in different countries, and so is more straightforward between arms' length economies that have flexible labour markets and similar institutional arrangements for developing high-level expertise.

It is also worth noting that constructing and changing expert teams for accomplishing complex and risky short-term projects requires efficient signalling of expertise and achievement, as discussed in Chapter 9. This means that firms will not find it easy to delegate authority to deal with complex cross-border problems to employees from economies without strong public credentialling systems and where expertise tends to be highly organization-specific, as in many large Japanese companies. As a result, authority sharing with foreign employees in cross-national problem-solving teams is likely to be greater in economies that share strong transnational technical communities and common ways of certifying skills.

In general, though, any such authority sharing by firms from arm's length economies is unlikely to extend much beyond senior professional and managerial staff, given similar limitations at home and the lack of strong international institutions that might restrain employer and employee opportunism. While their subsidiaries located in economies dominated by strong collaborative institutions may develop greater levels of authority sharing with skilled workers, this seems likely to be limited to local operations given the arms' length nature of the parent MNC's domestic business environment.

Similarly, few firms from these kinds of institutional frameworks are likely to make long-term career commitments to many foreign employees, especially at the international level. Since commitments in general are short term in such regimes, most employers will not feel able to offer cross-national organizational careers to more than a few senior foreign managers, nor would such offerings be viewed as highly credible, although Butler *et al.* (2006) did find that some of the US firms they studied were concerned to maintain an internal labour market across national boundaries for managers. Again, where host economy institutions encourage high levels of employer–employee commitment and firms have to offer organizational careers to skilled staff in order to attract the most capable, MNCs may well enter into long-term employer–employee commitments at the local level, as do many foreign firms in Japan, but such commitments are unlikely to be extended internationally.

Overall, then, we would not expect long-term commitment to building and improving cross-national problem-solving capabilities and skills, as opposed to extending domestic ones, to be high in most foreign subsidiaries of MNCs from arm's length economies. Loyalty to the parent company and investment in the enhancement of its knowledge and capabilities will be no more extensive than in its domestic operations, and so continuing organizational learning at the international level will probably be restricted to senior managerial levels.

In contrast, MNCs based in more collaborative market economies are embedded in a number of relatively long-term obligations with particular business partners, including skilled employees. However, few of the institutions leading to such commitments transcend national boundaries, and so foreign employees are not as locked into the fate of MNCs from these kinds of societies as are many domestic ones. This means that both employer and employee opportunism is likely to be less constrained across borders than within such economies. As a result, long-term employee willingness to invest in enhancing the capabilities of the MNC will probably be lower in foreign subsidiaries than in the domestic organization.

Furthermore, where such firms consider that their core capabilities are substantially derived from these long-term commitments and are highly specific to their home business environment, they will be reluctant to invest much in authority sharing with foreign staff. The more MNCs see their distinctive competences as being generated by their domestic organization and its particular pattern of employment relations, the less they are likely to involve foreign staff from quite different environments in substantial international problem-solving activities. This seems to be the case for many Japanese MNCs (see, e.g., Ernst, 2006; Kopp, 1999: Pucik, 1999).

However, some companies from collaborative institutional frameworks have become more willing to delegate considerable discretion to foreign managers and professionals in some subsidiaries, and to involve them extensively in international problem-solving teams as they seek to acquire new kinds of capabilities that their domestic business system appears unable to provide. In situations where the lock-ins encouraged by home economy institutions are seen to be inhibiting radical innovation and limiting growth, such MNCs may deliberately use foreign subsidiaries to try novel practices with the different kinds of approaches and skills developed in societies with contrasting institutional frameworks, such as Japanese investments in UK and US biotechnology facilities (Kneller, 2003; Lam, 2003). Some German companies seem to have tried to do this in the 1990s, although such plans have not always been realized in practice, particularly in the car industry (Fleury and Salerno, 1998; Jurgens, 1998; Lane, 2001).

MNCs from inclusive corporatist regimes that organize careers and identities around specialist skills and activities may well find this kind of authority sharing and joint problem solving with foreign employees easier to accomplish than do those from business corporatist ones whose internal labour markets are more structured around generalist competences.

This is because their home and host economy professional staff are more likely to share a common cognitive framework and approach to problem understanding than are employees in MNCs where engineers and other highly educated employees are encouraged to become organizational generalists.

This contrast in ease of collaboration in dealing with cross-border problems will be especially marked when professionals from highly coordinated economies are working with those in arm's length ones, since these latter tend to be more specialized and focused on their professional identity rather than that of their current employer. We would expect, then, MNCs from inclusive corporatist institutional regimes to be more willing to share authority with managers and professionals in arm's length economies than those from business corporatist ones, and to be more effective in managing international problem-solving teams.

They may also be more willing to develop long-term career commitments to foreign staff because of a greater specialization of organizational careers around professional expertise. However, for many MNCs from coordinated institutional frameworks, the importance of their considerable commitments to domestic skilled workers for the development of their firm-specific competences, and the lack of strong international institutions encouraging similar commitments to foreign staff, mean that extending long-term organizational careers abroad will be difficult, especially to workers in arm's length economies. Indeed, some may not wish to do so in order to increase their flexibility and ability to change competences in foreign subsidiaries at short notice. In effect, these kinds of MNCs develop contrasting employment relations in different environments in order to generate varied kinds of capabilities, as have perhaps some continental European investors in new technology firms in the USA.

MNCs from business corporatist institutional regimes are particularly unlikely to establish credible long-term organizational careers for foreign employees since their distinctive organizational capabilities are often generated by generalist career structures that reward long-term contributions to the organization as a whole rather than to the improvement of departmental knowledge. Weak professional identities and the highly firm-specific nature of careers and skills in such economies enable extensive rotation across functions and divisions, facilitating organization-wide communication and learning. Incorporating foreign employees into such career structures will clearly not be easy, especially if they have developed distinctive specialist identities in nationally well-regarded training systems. As a result, many large Japanese firms have become noted for relatively limited career opportunities for foreign staff including managers, especially when they remain heavily dependent upon domestic customers as do most banks (Morgan *et al.*, 2003; Sakai, 2000).

These points suggest that firms from arms' length economies could find it easier to develop multinational career structures for key foreign managers and technical experts than do MNCs originating in collaborative ones because their competitive capabilities are not so closely tied to home economy employee involvement in joint problem solving and knowledge development. Insofar, then, as the former companies do establish long-term organizational careers for key employees to gain their continuing commitment to organizational specific problem solving and knowledge development, they may extend them to some senior staff in overseas subsidiaries to a greater extent than would firms from more coordinated business environments.

However, this does not imply that most MNCs from arms' length economies are likely to share authority with foreign managers or to provide long-term organizational commitments for them. Indeed, some US firms have been as 'ethnocentric' (Perlmutter, 1969) in these respects as Japanese ones (Malnight, 1995), as the example of Henry Ford imposing his American manufacturing and pricing model on his British subsidiary in the 1920s and 1930s graphically illustrates (Tolliday, 2000). The variety of cross-border authority sharing and career commitments to foreign employees in MNCs from these kinds of institutional frameworks is, then, likely to be considerable (Ferner *et al.*, 2006).

These institutional influences on MNCs' varied patterns of international authority sharing and career commitments affect the extent to which, and how, they develop distinctive cross-national capabilities and competitive competences, as opposed to those generated by national and regional units. I now turn to consider the connections between variations in employer–employee commitment in MNCs and the sorts of distinct transnational competences they are likely to develop through an analysis of six ideal types of MNC that combine different degrees of authority sharing with foreign employees with varied kinds of international organizational careers.

Transnational Authority Sharing, Careers, and Capabilities in Six Types of MNC

In considering how different MNCs develop contrasting kinds of transnational organizational capabilities, it is helpful to distinguish three levels of cross-national authority sharing between the parent company and its foreign subsidiaries by drawing on Malnight's (1995) distinction between 'appendage', 'participant' and 'contributor' roles of major MNC subsidiaries. The lowest degree of authority sharing occurs in firms that are so home-centred as to regard domestically developed knowledge and skills as always being superior to those of foreign units (Westney and Zaheer, 2001). The core competences and business success of the MNC are seen here as deriving almost entirely from the domestic organization, such that foreign subsidiaries have to follow its policies and procedures. In these sorts of MNCs, most, if not all, host economy units are treated as appendages to the domestic organization that are given little discretion over what activities they carry out or how they manage them. Equally, they are rarely expected to contribute to problem solving or decision making in any other units.

Somewhat greater authority sharing with foreign managers and staff of the more significant subsidiaries occurs in more decentralized MNCs that grant them limited discretion to deal with local markets and provide resources to develop local capabilities. In his account of globalization at Eli Lilly, Malnight (1995) characterizes subsidiaries in this situation as being participants in meeting local needs, and describes how the parent firm provided resources for European subsidiaries to conduct clinical trials and marketing activities at the local level. However, such investments were centrally coordinated and controlled by a special unit at head office to ensure that they followed established procedures and were compatible with domestic practices. Authority sharing in this situation, then, is typically restricted to local issues and does not extend to decisions beyond subsidiary boundaries. It is often limited to subsidiaries that have demonstrated their reliability and/or are situated in clearly differently organized kinds of markets and societies, such as Japanese units of US firms.

Higher levels of authority sharing are involved when MNCs encourage managers and technical staff in major subsidiaries to develop capabilities and knowledge that contribute to international problem solving and strategies, and assess their performance partly in terms of such contributions. Here, successful local units are more able to experiment with alternative ways of doing things and develop novel approaches without needing to obtain prior approval from the parent company. Through membership of international project teams they diffuse these innovations to other units and head office. They become contributors to the international parent firm and other subsidiaries, in Malnight's

(1995) terminology, by, for instance, providing clinical data for regulatory processes in different countries and developing marketing practices that can be used elsewhere. Such contributions involve extensive information exchange, use of international project teams to deal with worldwide issues and considerable staff mobility across national and regional boundaries. In ABB, for instance, the extensive use of 'best practice' benchmarking in the 1990s enabled a number of subsidiaries to contribute significantly to process improvements in the power transformers business area (Belanger *et al.*, 1999).

The significance of international organizational careers in MNCs can similarly be distinguished in terms of the longevity of employer–employee commitments and the range of groups to whom they are extended. These kinds of careers are built around success in dealing with problems and issues in different national and regional locations as well as contributing to cross-national ones. In contrast, more domestic careers are focused on problem solving within the home organization. While this may include some foreign postings in subsidiaries that are closely integrated with the parent firm, success in these is typically regarded as being less important than domestic contributions in home-centric MNCs, and such mobility represents an extension of domestic career patterns more than constituting a distinct international structure.

Three patterns of international careers in MNCs can be distinguished in these terms. First, the least developed international career structure occurs in MNCs that offer few long-term commitments to foreign employees beyond their national subsidiaries, and usually rely on home country nationals to run them. Insofar as long-term careers are established in such firms, then, they are primarily organized within subsidiary boundaries, and expatriate postings form part of the domestic promotion system rather than constituting a separate international one. These can be described as domestically extended career structures.

Second, more established cross-national career patterns have developed in MNCs that encourage both foreign and domestic managers to move between subsidiaries and reward contributions to international corporate goals by promoting them abroad. However, such opportunities are usually restricted to senior foreign managers who rise to the top of host economy operations and then transfer to similar posts in other countries before joining the international managerial elite. They are not usually extended to middle managers and technical staff, and can be termed elite international career structures.

Third, more transnational career structures encourage long-term employer–employee commitment at the international level for a larger proportion of managers and professional employees by promoting them across subsidiaries and countries as much as within them and without privileging home country nationals. Here, successful organizational careers involve mid-career international mobility and the global internal labour market dominates local subsidiary ones. They encourage contributions to cross-national problem solving and the development of international organizational capabilities as much as, if not more than, national ones.

While some combinations of transnational authority sharing and cross-national organizational careers are quite feasible in MNCs, others are less so. For example, companies that offer long-term organizational careers to foreign managerial and technical staff seem likely to grant them considerable discretion and expect them to contribute to global problem solving once they have demonstrated their competence and commitment. As a result, not many MNCs will establish international managerial careers without some authority sharing with foreign employees, or reward long-term organizational commitments by foreign managers and professionals without involving them in cross-national decision making and development. This suggests that the combination of transnational career paths with low subsidiary discretion is empirically improbable.

However, high levels of authority sharing can be combined with limited organizational commitments to long-term careers, as we have seen with small firms in some industrial districts and new technology start-ups. Substantial delegation to foreign units and employees is quite consonant, then, with limited international career opportunities, especially in international project-based firms and professional service companies. Combining the three levels of authority sharing across borders in terms of the roles of major subsidiaries with three kinds of international organizational careers enables us to identify six types of MNC with varied levels of cross-national employee commitment to the parent organization. These are listed in Table 11.2.

In broad terms, we would expect MNCs that share authority with foreign subsidiary managers and experts, and provide them with international career opportunities, to elicit greater cross-national employee commitment to MNC problem solving and competence development than those that do not. They are more likely, then, to generate firm-specific international organizational capabilities as distinct from national ones. These involve novel routines and knowledge at the international

Table 11.2. Six types of MNCs with different degrees of cross-national authority sharing and organizational careers

Types of International Organizational Careers	International Authority Sharing: The Role of Major Foreign Subsidiaries		
	Appendage	Participant	Contributor
Domestic extended	Colonial	Domestically dominated	Delegated professional
Elite	Unlikely	Managerially integrated	Delegated managerial
Transnational	Unlikely	Unlikely	Highly integrated

level rather than simply extending domestic ones across national borders.

In this sense, international coordinating capabilities enable firms to integrate knowledge about internal and external processes throughout all major units, linking information about customer needs with development choices across national borders and ensuring that inputs and outputs are coordinated cross-nationally. International learning capabilities similarly transcend local boundaries and enable companies to codify, integrate and diffuse new understandings and approaches to problem solving across subsidiaries without privileging those from the home economy.

Equally, international reconfigurational capabilities involve the ability to restructure resources, skills and knowledge across national boundaries, rather than within them, and generate new kinds of products and services at the international level. They go beyond simply buying and selling businesses or hiring and firing employees in different countries to encompass the integrated cross-national development of new kinds of competences through, for instance, organizing international project teams of experts to work on new technologies and markets.

Developing these kinds of firm-specific international organizational capabilities—as opposed to more generic portfolio management skills—depends on quite high levels of employee commitment to the MNC. Consequently, we would not expect many of the six types of MNC listed above to generate them to any great extent. I now turn to consider their key characteristics and likely cross-national organizational capabilities, summarized in Table 11.3, in a little more detail.

First, the colonial MNC keeps key decision making over resources, skills and knowledge production at home, similarly to Perlmutter's (1969) ethnocentric MNC. Whether run as a highly centralized and personally controlled business from a particularistic institutional environment or a home-focused hierarchy from a more stable society, these kinds of MNCs

Table 11.3. International commitment and organizational capabilities in six types of MNC

	Type of MNC					
	Colonial	Domestically Dominated	Managerially Integrated	Delegated Professional	Delegated Managerial	Highly Integrated
Level of foreign employee commitment to MNC	Low	Low, except for a few senior managers	Some managerial, otherwise Low	Considerable in the short term for project teams	Considerable among managerial elite	Considerable
Extent of firm specific cross-national organizational capabilities						
(a) Coordinating	Low	Extensions of domestic routines	Some managerial routines	Considerable in project teams, low otherwise	Considerable	High
(b) Learning	Low	Limited to domestic organization	Limited to managerial elite	Considerable in project teams, limited otherwise	Considerable among senior managers	Considerable
(c) Reconfigurational	Low	Limited	Limited to portfolio management skills	Considerable in societies with strong codified skills	Some, especially in arm's length regimes	Some, but radical changes limited by transnational routines and skills

function as national companies with foreign operations that are highly subservient to the head office. Consequently, their capabilities will be largely those developed domestically, with few if any new ones being generated from their cross-border activities.

In some of these kinds of MNCs, career success is tied to the long-term cultivation of, and services for, large domestic customers. As a result, managers and other staff who work abroad can become regarded as second rate and become less successful in promotion tournaments, as in a number of Japanese banks in the 1980s and 1990s (Sakai, 2000). Knowledge and skills obtained from such assignments are not highly regarded and rarely impinge greatly on domestically developed capabilities. Such relegation is, of course, even more marked for foreign workers who rarely deal with home-based customers and are typically excluded from parent company-based organizational careers (Morgan *et al.*, 2003). Consequently, foreign-based capabilities are poorly developed, except perhaps for some projects involving highly paid foreign experts, and rarely make any impact on the parent company. As international companies, then, they are unlikely to generate any distinctive kinds of collective competences that distinguish them from their domestic competitors.

Second, in domestically dominated MNCs some authority sharing with foreign managers over local issues is combined with few, if any, international careers for foreigners. Here, the home economy and employer are dominant, with overseas subsidiaries either seen as peripheral in terms of collective competences and learning, or else built upon the domestically developed recipe. These firms tend to view their foreign operations as extensions of their domestic ones, and careers in the worldwide organization are largely based on success in the domestic business. Foreign managers may be involved in developing local business strategies, as well as being entrusted with handling personnel matters, but this is often after they have fully imbibed the parent firm's philosophy and can be trusted to follow the x company's 'way'. Such firms are unlikely to come from particularistic environments.

In the case of many Japanese car assembly MNCs in Europe and the USA, the 'hard side' of the production system, i.e. equipment, technical processes and standard operating procedures, is often transferred as a standard package with little flexibility for local staff to alter specifications or practices, although other features are adapted to local circumstances (Abo, 1994; Botti, 1995; Brannen *et al.*, 1999; Kenney and Florida, 1993). Authority sharing with foreigners is often considerably circumscribed by expatriate 'coordinators' who are in daily contact with head office (Pil and

MacDuffie, 1999). Although improvements to manufacturing processes in these companies derive from foreign operations as well as domestic ones, they are usually planned by engineers and managers in Japan on the basis of continuous feedback from overseas and home plants without much foreign involvement, as discussed in the next chapter.

Most managerial careers in these kinds of MNC remain predominantly national, or perhaps regional. Furthermore, domestically based career success dominates foreign performance since the domestic operations remain the primary source of collective competence development and location of the key succession tournaments. Even when foreign production exceeds domestic output, and successful domestic careers increasingly include some foreign experience, long-term contribution to organizational problem solving and success in the home economy usually remains more important than foreign success in such MNCs. As a result, foreign staff have limited incentives to invest in long-term MNC-specific knowledge and skill development, and are more likely to focus on demonstrating their expertise and effectiveness at a national or maybe regional level in ways that are externally visible.

Developing new and distinctive capabilities in foreign subsidiaries will not, then, be encouraged in domestically dominated MNCs, and any international competences they do generate will be highly dependent on those developed in their home economy. Strong coordinating and learning capabilities in these kinds of MNCs are more derived from their home economy than from their international operations as a whole, and so they are unlikely to develop separate transnational collective competences that are specific to the company as an international firm.

Third, managerially coordinated MNCs combine some authority sharing with foreign managers to deal with local needs and opportunities with the establishment of international careers for some foreign top managers. Commitments by leading subsidiary managers to such parent companies can thus be expected to be greater than in domestically dominated MNCs, and the creation of a more international managerial elite should help to develop distinctive routines for coordinating activities across national borders. However, the largely local focus of most subsidiary managers and professionals, coupled with their lack of involvement in cross-national problem solving in these kinds of firms limit the extent of international integration of knowledge and skills.

Most cross-national coordination, planning and innovation is accordingly based on home country routines and competences in these kinds of MNCs, with little input from foreign subsidiaries. However, the growth of a multinational managerial elite may encourage some cross-national learning as foreign managers become assimilated into the top management ranks and seek to build on their foreign experiences. This possibility will, though, be restricted by the strong pressures for conformity to the domestically dominated culture and domestically derived operating procedures (Butler *et al.*, 2006). The opening of some senior MNC posts to foreign employees in these kinds of firm does not necessarily alter their largely ethnocentric nature, as Perlmutter (1969) emphasizes. Similarly, while the limited extent of authority sharing enables the top managers of such companies to restructure subsidiaries relatively easily and speedily, especially those in arm's length institutional regimes, the lack of involvement of most foreign employees in cross-national activities means that reconfigurational capabilities are more derived from domestic practices than from international ones.

The limited autonomy granted to some foreign subsidiaries in these kinds of MNC does, however, allow them to develop more varied approaches to some organizational issues at the local level. As a result, local institutional environments can affect the nature of loyalties and commitments in subsidiaries. Employees in collaborative market economies, for example, may well be more loyal and committed to the success of their national organizational unit than to the parent company because there is only limited international authority sharing and long-term commitment. Equally, organizational careers and commitments to dealing with organizational problems will be more focused on the national or regional employer than the parent one. Problem solving efforts and collaboration are accordingly more likely to be easier to manage within these units than internationally, and so collective coordinating and learning capabilities more developed at the national level.

In contrast, employees of managerially coordinated MNCs in more arms' length market economies will limit their commitment to organization-specific problem solving at both national and international levels, and so restrict the development of distinctive, continually improving employer-specific competences. However, formal coordination of generic skills nationally and internationally should be relatively straightforward in these subsidiaries, and flexibility in changing direction considerable. Skilled staff here are likely to prefer to work on project-based problem-solving activities that enhance and display technically specialized expertise and so managerial integration of such projects across national labour markets should not be too difficult. They will not be encouraged, though, to commit considerable time and energy to learning about, and contributing to, MNC-wide activities on a long-term basis, and thus building organization-specific capabilities.

The variety of organizational commitments in different subsidiaries of such MNCs, then, can be considerable, but at the worldwide level they are unlikely to develop firm-specific collective competences through long-term cooperative problem solving and learning. Instead, the international managerial elite may well prefer to focus on refining formal coordination and control systems for realizing the benefits of integrating diverse national and regional capabilities, as well as dealing with international capital markets, suppliers and customers on a cross-national basis. A key 'global' organizational capability of such MNCs, then, may well be their ability to develop and implement standard routines and procedures for integrating diverse operations and competences located in different kinds of business environments, often building on those developed domestically.

The final three kinds of MNC to be discussed here share considerable authority with foreign employees over local and international issues and involve them extensively in cross-national problem solving, such that subsidiaries are expected to develop strong capabilities for contributing to global strategies. They differ, though, in their willingness to establish long-term international careers for managers and professionals, and hence in the likely longevity of their commitment to developing MNC specific competences and knowledge.

Considering first delegated professional MNCs, these share considerable authority with a number of foreign employees and delegate high levels of discretion to them, but limit the extent and scope of international careers. They mobilize managers and professionals from around the world to work on highly complex and often risky problems, as in, for instance, many business services, but are unable to offer long-term organizational commitments to most staff. This is often because they undertake highly uncertain activities that have unpredictable and risky outcomes, and so flexibility in developing and using skills is more important than the long-term development of organization-specific knowledge.

A major capability of such firms, then, is the capacity to create and direct cross-national project teams for specific, discrete problems with finite outcomes and clear performance criteria. International coordination is achieved primarily through such project teams that combine relatively standardized sets of expertise for dealing with particular, one-off problems. Long-term integration of activities and skills leading to the development of international organization-specific capabilities tends to be limited in such companies, especially their cross-national coordinating and learning capabilities. Although teams may contribute codified information to a central database, as in some consultancy firms, their short-term nature limits the extent to which the organization as a whole can build firm-specific knowledge internationally.

Since authority sharing with foreign managers and professionals is typically quite high in these companies, we would expect them to develop quite varied ways of dealing with the local environment and to innovate in ways that differ from the home economy. This is especially likely when the major institutions governing labour and capital markets vary significantly between countries so that the organizationally specific nature of skills and careers differs across subsidiaries. Given the disparity of commitments, skills and capabilities between teams in different kinds of market economies, such MNCs may well experience considerable coordination difficulties, and effectively decentralize decision making to national subsidiaries to a high degree, as in franchise-based professional service organizations.

However, their flexibility and ability to mobilize highly skilled staff to work on complex and risky problems can enable them to develop effective international abilities to transform key assets and skills. Particularly where there are strong technical communities and fluid labour markets across national boundaries, these kinds of MNCs should be able to adapt rapidly to changing circumstances, and their reconfigurational capabilities can be expected to be considerable, as in some business service companies. This is less likely in highly regulated professional service firms where skills and technologies are more standardized and problem solving is more a matter of applying current skills to particular client problems than inventing new technologies.

Next, delegated managerial MNCs combine considerable delegation of authority to managers and professionals in many foreign subsidiaries with international careers for senior subsidiary managers. These kinds of MNCs encourage foreign subsidiaries to develop distinctive capabilities that contribute to international strategies as well as meeting local targets. By delegating considerable discretion to local managers and professionals they enable them to innovate and adapt to local conditions, and so generated varied capabilities at the local level. By also involving them in international teams to deal with more global issues they are able to draw upon these different backgrounds and expertise. The establishment of international managerial careers here should ensure that commitments to the long-term development of the parent MNC is greater than in delegated professional MNCs and integration of activities through managerial routines and controls correspondingly more developed.

In the case of ABB in the 1990s, for instance, considerable local diversity in one division was combined with extensive use of benchmarking and imposition of common improvement programmes from the centre to upgrade process efficiencies and learn from the better performers (Belanger *et al.*, 1999). Here, a cadre of international managers was developed by rotating successful plant executives across countries and continents, and eventually to leading positions in global divisions. They transferred effective recipes and processes between subsidiaries and so were key components of the MNC's learning activities. Committed to the success of the parent company, these elite managers contributed to the development of its international knowledge and capabilities on a continuing, long-term basis.

The predominantly national nature of organizational careers for most foreign employees, however, means that their loyalties will be more focused on national labour markets than the parent company. This means that local institutional differences are likely to affect levels and foci of long-term commitments such that significant variations can be expected between, say, R&D teams in the UK and Japan that affect cross-national organizational learning, as some Japanese pharmaceutical firms have found out (Methe and Penner-Hahn, 1999; Lam, 2003).

While the international coordination of technology development activities through project planning and regular communication may be quite straightforward when problem-solving activities follow relatively predictable trajectories, it becomes more difficult as the importance of tacit knowledge increases and technical uncertainty grows (Cantwell, 2001). Long-term international cooperation to develop organization-specific knowledge and skills in situations of considerable uncertainty is obviously not easy to accomplish when labour market institutions in some countries discourage long-term organizational commitments—whether national or international—and key staff are as much concerned with enhancing their external reputations and generic skills as developing firm-specific knowledge.

Finally, highly integrated MNCs develop organizational careers and commitments that dominate those within national and regional subsidiaries, and reward both managerial and professional employees who demonstrate success in dealing with international problem solving and commitment to the parent organization. As a result, these firms develop distinctive knowledge and skills at the international level, and their organizational capabilities are transnational rather than national. In particular, complementary activities are here integrated across borders by technical experts, as well as by managers, whose loyalties and identities are as much focused on the MNC as a whole as on national subsidiaries or local labour markets. Technical careers are as international as senior managerial ones, and depend on internationally visible success in solving organization-specific problems cross-nationally.

Ambitious foreign professionals and managers in these kinds of MNCs seek to demonstrate their success cross-nationally in contributing to major parent company issues rather than focusing on enhancing their reputations in local labour markets. This should generate strong international coordinating and learning capabilities as professional and managerial elites compete in the transnational organizational labour market on the basis of their success in dealing with major MNC problems. Because international careers dominate purely national ones, complex and tacit knowledge is more likely to be transferred and built upon by technical experts across national units than in delegated managerial MNCs.

The more international nature of commitments and loyalties in highly integrated MNCs additionally encourages the development of customer-specific knowledge at the international level. While the lack of strong cross-national institutions encouraging authority sharing between suppliers and customers limits the extent of such cross-national linkages compared to those in collaborative institutional frameworks, the primacy of international careers and problem solving in these MNCs means that any investments in dealing with customers' problems will be cross-national rather than national. Similarly, they are as likely to compete with other MNCs at the international level as nationally, and so collectively develop an international competitive system that can, in some industries such as oil exploration, refining and distribution, dominate local markets.

For firms to be able to make credible commitments to key members of their international labour force such that they are encouraged to invest in long-term, firm-specific problem solving and knowledge development, they need to be large and stable enough to maintain employment over business cycles and to offer international promotion prospects that greatly exceed domestic ones. MNCs are only likely to want to develop distinctive transnational capabilities through such commitments when they have strong international coordination and learning needs that far outweigh national and regional market variations and labour costs considerations. These points suggest that the relatively few MNCs that do develop long-term international careers for key experts and managers will be in capital intensive industries with systemic technologies and worldwide markets for standardized products dominated by a few vertically integrated companies, such as the oil extraction, refining and distribution industry.

The primacy of international careers and commitments in such companies suggests that they may be more difficult to establish in the more coordinated economies than in arms' length ones because domestic organizational loyalties and authority sharing are greater in the former societies. Separating a relatively small group of highly trained employees for international careers from local colleagues, and rewarding cross-national competence development more than focusing on nationally specific issues is likely to be more difficult in these kinds of market economy. In contrast, because arm's length institutional regimes discourage high levels of employer–employee interdependence with the bulk of the workforce, they may enable MNCs from such domestic economies to provide organizational careers for technical and managerial staff. Additionally, low levels of authority sharing with business partners in these kinds of societies enables MNCs to develop a variety of linkages with customers and suppliers on a worldwide basis without having to integrate these with home economy ones.

Insofar, then, as companies are able to establish such integrated international organizations that generate distinctive cross-national capabilities, and I suspect that this is less common than much of the literature celebrating transnational MNCs suggests, they are more likely to originate in arm's length economies than collaborative ones. It is also worth pointing out that companies based in these kinds of economies will have had more experience of dealing with arm's length investors and capital markets than those from more collaborative regimes. Such MNCs may, then, be more adept at managing relations with international investors.

Conclusions

This analysis of the organizational capabilities of different kinds of MNCs in the light of differences in the institutional frameworks of home and host economies suggests a number of conclusions about their development of transnational competences. First, while many companies with major facilities in different countries may develop distinctive collective capabilities at the national and regional levels, by no means all of them do so internationally. Because of: (a) the relative weakness of international institutions governing employer and employee opportunism, (b) the common belief in the superiority of domestically developed competences, and (c) the variable nature of institutional frameworks across market economies, many companies are often reluctant to share authority with foreign managers and professionals or to offer them long-term organizational commitments. This means that their organizational capabilities as MNCs are little different from those of their domestic organization, together perhaps with those generated separately by some subsidiaries. The coordination of economic activities in different countries does not, then, necessarily produce distinctive cross-national collective capabilities, and so MNCs as such do not constitute a distinctive kind of company from the point of view of the competence-based view of the firm.

Second, the variety of organizational capabilities in MNCs reflects the varied nature of institutional regimes across market economies, and the resultant differences in kinds of firms that develop in them. Arm's length institutional frameworks may, for example, encourage firms to develop the ability to manage various kinds of businesses through managerial procedures and routines that do not involve the bulk of the workforce. This in turn leads MNCs from such backgrounds to extend these control and planning systems to operations in different countries, limiting any authority sharing and career commitments to senior managers. The kinds of international organizational capabilities that they develop are therefore likely to be quite similar to domestic ones.

Similarly, MNCs from highly coordinated economies that have developed strong organizational learning capabilities through considerable authority sharing with, and career commitments to, many domestic employees are likely to restrict such commitments to foreign staff because the institutions that constrained opportunism in the home economy are often missing in their societies. This is particularly probable when long-term careers in the domestic organization are both highly firm specific and general across specialisms, as in many MNCs from business corporatist regimes.

Additionally, the impact of host economy institutions governing skill formation and labour markets can affect the development of cross-national capabilities by varying in their standardization and certification of practical expertise, as well as in their control over employer and employee opportunism. In general, the more fluid are external labour markets in an economy, and the more standardized are skills through educational and/or professional development and certification, the more difficult it becomes to develop long-term employee commitment at both national and international levels. While such institutional arrangements do facilitate employers' ability to hire and fire staff with various kinds of skills, and so rapidly transform their knowledge and expertise base, they limit employees' willingness to invest in developing firm-specific capabilities on a continuing basis.

This suggests, third, that cross-national problem solving and learning should be easier when skill boundaries, knowledge bases and organizational structures are quite similar in different countries. In these circumstances, careers in both internal and external labour markets are likely to reward comparable kinds of technically specialized contributions, and externally certified skills are sufficiently standardized across labour markets to provide common languages for joint problem solving. Even when commitments to developing employer-specific knowledge and skills differ considerably between national subsidiaries, continuing communication and gaining the cooperation of specialists across borders on a long-term basis will be greatly facilitated by organizational career structures that reward expertise-based performance, as distinct from broader contributions to general organizational success. However, such specialist careers can, of course, inhibit cross-functional collaboration.

These kinds of expertise-based career structures are in turn encouraged by similar kinds of public skill formation and evaluation systems that generate social identities and loyalties around certified skills. For MNCs to develop distinctive cross-national learning capabilities that enable different kinds of knowledge production and problem solving to be transferred between subsidiaries—as opposed to the codified results of such activities—careers and commitments have to overlap across organizational subunits.

Overall, the more varied are subsidiaries' environments and their organization of careers, especially the kinds of contributions and skills that they reward, the more difficult it is likely to be for MNCs to develop distinctive international learning capabilities, particularly for developing new knowledge that is not readily codified. Establishing a common cross national career structure for some middle managers and professionals will contribute to the generation of these kinds of capabilities, but this requires the MNC to be able to offer credible commitments over business cycles and national differences.

Fourth, the few MNCs that do develop strong coordinating and learning capabilities across borders through long-term international employer–employee commitments are less likely than delegated professional MNCs to be able to reconfigure their skills and competences radically to deal with rapidly changing circumstances. This is because of their dependence on current employees' skills and their establishment of transnational integrating routines. Building and maintaining long-term firm specific organizational capabilities at the international level usually involves considerable investments in cross-national procedures, routines and competences. These are unlikely to encourage rapid and radical transformation of key skills and technologies that would enable firms to move effectively into quite novel industries with discontinuous technological trajectories and markets.

Delegated professional MNCs, in contrast, are more flexible, especially when their major operations are in fluid external labour markets, but tend to limit the international coordination of knowledge and skill development to cross-national teams working on discrete, one-off problems (Morgan and Quack, 2005). They are therefore able to adjust relatively quickly to changing technologies and markets, particularly when there are highly organized markets for technical specialists, but key competences are as much individual and team-based as organizationally-specific. International capabilities here involve coordinating teams of specialists across countries on a largely *ad hoc* opportunistic basis with little employer or employee commitment to organizational careers. Mobilizing and controlling such teams are here central organizational competences that depend on considerable knowledge of local labour markets and reputational networks, further encouraging authority sharing and delegation of operational control, as in many project-based firms in emerging industries (Grabher, 2002a; 2002b).

12

The Changing Japanese Multinational: Application, Adaptation, and Learning in Car Manufacturing and Financial Services

with Glenn Morgan, William Kelly, and Diana Sharpe

Introduction

Japanese multinational companies are commonly portrayed as sharing relatively little authority with foreign subsidiaries, and being reluctant to invest in transnational organizational careers for their foreign employees (see, e.g. Beechler and Bird, 1999), pursuing largely *colonial* or *domestically dominated* patterns of cross-national authority sharing and career development. Their foreign operations are often considered to function as delivery pipelines for centrally planned products and services, which replicate domestic production processes and management systems (see, e.g. Bartlett and Ghoshal, 1989: 51–2, 158–61). Relying extensively on expatriate managers to control subsidiaries tightly, and to teach foreign managers and workers the 'X company way' of working, such globally integrated MNCs have become renowned for limiting the promotion opportunities for non-Japanese staff (see, e.g. Kopp, 1999) and operating in a home country centric manner (Ernst, 2006; Westney, 2001b). In Abo's (1994) terms, these often rather reluctant and relatively late internationalizing organizations applied their successful domestic business recipe to overseas locations rather than adapting it to suit local conditions.

This broad view of the Japanese MNC has been modified somewhat by recent empirical research on how they manage their European and US subsidiaries, especially in the car manufacturing industries (see, e. g. Abo, 1994; Botti, 1995; Delbridge, 1998; Kenney and Florida, 1993; Liker *et al.*, 1999). While many features of their production systems, such as relying extensively upon Japanese production machinery and close connections to suppliers, using Japanese standard procedures and manuals, reducing job classifications, and limiting the role of labour unions, seem to be widely applied in foreign settings without a great deal of modification, others, such as job rotation, promoting production workers to maintenance and supervisory roles and involving them in problem solving, are not so standardized across foreign subsidiaries (Abo, 1994: 63; Adler, 1999; Dedoussis, 1994; Pil and MacDuffie, 1999).

Furthermore, there appear to be significant sectoral variations in how much of the domestic recipe is transferred to foreign operations, both across manufacturing industries and between the manufacturing and service sectors. In particular, many firms in the electronics industry have been less concerned to transfer the distinctive corporate way of doing things to their European and US subsidiaries than have car producers (Kenney, 1999). Whereas nearly all foreign plants in the latter industry have developed under the tutelage of domestic 'mother' plants, this was not the case in all electronics companies (Elger and Smith, 1994; Kenney and Florida, 1993; Liker *et al.*, 1999). Additionally, not all electronics manufacturing processes incorporate every component of what has become seen as the 'Japanese' system. For instance, Taylor *et al.* (1994) found that in one electronics firm, JIT was not highly developed either in the domestic parent or in the British subsidiary, and in general the latter had rather limited communication with head office.

One reason for this divergence between Japanese vehicle and electronics companies' policies in Europe and the USA is that car firms' investments in these markets have tended to be full-scale manufacturing plants that were capital-intensive and required a skilled and committed labour force to function effectively. In contrast, many manufacturing subsidiaries in the electronics industry had more limited, final assembly, plants, which required fewer resources, lower skills and less intensive coordination with component suppliers (Delbridge, 1998: 205–8; Emmott, 1992; Kenney, 1999). They were more similar to many car plants in developing countries that assembled knockdown kits.

As one manager in the Global Human Resource (GHR) division of a car assembly firm suggested to us during the study reported here, many of their plants in South East Asia required less investment and lower skills than those in more developed economies, and so the firm did not need to transfer all aspects of that company's specific production system to the region. The greater capital commitments and complexity of car production in industrialized countries encouraged firms to invest more managerial resources there to ensure the success of their foreign operations, especially in improving skills and establishing stable labour relations (Abo, 1994).

In the service sector, which accounts for by far the greatest amount of Japanese foreign direct investment (FDI) (Abo, 1994; Dicken *et al.*, 1997; Strange, 1993), foreign subsidiaries have usually been established to provide specific services for domestic clients. These included the provision of market information, trade finance and intermediation in the case of the general trading companies that established foreign offices before the First World War (Dicken and Miyamachi, 1998; Mason, 1994). As a result, they have been dominated by Japanese expatriate managers implementing agreements made in Tokyo or Osaka, with little adaptation to local conditions, except perhaps for the recruitment and management of junior staff. Here, foreign units were more outposts of domestic divisions than distinct organizations serving foreign markets. When these overseas units did hire local staff to deal with non-Japanese business, they tended to develop segmented organizations in which employment conditions, working practices and reward systems differed significantly between Japanese and local employees, such that some banks were described as constituting two banks under one roof (Sakai, 2000).

In general, then, while much Japanese FDI in Europe and North America in the 1980s was based on domestic recipes and involved the transfer of those frameworks to foreign operations, the extent of such transfer varied between sectors and the nature of each location (Westney, 1999; 2001b). Few Japanese firms sought to learn new managerial practices from their overseas subsidiaries, and rarely if ever transferred new routines developed abroad back to their domestic units (Fujimoto *et al.*, 1994). Their extensive use of expatriate managers, particularly in the car and financial services industries, reflected this focus on transfer and application rather than adaptation and learning. In a number of manufacturing industries, Japanese managers were used to train foreign managers and workers in specific manufacturing processes and techniques as well as in the corporate culture and philosophy, so that the primary sources of the firms' competitive advantages could be institutionalized throughout its operations. As new plants became more established and reliable, their roles became more concerned with ensuring effective coordination with Japanese plants and Head Office (Pucik, 1994).

Given the success of Japanese firms in the consumer electronics and vehicle manufacturing industries in world markets in the 1970s and 1980s, and the highly integrated nature of the postwar business system and its institutional context in Japan (Westney, 1996; Whitley, 1992a), it is not surprising that the prevalent pattern of managing foreign subsidiaries was one of application rather than learning from local institutions and practices. Although these firms had to adapt some of their practices to prevailing norms and practices, especially those governing labour markets, when investing substantial resources in the industrialized economies of Europe and the Americas, they were able to apply many components of their domestic recipe to subsidiaries in the relatively pluralistic and arms' length institutional environments of the UK and the USA (Kenney, 1999). Most, if not all, foreign subsidiaries were appendages in Malnight's (1995) terminology, rather than becoming participants, let alone contributors.

In the 1990s, however, the extension of 'owner-specific' advantages and organizational capabilities to gain competitive advantages in foreign markets became more questionable as the Japanese economy experienced its longest recession since 1950. Additionally, the international success of Japanese firms in new industries and the service sector has been less evident than in consumer electronics and motor vehicles. Furthermore, the domestic economy is beginning to be more accessible to foreign firms, albeit from a very low baseline, and a few have taken control of large Japanese companies such as Mazda and Nissan. This challenge of overseas firms and their different ways of working has also been evident in the financial services sector where many Japanese companies have been greatly weakened by the recession and undergone major reorganization.

The weakness and restructuring of the domestic economy have made foreign operations more important as possible sources of markets and profits in many Japanese MNCs, and encouraged some to use them to learn new skills and practices (see, e.g. Beechler et al., 1998). From being subsidiary to domestic sales and profits, and sometimes run at a loss to gain market share, overseas markets and customers have gained in importance for some companies as domestic growth has faltered. In a few manufacturing industries, rapid overseas investment in production and marketing operations, especially during the 1980s, seemed to be coming to fruition for some firms in the 1990s, in terms of both percentages of global market shares secured and percentage of overall profit accounted for by overseas operations.

These changes could be expected to alter some of the features of Japanese internationalization outlined above. As Japanese MNCs begin to produce a significant proportion of their outputs abroad, such that domestic markets and facilities constitute less than half of sales and value-added activities, they might consider developing a less centralized structure, and attempt to learn from local innovations. Some Japanese pharmaceutical companies, for instance, have invested in UK and US research facilities and biotechnology firms in order to gain direct access to new knowledge and research skills that are not readily available in Japan (Cairncross, 1994; Kneller, 2003; Lam, 2003; Methe and Penner-Hahn, 1999).

However, the extent of such changes is likely to vary considerably between firms in different sectors, according to both the relative success of their domestically developed competences in international markets and their dependence on domestic Japanese customers. Since many Japanese firms in the consumer electronics and car manufacturing industries continue to build market share in many parts of the world on the basis of home-based innovation and production capabilities, it seems improbable that they will radically change their centralized coordination and control system. On the other hand, rather less successful companies may be more open to more substantial changes, particularly where they have been taken over by foreign companies.

This is especially likely in sectors where the dominant framework and rules of the game are Anglo-Saxon rather than Japanese, as in international investment banking, and where changes in the international business environment are combined with domestic restructuring and deregulation (Dufey, 1994; Laurence, 2001; Morgan and Kubo, 2005). Here, some Japanese firms might invest in learning from their overseas branches and begin to operate in novel ways. Insofar as growing internationalization and the lengthy domestic recession are likely to have had major effects on Japanese MNCs, they should be more noticeable in these sectors. Such changes have major implications for the use of expatriate managers, especially their selection, training and career patterns.

In particular, the increasing internationalization of production and distribution activities of many Japanese MNCs could encourage a more systematic approach to the selection and management of expatriates than has tended to be the case, as well perhaps as more active use of non-Japanese managers in jobs outside their native country, including Japan (Kopp, 1999). In addition to foreign postings becoming part of the usual pattern of rotating future senior managers between sections and departments, it might lead Head Office personnel departments to develop more specific training programmes for international managers and to ensure that future appointments reflected the benefits gained from foreign experiences.

However, the continued concentration of key resources and activities in Japan in many, if not most, successful manufacturing companies seem likely to limit the significance of overseas postings for Japanese managers as well as the development of a separate international management cadre integrating foreign employees with Japanese ones. The generation of distinctive transnational organizational capabilities through international careers that would encourage long-term employer-specific commitment amongst foreign as well as Japanese senior managers appears, then, rather improbable in successful Japanese car assembly firms.

In contrast, where domestic restructuring and deregulation is combined with a lack of success in international markets, we might expect the traditional pattern of expatriate rotation through senior positions in foreign units to be more radically altered. In the financial services industry, for example, the superior status of domestic 'generalist' bankers compared to international 'specialist' ones (Sakai, 2000), could change as expertise in international capital markets became more highly valued and the home economy remained in recession. Generalist managerial careers in Japanese banks might become less attractive to junior staff than developing specialist skills in, say, investment analysis, that would enable them to move to more attractive opportunities, including foreign employers (Morgan and Kubo, 2005).

With the continuing restructuring and mergers between banks and related financial service companies in the 1990s, and the appearance of US investment banks recruiting new graduates from the better universities in Japan, international assignments and experience could become more valued by both Japanese banks and their employees. This is especially probable where such banks have become committed to competing in international capital markets. Careers and commitments could, then, be expected to have changed more in the 1990s in the banking sector than in car assembly and electronics, particularly with respect to the importance of overseas experience and knowledge.

In particular, we might anticipate Japanese banks and other financial companies would begin to use expatriate managers in London and New York to learn about international capital market risks and opportunities, and so develop new kinds of expertise and knowledge. However, this could lead to conflicts with established generalist career patterns and prestige hierarchies in these organizations. Together with the continued predominance of domestic clients and markets, such difficulties are likely to limit organizational adaptation and learning in many Japanese banks, depending on their long-term strategic objectives. Adaptation and learning may then be more apparent in the banking sector than in manufacturing, but will be restricted by current career paths and skill development practices.

In this chapter we consider how international managerial careers and attitudes are changing in Japanese companies in two quite different industries, car manufacturing and banking, as revealed by a series of interviews with Japanese and British managers in Japanese firms in the UK, and with head office managers of these MNCs. These were conducted in 2000 and 2001 as part of a larger study of expatriate Japanese and Korean managers in the UK. Most interviews were conducted in English, though occasionally the meaning of replies would be clarified in Japanese, and were recorded to be subsequently transcribed. Detailed interviews were held with twenty-one managers of three car assembly firms in the UK, eight of whom were British, and with ten managers in the Head Offices of these companies in Japan. Fifteen managers of eleven Japanese banks and securities companies were interviewed in London, two of whom were British, and a further nine in Japan.

In addition to enquiring about their roles and careers, we discussed changes in head office-subsidiary relationships, coordination among subsidiaries, and the practical problems of working in different countries. At head office, we focused on the strategic use of expatriates, whether they were systematically trained before going abroad, how firms used them upon returning, changes in their career paths, and the overall development of the companies' international operations. In the next section we shall discuss our findings from the car manufacturing firms, and subsequently consider the banking sector.

Changing Managerial Careers and Roles in Japanese Car Manufacturing MNCs

Japanese car manufacturers established major production facilities in Europe later than their electronics counterparts who began assembly operations in the UK in the 1970s (Strange, 1993). This was partly because of the larger cost involved and partly because of the complexity of transferring their firm-specific production systems to quite different environments. Nissan started production from knockdown kits in Sunderland in 1986, while Honda developed its joint venture with Rover from 1989 with commercial production of Honda cars starting in 1992 and full-scale manufacturing achieved in 1995. Toyota began assembling cars in Burnaston in 1993. The number of employees at each of these car plants is considerable, typically over 3000.

In the three car manufacturing companies considered here, our interviewees identified three distinct stages in the role and importance of expatriate managers in foreign subsidiaries. During the initial phase of building the plants and increasing production up to full capacity there was considerable reliance on Japanese managers, engineers, and supervisors. This was not only to train British staff in the correct use of the machinery, but also to establish the parent company's way of producing vehicles, and to instil its philosophy and way of thinking in the local workforce. Typically, expatriates took the main line management roles at this stage, although personnel management was often left to local managers. The dominant role of Japanese managers and engineers was clearly understood as a teaching one.

Second, after the plant and related facilities were up and running at a comparable level of efficiency as domestic ones—though rarely at the identical level—the number of Japanese managers on long-term assignments declined and their role became more advisory. Most senior management posts were given to local staff and the bulk of the expatriates were designated as coordinators or advisors, often shadowing each British manager or senior engineer. However, since they often reported directly to head office as well as to the local top management, some of the British managers we spoke to felt that these coordinators were the dominant partners in practice. This was confirmed by a number of Japanese managers at the head offices of these companies. As one general manager of an international relations department in a leading Japanese electronics firm suggested, the use of local managing directors was a 'gimmick' to disguise the real control exerted by their coordinator 'partners'.

In the third stage, which few had reached, the numbers of expatriates were further reduced and their function was perceived as being more supportive than directive. This portrayal of the declining importance of Japanese managers in foreign subsidiaries as the latter gain experience and the trust of head offices has not been reflected in the experience of all local managers in US subsidiaries (Brannen *et al.*, 1999; Pil and MacDuffie, 1999; Pucik, 1994), and can be expected to vary in its accuracy in Europe as well.

In 2000, all three of the car manufacturing firms we studied had established their UK plants successfully, and had reduced the number of expatriate managers from the levels of the early 1990s. However, there were some significant variations between them, as Abo (1994) and his colleagues found in the USA. One plant had less than one per cent of its workforce who were Japanese, but a further thirty-seven were working in R&D at another location. Two per cent of the employees of another car plant were expatriates but the third one had six per cent who were Japanese.

The oldest plant had the lowest number of Japanese staff, as was the case also with that firm's American subsidiaries, and one manager there claimed that it was a more international company than the other two. However, the large difference in the number of expatriates between the other two firms did not seem due to the age of their foundation, but probably reflected different strategies for managing overseas operations, as well as investment in a second production line due to start in 2001. The firm with the greatest proportion of Japanese staff at its main UK plant also had more Japanese managers working overseas throughout the organization (1,500) than did the other two (1,000 and 700), despite its smaller overall size and earlier establishment of plants in the USA.

This company also had main board directors of the parent firm heading their European and North American regional head offices and claimed that these units had more autonomy than most Japanese subsidiaries. However, product development, finance and other strategic roles seemed to be as centralized in Japan as in the other companies, and equally strong emphasis was placed on instilling the corporate philosophy throughout the business. The mother plant system for training foreign units was also used in much the same way in this company as elsewhere.

Expatriate managers and technical staff in these car manufacturing firms were predominantly in coordinating roles in 2000, combining intensive liaison with head office and the mother plant with monitoring of quality control and product consistency. In addition to technical integration of UK operations with Japanese ones, they performed what one British manager termed 'corporate governance', or control, functions. Often younger and less experienced than the first wave of Japanese staff, they sometimes had difficulties in dealing with their British counterparts, some of whom were unclear about the benefits gained from their presence, as were their US equivalents according to a human resources manager in Tokyo. Feedback to Japan was equally important as feed forward from Japan, and many expatriates were acting as much as windows on foreign markets for head office as windows on Japan for subsidiaries. Some firms also distinguished between younger managers, usually single men in their twenties, who were sent overseas as part of their training, and senior ones who were assigned to more specific roles.

These changes in expatriate roles, coupled with the growing significance of foreign assembly and markets relative to domestic activities, had stimulated one major car manufacturer to establish a GHR management division that had started a new programme for developing international leaders, in cooperation with a US business school. Whereas the traditional pattern of expatriate assignments in this company was—and typically remained—to send domestic managers to overseas units in answer to the latters' requests on a largely ad hoc basis, without much building on that experience, this new group was thinking about a more systematic selection and training of a cadre of international managers.

Accordingly, they were actively encouraging the serial posting of high-quality managers from one overseas post to another, and they claimed that successful foreign experience was in the process of becoming a necessary condition for promotion into senior management. The development programme was linked to the systematic assessment of the qualities needed to fill the top 400 positions in foreign affiliates, and the planning of managers' careers in such a way that they would be suitable for them.

A major reason for such programmes being developed, and indeed for the establishment of this particular division, was the difficulty that the company was having in retaining the best local managers of their foreign operations. As they often saw limited opportunities with this firm beyond their national subsidiary, they tended to leave once the top management level of their country's operations had been achieved. Whether the new division will succeed in developing an international cadre of foreign and Japanese managers to constitute the top management group of the whole firm, and so create an elite pattern of international organizational careers, remains to be seen. At the moment, it is concentrating on developing deputy managing directors and above, and does not seem to have altered the prevalent domestically extended pattern of sending Japanese managers abroad on one or two assignments at the request of subsidiaries in a rather reactive and unsystematic manner.

While GHR managers at the other two car firms also mentioned the growing importance of foreign experience for domestic promotion, it did not seem yet to have become a necessary condition. Additionally, neither company had established a systematic career structure for expatriate managers—or considered setting up a process for creating an international cadre of elite managers. Indeed, we were told by GHR managers in two of these car companies that quite a number of expatriates had returned to the same job in the same section when they went back to Japan, and that this pattern had led to a number of resignations in one of these firms.

The prevalent impression we gained from interviews with GHR staff in the UK and at Head Office in all three companies was that the rather ad hoc process of selection and assignment of expatriate managers, and limited attempts to learn systematically from their experiences when they went back to Japan, remained dominant. International postings were not regarded as being particularly different from domestic ones, and typically involved little preparation. One Japanese manager told us that he had had only one month's notice and twenty hours language instruction before coming to the UK. While, then, the establishment of a GHR division in one firm certainly suggested a commitment to integrating senior managerial careers in Japan with those elsewhere, that unit was still attempting to gain control over local managerial careers in foreign subsidiaries and to standardize compensation arrangements for their top managers.

All three car manufacturers had additionally experimented with sending a few UK and US managers to work in Japan for periods of several years to encourage a more integrated career structure, but the results had been rather mixed. As one Japanese senior GHR manager told us, this was partly because of different family expectations and commitments. In addition to difficulties in making suitable arrangements for their children's education, divorce rates were much higher in European and American families than in Japanese ones. A British director of one firm's UK subsidiary suggested that many foreigners who moved to Japan with their families for substantial periods found it difficult to adjust to living in the quite different environment. Although some Japanese managers with children in secondary school worked abroad for several years on their own, as *tanshin funin* (unaccompanied posting), leaving their wives and children in Japan, such behaviour was less acceptable among other nationalities.

These incremental changes in GHR policies were accompanied by moves to establish separate regional head offices for sales and manufacturing in Europe and the Americas. While regional sales offices had been set up a few years earlier in most cases, the manufacturing ones were quite recent, with one only beginning operations in 2000. They were usually responsible for coordinating some sales, production planning and purchasing activities, but design and technology development remained dominated by domestic plants and functions, as did most GHR management.

On the whole, these new regional offices did not seem to increase subsidiary autonomy greatly, and reporting to head office often remained through functional hierarchies as well as through the new structure, although some car manufacturers claimed that they were about to coordinate supply chains at the European level. This pattern of combining direct responsibility to head office with regional reporting was also found in the general trading companies studied by Dicken and Miyamachi (1998), and suggests that, in practice, senior managers in Japan were reluctant to cede much authority to regional units. As one Japanese senior coordinator for GHR told us, regional offices' authority was not very clearly specified, and this led to some confusion of different groups' roles and responsibilities (see, also, Schutte, 1998). In no company did these offices seem to have integrated management control of all production, marketing and sales activities in North America and Europe, and in general, functional reporting to divisional head offices in Japan remained the dominant pattern.

One expatriate manager also suggested that if his company was to become truly 'global', it should separate the domestic operations from a new global head office and treat them as part of their Asian regional division. Given the continued use of domestic Japanese plants as mother—or sister—plants for foreign ones, the continued centralization of research and product development in Japan, and the widespread belief that the competitive advantages of the more successful Japanese car firms are closely dependent on their domestically developed production systems, this seems unlikely to happen in the near future.

In general, then, the internationalization of the leading Japanese car manufacturers remains based on their distinctive domestic recipes. Foreign subsidiaries are more *appendages* than *participants* in transnational problem solving, and international careers more *domestically extended* than *elite*. However, it should be noted that while the organizational template remains relatively constant, the principle of continuous improvement means that the Japanese designers of each new plant build on earlier experiences, just as new machinery incorporates suggestions and adjustments made during previous use (Fujimoto, 2000). As a result, no two plants are laid out in the same way since these companies incorporate improvements in the floorplans and other design aspects of new factories.

For instance, the British General Manager of car manufacturing in one plant pointed out with reference to a new European plant that:

the physical layout of the plant depends upon what [X firm] learned from the last ones and every new one they build is completely different and the one they're building in France is completely and utterly different to this one.

While, then, the fundamental philosophy and approach to production control, procurement, work organization, and employment relations have been developed in Japan, the actual production machinery and its layout in new locations are being continuously updated and modified, typically by Japanese engineers and managers. Organizational learning here seemed to take place predominantly in Japan on the basis of information provided by expatriate staff about foreign plants and markets rather than relying on the knowledge and skills of local employees.

In a few cases, some transfer of information and skills did take place between subsidiaries, and one expatriate director of GHR and legal affairs suggested that coordination of new product launches was easier between the UK and USA than with Japanese plants. Additionally, more established plants in Europe have acted as training sites for newer ones, albeit with some resistance by the French employees according to an expatriate general manager in the accounting and finance division of one company. Some cross-subsidiary learning is developing, then, especially between the English-speaking countries (Fujimoto *et al.*, 1994), but head office remains closely involved in such developments and control over the careers of Japanese managers is still centralized in Japan.

On the whole, managerial careers in these car companies remain relatively generalist, intended to develop extensive firm-specific knowledge of different departments and divisions and reward contributions to organizational problem solving within and across different functions. Many rotated between quite different departments over the course of a working lifetime, for example between production control, GHR and accounting and finance, and managerial expertise is more organization-specific than generic across employers. International assignments and success were treated much the same as domestic ones, with little evidence of substantial investment in developing a separate group of international managers despite the formation of a GHR division in one firm. While success in a foreign post was becoming seen by some of the Japanese managers we interviewed as a useful component of their careers, none of the GHR managers confirmed that it was a necessary condition for promotion, at least in 2000.

Since all three Japanese car companies, including the one that had recently come under foreign control, saw the firm-specific way of managing as crucial to their success in all markets, and a critical function of expatriate managers to develop a deep understanding of the X company Way in all managerial staff, it is perhaps not too surprising that managers' careers should continue to follow the established pattern, whether national or international. This also implies that foreign managers have to become fully integrated into that culture, and not just successful in their current post, if they are to be regarded as worthy of high-level promotions. Given the very different labour market structures and practices in the UK and USA, it seems unlikely that many local managers of Japanese car firms in these countries will make the commitments required to demonstrate such integration. This disjunction between local labour markets and Japanese managerial careers is even more marked in the financial services sector.

Changing Managerial Careers and Roles in Japanese Financial MNCs

Many of the leading Japanese financial firms initially established foreign offices and branches in the late 19th century to fund trade and to access international capital markets for their domestic clients, including the Japanese state (Sakai, 2000: 30). After the Second World War, they provided working capital and trade finance for Japanese firms who were often members of their business group, and also invested abroad to escape from domestic regulatory restrictions on the kinds of business they could undertake (Dufey, 1994: Laurence, 2001). As restrictions on foreign lending were lifted in the 1970s and 1980s, they also developed services for Japanese investors who wished to gain exposure to overseas borrowers. Banks, for example, established units to underwrite Japanese corporate bonds in the Euromarkets while brokers such as Nomura undertook investment banking and other activities in London and New York (Hawawini and Schill, 1994).

The burgeoning trade surplus and rising value of the yen after the 1985 Plaza Accord led to rapid increases in capital exports to Europe and the USA in the 1980s. According to Emmott (1992: 146) Japanese firms bought up to 40 per cent of new US Treasury bonds issued in the mid-1980s for their domestic clients, and Japanese banks accounted for over 30 per cent of all non-sterling loans issued in London between 1984 and 1991 (*ibid.* 156). By the time the stock market and property bubble burst in 1990–1, Japanese banks in the City of London were lending to non-Japanese companies and to local municipalities, engaging in financial advice in mergers and acquisitions, and providing capital for aircraft leasing, syndicated loans and project finance, in addition to their support of Japanese companies (Hawawini and Schill, 1994; Sakai, 2000: 35).

315

However, they rarely led loan syndicates and often found it difficult to gain access to the best quality business, partly because they were relative newcomers to the City and were perceived to be reluctant to innovate in a similar way to the US and UK banks. As one of Sakai's (2000: 36) interviewees put it: 'we are cheap money suppliers, but we are not respected by western bankers.' As long as the Tokyo stock market continued to rise and property values in Japan remained high, they could provide cheap capital for foreign markets and were highly competitive in terms of interest rate spreads, but failed to appreciate the implications of different ways of doing business in London and New York, especially when it came to evaluating risk.

In Haye's (2000: 109) colourful account, the list of their overseas failures includes their

'real estate-related losses, their leveraged buy-out (LBO) loans made without even perfunctory local knowledge; their abysmal acquisition and joint venture strategies; their pathetically low or negative returns on equity in their overseas operations; their disdain for perfunctory let alone proper research; their failure to employ hedging techniques in investment or trading areas; their lack of focus and planning in establishing their overseas businesses; their failure to produce a skilled and knowledgeable personnel base to handle sophisticated business transactions; their fixation on mindless asset growth.'

Accordingly, they were left with large problem loans in the recession of the early 1990s that were compounded by the collapse of the domestic stock market and property values.

While these firms relied extensively on Japanese staff in London and New York to deal with domestic clients with whom they typically had long-standing relationships, they usually hired local professionals to handle non-Japanese clients and products. As that business expanded in the 1980s, the numbers of local staff grew considerably and the cultures of many banks changed, although many Japanese financial companies found it difficult to attract high-quality local professional staff (Hawawini and Schill, 1994).

Because the labour markets and organization of skills in financial services in London and New York are quite different from those in large Japanese firms, in being more structured around specialist expertise developed by individuals and small groups to deal with particular problems and clients rather than highly organizationally-specific, these local staff had quite different career patterns to Japanese expatriates (Flood, 2001; Morgan and Kubo, 2005). Even if the Japanese banks and securities firms had wanted to develop a more open pattern of staff development for senior posts, it is not at all clear that the more successful British professionals would have wanted to become committed to a single employer, especially if that meant investing in firm-specific knowledge and skills at the expense of enhancing their reputations on external labour markets.

The reluctance of many Japanese companies to promote local staff to senior managerial posts, and to encourage them to develop careers with them, was not, then, just a matter of cultural differences and contrasting ways of working, but also reflected the quite different labour market structures and reward systems institutionalized in the UK and Japan. Given the dominant role of London and New York in the world's capital markets, and Tokyo's perceived provincial status, it was not realistic to expect highly skilled and rewarded bankers, dealers and other specialists to commit themselves to working for a Japanese firm in the long term if that meant learning the details of that company's varied businesses in Japan and elsewhere over 20 or 30 years, not to mention learning the Japanese language.

As one Japanese Assistant General Manager of a leading Japanese City bank told us, they hire individual local staff with specialist skills to do specific jobs at the going rate, even if that involves paying them much more than the expatriate staff, and do not expect them to stay if other opportunities arise elsewhere. They did not recruit British university graduates who were expected to commit themselves to the bank for many decades. Thus, the careers of, and rewards for, local and expatriate staff in the financial services industry have been quite different in these Japanese companies, to the extent that some have seen them as containing two quite distinct cultures, exacerbating coordination problems and leading to poor decision making (Sakai, 2000).

The importance of Japanese customers, whether as borrowers, issuers, or investors, to these firms meant that they had much higher numbers of expatriate managers than the manufacturing firms we studied. As Sakai (2000) shows, the proportion of Japanese staff in banks, securities companies and other financial firms in London in the early 1990s ranged from 7.5 per cent to 50 per cent, while most factories had under 5 per cent (Abo, 1994). Smaller units had proportionately more Japanese staff, but even those with total employment of 500 had over 50 expatriates. In general, these did not become involved with non-Japanese customer relationships, but would monitor the local staff who did deal with British and other clients, and reported to Head Office about them.

The internationalization of Japanese banks and other financial companies in the 1970s and 1980s, then, was even more tied to their domestic
business system and customers than was the case for manufacturing firms.
Initially concerned with obtaining financial resources for Japanese clients,
they subsequently functioned as channels for Japanese investors to dis-
tribute financial surpluses to Japanese and foreign borrowers at highly
competitive rates. Despite increasing their share of world capital markets
with these low-cost funds, most banks did not invest substantially in
learning about new products or ways of doing business in these rather
different markets. They were not renowned for their innovativeness or
technical sophistication (Hawawini and Schill, 1994). As one expatriate
manager in the investment banking division of a major Japanese bank
put it, when he was working in Europe he 'just lend money, in a good
time. I never recover money'.

Because they were essentially operating their international businesses
as extensions of domestic ones, they failed to develop new competences
and routines that would have enabled them to compete effectively with
the dominant financial companies in these markets, which were mostly
European and North American (Sakai, 2000: 43–50). Even when they did
take a leading role in a specialist area of banking, as for example they
did in aircraft leasing, this was largely because of their access to cheap
capital provided by Japanese investors who bought leasing companies'
bonds, and perhaps also because of tax advantages (Dufey, 1994; Sakai,
2000: 53–4). As a result, they often lost money on lending to foreign borrowers, partly because of the highly centralized nature of decision making
that delayed major transactions, and this reinforced their preference for
dealing with domestic clients.

Similarly, the dominant role of domestic customers and investors for
these companies meant that foreign experience and expertise was not
highly valued. Indeed, in some banks to be posted abroad was a sign
of inferior status since all important decisions and developments were
made in Tokyo and Osaka, and career chances could be affected by being
away from the informal networks at head office (Sakai, 2000). To be an
international banker was to be regarded as a specialist in an organization
that valued generalist skills and the development of close relationships
with large Japanese companies, which of course made key decisions at
their head offices in Japan.

Careers were, and remain, tightly controlled by central GHR
departments—even more so in banking than in manufacturing according
to a number of informants—who sent managers abroad on a largely

ad hoc basis, and often reassigned them to the same post and section when they returned to Japan. Overseas branches and activities were not differentiated greatly from domestic ones in terms of assignments and career development. Although a number of the large banks did invest considerably in foreign education, sending up to 20 junior staff abroad to do MBAs or masters degrees in economics or law a year, there seemed to be little evidence that their new skills were used systematically to develop the business. As one interviewee who had suffered from this attitude towards foreign education and business told us, this was partly because they were regarded as being too young and inexperienced to deviate from the established career pattern in the bank. Learning from their foreign operations was not, then, a high priority for Japanese banks in the 1980s, not least because, as an expatriate Assistant General Manager of the corporate research department of a major bank told us, the vast majority (90 per cent) of their business was domestically based.

This began to change in the 1990s as the result of a number of domestic and external events. Probably the most important was the collapse of the Tokyo stock market and of property values in much of Japan. This affected both the value of the banks' capital base and their assets since a considerable amount of lending during the bubble economy had been secured against land and buildings, especially that by the Trust and Long Term Credit banks (Ueda, 1994). Together with the implementation of the Bank for International Settlements (BIS) agreement that international banks had to have 8 per cent of their assets as capital by 1993, the radical decline in banks' share prices as well as those of the firms they invested in meant that they suddenly had much less money to lend and the quality of loans became more important. The decline of the stock market additionally reduced the amount of capital that Japanese investors had available for international investment so that the basis of much of the banks' foreign business was severely cut back.

There were also recessions in the UK and the USA in the early 1990s, which put pressure on many of the customers to whom Japanese banks had made large loans, and increasing external, especially US, efforts to open up the Japanese financial markets to foreign companies. At the same time, then, as the values of their assets at both home and abroad were clearly declining, their large customers were experiencing downturns in business, and their capital bases were being severely reduced, Japanese financial companies were having to deal with a more deregulated domestic environment and the entry of international competitors who were more skilled at operating in such contexts.

Their responses to this situation—and the continuing Japanese recession throughout the 1990s coupled with the Asian financial crises of 1997–8—were varied. Most Japanese banks were, at the time of our interviews in 2001, involved in major restructuring efforts that involve merging across business group boundaries, closing branches and other units and reducing staff. These closures have been especially noticeable in Europe and the USA, with many local branches being turned into representative offices under the control of regional head offices. Two banks have actually withdrawn from foreign operations completely, in one case because the bank lost its banking licence as a result of a scandal in the 1980s.

A second reaction has been to concentrate their recovery plans on serving Japanese customers, usually within their network of associated companies that are also being restructured, and to reduce greatly the amount of non-Japanese business they undertake. Two of the three banks in our study that were pursuing this strategy had only established their European operations since the Second World War, partly because their main domestic competitors were doing so. As the legal advisor to one of these banks told us: 'other banks do it, so we follow.' This strategy meant closing many foreign offices and reducing local staff numbers as well as sending many expatriate managers back to Japan. These latter often felt a sense of failure—or at least of being regarded as having experience and skills that were not valued—and were concerned about how they would be treated by the highly domestically oriented bank.

For instance, one banker at the head office of a large city bank suggested that some employees returning from overseas were leaving the company after a few years as they 'believe that the bank cannot use their speciality' (as international bankers). As did other respondents, this banker also referred to the problems that returning expatriates had in fitting into a company that was primarily domestically oriented:

People that work in international operations has some kind of cultures. (*There is*) not an international culture in a very typical Japanese bank, and...some cases they don't understand each other, their way of thinking or you know their manner...Sometimes the people...just come back from foreign operation, at senior level, assigned to Japan as domestic Branch manager and normally...when assigned they spend two years, it's normal, you know, period for being general manager for a domestic branch. But that kind of general manager, just come back from the foreign operation, sometimes reassigned to the Headquarters just after one year or so. I believe this is because there is some kind of struggle between the General Manager and the branch staff.

A third group of financial firms, four of the eleven we studied, were combining retrenchment and restructuring with a more positive approach to international business. Two of these were large city banks that had a long history of operations in London, and one was a long-term credit institution. At the time of the interviews they were all engaged in large-scale mergers that often crossed traditional business group boundaries. The fourth firm was the investment banking division of a leading securities company. Despite domestic business remaining by far the dominant source of sales and profits, these companies were committed to developing a more international cadre of managers who were successful in London and New York, becoming skilled in particular areas of finance and who could compete with European and American bankers for non-Japanese business.

As the expatriate Chief Credit Officer for a long-term corporate finance bank that had become quite active in international markets since the 1960s suggested:

the ideal... manager will combine foreign experience with fluency in a foreign language and specialist expertise.

The same manager also thought that a key role of expatriates was to learn new techniques in London and New York and then transfer them to Tokyo so that his bank would become more competitive. However, it was not clear whether in fact his domestic colleagues saw things similarly, and there seemed little evidence that the GHR department at head office was systematically using expatriates for this purpose. More often, these returning internationally experienced bankers were having to adapt to the rapidly changing domestic environment.

To implement such changes in the traditional career patterns of generalist bankers, and in attitudes towards foreign subsidiaries, is not easy for these Japanese banks, especially when combined with quite radical organizational changes in the domestic industry. Indeed, the development of a separate international division, with its own career structure and reward systems, as some banks had done, may well limit head office learning and controls.

The two city banks that were committed to developing more international business had established regional head offices in London and New York to coordinate local branches, instead of these latter reporting direct to Tokyo or Osaka. These offices were headed by main board directors who could make most decisions without needing to check with head office. This was intended both to speed up decision making and to increase the effectiveness of central control over these important activities. Closing or reducing the significance of local branches enabled these banks to send many expatriates home, and so reduce costs. They aimed to reduce the proportion of non-Japanese business from around 70 per cent to about half in order to improve profits that were usually greater with domestic customers, but were also committed to increasing the use of local staff in managerial positions.

The Deputy General Manager of the International Planning Department in one of these banks, who was based in Japan, stated that the bank's

purpose was to localize activities. Localization, meaning, instead of depending on a lot of expats, rather having local people do their own job instead... if you have locally hired professionals, they know what they are talking about, they know what's happening. That's the purpose. And also quick decision if you have given authority to local headquarters. They can do whatever is needed instead of having to come to Tokyo for approval. It takes a few days... localization speeds up the process. And also cost reduction.

One British interviewee—who had herself been appointed as a Deputy General Manager—commented on the changes that this bank was making as follows:

When I first joined the bank I don't think there was anyone Japanese reporting to a non-Japanese so that's changed. Now there are a number dotted around. Not very many when I think about it but you know.... At least you think, well there's no reason as such why I shouldn't end up being GM. Now whether that's the pinnacle of my ambitions, who knows? But I can, you know, aspire to that. I can't aspire to be a member of the Board, but that would be rather far-fetched, but when I joined the Bank, we had one General Manager, who was head of the branch, he was going to be Japanese. No question. No-one would ever question that. And now people talk about it. I mean to say everybody happens to be Japanese. It may change... We've become a bit less Japanesy and again more, I don't know, international.

The sense was that the company was encouraging Japanese and non-Japanese to work together more closely and not simply split themselves between Japanese and non-Japanese corporate clients, at least in the London and New York offices. However, it should be noted that, although the proportion of Japanese managers in these financial companies in general had been reduced from the figure found by Sakai (2000) for the early 1990s, it still remained considerable. In the six firms still maintaining a significant presence in London, all but one had more than 10 per cent Japanese staff, and the other had 5 per cent. As the balance of business shifts back towards Japanese clients, this figure is unlikely to decline further, and may well increase.

An important aspect of these changes was the increasing recognition accorded to specialist technical skills in international banking. This could potentially cut across the Japanese/non-Japanese business divide but also threatened the traditional image of the banking generalist that was so dominant in Japan. The expatriate General Manager of the Planning Department of one large City bank stated:

The tendency is more like specialized units than before. When I joined the bank 25 years ago, I was told that the banker should be a generalist. Then the trend changed and because we are establishing that Europe division so my concern is more narrowly focused to Europe.... so in the future it may be very difficult to transfer from one division to another. So I think the tendency for the future is more likely to be hire the specialized person from the start.

The need for specialist expertise was also recognized by more junior bankers in this firm. One Japanese informant had built himself a reputation in the field of aircraft leasing where he was dealing with Europeans, Africans, Middle Easterners as well as British and Japanese. He spoke of wanting to focus on this and make his career in financing:

So long as the Bank allows me Aircraft Financing the opportunity, which I am quite keen on pursuing I will be with the Bank. If they switch me to some other job I would evaluate that option against the options I would have in pursuing a career in Aircraft Financing in others companies and then make a judgement there. Both ways I can feed my family definitely whether I decide to work my way in the Bank, I am pretty sure unless I really, really make a big mistake, I'm pretty sure I will go up the ladder. In Aircraft Financing I am sure there will be jobs available for me to pursue whether I change the institution to another, you know, every two or three years, there is a career path for that.

For some, then, becoming a specialist in a particular area of banking was an increasingly attractive option and perhaps the best way to cope with the uncertainties of a banking sector that had to retrench drastically. Another expatriate banker, for example, stated that:

When I finished my undergraduate in 1985, people were proud to believe that... you know, working for a banking company or working for a life insurance company is quite a good job. It's secure and people privately believed that secure situation will last on forever. But you know things are changing dramatically after the collapse of the economy. So all the people started to think about, say, job protection, how they get a job or how they protect their job and things like that.

So one solution is like . . . say it will be working as specialist, say getting a CPA and working as a specialist, things like that. So especially after 1990, that kind of tendency is getting stronger and stronger. It was quite natural.

This trend towards greater skill specialization appeared to be spreading from the experience of the banks in the City of London back to the head offices. For example, Sumitomo has recently introduced differentiated pay scales to attract specialist derivative and currency traders and fund managers in Tokyo (Hayes, 2000: 120). Similarly, company analysts are developing a distinct specialist identity in some investment banks in Tokyo, specially the foreign ones, and there is some evidence of a separate labour market becoming institutionalized for such skills (Morgan and Kubo, 2005). Additionally, at least a few financial institutions have attempted to learn from their foreign operations. As one Japanese informant in an investment banking division suggested:

our department is basically introducing financial idea, techniques to Japan.

In this case, a very specific example was given in terms of learning from the UK government's development of the Private Finance Initiative for public works.

These relatively more internationally focused firms were, then, becoming complex arenas for the negotiation of power between Japanese managers themselves as well as between Japanese and non-Japanese managers. This was reinforced by the sense that the protected Tokyo market was now being opened up to outsiders and therefore the Japanese banks would have to be more innovative, or at least better able to copy Western capital market techniques than previously. Therefore international experience was becoming more necessary at a time when it was actually becoming scarcer, given the retrenchment that was occurring in these firms.

These sorts of developments appeared to have gone furthest in the investment banking division of a large securities firm. Here, the balance of business had shifted from 90 per cent of profits coming from Japanese corporate clients in 1990 to less than 30 per cent from them in 2000, with much of the remainder stemming from deal making in European capital markets, often by local managers. This bank had recently reorganized itself around global product lines and established regional head offices in London and New York run by main board directors. Reporting was dual, to both the regional management and to global product leaders in Tokyo.

Unlike most Japanese companies, however, the heads of these global product lines had had extensive experience of working successfully in

London and New York and, as a result, had considerable credibility with staff in overseas offices. As the Head of Equity Capital Markets in this division put it, the:

head of Tokyo is person usually who has been head of like Europe or States. They know what they're talking about, less the local office won't listen to them.

While top managers in this firm were no more likely to be non-Japanese than elsewhere, they were increasingly likely to have had direct experience of competing with their European and American rivals abroad, especially if they were in charge of Anglo-Saxon style investment banking activities.

This division had adapted considerably to the dominant approach to investment banking in world capital markets, and altered its authority structures and use of foreign branches as a result. Not only were the London and New York offices regarded as integral and strategic components of the division, but they were also important learning locations for future top managers, and thus developing more of a participant, and perhaps even contributor, role in the future, than remaining mere appendages to the Japanese operation. While scarcely a global transnational firm, this division had internationalized the most of the units we studied, especially in terms of its competitive strategies and development of organizational capabilities. Whether this will continue as business in investment banking declines remains to be seen, but as long as the domestic market remains depressed there is little incentive to return to the earlier structure.

These changes rely on Japanese managers learning from foreign experiences rather than on foreign staff working in Japan, and so the continuance of domestic extended international career patterns. While this may be partly because of the difficulty of learning Japanese and adapting to a very different work culture, it also reflects the centrality of London and New York to investment banking and the limited attractions of Tokyo as a location for making one's career as an investment banker. Even some large Japanese companies are moving many of their central treasury activities to London, as Sony announced it would in June 2001.

In this industry, then, learning from abroad involves expatriate managers working with locals in world centres rather than parachuting foreigners into domestic operations and establishing elite patterns of international organizational careers. This means that the previous barriers between locals and expatriates that were typical of many Japanese banks in the 1980s had to be transcended, and local managers given incentives to work with Japanese staff long enough for the latter to learn new skills. This often means paying them higher salaries and success bonuses that lock them in for several years, as well as granting them much greater autonomy than Japanese top managers have been prone to do, to some extent moving away from integrated hierarchies to more project-based structures.

It is not surprising then that the only financial organization to have made such innovative moves was a securities company rather than an established bank in one of the ex-zaibatsu business groups. Firms in this subsector of the financial services industry have traditionally been viewed as less prestigious and respectable than most large banks, and recruited from the lower prestige universities. As Dore (2000: 123) puts it: 'their shady-dealing image severely limited their power to recruit from the top universities'.

A further point to note about this example of internationalization is that the bank remains clearly run by Japanese managers, and is highly integrated with head office, despite some local autonomy being granted to London and New York. There is no integrated Japanese and foreign managerial cadre being developed. Equally, although London and New York contribute considerably to the development of the firm as a whole, global product heads are part of top management in Tokyo that coordinates major decisions. Furthermore, the domestic brokerage operation remains the major part of the firm's activities, if not quite as dominant as it was in the early 1980s.

Overall, then, the rapid international expansion of the 1980s and the retrenchment of the 1990s had led to increased differences in the strategies and structures of Japanese financial companies. Before the growth of international operations, they shared many characteristics, such as long-term employment, the development of firm-specific knowledge on the part of the employees and job rotation which fostered the development of general skills in banking, coupled with close long-term relationships with their major customers, who were often members of the same business group (Sunamura, 1994).

In the 1980s, however, managers' careers and skills became more differentiated. In particular, relocation to an overseas subsidiary became increasingly common—up to 30 per cent of the cohorts of recruits in the 1980s were sent on overseas assignments. For some bankers, this was a welcome move and fitted in with their hopes for international experience. Amongst this group, there was a further select elite who had been given scholarships by the banks to study business, economics and finance at

Western universities with the expectation that they would utilize these skills in subsidiaries as well as in the Japanese head office. Although international banking was not then marked out as a distinctive career path, a division of expertise and skill began to develop between those who had experienced an overseas assignment (and possibly overseas education) and those, still by far the majority, who remained in the domestic banking system.

In the early stages of internationalization, the favourable economic conditions for the banks at home and abroad enabled different career patterns to be accommodated. From the collapse of the bubble economy, however, conditions inside the banks became more stringent. In many of the Japanese city banks, the scale of the losses that became apparent meant that overseas operations had to be closed down or reduced to representative offices (Wood, 1992), with just a few local and Japanese managers serving Japanese corporate clients in a limited capacity. This was especially the case for those banks that had the least experience of foreign capital markets and had moved abroad more as part of the general internationalization of Japanese banking than as a long-term strategic investment.

For international managers who returned home in the wake of these closures, their career appeared to be seriously damaged. They felt that they had developed skills as international bankers that were no longer relevant to their company. Those who felt that international experience had equipped them with a specialist skill were more optimistic about this than those who felt trapped with the label of a 'generalist' banker. It is unclear whether these banks will be able to utilize these returnees' skills and knowledge to deal effectively with the changing business environment in Japan, especially with the slow but continuing deregulation of financial markets and increasing foreign competition (Laurence, 2001). In 2001 it did not appear that they were making sustained efforts to do so.

In the banks that combined cost cutting and rationalization of the international branch structure with a commitment to remaining active in world capital markets, a new group of Japanese expatriate managers has emerged who are increasingly identifying themselves with the activity of international banking, in some cases in newly created or reinforced international banking divisions. This identification implies a belief in the importance of the international dimension for the future of the company, both as a way of growing outside Japan but also in terms of defending home markets by having experience and knowledge of techniques and products drawn from the US and UK capital markets. This is also

327

associated with a growing belief amongst this group that banking in Japan itself is becoming more specialized. They are therefore increasingly looking to develop specialist expertise themselves, which in turn may serve to be the basis of increasing mobility between firms, a highly unusual step in the Japanese context. Thus an emerging tension between generalist and specialists within these banks might be expected to arise, partly overlapping the tension between international and domestic bankers.

The role of local managers in overseas subsidiaries is also becoming more significant. These banks talk about the localization of key decisions and this implies a greater involvement of local managers. However, it is also clear that it involves a tighter integration between the head office and the local subsidiary. In particular, the head offices are locating members of the Main Board in London and New York to ensure that there is strong control exercised over the local managers within a framework that allows more decisions to be made quickly at the local level but where the head office has confidence that its concerns will have been taken into account. Local managers see this as opening up some small possibilities for extending their role, though their specialist skills inevitably make them more mobile than their Japanese employers would like, a process that also serves as a lesson to those Japanese with whom they work that developing specialized skills is a way to obtain increased autonomy and control over careers in fluid, dynamic labour markets.

Discussion and Conclusions

These contrasts highlight the variety of responses of Japanese companies to their increasing internationalization during the 1980s and 1990s, especially in Europe and North America, and to the continuing domestic recession since 1991. While some appear to be developing—or at least some managers in these firms are talking about—novel international management career patterns, others are content to reproduce domestically extended ones. Similarly, the extent to which Japanese firms are committed to competing in international markets in the financial services industry differs considerably, especially when that involves developing new types of capabilities and expertise. Where such commitment is relatively high, companies are being pressured to reconfigure their organization structure, often while engaged in large-scale mergers. These differences reflect variations in firm-specific capabilities and local labour and product market characteristics, as well as sectoral contrasts.

The car manufacturing companies we studied had invested considerable resources in transferring the key sources of their comparative advantages in production to UK plants—their distinctive way of managing complex production processes, including close integration of suppliers' operations—through the extensive use of expatriates. Despite significant differences in skill levels and labour market institutions, as well as the more fragmented European market compared to Japan and the USA, all three firms were very concerned to teach their particular recipe for obtaining high levels of productivity and quality, which depends considerably upon core worker commitment to the company and the development of firm-specific knowledge and expertise. While they had begun to localize the management structure of their British subsidiaries to a significant degree compared to the start-up period, substantial numbers of Japanese staff remained in coordinator and advisory roles. Furthermore, whenever new production lines were developed, over a hundred engineers and managers were commonly sent from Japan to ensure their correct and effective operation.

The growing importance of these firms' foreign subsidiaries in the industrialized countries, at least in terms of sales and employees if not design and development (Cairncross, 1994; Kenney, 1999), was, however, beginning to change perceptions of core managerial skills and appropriate international structures, especially when coupled with the high costs of relying extensively on expatriate staff and growing trust in local managers. Regional offices headed by top managers from the parent firm were being established, although it was not clear that these fully integrated manufacturing with sales, or that they had complete line management authority over national units. The tendency of successful local managers to leave once they had reached the top positions in national subsidiaries was additionally encouraging some of these companies to consider internationalizing their management development programmes so that effective managers could be offered longer career paths within the organization.

Concomitantly, foreign subsidiaries were beginning to exchange ideas and practices between themselves, especially those in the UK and USA, occasionally without direct control from Japan. While these moves scarcely indicate a radical transformation towards a more 'transnational' framework for these firms—and in any case only one of the three had gone so far as establishing a global GHR division—they do indicate a change from the straightforward transfer of the domestic recipe to foreign locations.

However, as long as domestic plants and their associated design and development 'knowledge works' (Fruin, 1997; 1999) remain the pre-eminent models for international operations, as well as their key sources of competitive advantages, it is unlikely that these companies will distinguish systematically between their Japanese units and global head office, or that international careers will become more important than domestic ones for Japanese managers. Furthermore, foreign postings remained unattractive for the most valued engineering and production staff in all three firms because key developments took place in Japan and learning from abroad was not as important as demonstrating success in dealing with technical and organizational issues at home. Insofar as distinctly international careers do become established in these companies, then, they are likely to be dominated by sales and marketing staff, and only rarely involve non-Japanese managers.

Overall, then, it seems that these Japanese car firms were primarily using expatriate managers to apply their domestically developed recipes to foreign subsidiaries, and then to transmit new information about plant operations to Japan to improve them. They were not, however, encouraging them to develop novel kinds of capabilities in diverse environments that could lead to the adaptation of the basic business recipe. Authority sharing with foreign managers and skilled workers remained quite limited and most if not all subsidiaries functioned as appendages rather than participants in organizational problem solving, let alone contributors to MNC development.

Equally, despite some discussion of the possibility, they also have yet to establish elite international career structures that would generate long-term employer-specific problem solving and skill enhancement commitments across subsidiaries, and so transnational organizational capabilities. Strong international coordination capabilities were largely developed and maintained through expatriate managers and engineers, who also were the primary means by which the parent company learnt about foreign markets and process improvements.

In the case of Japanese banking, the central position of the City and Long-term Credit banks in the domestic business system, together with their largely domestic client-driven internationalization in the 1970s and 1980s, limited their adaptation to, and learning from, foreign operations. The changed conditions of the 1990s have mostly resulted in a retreat to traditional customers and sources of competitive advantage, i.e. their knowledge of, and centrality to, the domestic business system, and so foreign subsidiaries are greatly subordinated to domestic decisions and routines. This was especially the case for banks that had the least experience of foreign operations and appeared to have followed others abroad in the 1970s and 1980s.

Even where some attempts were being made to learn from foreign competitors and locations, substantial divisions remained between international groups and managers and domestic ones. Thus, while parts of these companies might be changing through their involvement with overseas markets and institutional arrangements, they may become more separated from domestic operations rather than diffusing new routines throughout the entire organization.

In the short to medium term it may be feasible for banks that remain committed to competing in foreign markets to develop largely separate international divisions with more specialized staff than those working domestically, as long as pressures to realize economies of knowledge and skill across the organization are limited. These divisions will probably retain long-term commitments between Japanese employees and the company but encourage the development of more generic technical expertise, and careers based on using those skills in different locations. Expatriate managers in such units will spend as much time away from Japan as in it, and their domestic jobs focus more on integrating international operations than on carrying out home-focused duties.

However, as long as the primary sources of business and profits remain concentrated in their home economy, and the organization of the financial services industry in that economy remains highly distinctive, international careers and expertise are likely to continue to be less valued than domestic ones. Even if some Japanese banks do manage to develop organizational capabilities in international financial markets, then, the separation of foreign from home-based careers will restrict learning from abroad and the generation of new kinds of capabilities in these organizations as a whole.

The different pattern of internationalization followed by Japanese car firms and banks, and their contrasting success, highlights the distinctive nature of the Japanese domestic financial system and the limited transferability of the skills and competences it has encouraged. Many of the car companies developed strong organizational capabilities for designing, engineering, producing and marketing cars through competition in domestic markets, and then began to compete increasingly successfully in international markets. Subsequently they transferred some of these organizational competences to facilities in major industrialized countries.

The banks and other financial companies, on the other hand, developed in a more state-organized environment that rewarded conformity with Ministry of Finance guidance rather than competitive success in gaining funds and clients from other firms (Hayes, 2000; Laurence, 2001; Wood, 1992). As Ueda (1994: 105) suggests, the state protected the banks during much of the postwar period in three ways: 'discouragement of competition, sharing of credit risks by the government and the restriction of direct finance'.

Playing a central and highly valued role in the postwar reconstruction of the Japanese economy, the major banks channelled funds to favoured industries and monitored firms' behaviour as their 'main bank' (Aoki and Patrick, 1994). They attracted the best graduates of the top universities and have been seen as more prestigious employers than most manufacturing firms (Dore, 2000). Rather similar to their counterparts in France for much of the postwar era (Salomon, 1997; 1999; Zysman, 1983), they have administered the highly segmented financial system rather than competed for customers and funds in a competitive market. Their key capabilities, then, have tended to be highly specific to the postwar Japanese political economy and of limited use in different kinds of environments.

Consequently, the internationalization of these companies has not usually involved the export of a domestically competitive recipe, but rather the channelling of surplus funds from the Japanese financial system to foreign borrowers—as well as to domestic ones seeking to escape from government restrictions—at cheap rates to build market share. It was, and remains, subsidiary to domestic business, both in terms of size and profitability, in contrast to the car companies that are competing with foreign firms in their domestic markets as major parts of their overall strategies. As long as Japanese banks and other financial firms remain concentrated on domestic markets as their primary source of business and earnings, and those markets remain organized in highly specific ways, it is difficult to see how they will develop competitive competences in overseas markets to the same extent as their manufacturing colleagues.

In general, the largely incremental changes that have occurred in most Japanese MNCs emphasize the continued importance of domestic facilities and competences. They additionally highlight the difficulty that some MNCs have in developing integrated career structures and distinctive organizational competences across differently organized labour markets. Firms that encourage key staff to develop organization-specific, generalist, skills and knowledge through long-term careers, as in Japan, find it difficult to attract and retain highly skilled specialists who seek to enhance their generic competences on external labour markets.

While such companies are able to extend their domestic organizational capabilities to foreign locations, as is shown by Japanese car companies, developing new organization-wide capabilities through incorporating the knowledge and skills of overseas subsidiaries into novel managerial routines is more problematic, especially where labour market institutions discourage long-term employer–employee commitments. This also suggests that, as argued in previous chapters, companies with generalist career structures may be at some disadvantage in industries primarily organized around project teams composed of specialized experts in highly fluid labour markets.

This raises other questions about how MNCs can develop distinctive organization capabilities through genuinely transnational managerial hierarchies and skills. To the extent that competitive competences depend on problem-solving routines and knowledge being generated by long-term commitments from key staff in differently structured labour markets, MNCs may struggle to develop distinctively transnational abilities, as opposed to multidomestic ones. Competitive competences based on employee commitment to collective problem solving gained through organizational careers are likely, then, to be as much national as international, at least where labour market institutions vary as much as they do between Japan and the UK.

References

Abo, Tetsuo (ed.) (1994) *Hybrid Factories: The Japanese Production System in the United States*, Oxford: Oxford University Press.

Abramson, H. Norman, Jose Encarmacao, Proctor R. Reid, and Ulrich Schmoch (eds.) (1997) *Technology Transfer Systems in the United States and Germany*, Washington, DC: National Academy Press.

Adelberger, K. E. (2000) 'Semi-Sovereign Leadership? The State's Role in German Biotechnology and Venture Capital Growth', *German Politics*, 9, 103–22.

Adler, Paul S. (1999) 'Hybridization: Human Resource Management at Two Toyota Transplants', pp. 75–116 in J. K. Liker, W. M. Fruin and P. S. Adler (eds.) *Remade in America*.

Aguilera, Ruth and G. Jackson (2003) 'The Cross-National Diversity of Corporate Governance: Dimensions and Determinants', *Academy of Management Review*, 28, 447–65.

Allen, Matthew (2004) 'The Varieties of Capitalism Paradigm: Not Enough Variety?' *Socio-Economic Review*, 2, 87–107.

Almeida, Paul and Bruce Kogut (1999) 'Localization of Knowledge and the Mobility of Engineers in Regional Networks', *Management Science*, 45, 905–17.

Almond, Phil and Anthony Ferner (eds.) (2006) *American Multinationals in Europe: Managing Employment Relations Across National Borders*, Oxford: Oxford University Press.

Amable, Bruno (2003) *The Diversity of Modern Capitalism*, Oxford: Oxford University Press.

Amsden, A. H. (1989) *Asia's Next Giant*, Oxford: Oxford University Press.

Andersen, P. H. and P. R. Christensen (1999) 'Internationalization in Loosely Coupled Business Systems: The Danish Case', pp. 205–31 in P. Karnoe, P. H. Kristensen and P. H. Andersen (eds.) *Mobilizing Resources and Generating Competencies*, Copenhagen: Copenhagen Business School Press.

Andersen, Esben and Asger Braendgaard (1992) 'Integration, Innovation and Evolution', pp. 242–64 in B-A Lundvall (ed.) *National Systems of Innovation*, London: Pinter.

Angel, David P. (2000) 'High-technology Agglomeration and the Labor Market: The Case of Silicon Valley', pp. 124–40 in Martin Kenney (ed.) *Understanding Silicon Valley*.

Aoki, Masahiko (2001) *Toward a Comparative Institutional Analysis*, Cambridge, Mass.: MIT Press.

Aoki, Masahiko and Hugh Patrick (eds.) (1994) *The Japanese Main Bank System: Its Relevance for Developing and Transforming Economies*, Oxford: Clarendon Press.

Armingeon, Klaus (2004) 'Institutional Change in OECD Democracies, 1970–2000', *Comparative European Politics*, 2, 212–38.

Arthur, Brian (1994) *Increasing Returns and Path Dependence in the Economy*. Ann Arbor: University of Michigan Press.

Arvidsson, Niklas (1999) *The Ignorant MNE: The Role of Perception Gaps in Knowledge Management*, Stockholm: Stockholm School of Economics.

Bache, Ian and Matthew Flinders (eds.) (2004) *Multi-level Governance*, Oxford: Oxford University Press.

Bahrami, H. and S. Evans, (1995) 'Flexible Re-cycling and High Technology Entrepreneurship', *California Management Review*, 37, 62–88.

Barca, Fabrizio and Marco Becht (eds.) (2001) *The Control of Corporate Europe*, Oxford: Oxford University Press.

Bartlett, C. A., Y. Doz, and G. Hedlund (eds.) (1990) *Managing the Global Firm*, London: Routledge.

Bartlett, C. A. and S. Ghoshal (1989) *Managing Across Borders: The Transnational Solution*, London: Hutchinson Business Books.

Bauer, Michel and Elie Cohen (1981) *Qui gouverne les groupes industriels?* Paris: Seuil.

Beechler, S. L. and Bird, A. (eds.) (1999) *Japanese Multinationals Abroad: Individual and Organizational Learning*, Oxford: Oxford University Press.

Beechler, Schon, Allan Bird, and Sully Taylor (1998) 'Organizational Learning in Japanese MNCs: Four affiliate archetypes', pp. 333–66 in Julian Birkinshaw and Neil Hood (eds.) *Multinational Corporate Evolution and Subsidiary Development*, London: Macmillan.

Beetham, David (1991) *The Legitimation of Power*, London: Macmillan.

Belanger, Jacques, Christian Berggren, Torsten Bjorkman, and Cristoph Kohler (eds.) (1999) *Being Local Worldwide: ABB and the Challenge of Global Management*, Ithaca, N. Y.: Cornell University Press.

Berghahn, Volker (1986) *The Americanisation of West German Industry 1945–1973*, Leamington Spa: Berg.

Bieler, Andreas (2005) 'European Integration and the Transnational Restructuring of Social Relations: The Emergence of Labour as a Regional Actor?' *Journal of Common Market Studies*, 43, 461–84.

Biggart, Nicole and Mauro Guillen (1999) 'Developing Difference: Social Organization and the Rise of the Auto Industries of South Korea, Taiwan, Spain and Argentina', *American Sociological Review*, 64, 722–47.

Birkinshaw, Julian (2001) 'Strategy and Management in MNE Subsidiaries', pp. 380–401 in A. Rugman and T. Brewer (eds.) *The Oxford Handbook of International Business*.

References

Birkinshaw, Julian and Hood, Neil (eds.) (1998) *Multinational Corporate Evolution and Subsidiary Development*, London: Macmillan.

Botti, Hope (1995) 'Misunderstandings: A Japanese Transplant in Italy Strives for Lean Production', *Organization*, 2, 55–86.

Boudon, Raymond (1998) 'Social Mechanisms without Black Boxes', pp. 172–203 in Peter Hedstrom and Richard Swedberg (eds.) *Social Mechanisms: An Analytical Approach to Social Theory*, Cambridge: Cambridge University Press.

—— (2003) 'Beyond Rational Choice Theory', *Annual Review of Sociology*, 29, 1–21.

Bowman, John R (2002) 'Employers and the Persistence of Centralized Wage Setting: The Case of Norway', *Comparative Political Studies*, 35, 995–1026.

Boyer, Robert (2004) 'New Growth Regimes, but still Institutional Diversity', *Socio-economic Review*, 2, 1–32.

Boyer, Robert and Durand, J.-P. (1997) *After Fordism*, London: Macmillan.

Braczyk, Hans-Joachim, Philip Cooke, and Martin Heidenreich (eds.) (1998) *Regional Innovation Systems: The Role of Governances in a Globalized World*, London: UCL Press, republished by Routledge in 2003.

Braithwaite, John and Peter Drahos (2000) *Global Business Regulation*, Cambridge: Cambridge University Press.

Brannen, Mary Yoko, Jeffrey K. Liker, and W. Mark Fruin (1999) 'Recontextualization and Factory-to-Factory Knowledge Transfer from Japan to the United States: The Case of NSK', pp. 117–53 in J. K. Liker, W. M. Fruin and P. S. Adler (eds.) *Remade in America: Transplanting and Transforming Japanese Management Systems'*, New York: Oxford University Press.

Branscomb, Lewis, Fumio Kodama, and Richard Florida (eds.) (1999) *Industrializing Knowledge: University–Industry Linkages in Japan and the United States*, Cambridge, Mass: MIT Press.

Breschi, Stefano and Franco Malerba (1997) 'Sectoral Innovation Systems: Technological Regimes, Schumpeterian Dynamics and Spatial Boundaries', pp. 130–56 in Charles Edquist (ed.) *Systems of Innovation*, London: Pinter.

Bresnen, Mike, Anna Goussevskaia, and Jacky Swan (2004) 'Embedding New Management Knowledge in Project-Based Organizations', *Organization Studies*, 25, 1535–55.

Brown, John Seely and Paul Duguid (2000) 'Mysteries of the Region: Knowledge dynamics in Silicon Valley', pp. 16–39 in Chong-Moon Lee *et al.* (eds.) *The Silicon Valley Edge*.

Bunge, Mario (2004) 'How Does It Work? The Search for Explanatory Mechanisms', *Philosophy of the Social Sciences*, 34, 182–210.

Burroni, Luigi and Carlo Trigilia (2001) 'Italy: Economic Development Through Local Economies', pp. 46–78 in Colin Crouch *et al.* (eds.) *Local Production Systems in Europe*.

Butler, Peter, David Collings, Rene Peters, and Javier Quintanilla (2006) 'The Management of Managerial Careers', pp. 172–94 in P. Almond and A. Ferner (eds.) *American Multinationals in Europe*.

Cairncross, David (1994) 'The Strategic Role of Japanese R&D Centres in the UK', pp. 98–112 in N. Campbell and F. Burton (eds.) *Japanese Multinationals: Strategies and Management in the Global Kaisha*, London: Routledge.

Calder, Kent E. (1993) *Strategic Capitalism: Private Business and Public Purpose in Japanese Industrial Finance*, Princeton: Princeton University Press.

Campbell, John (2005) *Institutionalization Change and Globalization*, Princeton: Princeton University Press.

Campbell, John L. and Ove Kaj Pedersen (eds.) (2001) *The Rise of Neoliberalism and Institutional Analysis*, Princeton: Princeton University Press.

Campbell, John, John Hall, and Ove Pedersen (eds.) (2006) *National Identity and the Varieties of Capitalism: The Danish Experience*, Montreal: McGill-Queen's University Press.

Cantwell, John (2001) 'Innovation and Information Technology in the MNE', pp. 431–56 in A. Rugman and T. Brewer (eds.) *The Oxford Handbook of International Business*.

Carlsson, Bo, Staffan Jacobsson, Magnus Holmen, and Annika Rickne (2002) 'Innovation Systems: Analytical and Methodological Issue', *Research Policy*, 31, 233–45.

Casper, Steven (2000) 'Institutional Adaptiveness, Technology policy and the Diffusion of New Business Models: The Case of German Biotechnology', *Organization Studies*, 21, 887–914.

—— (2003) 'The German Internet Economy and the Silicon Valley Model: Convergence, Divergence, or Something Else?' in B. Kogut (ed.) *The Global Internet Economy*, Cambridge, Mass.: MIT Press.

Casper, Steven and Henrik Glimstedt (2001) 'Economic Organization, Innovation Systems, and the Internet', *Oxford Review of Economic Policy*, 17, 265–81.

Casper, Steven and Hannah Kettler (2001) 'National Institutional Frameworks and the Hybridization of Entrepreneurial Business Models: The German and UK Biotechnology Sectors', *Industry and Innovation*, 8, 5–30.

Casper, Steven and Catherine Matraves (2003) 'Institutional Frameworks and Innovation in the German and UK Pharmaceutical Industry', *Research Policy*, 32, 1865–79.

Casper, Steven and Fiona Murray (2004) 'Examining the Marketplace for Ideas: How local are Europe's biotechnology clusters?' pp. 326–55 in M. McKelvey, A. Rickne, and J. Laage-Hellman (eds.) *The Economics of Modern Biotechnology*, Cheltenham: E. Elgar.

—— (2005) 'Careers and Clusters: Analyzing the Career Network Dynamics of Biotechnology Clusters', *Journal of Engineering and Technology Management*, 22, 51–74.

Casper, Steven, Mark Lehrer, and David Soskice (1999) 'Can High-Technology Industries Prosper in Germany: Institutional Frameworks and the Evolution of the German Software and Biotechnology Industries', *Industry and Innovation* 6, 6–23.

Casper, Steven and Sigurt Vitols (2006) 'Managing Competences Within Entrepreneurial Technologies: A Comparative Institutional Analysis of Software Firms in Germany and the UK', pp. 205–35 in M. Miozzo and D. Grimshaw (eds.) *Knowledge Intensive Business Services: Organizational Forms and National Institutions*, Cheltenham: E. Elgar.

Chandler, Alfred (1990) *Scale and Scope*, Cambridge, Mass.: Harvard University Press.

Chesbrough, Henry (1999) 'The Organizational Impact of Technological Change: A Comparative Theory of Institutional Factors', *Industrial and Corporate Change*, 8, 447–85.

Child, J., M. Fores, I. Glover, and P. Lawrence (1983) 'A Price to Pay? Professionalism in Work Organization in Britain and West Germany', *Sociology*, 17, 63–78.

Christensen, Clayton M. (1997) *The Innovator's Dilemma: When New Technologies Cause Great Firms to Fail*, Boston: Harvard Business School Press.

Christopherson, Susan (2002a) 'Why do National Labor Market Practices Continue to Diverge in the Global Economy? The 'Missing Link' of Investment Rules', *Economic Geography*, 78, 1–20.

—— (2002b) 'Project Work in Context: Regulatory Change and the New Geography of Media', *Environment and Planning A*, 34, 2003–15.

Clark, Burton R. (1995) *Places of Inquiry: Research and Advanced Education in Modern Universities*, Berkeley: University of California Press.

Clark, Rodney (1979) *The Japanese Company*, Yale University Press.

Clark, Timothy and Robin Fincham (2002) (eds.) *Critical Consulting: New Perspectives on the Management Advice Industry*, Oxford: Blackwell.

Cohen, Stephen S. and Gary Fields (2000) 'Social Capital and Capital Gains: An Examination of Social Capital in Silicon Valley', pp. 190–217 in Martin Kenney (ed.) *Understanding Silicon Valley*.

Cohen, Wesley M. and Daniel A. Levinthal (1990) 'Absorptive Capacity: A new Perspective on Learning and Innovation', *Administrative Science Quarterly*, 35, 128–52.

Cohen, Wesley M., Richard Nelson, and John Walsh (2003) 'Links and Impacts: The Influence of Public Research on Industrial R&D', pp. 109–46 in Aldo Geuna, Ammon Salter and Edward Steinmuller (eds.) *Science and Innovation: Rethinking the Rationales for Funding and Governance*, Cheltenham: Edward Elgar.

Coleman, Samuel (1999) *Japanese Science: View from the Inside*, London: Routledge.

Cooke Phillip (1999) 'Biotechnology Clusters in the UK: Lessons from Localization in the Commercialization of Science', Centre for Advanced Studies, Cardiff University, Cardiff.

Coriat, Benjamin and Olivier Weinstein (2002) 'Organizations, Firms and Institutions in the Generation of Innovation', *Research Policy*, 31, 273–90.

Creplet, F., O. Dupouet, F. Kern, B. Mehmanpazir, and F. Munir (2001) 'Consultants and Experts in Management Consulting Firms', *Research Policy*, 30, 1517–35.

Crouch, Colin (1999) *Social Change in Western Europe*, Oxford: Oxford University Press.

—— (2003) 'Comparing Economic Interest Organizations', pp. 192–207 in J. Hayward and A. Menon (eds.) *Governing Europe*.

—— (2005) *Capitalist Diversity and Change: Recombinant Governance and Institutional Entrepreneurs*, Oxford: Oxford University Press.

Crouch, Colin and Carlo Trigilia (2001) 'Conclusions: Still Local Economies in Global Capitalism?' pp. 212–37 in Colin Crouch *et al.* (eds.) *Local Production Systems in Europe*.

Crouch, Colin and Wolfgang Streeck (eds.) (1997) *Political Economy of Modern Capitalism*, London: Sage.

Crouch, Colin, David Finegold, and Mari Sako (1999) *Are Skills the Answer? The Political Economy of Skill Creation in Advanced Industrial Countries*, Oxford: Oxford University Press.

Crouch, Colin, Patrick le Gales, Carlo Trigilia, and Helmut Voelzkow (2001) *Local Production Systems in Europe: Rise or Demise?* Oxford: Oxford University Press.

—— (2004) *Changing Governance of Local Economies: Responses of European Local Production Systems*, Oxford: Oxford University Press.

Culpepper, Pepper D. (1999) 'Individual Choice, Collective Action, and the Problem of Training Reform: Insights from France and Eastern Germany', pp. 269–325 in Pepper Culpepper and David Finegold (eds.) *The German Skills Machine: Sustaining Comparative Advantage in a Global Economy*, New York: Berghahn Books.

—— (2001) 'Employers' Associations, Public Policy and the Politics of Decentralized Cooperation', in Peter Hall and David Soskice (eds.) *Varieties of Capitalism*.

Culpepper, Pepper D., and David Finegold (1999) (eds.) *The German Skills Machine: Sustaining Comparative Advantage in a Global Economy*, New York: Berghahn Books.

Cusumano, M. A. (1985) *The Japanese Automobile Industry: Technology and Management at Nissan and Toyota*, Harvard University Press.

Czaban, Laszlo and Richard Whitley (1998) 'The Transformation of Work Systems in Emergent Capitalism: The case of Hungary', *Work, Employment and Society*, 12, 1–26.

Davenport, John (2005) *Project-Based Firms in the UK Film Industry: Causes and Consequences*, PhD thesis. Manchester Business School, University of Manchester.

Davenport, John and Laszlo Czaban (2005) 'Freelance Working in a Project-based Industry: The influence of the institutional system in the British film industry', presented to the 21st EGOS colloquium, Berlin, July.

Davies, Andrew (2003) 'Integrated Solutions: The Changing Business of Systems Integration', pp. 333–68 in A. Principe, A. Davies and M. Hobday (eds.) *The Business of Systems Integration*, Oxford: Oxford University Press.

Davies, Andrew and T. Brady (2000) 'Organizational Capabilities and Learning in Complex Product Systems', *Research Policy*, 29, 931–53.

Davis, Gerald F., Kristine Diekmann, and Catherine Tinsley (1994) 'The Decline and Fall of the Conglomerate Firm in the 1980s: The Deinstitutionalization of an Organizational Form', *American Sociological Review*, 59, 547–70.

Dedousssis, Vagelis (1994) 'The Core Workforce—Peripheral Workforce Dichotomy and the Transfer of Japanese Management Practices', pp. 186–217 in N. Campbell and F. Burton (eds.) *Japanese Multinationals*, London: Routledge.

Deeg, Richard (2005a) 'Path Dependency, Institutional Complementarity, and Change in National Business Systems', pp. 21–52 in G. Morgan, R. Whitley and E . Moen (eds.) *Changing Capitalisms?*

—— (2005b) 'Change from Within: German and Italian Finance in the 1990s', pp. 169–202 in W. Streeck and K. Thelen (eds.) *Beyond Continuity*.

DeFillippi, R. and M. Arthur (1998) 'Paradox in Project-based Enterprise: The Case of Film Making', *California Management Review*, 40, 125–39.

Delbridge, Rick (1998) *Life on the Line in Contemporary Manufacturing*, Oxford: Oxford University Press.

Deutsche Bundesbank (1998) *Monthly Report*, April.

Deyo, F. C. (1989) *Beneath the Miracle: Labour Subordination in the New Asian Industrialism*, Berkeley: University of California Press.

Dicken, P. (1998) *Global Shift*, London: Paul Chapman Publishing.

Dicken, P., M. Forsgren, and A. Malmberg (1994) 'The Local Embeddedness of Transnational Corporations', in Amin A. and N. Thrift (eds.) *Globalization, Institutions and Regional Development in Europe*, Oxford University Press.

Dicken, Peter and Yoshihiro Miyamachi (1998) ' "From Noodles to Satellites": The Changing Geography of the Japanese *Sogo Shosha*', *Trans. Inst. Br. Geog.* 23, 55–78.

Dicken, Peter, Adam Tickell, and Henry Yeung (1997) 'Putting Japanese Investment in Europe in its Place', *Area*, 29, 200–12.

DiMaggio, Paul (ed.) (2001a) *The Twenty-First-Century Firm*, Princeton: Princeton University Press.

DiMaggio, Paul (2001b) 'Conclusion: The Futures of Business Organization and Paradoxes of Change', pp. 210–43 in Paul DiMaggio (ed.) *The Twenty-First-Century Firm*.

Djelic, Marie-Laure (1998) *Exporting the American Model*, Oxford: Oxford University Press.

Djelic, Marie-Laure and Sigrid Quack (2003a) 'Introduction: Governing Globalization-Bringing Institutions Back In', pp. 1–14 in Djelic and Quack (eds.) 2003.

—— (2003b) 'Conclusion: Globalization as a Double Process of Institutional Change and Institution Building', pp. 302–33 in Djelic and Quack (eds.) 2003.

—— (2005) 'Rethinking Path Dependency from an Open Systems Perspective: The Crooked Path of Institutional Change in Postwar Germany', pp. 137–66 in Morgan, Whitley and Moen (eds.) *Changing Capitalisms?*

—— (eds.) (2003) *Globalization and Institutions: Redefining the Rules of the Economic Game*, Cheltenham: Edward Elgar.

Dobbin, Frank (1994) *Forging industrial policy: the United States, Britain, and France in the Railway Age*, Cambridge: Cambridge University Press.

Dore, Ronald (2000) *Stock Market Capitalism: Welfare Capitalism*, Oxford: Oxford University Press.

Doremus, P. N., W. W. Keller, L. W. Pauly, and S. Reich (1998) *The Myth of the Global Corporation*, Princeton, N. J.: Princeton University Press.

Dosi, G. (1988) 'Sources, Procedures, and Microeconomic Effects of Innovation', *Journal of Economic Literature*, Vol. 26, No. 3, pp. 1120–71.

Dosi, Giovanni, Richard Nelson, and Sidney Winter (eds.) (2000) *The Nature and Dynamics of Organizational Capabilities*, Oxford: Oxford University Press.

Dufey, Gunter (1994) 'Comment' pp. 288–92 in M. Mason and D. Encarnation (eds.) *Does Ownership Matter? Japanese Multinationals in Europe*, Oxford: Oxford University Press.

Dunning, John (1993) 'The Governance of Japanese and U.S. Manufacturing Affiliates in the U.K: Some country-specific differences', pp. 203–24 in B. Kogut (ed.) Country Competitiveness, New York: Oxford University Press.

Eccleston, B. (1989) *State and Society in Post-War Japan*, Cambridge: Polity Press.

Eckstedt, Eskil, Rolf Lundin, Anders Soderholm, and Hans Wirdenius (1999) *Neo-Industrial Organizing: Renewal by Action and Knowledge Formation in a Project-Intensive Economy*, London: Routledge.

Edquist, Charles (2005) 'Systems of Innovation: Perspectives and Challenges', pp. 181–208 in Jan Fagerberg, David C. Mowery and Richard R. Nelson (eds.) *The Oxford Handbook of Innovation*, Oxford: Oxford University Press.

—— (ed.) (1997) *Systems of Innovation: Technologies, Institutions and Organizations*, London: Pinter.

Edwards, Tony, David Collings, Javier Quintanilla, and Anne Tempel (2006) 'Innovation and the Transfer of Organizational Learning', pp. 223–47 in P. Almond and A. Ferner (eds.) *American Multinationals in Europe*.

Elger, Tony and Chris Smith (1994) 'Global Japanization? Convergence and Competition in the Organization of the Labour Process', pp. 31–59 in T. Elger and C. Smith (eds.) *Global Japanization? The Transnational Transformation of the Labour Process*, London: Routledge.

Emmott, Bill (1992) *Japan's Global Reach: The Influence, Strategies and Weaknesses of Japan's Multinational Companies*, London: Century Business.

Enright, Michael, Edith Scott, and David Dodwell (1997) *The Hong Kong Advantage*, Hong Kong: Oxford University Press.

Ergas, Henry (1987) 'Does Technology Policy Matter?' in Bruce R. Guile and Harvey Brooks (eds.) *Technology and Global Industry: Companies and Nations in the World Economy*, Washington, D.C.: National Academy Press.

References

Ernst, Dieter (2006) 'Searching for a New Role in East Asian Regionalization-Japanese Production Networks in the Electronics Industry', pp. 161–87 in P. J. Katzenstein and T. Shiraishi (eds.) *Beyond Japan.*

Ernst & Young (1999) *European Life Sciences 1999*, London: Ernst & Young International.

Ernst & Young (2001) *European Life Sciences 2001*, London: Ernst & Young.

Ernst and Young (2006) *Beyond Borders: The Global Biotechnology Report*, Ernst and Young.

Evans, Peter (1994) *Embedded Autonomy: States and Industrial Transformation*, Princeton, New Jersey: Princeton University Press.

Fafchamps, Marcel (1996) 'The Enforcement of Commercial Contracts in Ghana', *World Development*, 24, 427–48.

Farrell, Henry and Ann-Louise Holten (2004) 'Collective Goods in the Local Economy: The Packaging Machinery Cluster in Bologna', pp. 23–45 in C. Crouch *et al.*, *Changing Governance of Local Economies.*

Faulkner, Robert and Andy Anderson (1987) 'Short Term Projects and Emergent Careers: Evidence from Hollywood', *American Journal of Sociology*, 92, 879–909.

Feller, Irwin (1999) 'The American University System as a Performer of Basic and Applied Research', pp. 65–101 in Lewis Branscomb, Fumio Kodama and Richard Florida (eds.) *Industrializing Knowledge*, Cambridge, Mass.: MIT Press.

Ferguson, Charles (1999) *High Stakes, No Prisoners: A Winner's Tale of Greed and Glory in the Internet Wars*, New York: Random House.

Ferner, Anthony, Paddy Gunnigle, Javier Quintanilla, Hartmut Wachter and Tony Edwards (2006) 'Centralization', pp. 197–222 in P. Almond and A. Ferner (eds.) *American Multinationals in Europe.*

Fields, Karl J. (1995) *Enterprise and the State in Korea and Taiwan*, Ithaca, N.Y.: Cornell University Press.

Finegold, Stephen and Karin Wagner (1999) 'The German Skill-Creation System and Team-based Production: Competitive Asset or Liability?' pp. 115–55 in P. D. Culpepper and D. Finegold (eds.) *The German Skills Machine*, Oxford: Berghahn.

Fioretos, Orfeo (2001) The Domestic Sources of Multilateral Preferences: Varieties of Capitalism in the European Community', pp. 213–44 in P. Hall and D. Soskice (eds.) *Varieties of Capitalism: the Institutional Foundations of Comparative Advantage*, Oxford: Oxford University Press.

Fleury, Alfonso and Mario Sergio Salerno (1998) 'The Transfer and Hybridization of New Models of Production in the Brazilian Automobile Industry', pp. 278–94 in Robert Boyer, Elsie Charron, Ulrich Jurgens and Steven Tolliday (eds.) *Between Imitation and Innovation: The Transfer and Hybridization of Productive Models in the International Automobile Industry*, Oxford: Oxford University Press.

Fligstein, Neil (1990) *The Transformation of Corporate Control*, Cambridge, Mass.: Harvard University Press.

Flood, John (2001) 'Capital Markets: Those who Can and Cannot do the Purest Global Law Markets', pp. 249–72 in R. Applebaum, W. Felstiner, and V. Gessner (eds.) *Rules and Networks: The Legal Culture of Global Business Transactions*, Oxford: Hart.

Foss, Nicolai and Christian Knudsen (eds.) (1996) *Towards a Competence Theory of the Firm*, London: Routledge.

Freeland, Robert F. (2001) *The Struggle for Control of the Modern Corporation: Organizational Change at General Motors, 1924–1970*, Cambridge: Cambridge University Press.

Friedman, David (1988) *The Misunderstood Miracle*, Ithaca, N.Y.: Cornell University Press.

Fruin, Mark (1992) *The Japanese Enterprise System*. Oxford University Press.

—— (1997) *Knowledge Works*, Oxford: Oxford University Press.

—— (1999) 'Site-Specific Organizational Learning in International Technology Transfer', pp. 232–55 in J. K. Liker, W. M. Fruin and P. S. Adler (eds.) *Remade in America: Transplanting and Transforming Japanese Manufacturing Systems*, New York: Oxford University Press.

Fujimoto, T. (2000) 'Evolution of Manufacturing Systems and *Ex Post* Dynamic Capabilities', pp. 244–80 in G. Dosi *et al.* (eds.) *The Nature and Dynamics of Organizational Capabilities*.

Fujimoto, T., T. Nishiguchi, and S. Sei (1994) 'The Strategy and Structure of Japanese Automobile Manufacturers in Europe', pp. 367–406 in M. Mason and D. Encarnation (eds.) *Does Ownership Matter? Japanese Multinationals in Europe*, Oxford: Oxford University Press.

Gambardella, Alfonso (1995) *Science and Innovation: The US Pharmaceutical Industry During the 1980s*, Cambridge: Cambridge University Press.

Gann, David and Ammon Salter (2000) 'Innovation in Project-based, Service Enhanced Firms: The Construction of Complex Products and Systems', *Research Policy*, 29, 955–72.

—— (2003) 'Project Baronies: Growth and Governance in the Project-Based Firm', presented to the 19th EGOS Colloquium, Copenhagen, July.

Gao, Bai (2001) *Japan's Economic Dilemma: The Institutional Origins of Prosperity and Stagnation*, Cambridge: Cambridge University Press.

Garcia-Fontes, Walter and Aldo Geuna (1999) 'The dynamics of research networks in Europe', pp. 343–66 in Alfonso Gambardella and Franco Malerba (eds.) *The Organization of Economic Innovation in Europe*, Cambridge: Cambridge University Press.

Garon, Sheldon (1987) *The State and Labor in Modern Japan*, Berkeley, California: University of California Press.

Gates, H. (1996) *China's Motor: A Thousand Years of Petty Capitalism*, New York: Cornell University Press.

George, Stephen (2004) 'Multi-Level Governance and the European Union', pp. 107–26 in I. Bache and M. Flinders (eds.) *Multi-level Governance*.

Gerlach, Michael (1992) *Alliance Capitalism*, Berkeley, CA: University of California Press.

German Venture Capital Association (1999) 'Venture Capital in Europe 1998', Special Report, July 9.

Geuna, Aldo (1999) *The Economics of Knowledge Production: Funding and the Structure of University Research*, Cheltenham: Edward Elgar.

Geuna, Aldo and Ben Martin (2003) 'University Research Evaluation and Funding: An International Comparison', *Minerva*, 41, 277–304.

Ghoshal, S. and E. Westney (1993) 'Introduction and Overview', in Ghoshal, S. and E. Westney (eds.) *Organization Theory and the Multinational Corporation*, London: Macmillan.

Gilardi, Fabrizio (2005) 'The Institutional Foundation of Regulatory Capitalism: The Diffusion of Independent Regulatory Agencies in Western Europe', *Annals of the American Academy of Political and Social Science*, 598, 84–101.

Gilpin, Robert (2000) *The Challenge of Global Capitalism*, Princeton: Princeton University Press.

Glassmann, Ulrich (2004) 'Refining National Policy: The Machine-Tool Industry in the Local Economy of Stuttgart', pp. 46–73 in C. Crouch *et al.*, *Changing Governance of Local Economies*.

Glimstedt, H. (2001) 'Competitive Dynamics of Technological Standardization: The Case of Third Generation Cellular Communications', *Industry and Innovation*, 8, 49–78.

Glimstedt, H. and U. Zander, (2003) 'Sweden's Wireless Wonders: Defining the Swedish Internet Economy', in B. Kogut, ed., *The Global Internet Economy*, Cambridge: MIT Press.

Gordon, Jeffrey N. (2003) 'Convergence on Shareholder Capitalism: An Internationalist Perspective', pp. 214–56 in C. J. Milhaupt (ed.) *Global Markets, Domestic Institutions: Corporate Law and Governance in a New Era of Cross-Border Deals*, New York: Columbia University Press.

Goshen, Zohar (2003) 'Controlling Corporate Self-dealing: Convergence or Path Dependency?' pp. 17–45 in C. Milhaupt (ed.) *Global Markets, Domestic Institutions: Corporate Law and Governance in a New Era of Cross-Border Deals*, New York: Columbia University Press.

Goyer, Michel (2003) 'Corporate Governance, Employees and the Focus on Core Competences in France and Germany', pp. 183–213 in C. J. Milhaupt (ed.) *Global Markets, Domestic Institutions: Corporate Law and Governance in a New Era of Cross-Border Deals*, New York: Columbia University Press.

Grabher, Gernot (2002a) 'Cool Projects, Boring Institutions: Temporary Collaboration in Social Context', *Regional Studies*, 36, 204–14.

—— (2002b) 'The Project Ecology of Advertising: Tasks, Talents and Teams', *Regional Studies*, 36, 245–62.

—— (2002c) 'Fragile Sector, Robust Practices: Project Ecologies in New Media', *Environment and Planning A*, 34, 1911–26.

Grabher, Gernot (2004a) 'Learning in Projects, Remembering in Networks? Communality, Sociality and Connectivity in Project Ecologies', *European Urban and Regional Studies*, 11, 99–119.

—— (2004b) 'Temporary Architectures of Learning: Knowledge Governance in Project Ecologies', *Organization Studies*, 25, 1491–514.

Graham, Hugh Davis and Nancy Diamond (1997) *The Rise of the American Research Universities*, Baltimore: Johns Hopkins University Press.

Granovetter, Mark (2005) 'Business Groups and Social Organization', pp. 429–50 in Neil Smelser and Richard Swedberg (eds.) *The Handbook of Economic Sociology*, Princeton: Princeton University Press. Second edition.

Grimshaw, Damian and Marcela Miozzo (2006) 'Institutional Effects on the Market for IT Outsourcing: Analysing Clients, Suppliers and Staff Transfer in Germany and the UK', pp. 151–86 in M. Miozzo and D. Grimshaw (eds.) *Knowledge Intensive Business Services*, Cheltenham: E. Elgar.

Guerrieri, Paolo and Andrew Tylecote (1997) 'Interindustry Differences in Technical Changes and National Patterns of Technological Accumulation', pp. 107–29 in C. Edquist (ed.) *Systems of Innovation*, London: Pinter.

Hall, Peter and David Soskice (2001a) 'An Introduction to Varieties of Capitalism', pp. 1–68 in P. Hall and D. Soskice (eds.) *Varieties of Capitalism: the Institutional Foundations of Comparative Advantage*, Oxford: Oxford University Press.

—— (eds.) (2001b) *Varieties of Capitalism: the Institutional Foundations of Comparative Advantage*, Oxford: Oxford University Press.

Hamilton, Gary (1997) 'Organization and Market Processes in Taiwan's Capitalist Economy' pp. 237–93 in Marco Orru, Nicole Woolsey Biggart and Gary Hamilton (eds.), *The Economic Organization of East Asian Capitalism*, Thousand Oaks, CA: Sage, pp. 237–93.

Hamilton, Gary and Cheng–Shu Kao (1990) 'The Institutional Foundation of Chinese Business: The Family Firm in Taiwan', *Comparative Social Research*, 12, 95–112.

Hamilton, Gary and Robert C. Feenstra (1997) 'Varieties of Hierarchies and Markets: An Introduction' in Marco Orru, Nicole Woolsey Biggart and Gary Hamilton, *The Economic Organization of East Asian Capitalism*, Thousand Oaks, CA: Sage.

Hancke, Robert (2002) *Large Firms and Institutional Change*, Oxford: Oxford University Press.

Hancke, Robert and Michel Goyer (2005) 'Degrees of Freedom: Rethinking the Institutional Analysis of Economic Change', pp. 53–77 in G. Morgan, R. Whitley and E. Moen (eds.) *Changing Capitalisms?*

Hart, Jeffrey A. (1992) *Rival Capitalists: International Competitiveness in the United States, Japan, and Western Europe*, Ithaca, New York: Cornell University Press.

Hawawini, Gabriel and Michael Schill (1994) 'The Japanese Presence in the European Financial Services Sector', pp. 235–87 in M. Mason and D. Encarnation (eds.) *Does Ownership Matter? Japanese Multinationals in Europe*, Oxford: Oxford University Press.

Hayes, Declan (2000) *Japan's Big Bang: The Deregulation and Revitalization of the Japanese Economy*, Boston and Tokyo: Tuttle.

Hayward, Jack and Anand Menon (eds.) (2003) *Governing Europe*, Oxford: Oxford University Press.

Hedlund, Gunnar (1993) 'Assumptions of Hierarchy and Heterarchy, with Applications to the Management of the Multinational Corporation', pp. 211–36 in S. Ghoshal and E. Westney (eds.) *Organization Theory and the Multinational Corporation*, London: Macmillan.

Hedlund, Gunnar and J. Ridderstale (1998) 'Toward a Theory of the Self-renewing MNC', in Egelhoff, W. G. (ed.) *Transforming International Organizations*, Cheltenham: E. Elgar.

Held, D., A. McGraw, D. Goldblatt and J. Perraton (1999) *Global Transformations*, Cambridge: Polity Press.

Hellman, Thomas (2000) 'Venture Capitalists: The Coaches of Silicon Valley', pp. 276–94 in C.-M. Lee *et al.* (eds.) *The Silicon Valley Edge*.

Henderson, Rebecca, Luigi Orsenigo, and Gary Pisano (1999) 'The Pharmaceutical Industry and the Revolution in Molecular Biology: Interactions Among Scientific, Institutional, and Organizational Change', pp. 267–311 in David Mowery and Richard Nelson (eds.) *Sources of Industrial Leadership*, Cambridge: Cambridge University Press.

Hendriksen, Lars Bo (1999) 'The Danish Furniture Industry: A Case of Tradition and Change', pp. 233–58 in P. Karnoe, P. H. Kristensen and P. H Andersen (eds.) *Mobilizing Resources and Generating Competencies*, Copenhagen: Copenhagen Business School Press.

Hendrischke, Hans (2007) 'Networks and Business Networks' in Barbara Krug and Hans Hendrischke (eds.) *China's Economy in the 21st Century*, Cheltenham: E. Elgar.

Hennart, Jean-Francois (2001) 'Theories of the Multinational Enterprise', pp. 127–49 in A. Rugman and T. Brewer (eds.) *The Oxford Handbook of International Business*, Oxford: Oxford University Press.

Herrigel, Gary (1993) 'Large Firms, Small Firms, and the Governance of Flexible Specialization: the Case of Baden Württemberg and Socialized Risk', pp. 15–35 in Bruce Kogut (ed.) *Country Competitiveness: Technology and the Organizing of Work'*, Oxford: Oxford University Press.

—— (1994) 'Industry as a Form of Order' in R. Hollingsworth, P. Schmitter and W. Streeck, (eds.) (1994) *Governing Capitalist Economies*, Oxford University Press.

—— (1996) *Industrial Constructions*, Cambridge: Cambridge University Press.

Herrigel, Gary and Charles Sabel (1999) 'Craft Production in Crisis: Industrial Restructuring in Germany During the 1990s', pp. 77–114 in P. D. Culpepper and D. Finegold (eds.) *The German Skills Machine*, Oxford: Berghahn.

Herrigel, Gary and Volker Wittke (2005) 'Varieties of Vertical Disintegration: The Global Trend Towards Heterogeneous Supply Relations and the Reproduction of Difference in US and German Manufacturing', in G. Morgan, R. Whitley and E. Moen (eds.) *Changing Capitalisms?*

Herrmann, Andrea (2005) 'Converging Divergence: How Competitive Advantages Condition Institutional Change Under EMU', *Journal of Common Market Studies*, 43, 287–310.

Heydebrand, Wolf and Annalisa Miron (2002) 'Constructing Innovativeness in New Media Start-up Firms', *Environment and Planning A*, 34, 1951–84.

Higgins, Monica (2005) *Career Imprints: Creating Leaders Across an Industry*, San Francisco: Jossey-Bass.

Hinz, Thomas (1999) 'Vocational Training and Job Mobility in Comparative Perspective', pp. 159–88 in P. D. Culpepper and D. Finegold (eds.) *The German Skills Machine*, New York: Berghahn Books.

Hirsch, Paul M. (1972) 'Processing Fads and Fashions: An Organization Set Analysis of Cultural Industry Systems', *American Journal of Sociology*, 77, 639–59.

Hirst, Paul and Grahame Thompson (1996) *Globalization in Question*, Oxford: Polity Press.

Hobday, Mike (2000) 'The Project-Based Organization: An Ideal Form for Managing Complex Products and Systems?' *Research Policy*, 29, 871–93.

Hodgson, Geoffrey (1996) 'Varieties of Capitalism and Varieties of Economic Theory', *Review of International Political Economy*, 3, 381–434.

Hollingsworth, J. Rogers (1991) 'The Logic of Coordinating American Manufacturing Sectors' pp. 35–73 in J. L. Campbell, J. R. Hollingsworth and L. Lindbergh (eds.) *Governance of the American Economy*, Cambridge: Cambridge University Press.

Hollingsworth, J. Rogers, and Robert Boyer (eds.) (1997) *Contemporary Capitalism: The Embeddedness of Institutions*, Cambridge University Press.

Hollingsworth, J. Rogers, Karl H. Muller, and Ellen Jane Hollingsworth (eds.) (2002) *Advancing Socio-Economics: An Institutionalist Perspective*, Lanham, Maryland: Rowman and Littlefield.

Hollingsworth, J. Rogers, Philippe Schmitter, and Wolfgang Streeck (eds.) (1994) *Governing Capitalist Economies*, Oxford: Oxford University Press.

Hollingsworth, J. Rogers, and Wolfgang Streeck (1994) 'Counties and Sectors: Concluding Remarks on Performance, Convergence and Competitiveness' in J. Rogers Hollingsworth *et al.* (eds.) *Governing Capitalist Economies*, Oxford University Press.

Holm, Ulf and Torben Pedersen (eds.) (2000) *The Emergence and Impact of MNC Centres of Excellence: A Subsidiary Perspective*, London: Macmillan.

Hopner, James (1999) 'The Danish Banking System: Concentration, Local Autonomy and the Financing of Small and Medium-Sized Enterprises', pp. 113–35 in P. Karnoe *et al.* (eds.) *Mobilizing Resources and Generating Competencies*.

References

Howells, J. (1998) 'Innovation and Technology Transfer within Multinational Firms' in Michie, J. and J. Grieve Smith (eds.) *Globalization, Growth and Governance*, Oxford: Oxford University Press.

Hu, Y-S. (1992) 'Global Firms are National Firms with International Operations', *California Management Review*, 34, 107–26

Humphrey, John, and Hubert Schmitz (1998) 'Trust and Inter-firm Relations in Developing and Transition Economies', *Journal of Development Studies*, 34, 32–61.

Hung, S. and R. Whittington (1997) 'Strategies and Institutions: A Pluralistic Account of Strategies in the Taiwanese Computer Industry', *Organization Studies*, 18, 551–75.

Hurrell, Andrew and Anand Menon (2003) 'International Relations, International Institutions, and the European State', pp. 395–412 in J. Hayward and A. Menon (eds.) *Governing Europe*.

Ibert, Oliver (2004) 'Projects and Firms as Discordant Complements: Organizational Learning in the Munich Software Ecology', *Research Policy*, 33, 1529–46.

Imai, K. and H. Itami (1984) 'Interpretation of Organization and Market: Japan's Firm and Market in Comparison with the U.S.' *International Journal of Economic Organization*, 2, 285–310.

Iterson, A. van and R. Olie (1992) 'European Business Systems: the Dutch Case', in R. Whitley (ed.) *European Business Systems: Firms and Markets in their National Contexts*, London: Sage.

Jackson, Gregory (2003) 'Corporate Governance in Germany and Japan: Liberalization Pressures and Responses During the 1990s', pp. 261–305 in K. Yamamura and W. Streeck (eds.) (2003) *The End of Diversity?*

Jackson, Tim (1997) *Inside Intel*, London: Harper Collins.

Jacoby, Sanford (2005) *The Embedded Corporation: Corporate Governance and Employment Relations in Japan and the United States*, Princeton: Princeton University Press.

Janelli, R. L. (1993) *Making Capitalism: the Social and Cultural Construction of a South Korean Conglomerate*, Stanford: Stanford University Press.

Jessop, Bob (2004) 'Multi-level Governance and Multi-level Metagovernance', pp. 49–74 in I. Bache and M. Flinders (eds.) *Multi-level Governance.*

Johnson, Chalmers (1982) *MITI and the Japanese Miracle*, Stanford University Press.

Jones, Candace (1996) 'Careers in Project Networks: The Case of the Film Industry', pp. 58–75 in M. B. Arthur and D. M. Rousseau (eds.) *The Boundaryless Career: A New Employment Principle for a New Organizational Era*, New York: Oxford University Press.

—— (2002) 'Signalling Expertise: How Signals Shape Careers in Creative Industries', pp. 209–28 in M. A. Peiperl, M. B. Arthur and N. Anand (eds.) *Career Creativity: Explorations in the Remaking of Work*, Oxford: Oxford University Press.

Jones, Candace, W. S. Hesterly, and S. P. Borgatti (1997) 'A General Theory of Network Governance: Exchange Conditions and Social Mechanisms', *Academy of Management Review*, 22, 911–45.

Jones, Geoffrey (1996) *The Evolution of International Business: An Introduction*, London: Routledge.

Jones, Geoffrey (2005) *Multinationals and Global Capitalism from the Nineteenth to the Twenty-First Century*, Oxford: Oxford University Press.

Jurgens, Ulrich (1998) 'Implanting Change: The Role of "Indigenous Transplants" in Transforming the German Productive Model', pp. 319–60 in Robert Boyer *et al.* (eds.) *Between Imitation and Innovation*, Oxford: Oxford University Press.

Kaiser, Robert and Heiko Prange (2004) 'The Reconfiguration of National Innovation Systems–the Example of German Biotechnology,' *Research Policy*, 33, 395–408.

Karnoe, Peter (1999) 'The Business Systems Framework and Danish SMEs', pp. 7–72 in P. Karnoe, P. H. Kristensen, and P. H. Andersen (eds.) *Mobilizing Resources and Generating Capabilities*, Copenhagen: Copenhagen Business School Press.

Karnoe, Peter, P. H. Kristensen, and P. H. Andersen (eds.) (1999) *Mobilizing Resources and Generating Capabilities*, Copenhagen: Copenhagen Business School Press.

Katzenstein, Peter (1985) *Small States in World Markets*. Ithaca, New York: Cornell University Press.

—— (2006) 'East Asia-Beyond Japan', pp. 1–33 in P. Katzenstein and T. Shiraishi (eds.) *Beyond Japan*.

Katzenstein, Peter and Takashi Shiraishi (eds.) (2006) *Beyond Japan: The Dynamics of East Asian Regionalism*, Ithaca, N.Y.: Cornell University Press.

Kelly, William W. and Merry White (2006) 'Students, Slackers, Singles, Seniors and Strangers', pp. 63–82 in P. Katzenstein and T. Shiraishi (eds.) *Beyond Japan*.

Kenney, Martin (1986) *Biotechnology: The University-Industry Complex*, New Haven: Yale University Press.

—— (1999) 'Transplantation? A Comparison of Japanese Television Assembly Plants in Japan and the United States', pp. 256–93 in J. K. Liker *et al.* (eds.) *Remade in America*, New York: Oxford University Press.

—— (ed.) (2000) *Understanding Silicon Valley: The Anatomy of an Entrepreneurial Region*, Stanford: Stanford University Press.

Kenney, M. and R. Florida (1993) *Beyond Mass Production*, Oxford University Press.

—— (2000) 'Venture Capital in Silicon Valley: Fuelling New Firm Formation', pp. 98–123 in Martin Kenney (ed.) *Understanding Silicon Valley*.

Kenworthy, Lane (1997) 'Globalization and Economic Convergence', *Competition and Change*, 2, 1–64.

Kenworthy, Lane (2005) 'Institutional Coherence and Macroeconomic Performance', *Socio-Economic Review*, 4, 69–91.

Kim, Eun Mee (1997) *Big Business, Big State: Collusion and Conflict in South Korean Development, 1960–1990*, Albany, New York: State University of New York Press.

King, Lawrence and Ivan Szelenyi (2005) 'Post-Communist Economic Systems', pp. 205–229 in Neil Smelser and Richard Swedberg (eds.) *The Handbook of Economic Sociology*, Princeton: Princeton University Press, second edition.

References

Kipping, Matthias and Lars Engwall (eds.) (2002) *Management Consulting: Emergence and Dynamics of a Knowledge Industry*, Oxford: Oxford University Press.

Kitschelt, Herbert (1991) 'Industrial Governance, Innovation Strategies, and the Case of Japan: Sectoral Governance or Cross-National Comparative Analysis?' *International Organization*, 45, 453–93.

Kitschelt, Herbert, Peter Lange, Gary Marks, and John D. Stephens (1999) 'Convergence and Divergence in Advanced Capitalist Economies', pp. 427–60 in H. Kitschelt, P. Lange, G. Marks, and J. D. Stephens (eds.) *Continuity and Change in Contemporary Capitalism*, Cambridge University Press.

Kleiner, Thibault (2003) 'Building Up an Asset Management Industry: Forays of an Anglo-Saxon Logic into the French Business System', pp. 57–82 in M-L. Djelic and S. Quack (eds.) *Globalization and Institutions*, Cheltenham: E. Elgar.

Kneller, Robert (1999) 'University-Industry Cooperation in Biomedical R&D in Japan and the United States', pp. 410–38 in L. Branscomb, F. Kodama and R. Florida (eds.) (1999) *Industrializing Knowledge: University-Industry Linkages in Japan and the United States*, Cambridge, Mass: MIT Press.

—— (2003) 'Autarkic Drug Discovery in Japanese Pharmaceutical Companies: Insights into National Differences in Industrial Innovation', *Research Policy*, 32, 1805–27.

Knill, Christoph and Andrea Lenschow (2005) 'Compliance, Competition and Communication: Different Approaches of European Governance and their Impact on National Institutions', *Journal of Common Market Studies*, 43, 583–606.

Knill, Christoph and Dirk Lehmkuhl (2002) 'The National Impact of European Regulatory Policy: Three Europeanization Mechanisms', *European Journal of Political Research*, 41, 255–80.

Koechlin, T. (1995) 'The Globalization of Investment', *Contemporary Economic Policy*, 13, 92–100.

Kogut, Bruce (1993) 'Learning, or the Importance of Being Inert: Country Imprinting and International Competition', in Ghoshal, S. and E. Westney (eds.) *Organization Theory and the Multinational Corporation*, London: Macmillan.

—— (ed.) (2003) *The Global Internet Economy*, Cambridge: MIT Press.

Kogut, Bruce and Udo Zander (1992) 'Knowledge of the Firm, Combinative Capabilities, and the Replication of Technology', *Organization Science*, 3, 383–97.

—— (1993) 'Knowledge of the Firm and the Evolutionary Theory of the Multinational Corporation', *Journal of International Business Studies*, 24, 625–45.

—— (1996) 'What Do Firms Do? Coordination, Identity and Learning', *Organization Science*, 7, 502–18.

Koike, K. (1987) 'Human Resource Development and Labour Management Relations', in K. Yamamura and Y. Yasuba (eds.) *The Political Economy of Japan I*. Stanford University Press.

Kopp, R. (1999) 'The Rice-Paper Ceiling in Japanese Companies: Why It Exists and Persists', pp. 107–28 in S. L. Beechler, and A. Bird (eds.) *Japanese Multinationals*

Abroad: Individual and Organizational Learning, New York: Oxford University Press.

Kraakman, Reinier (2001) 'The Durability of the Corporate Form', pp. 147–60 in Paul DiMaggio (ed.) *The Twenty-First-Century Firm*, Princeton: Princeton University Press.

Kristensen, Peer Hull (1992) 'Strategies against Structure: Institutions and Economic Organization in Denmark', pp. 117–36 in R. Whitley (ed.) *European Business Systems*, London: Sage.

—— (1994) 'Strategies in a Volatile World', *Economy and Society*, 23, 305–34.

—— (1996) 'On the Constitution of Economic Actors in Denmark: Interacting Skill Container and Project Coordinators', pp. 118–58 in R. Whitley and P. H. Kristensen (eds.) *The Changing European Firm: Limits to Convergence*, London: Routledge.

—— (1999) 'When Labour Defines Business Recipes', pp. 73–112 in P. Karnoe *et al.* (eds.) *Mobilizing Resources and Generating Competencies*.

—— (2006) 'Business Systems in the Age of the 'New Economy': Denmark facing the challenge', pp. 295–320 in J. Campbell, J. Hall and O. Pedersen (eds.) *National Identity and the Varieties of Capitalism.*

Kristensen, Peer Hull and Jonathan Zeitlin (2005) *Local Players in Global Games: The Strategic Constitution of a Multinational Corporation*, Oxford: Oxford University Press.

Krug, Barbara and Hans Hendrischke (eds.) (2007) *China's Economy in the 21st Century*, Cheltenham: E. Elgar.

Lam, Alice (2003) 'Organizational Learning in Multinationals: R&D Networks of Japanese and U.S. MNEs in the U.K.' *Journal of Management Studies*, 40, 673–704.

Lane, Christel (1998) 'European Companies between Globalization and Localization: A Comparison of Internationalization Strategies of British and German MNCs', *Economy and Society*, 27, 462–85.

—— (2001) 'The Emergence of German Transnational Companies: A Theoretical Analysis and Empirical Study of the Globalization Process, pp. 69–96 in G. Morgan, P. H. Kristensen and R. Whitley (eds.) *The Multinational Firm: Organizing Across Institutional and National Divides*, Oxford: Oxford University Press.

Langlois, Richard (2003) 'The Vanishing Hand: The Changing Dynamics of Industrial Capitalism', *Industrial and Corporate Change*, 12, 351–85.

Langlois, Richard and David Mowery (1996) 'The Federal Government Role in the Development of the U.S. Software Industry', pp. 53–85 in David Mowery (ed.) *The International Computer Software Industry: A Comparative Study of Industry Evolution and Structure*, Oxford: Oxford University Press.

Langlois, Richard and Paul Robertson (1995) *Firms, Markets and Economic Change*, London: Routledge.

Laurence, Henry (2001) *Money Rules: The New Politics of Finance in Britain and Japan*, Ithaca, NY: Cornell University Press.

References

Lazonick, W. (1990) *Competitive Advantage on the Shop Floor*, Cambridge, Mass.: Harvard University Press.

—— (1991) *Business Organization and the Myth of the Market Economy*, Cambridge: Cambridge University Press.

Lazonick, W. and Jonathan West (1998) 'Organizational Integration and Competitive Advantage', in G. Dosi, D. J. Teece, and J. Chytry (eds.) *Technology, Organization and Competitiveness*, Oxford University Press.

Lazonick, W. and Mary O'Sullivan (1996) 'Organization, Finance and International Competition', *Industrial Corporate Change*, 5, 1–49.

—— (1997) 'Big Business and Skill Formation in the Wealthiest Nations: The Organizational Revolution in the Twentieth Century', pp. 497–521 in A. D. Chandler, F. Amatori, and T. Hikino (eds.) *Big Business and the Wealth of Nations*, Cambridge: Cambridge University Press.

Le Gales, Patrick and Helmut Voelzkow (2001) 'Introduction: The Governance of Local Economies', pp. 1–24 in Crouch *et al.*, *Local Production Systems in Europe*.

Lee, Chong-Moon (2000) 'Four Styles of Valley Entrepreneurship', pp. 94–123 in Lee, Chong-Moon, William F. Miller, Marguerite Gong Hancock, and Henry S. Rowen (2000) (eds.) *The Silicon Valley Edge: A Habitat for Innovation and Entrepreneurship*, Stanford: Stanford University Press.

Lehmbruch, Gerhard (2001) 'The Institutional Embedding of Market Economies: the German "Model", and its Impact on Japan', pp. 39–93 in W. Streeck and K. Yamamura (eds.) *The Origins of Nonliberal Capitalism: Germany and Japan in Comparison*, Ithaca, N.Y.: Cornell University Press.

Lehrer, Mark, (2000) 'Has Germany Finally Solved Its High-Tech Problem? The Recent Boom in German Technolology-based Entrepreneurism', *California Management Review*, 42, 89–107.

—— (2006) 'Two Types of Organizational Modularity: SAP, ERP Product Architecture and the German Tipping Point in the Make/Buy Decision for IT Services', pp. 187–204 in M. Miozzo and D. Grimshaw (eds.) *Knowledge Intensive Business Services: Organizational Forms and National Institutions*, Cheltenham: E. Elgar.

Leslie, Stuart W. (2000) 'The Biggest "Angel" of Them All: The Military and the Making of Silicon Valley', pp. 48–67 in M. Kenney (ed.) *Understanding Silicon Valley*.

Levi-Faur, David and Jacint Jordana (eds.) (2005) *The Rise of Regulatory Capitalism: The Global Diffusion of a New Order*, Annals of the American Academy of Political and Social Science, 598, 4–197.

Levy, Jonah D. (2005) 'Redeploying the State: Liberalization and Social Policy in France', pp. 103–26 in W. Streeck and K. Thelen (eds.) *Beyond Continuity*.

Lewis, Michael (1999) *The New New Thing: A Silicon Valley Story*, London: Hodder and Stoughton.

Liker, Jeffrey K., Mark Fruin, and Paul Adler (eds.) (1999) *Remade in America: Transplanting and Transforming Japanese Management Systems*, Oxford: Oxford University Press.

Lilja, Kari and Risto Tainio (1996) 'The Nature of the Typical Finnish Firm', pp. 159–91 in R. Whitley and P. H. Kristensen (eds.) *The Changing European Firm*, London: Routledge.

Lilja, Kari, Keijo Rasanen, and Risto Tainio (1992) 'A Dominant Business Recipe: The Forest Sector in Finland', pp. 137–54 in R. Whitley (ed.) *European Business Systems*, London: Sage.

Lincoln, James and Michael Gerlach (2004) *Japan's Network Economy: Structure, Persistence and Change*, Cambridge: Cambridge University Press.

Loriaux, Michael (2003) 'France: A New "Capitalism of Voice"?' pp. 101–20 in L. Weiss (ed.) *States in the Global Economy*.

Lundvall, Bengt-Ake (ed.) (1992) *National Systems of Innovation*, London: Pinter.

Lundvall, Bengt-Ake, Bjorn Johnson, Esben Sloth Andersen, and Bent Dalum (2002) 'National Systems of Production, Innovation and Competence Building', *Research Policy*, 31, 213–31.

Lutz, Susanne (2004) 'Convergence within National Diversity: The Regulatory State in Finance', *Journal of Public Policy*, 24, 169–97.

Majone, Giandomenico (2003) 'The Politics of Regulation and European Regulatory Institutions', pp. 297–312 in J. Hayward and A. Menon (eds.) *Governing Europe*.

—— (2005) *Dilemmas of European Integration: The Ambiguities and Pitfalls of Integration by Stealth*, Oxford: Oxford University Press.

Malerba, Franco (2002) 'Sectoral Systems of Innovation and Production', *Research Policy*, 31.

Malerba, Franco and Luigi Orsenigo (1993) 'Technological Regimes and Firm Behaviour', *Industrial and Corporate Change*, 2, 45–71.

Malnight, Thomas, W. (1995) 'Globalization of an Ethnocentric Firm: An Evolutionary Perspective', *Strategic Management Journal*, 16, 119–41.

Mansfield, Edwin (1995) 'Academic Research Underlying Industrial Innovations: Sources, Characteristics, and Financing', *The Review of Economics and Statistics*, 77, 55–65.

Marks, Gary and Liesbet Hooghe (2004) 'Contrasting Visions of Multi-Level Governance', pp. 93–106 in I. Bache and M. Flinders (eds.) *Multi-Level Governance*.

Marsden, David (1999) *A Theory of Employment Systems*, Oxford: Oxford University Press.

Martin, Cathy Jo (2006) 'Corporatism in the Post-industrial Age: Employers and Social Policy in the Little Land of Denmark', pp. 271–94 in J. Campbell, J. Hall and O. Pedersen (eds.) *National Identity and the Varieties of Capitalism*.

Mason, Mark (1994) 'Historical Perspectives on Japanese Direct Investment in Europe', pp. 3–38 in M. Mason and D. Encarnation (eds.) *Does Ownership Matter? Japanese Multinationals in Europe*, Oxford: Oxford University Press.

Mazey, Sonia and Jeremy Richardson (2003) 'Interest Groups and the Brussels Bureaucracy', pp. 208–27 in J. Hayward and A. Menon (eds.) *Governing Europe*.

References

McKelvey, Maureen (1996) *Evolutionary Innovations: The Business of Biotechnology*, Oxford: Oxford University Press.

McKelvey, Maureen, Annika Rickne, and Jens Laage-Hellman (2004) 'Stylized Facts about Innovation Processes in Modern Biotechnology', pp. 43–75 in M. McKelvey, A. Rickne and J. Laage-Hellman (eds.) *The Econoimic Dynamics of Modern Biotechnology*, Cheltenham: E Elgar.

McNichol, James and Jabril Bensedrine (2003) 'Multilateral Rulemaking: Transatlantic Struggles Around Genetically Modified Food', pp. 220–44 in M-L. Djelic and S. Quack (eds.) *Globalization and Institutions*.

Menkhoff, Thomas (1992) 'Xinyong or How to Trust Trust? Chinese Non-Contractual Business Relations and Social Structure: The Singapore Case', *Internationales Asienforum*, 23, 262–88.

Menz, Georg (2005) *Varieties of Capitalism and Europeanization*, Oxford: Oxford University Press.

Metcalfe, J. Stanley and Andrew James (2000) 'Knowledge and Capabilities: A New View of the Firm', pp. 31–52 in Nicolai Foss and Paul Robertson (eds.) *Resources, Technology and Strategy: Explorations in the Resource Based Perspective*, London: Routledge.

Methe, David P. and Joan D. Penner-Hahn (1999) 'Globalization of Pharmaceutical Research and Development in Japanese Companies', pp. 191–210 in S. L. Beechler and A. Bird (eds.) *Japanese Multinationals Abroad: Individual and Organizational Learning*, Oxford: Oxford University Press.

Migdal, Joel (1988) *Strong Societies and Weak States*, Princeton: Princeton University Press.

Milhaupt, Curtis J. (ed.) (2003) *Global Markets, Domestic Institutions: Corporate Law and Governance in a New Era of Cross-Border Deals*, New York: Columbia University Press.

Miller, Gary, (1992) *Managerial Dilemmas*, Cambridge: Cambridge University Press.

Mintzberg, Henry (1983) *Structure in Fives: Designing Effective Organizations*, Englewood Cliffs, New Jersey: Prentice-Hall.

Miozzo, Marcela and Damian Grimshaw (2006) 'Modularity and Innovation in Knowledge Intensive Business Services: IT Outsourcing in Germany and the UK', pp. 82–120 in M. Miozzo and D. Grimshaw (eds.) *Knowledge Intensive Business Services*, Cheltenham: E Elgar.

Miyazaki, Kumiko (1995) *Building Competences in the Firm: Lessons from Japanese and European Optoelectronics*, London: Macmillan.

Monks, Robert and Neil Minow (1995) *Corporate Governance*, Oxford: Blackwell.

Morgan, Glenn (1997) 'The Global Context of Financial Services: National Systems and the International Political Economy', pp. 14–41 in G. Morgan and D. Knights (eds.) *Regulation and Deregulation in European Financial Services*, London: Macmillan.

Morgan, Glenn and David Knights (eds.) (1997) *Regulation and Deregulation in European Financial Services*, London: Macmillan.

Morgan, Glenn and Izumi Kubo (2005) 'Beyond Path Dependency? Constructing New Models for Institutional Change: The Case of Capital Markets in Japan', *Socio-Economic Review*, 3, 55–82.

Morgan, Glenn and Lars Engwall (eds.) (1999) *Regulation and Organizations: International Perspectives*, London: Routledge.

Morgan, Glenn and Sigrid Quack (2000) 'Confidence and Confidentiality: The Social Construction of Performance Standards in Banking', pp. 131–58 in S. Quack, G. Morgan and R. Whitley (eds.) *National Capitalisms, Global Competition and Economic Performance*, Amsterdam: John Benjamins.

—— (2005) 'Internationalization and Capability Development in Professional Service Firms', pp. 277–311 in G. Morgan, R. Whitley and E. Moen (eds.) *Changing Capitalisms?*

Morgan, Glenn, Bill Kelly, Diana Sharpe, and Richard Whitley (2003) 'Global Managers and Japanese Multinationals: Internationalization and Management in Japanese Financial Institutions', *Journal of International Human Resource Management* 14, 1–19.

Morgan, Glenn, Richard Whitley, and Eli Moen (eds.) (2005) *Changing Capitalisms? Internationalization, Institutional Change and Systems of Economic Organization*, Oxford: Oxford University Press.

Morris-Suzuki, Tessa (1994) *The Technological Transformation of Japan: From the Seventeenth to the Twenty-First Century*, Cambridge: Cambridge University Press.

Mowery, David C. (1999) 'The Computer Software Industry', pp. 133–68 in D. Mowery and R. Nelson (eds.) *Sources of Industrial Leadership*, Cambridge: Cambridge University Press.

Mowery, David C., Richard Nelson, Bhaven Sampat, and Arvids Ziedonis (1999) 'The Effects of the Bayh-Dole Act on US University Research and Technology Transfer', pp. 269–306 in Lewis Branscomb, Fumio Kodama and Richard Florida (eds.) *Industrializing Knowledge: University-Industry Links in Japan and the United States*, Cambridge, Mass.: MIT Press.

—— (2004) *Ivory Tower and Industrial Innovation: University-Industry Technology Transfer Before and After the Bayh-Dole Act*, Stanford, California: Stanford University Press.

Mueller, F. (1996) 'National Stakeholders in the Global Contest for Corporate Investment', *European Journal of Industrial Relations*, 2, 345–68.

Mueller, F. and R. Loveridge (1997) 'Institutional, Sectoral and Corporate Dynamics in the Creation of Global Supply Chains', pp. 139–57 in Whitley, R. and P. H. Kristensen (eds.) *Governance at Work*, Oxford: Oxford University Press.

Narin, Francis, Kimberly Hamilton, and Dominic Olivastro (1997) 'The Increasing Link Between US Technology and Public Science', *Research Policy*, 26, 317–30.

Nelson, Richard (ed.) (1993) *National Innovation Systems*, Oxford University Press.

Nohria, Nitin and Ghoshal, Sumantra (1997) *The Differentiated Network: Organizing Multinational Corporations for Value Creation*, San Francisco: Jossey-Bass.

Nonaka, Ikujiro and Hirotaka Takeuchi (1995) *The Knowledge-Creating Company: How Japanese Companies Create the Dynamics of Innovation*, Oxford: Oxford University Press.

Nooteboom, Bart (2000) 'Institutions and Forms of Cooperation', *Organization Studies*, 21, 915–40.

O' Riain, Sean (2000) 'States and Markets in an Era of Globalization', *Annual Review of Sociology*, 26, 187–213.

Odagiri, Hiroyuki and Akira Goto (1996) *Technology and Industrial Development in Japan: Building Capabilities by Learning, Innovation and Public Policy*, Oxford: Oxford University Press.

OECD (2002) *Benchmarking Industry-Science Relations*, Paris: OECD.

Ogura, Seiritsu and Hiroto Kotake (1999) 'Public Policies for Japanese Universities and the Job Market for Engineers', pp. 547–76 in Lewis Branscomb *et al.* (eds.) *Industrializing Knowledge*.

Okimoto, Daniel (1989) *Between MITI and the Market: Japanese Industrial Policy for High Technology*, Stanford, California: Stanford University Press.

Orru, Marco, Nicole Biggart, and Gary Hamilton (1997) *The Economic Organization of East Asian Capitalism*, Thousand Oaks, California: Sage.

O'Sullivan, Mary (2000) *Contests for Corporate Control*, Oxford: Oxford University Press.

Page, Edward C. (2003) 'Europeanization and the Persistence of Administrative Systems', pp. 162–76 in J. Hayward and A. Menon (eds.) *Governing Europe*.

Patrick, Hugh and Thomas Rohlen (1987) 'Small-Scale Family Enterprises' pp. 331–84 in K. Yamamura and Y. Yasuba (eds.) *The Political Economy of Japan Volume 1: The Domestic Transformation*, Stanford, California: Stanford University Press.

Pedersen, Ove (2006) 'Corporatism and Beyond: The Negotiated Economy', pp. 245–70 in J. Campbell, J. Hall and O. Pedersen (eds.) *National Identity and the Varieties of Capitalism*.

Pempel, T. J. (1998) *Regime Shift: Comparative Dynamics of the Japanese Political Economy*, Ithaca, New York: Cornell University Press.

—— (2006) 'A Decade of Political Torpor: When Political Logic Trumps Economic Rationality', pp. 37–62 in P. Katzenstein and T. Shiraishi (eds.) *Beyond Japan*.

Penan, Hervé (1996) 'R&D Strategy in a Techno-Economic Network: Alzheimer's Disease Therapeutic Strategies', *Research Policy*, Vol. 25, 337–58.

Penrose, E. (1959) *The Theory of the Growth of the Firm*, Oxford: Blackwell.

Perlmutter, Howard (1969) 'The Tortuous Evolution of the Multinational Corporation', *Columbia Journal of World Business*, 4, 9–18.

Perraton, Jonathon and Peter Wells (2004) 'Multi-level Governance and Economic Policy', pp. 179–94 in I. Bache and M. Flinders (eds.) *Multi-Level Governance*.

Perrow, Charles (1967) 'A Framework for the Comparative Analysis of Organizations', *American Sociological Review*, 32. 1968. 194–208.

Peterson, Mark F., T. K. Peng, and Peter B. Smith (1994) 'Using Expatriate Supervisors to Promote Cross-border Management Practice Transfer', pp. 294–327 in J. K. Liker *et al.* (eds.) *Remade in America*, New York: Oxford University Press.

Pierson, Paul (1996) 'The Path of European Integration: A Historical Institutionalist Analysis', *Comparative Political Studies*, 29, 123–63.

Pil, Frits and John Paul MacDuffie (1999) 'Transferring Competitive Advantage Across Borders: A Study of Japanese Auto Transplants in North America', pp. 39–74 in J. K. Liker, W. M. Fruin and P. S. Adler (eds.) *Remade in America: Transplanting and Transforming Japanese Management Systems*.

Piore, M. J. and Sabel, C.F. (1984) *The Second Industrial Divide*. New York: Basic Books.

Plehwe, Dieter and Stefano Vescovi (2003) 'Europe's Special Case: The Five Corners of Business-State Interactions', pp. 193–219 in M-L. Djelic and S. Quack (eds.) (2003) *Globalization and Institutions: Redefining the Rules of the Economic Game*, Cheltenham: Edward Elgar.

Polanyi, Karl (1957) *The Great Transformation*, Boston: Beacon Press.

Pollack, Mark A. (1998) 'The Engines of Integration? Supranational Autonomy and Influence in the European Union', pp. 217–49 in W. Sandholtz and A. Stone Sweet (eds.) *European Integration and Supranational Governance*.

Pontusson, Jonas and Peter Swenson (1996) 'Labor Markets, Production Strategies and Wage Bargaining Institutions: The Swedish Employer Offensive in Comparative Perspective', *Comparative Political Studies*, 29, 223–50.

Porter, M. E. (1986) 'Competition in Global Industries: A Conceptual Framework', in Porter, M. E. (ed.) *Competition in Global Industries*, Boston: Harvard Business School Press.

Powell, Walter (1996) 'Inter-Organizational Collaboration in the Biotechnology Industry', *Journal of Institutional and Theoretical Economics*, 152, 197–215.

—— (2001) 'The Capitalist Firm in the Twenty-First Century: Emerging Patterns in Western Perspective', pp. 33–68 in Paul DiMaggio (ed.) *The Twenty-First Century Firm*, Princeton: Princeton University Press.

Powell, Walter, K. Koput, J. F. Bowie, and L. Smith-Doerr (2002) 'The Spatial Clustering of Science and Capital: Accounting for Biotech Firm-Venture Capital Relationships', *Regional Studies*, 36, 291–305.

Powell, Walter, Kenneth Koput, and Laurel Smith-Doerr (1996) 'Interorganizational Collaboration and the Locus of Innovation: Networks of Learning in Biotechnology', *Administrative Science Quarterly*, 41, 116–45.

Prencipe, Andrea and Fredrik Tell (2001) 'Inter-Project Learning: Processes and Outcomes on Knowledge Codification in Project-Based Firms', *Research Policy*, 30, 1373–94.

Pucik, Vladimir (1994) 'The Challenges of Globalization: The Strategic Role of Local Managers in Japanese-Owned US Subsidiaries', pp. 218–39 in Nigel Campbell and Fred Burton (eds.) *Japanese Multinationals*, London: Routledge.

Pucik, Vladimir (1999) 'When Performance Does Not Matter: Human Resource Management in Japanese-Owned US Affiliates', pp. 169–88 in S. L. Beechler and A. Bird (eds.) *Japanese Multinationals Abroad*, Oxford: Oxford University Press.

Quack, Sigrid and Glenn Morgan (2000) 'Institutions, Sector Specialization and Economic Performance' pp. 27–52 in Sigrid Quack, Glenn Morgan and Richard Whitley (eds.) *National Capitalisms, Global Competition and Economic Performance*, Amsterdam: John Benjamins.

Rabinow, P. (1996). *Making PCR: A Story of Biotechnology*, Chicago: University of Chicago Press.

Ramseyer, J. Mark (1994) 'Explicit Reasons for Implicit Contrasts: The Legal Logic to the Japanese Main Bank System', pp. 231–57 in M. Aoki and H. Patrick (eds.) *The Japanese Main Bank System: Its Relevance for Developing and Transforming Economies*, Oxford: Clarendon Press.

Reberioux, Antoine (2002) 'European Style of Corporate Governance at the Crossroads: The Role of Worker Involvement', *Journal of Common Market Studies*, 40, 111–34.

Redding, S. G. (1990) *The Spirit of Chinese Capitalism*, Berlin: de Gruyter.

Riccaboni, Massimo, Walter Powell, Fabio Pammolli, and Jason Owen-Smith (2003) 'Public Research and Industrial Innovation: A Comparison of US and European Innovation Systems in the Life Sciences', pp. 169–201 in A. Geuna, A. Salter and E. Steinmuller (eds.) *Science and Innovation*, Cheltenham: E. Elgar.

Richardson, George (1972) 'The Organization of Industry', *Economic Journal*, 82, 883–96.

—— (1998) 'Some Principles of Economic Organization', pp. 44–62 in N. Foss and B. Loasby (eds.) *Economic Organization, Capabilities and Coordination*, London: Routledge.

Roe, Mark (2003) *Political Determinants of Corporate Governance*, Oxford: Oxford University Press.

Rosenbloom, Richard S. and Clayton M. Christensen (1998) 'Technological Discontinuities, Organizational Capabilities, and Strategic Commitments', pp. 215–46 in G. Dosi, D. J. Teece and J. Chytry (eds.) *Technology, Organization and Competitiveness: Perspectives on Industrial and Corporate Change*, Oxford: Oxford University Press.

Rosenzweig, P. M. and N. Nohria (1994) 'Influences on Human Resource Management Practices in Multinational Corporation', *Journal of International Business Studies*, 25, 229–51.

Roy, William G. (1997) *Socializing Capital: The Rise of the Large Industrial Corporation in America*, Princeton, N. J.: Princeton University Press.

Rugman, Alan and Alain Verbeke (2001) 'Location, Competitiveness and the Multinational Enterprise', pp. 150–77 in A. Rugman and T. Brewer (eds.) *The Oxford Handbook of International Business*.

Rugman, Alan and Thomas Brewer (eds.) (2001) *The Oxford Handbook of International Business*, Oxford: Oxford University Press.

Ruigrok, W. and R. van Tulder (1995) *The Logic of International Restructuring*, London: Routledge.

Sabel, Charles (1994) 'Learning by Monitoring: The Institutions of Economic development', pp. 137–85 in N. J. Smelser and R. Swedberg (eds.) *The Handbook of Economic Sociology*, Princeton: Princeton University Press.

Sakai, J. (2000) *Japanese Bankers in the City of London*, London: Routledge.

Sally, R. (1995) *States and Firms: Multinational Enterprises in Institutional Competition*, London: Routledge.

Salomon, Danielle (1997) 'The Problematic Transformation of the Banking Sector in France: The Case of Consumer Credit', pp. 133–53 in G. Morgan and D. Knights (eds.) *Regulation and Deregulation in European Financial Services*, London: Macmillan.

—— (1999) 'Deregulation and Embeddedness: The Case of the French Banking System', pp. 69–81 in G. Morgan and L. Engwall (eds.) *Regulation and Organization: International Perspectives*, London: Routledge.

—— (2000) 'Changing Performance Standards in the French Banking System', pp. 159–72 in S. Quack, G. Morgan and R. Whitley (eds.) *National Capitalisms, Global Competition and Economic Performance*, Amsterdam: John Benjamins Publishing Company.

Samuels, R. J. (1987) *The Business of the Japanese State*, Ithaca, New York: Cornell University Press.

Sandholtz, Wayne and Alec Stone Sweet (eds.) (1998) *European Integration and Supranational Governance*, Oxford: Oxford University Press.

Saxenian, Annalee (1994) *Regional Advantage: Culture and Competition in Silicon Valley and Route 128*, Cambridge, Mass: Harvard University Press.

—— (2000) 'Transnational Entrepreneurs and Regional Industrialization: the Silicon Valley and Hsinchu connection', pp. 283–302 in Rueyling T. and B. Uzzi (eds.) *Embeddedness and Corporate Change in a Global Economy*, New York: Peter Lang.

Scarborough, Harry, Jacky Swan, Stephane Laurent, Mike Bresnen, Linda Edelman and Sue Newell (2004) 'Project-Based Learning and the Role of Learning Boundaries', *Organization Studies*, 25, 1579–698.

Schmidt, Vivien A. (2002) *The Futures of European Capitalism*, Oxford: Oxford University Press.

Schmitter, Philippe (1997) 'The Emerging Europolity and its Impact upon National Systems of Production', pp. 395–430 in J. R. Hollingsworth and R. Boyer (eds.) *Contemporary Capitalism: The Embeddedness of Institutions*, Cambridge: Cambridge University Press.

Schutte, Helmut (1998) 'Between Headquarters and Subsidiaries: the RHQ solution', pp. 102–37 in J. Birkinshaw and N. Hood (eds.) *Multinational Corporate Evolution and Subsidiary Development*, London: Macmillan.

Senker, Jacqueline (1996) 'National Systems of Innovation, Organizational Learning and Industrial Biotechnology', *Technovation*, Vol. 16, 219–29.

Shapiro, Carl and Hal R. Varian (1999) *Information Rules: A Strategic Guide to the Network Economy*, Boston: Harvard Business School Press.

Sheard, Paul (1994) 'Interlocking Shareholdings and Corporate Governance in Japan', pp. 310–49 in M. Aoki and R. Dore (eds.) *The Japanese Firm: The Sources of Competitive Strength*, Oxford: Oxford University Press.

Sheridan, Kyoko (1993) *Governing the Japanese Economy*, Cambridge: Polity.

Shieh, G. S. (1992) *'Boss' Island: The Subcontracting Network and Micro-Entrepreneurship in Taiwan's Development*, New York: Peter Lang.

Shiraishi, Takashi (2006) 'The Third Wave: Southeast Asia and Middle-Class Formation in the Making of a Region', pp. 237–71 in P. J. Katzenstein and T. Shiraishi (eds.) *Beyond Japan*.

Sienko, Tanya (1997) *A Comparison of Japanese and U.S. Graduate Programs in Science and Engineering*, Tokyo: National Institute of Science and Technology Policy, Discussion Paper no. 3.

Silin, R. H. (1976) *Leadership and Values: The Organization of Large Scale Taiwanese Enterprises*, Harvard University Press.

Smith, Jackie (2005) 'Globalization and Transnational Social Movement Organization', pp. 226–48 in G. F. Davis, D. McAdam, W. R. Scott and M. Zald (eds.) *Social Movements and Organization Theory*, Cambridge: Cambridge University Press.

Smitka, M. (1991) *Competitive Ties: Subcontracting in the Japanese Automotive Industry*. New York: Columbia University Press.

Solvell, Orjan and Ivo Zander (1998) 'International Diffusion of Knowledge: Isolating mechanisms and the role of the MNE', pp. 402–16 in A. D. Chandler, P. Hagstrom and O. Solvell (eds.) *The Dynamic Firm: The Role of Technology, Strategy, and Regions*, Oxford: Oxford University Press.

—— (1996) 'Societal Effects in Cross-national Organizing Studies: Conceptualizing Diversity in Actors and Systems, pp. 67–86 in R. Whitley and P. H. Kristensen (eds.) *The Changing European Firm: Limits to Convergence*, London: Routledge.

—— (2005) *The Global and the Local*, Oxford: Oxford University Press.

Soskice, D. (1997) 'German Technology Policy, Innovation, and National Institutional Frameworks', *Industry and Innovation*, 4, 75–96.

—— (1999) 'Divergent Production Regimes: Coordinated and Uncoordinated Market Economies in the 1980s and 1990s', pp. 101–34 in Kitschelt, H. P. Lange, G. Marks and J. Stephens (eds.) *Continuity and Change in Contemporary Capitalism*, Cambridge: Cambridge University Press.

Steers, R. M., Shin, Y. K., and Ungson, G. R. (1989) *The Chaebol*. New York: Harper and Row.

Stewart, Rosemary, Jean-Louis Barsoux, Alfred Kieser, Hans-Dieter Ganter and Peter Walgenbach (1994) *Managing in Britain and Germany*, London: Macmillan.

Stokes, Donald E. (1997) *Pasteur's Quadrant: Basic Science and Technological Innovation*, Washington, D.C. : Brookings Institution Press.

Storper, Michael (1989) 'The Transition to Flexible Specialization in the US Film Industry: External Economies, the Division of Labour and the Crossing of Industrial Divides', *Cambridge Journal of Economics*, 13, 273–305.

Strange, Roger (1993) *Japanese Manufacturing Investment in Europe*, London: Routledge.

Streb, Jochen (2003) 'Shaping the National System of Inter-industry Knowledge Exchange: Vertical Integration, Licensing and Repeated Knowledge Transfer in the German Plastics Industry', *Research Policy*, 32, 1125–40.

Streeck, Wolfgang (1984) *Industrial Relations in West Germany: A Case Study of the Car Industry*. New York: St Martin's Press.

—— (1992) *Social Institutions and Economic Performance: Studies of Industrial Relations in Advanced Capitalist Economies*, London: Sage.

—— (1997) 'German Capitalism: Does it exist? Can it survive?' pp. 33–54 in Colin Crouch and Wolfgang Streeck (eds.) *Political Economy of Modern Capitalism*, London: Sage.

Streeck, Wolfgang and Kathleen Thelen (eds.) (2005a) *Beyond Continuity: Institutional Change in Advanced Political Economies*, Oxford: Oxford University Press.

—— (2005b) 'Institutional Change in Advanced Political Economies', pp. 1–39 in W. Streeck and K. Thelen (eds.) *Beyond Continuity*.

Streeck, Wolfgang and Philippe Schmitter (eds.) (1985) *Private Interest Government: Beyond Market and State*, London: Sage.

Streeck, Wolfgang and Kozo Yamamura (2003) 'Introduction: Convergence or Diversity? Stability and Change in German and Japanese Capitalism', pp. 1–50 in K. Yamamura and W. Streeck (eds.) (2003) *The End of Diversity?*

Sturgeon, Timothy (2002) 'Modular Production Networks: A New American Model of Industrial Organization', *Industrial and Corporate Change*, 11, 451–96.

Suchman, Mark (2000) 'Dealmakers and Counsellors: Law Firms as Intermediaries in the Development of Silicon Valley', pp. 71–97 in M. Kenney (ed.) *Understanding Silicon Valley*.

Sunamura, Satoshi (1994) 'The Development of Main Bank Managerial Capacity', pp. 295–324 in M. Aoki and H. Patrick (eds.) *The Japanese Main Bank System*.

Swank, Duane (2003) 'Withering Welfare? Globalization, political economic institutions, and Contemporary Welfare State', pp. 58–82 in L. Weiss (ed.) *States in the Global Economy*.

Sydow, Jorg, Lars Lindkvist, and Robert DeFillippi (2004) 'Project-Based Organizations, Embeddedness and Repositories of Knowledge', *Organization Studies*, 25, 1475–88.

Szulanski, G. (1996) 'Exploring Internal Stickiness: Impediments to the Transfer of Best Practices Within the Firm', *Strategic Management Journal*, 17, 27–44.

Tate, J. (2001) 'National Varieties of Standard-setting', in Hall, P. and D. Soskice (eds.) *Varieties of Capitalism: The Institutional Foundations of Comparative Advantage*, Oxford: Oxford University Press.

Taylor, Bill, Tony Elger, and Peter Fairbrother (1994) 'Transplants and Emulators: the Fate of the Japanese Model in British Electronics', pp. 196–225 in Tony Elger and Chris Smith (eds.) *Global Japanization?* London: Routledge.

Teece, David (1986) 'Profiting from Technological Innovation: Implications for Integration, Collaboration, Licensing and Public Policy', *Research Policy*, 15, 285–305.

Teece, David and Gary Pisano (1994) 'The Dynamic Capabilities of Firms: An Introduction', *Industrial and Corporate Change*, 3, 537–56.

Teece, David, Gary Pisano, and Amy Shuen (2000) 'Dynamic Capabilities and Strategic Management', pp. 334–62 in G. Dosi *et al.* (eds.) *The Nature and Dynamics of Organizational Capabilities*.

Teece, David, Richard Rumelt, Giovanni Dosi, Sidney Winter (1994) 'Understanding Corporate Coherence: Theory and Evidence', *Journal of Economic Behavior and Organization*, 23, 1–30.

Teubner, Günther (1998) 'Legal Irritants: Good Faith in British Law or How Unifying Laws Ends up in New Divergences', *The Modern Law Review*, 61, 11–32.

Thatcher, Mark (2004) 'Varieties of Capitalism in an Internationalized World: Domestic Institutional Change in European Telecommunications', *Comparative Political Studies*, 37, 751–80.

Thelen, Kathleen (2001) 'Varieties of Labour Politics in the Developed Democracies', pp. 71–103 in P. Hall and D. Soskice (eds.) *Varieties of Capitalism*, Oxford: Oxford University Press.

—— (2004) *How Institutions Evolve: The Political Economy of Skills in Germany, Britain, the United States and Japan*, Cambridge: Cambridge University Press.

Thelen, Kathleen and Christa van Wijnbergen (2003) 'The Paradox of Globalization: Labor Relations in Germany and Beyond', *Comparative Political Studies*, 36, 859–80.

Thelen, Kathleen and Ikuo Kume (2001) 'The Rise of Nonliberal Training Regimes: Germany and Japan Compared', pp. 200–28 in W. Streeck and K.Yamamura (eds.) *The Origins of Nonliberal Capitalism: Germany and Japan in Comparison*, Ithaca: Cornell University Press.

—— (2003) 'The Future of Nationally Embedded Capitalism: Industrial Relations in Germany and Japan', pp. 183–211 in K. Yamamura and W. Streeck (eds.) (2003) *The End of Diversity?*

Thomas, L. G. III (1994) 'Implicit Industrial Policy: The Triumph of Britain and the Failure of France in Global Pharmaceuticals', *Industrial and Corporate Change*, 3, 451–89.

—— (2001) *The Japanese Pharmaceutical Industry: The New Drug Lag and the Failure of Industrial Policy*, Cheltenham, U.K.: Edward Elgar.

Tolliday, Steven (2000) 'Transplanting the American Model? US Automobile Companies and the Transfer of Technology and Management to Britain, France, and Germany, 1928–1962', pp. 76–119 in J. Zeitlin and G. Herrigel (eds.)

Americanization and its Limits: Reworking US Technology and Management in Post-War Europe and Japan, Oxford: Oxford University Press.

Tsoukalis, Loukas (2003) 'Monetary Policy and the Euro', pp. 330–45 in J. Hayward and A. Menon (eds.) *Governing Europe.*

Tushman, Michael L. and Philip Anderson (1986) 'Technological Discontinuities and Organizational Environments', *Administrative Science Quarterly*, 31, 439–65.

Tylecote, A. and E. Conesa (1999) 'Corporate Governance, Innovation Systems and Industrial Performance', *Industry and Innovation*, 6, 25–50.

Ueda, Kazuo (1994) 'Institutional and Regulatory Frameworks for the Main Bank System', pp. 89–108 in M. Aoki and H. Patrick (eds.) *The Japanese Main Bank System.*

Ventresca, Marc, Dara Szyliowicz, and M. Tina Dacin (2003) 'Innovations in Governance: Global Structuring and the Field of Public Exchange-Traded Markets', pp. 245–77 in M-L. Djelic and S. Quack (eds.) (2003) *Globalization and Institutions.*

Vitois, Sigurt (2003) 'From Banks to Markets: The Political Economy of Liberalization of the German and Japanese Financial Systems', pp. 240–60 in K. Yamamura and W. Streeck (eds.) (2003) *The End of Diversity?*

Voelzkow, Helmut (2004) 'The Reconstruction of Declining Local Economies in Europe', pp. 131–8 in C. Crouch *et al., Changing Governance of Local Economies.*

Vogel, Ezra (1988) *Japan As Number One*, Cambridge, Mass: Harvard University Press.

Vogel, Steven K. (2001) 'The Crisis of German and Japanese Capitalism: Stalled on the Road to the Liberal Market Economy?' *Comparative Political Studies*, 34, 1103–33.

Wade, R. (1996) 'Globalization and its Limits: Reports of the Death of the National Economy are Greatly Exaggerated', in S. Berger and R. Dore (eds.) *National Diversity and Global Capitalism*, Cornell University Press.

Wank, David (1999) *Commodifying Communism, Business, Trust and Politics in a Chinese City*, Cambridge: Cambridge University Press.

Watson, Hamish (1976) *Organizational Bases of Professional Status: A Comparative Study of the Engineering Profession.* Unpublished PhD thesis, London School of Economics.

Way, Christopher R. (2005) 'Political Insecurity and the Diffusion of Financial Market Regulation', *Annals of the American Academy of Political and Social Science*, 598, 125–44.

Weiss, Linda (ed.) (2003a) *States in the Global Economy: Bringing Institutions Back In*, Cambridge: Cambridge University Press.

—— (2003b) 'Introduction: Bringing Domestic Institutions Back In', pp. 1–33 In L. Weiss (ed.) *States in the Global Economy.*

Werr, Andreas (2002) 'The Internal Creation of Consulting Knowledge: A Question of Structuring Experience', pp. 91–108 in M. Kipping and L. Engwall (eds.) *Management Consulting.*

References

Werth, Barry (1994) *The Billion-Dollar Molecule*. New York: Touchstone, Simon & Schuster.

Westney, Eleanor (1993a) 'Institutionalization Theory and the Multinational Corporation', pp. 53–76 in S. Ghoshal and E. Westney (eds.) *Organization Theory and the Multinational Corporation*, London: Macmillan.

—— (1993b) 'Country Patterns in R&D Organization: The United States and Japan', pp. 36–53 in Bruce Kogut (ed.) *Country Competitiveness*, Oxford: Oxford University Press.

—— (1996) 'The Japanese Business System: Key Features and Prospects for Changes', *Journal of Asian Business*, 12, 21–50.

—— (1999) 'Organization Theory Perspectives on the Cross-border Transfer of Organizational Practices', pp. 385–406 in J. K. Liker, W. M. Fruin and P. S. Adler (eds.) *Remade in America: Transplanting and Transforming Japanese Management Systems'*, Oxford: Oxford University Press.

—— (2001a) 'Japanese Enterprise Faces the Twenty-First Century', pp. 105–43 in Paul DiMaggio (ed.) *The Twenty-First-Century Firm*.

—— (2001b) 'Japan', pp. 623–51 in A. Rugman and T. Brewer (eds.) *Oxford Handbook of International Business*, Oxford: Oxford University Press.

Westney, Eleanor and Srilata Zaheer (2001) 'The Multinational Enterprise as an Organization', pp. 349–79 in A. Rugman and T. Brewer (eds.) *The Oxford Handbook of International Business*.

Whitley, Richard (1992a) *Business Systems in East Asia: Firms, Markets and Societies*, London: Sage.

—— (1998) 'Internationalization and Varieties of Capitalism: The Limited Effects of Cross-National Coordination of Economic Activities on the Nature of Business Systems', *Review of International Political Economy*, 5, 445–81.

—— (1999) *Divergent Capitalisms: The Social Structuring and Change of Business Systems*, Oxford: Oxford University Press.

—— (2000a) 'The Institutional Structuring of Innovation Strategies', *Organization Studies*, 21, 855–86.

—— (2000b) *The Intellectual and Social Organization of the Sciences*, Oxford: Oxford University Press. Second edition (first edition, 1984).

—— (2003a) 'Changing Transnational Institutions and the Management of International Business Transactions', pp. 108–33 in M-L. Djelic and S. Quack (eds.) *Globalization and Institutions: Redefining the Rules of the Game*, Cheltenham: E. Elgar.

—— (2003b) 'Competition and Pluralism in the Public Sciences: The Impact of Institutional Frameworks on the Organizationof Academic Science', *Research Policy*, 32, 1015–29.

—— (ed.) (1992b) *European Business Systems: Firms and Markets in their National Contexts*, London: Sage.

Whitley, Richard and Laszlo Czaban (1998) 'Institutional Transformation and Enterprise Change in an Emergent Capitalist Economy: The Case of Hungary' *Organization Studies*, 19, 259–80.

Whitley, R., J. Henderson, L. Czaban and G. Lengyel (1996) 'Trust and Contractual Relations in an Emerging Capitalist Economy' *Organization Studies*, 17, 397–420.

Whitley, Richard and Peer Hull Kristensen (eds.) (1996) *The Changing European Firm: Limits to Convergence*, London: Routledge.

—— —— (1997) *Governance at Work: The Social Regulation of Economic Relations*, Oxford: Oxford University Press.

Whitley, Richard, and Jochen Glaser (eds.) (2007) *The Changing Governance of the Sciences*, Dordrecht: Kluwer/Springer.

Wilkins, Mira (2001) 'The History of Multinational Enterprise', pp. 3–35 in A. Rugman and T. Brewer (eds.) *The Oxford Handbook of International Business*, Oxford: Oxford University Press.

Woo, Jung-en (1991) *Race to the Swift: State and Finance in Korean Industrialization*, New York: Columbia University Press.

Wood, Christopher (1992) *The Bubble Economy: The Japanese Economic Collapse*, London: Sidgwick and Jackson.

Yamamoto, Shinichi (1997) 'The Role of the Japanese Higher Education System in Relation to Industry', pp. 294–307 in A. Goto and H. Odagiri (eds.) *Innovation in Japan*. Oxford: Oxford University Press.

Yamamura, Kozo and Wolfgang Streeck (eds.) (2003) *The End of Diversity? Prospects for German and Japanese Capitalism*, Ithaca, New York: Cornell University Press.

Yeung, H. W. and K. Olds (eds.) (2000) *Globalization of Chinese Business Firms*, London: Macmillan.

Yoshihara, Mariko and Katsuya Tamai (1999) 'Lack of Incentive and Persisting Constraints: Factors Hindering Technology Transfer at Japanese Universities', pp. 348–64 in Lewis Branscomb *et al.* (eds.) *Industrializing Knowledge*.

Yoshino, M. Y. and T. B. Lifson (1986) *The Invisible Link: Japan's Sogo Shosha and the Organization of Trade*, Cambridge, Mass.: MIT Press.

Zander, Ivo and Orjan Solvell (2002) 'The Phantom Multinational', pp. 81–106 in V. Havila, M. Forsgren and H. Hakansson (eds.) *Critical Perspectives on Internationalization*, Oxford: Pergamon.

Zucker, Lynne and Michael Darby (1997) 'Present at the Biotechnological Revolution: Transformation of Technological Identity for a Large Incumbent Pharmaceutical Firm', *Research Policy*, 26, 429–46.

Zuckerman, Ezra W. (2004) 'Do Firms and Markets Look Different? Repeat Collaboration in the Feature Film Industry, 1935–1995', unpublished paper, MIT Sloan School of Management.

Zysman, John (1983) *Governments, Markets and Growth: Financial Systems and the Politics of Industrial Change*, Ithaca: Cornell University Press.

Index

366